Markets for Clean Air

Markets for Clean Air provides a comprehensive, in-depth description and evaluation of the first three years' experience with the U.S. Acid Rain Program. This environmental control program is the world's first large-scale use of a tradable emission permit system for achieving environmental goals. The book analyzes the behavior and performance of the market for emissions permits, called allowances in the Acid Rain Program, and quantifies emission reductions, compliance costs, and cost savings associated with the trading program. The book also includes chapters on the historical context in which this pioneering program developed and the political economy of allowance allocations. Finally, the book discusses the program's successes, its weaknesses, and the lessons learned regarding application of the emissions-trading approach to controlling other types of emissions, including greenhouse gases. The volume is an indispensable addition to the library of all interested in the application of market principles for meeting environmental goals.

A. Denny Ellerman is Senior Lecturer at the Sloan School of Management, Massachusetts Institute of Technology (MIT), and Executive Director of MIT's Center for Energy and Environmental Policy Research (CEEPR). Dr. Ellerman specializes in the economics of energy with a particular interest in the American coal industry. He was an executive vice president of the National Coal Association during most of the time that acid rain legislation was being debated in the U.S. Congress.

Paul L. Joskow is Elizabeth and James Killian Professor of Economics and Management, Department of Economics and Sloan School of Management at MIT, and Director of the CEEPR. Professor Joskow specializes in the economics of government regulation, industrial organization, and competition policy. He has published two books and numerous articles on economic and regulatory issues related to the electric power industry. He was a member of the Environmental Protection Agency's Acid Rain Advisory Committee and is currently a member of the EPA's Science Advisory Board.

Richard Schmalensee is Gordon Y. Billard Professor of Economics and Management, Dean of the MIT Sloan School of Management, and former Director of CEEPR. Dean Schmalensee specializes in industrial economics, regulation and antitrust, and environmental policy analysis. He served as a member of President Bush's Council of Economic Advisers during development of the 1990 Clean Air Act Amendments and was heavily involved in the design of the Acid Rain Program.

Juan-Pablo Montero is Associate Professor of Industrial Economics in the Department of Industrial Engineering at the Catholic University of Chile, and CEEPR Research Associate. Professor Montero specializes in industrial organization and environmental economics and policy. He has been involved in CEEPR's Title IV research from the beginning and devoted his doctoral dissertation at MIT to emissions trading.

Elizabeth M. Bailey is a consultant at National Economic Research Associates, Inc., Washington, D.C. Dr. Bailey's research as a graduate student in the Economics Department of MIT and a Research Associate at CEEPR concerned the analysis of the U.S. Acid Rain Program during its formative stages.

Markets for Clean Air
The U.S. Acid Rain Program

A. DENNY ELLERMAN
Massachusetts Institute of Technology

RICHARD SCHMALENSEE
Massachusetts Institute of Technology

ELIZABETH M. BAILEY
National Economic Research Associates, Inc.

PAUL L. JOSKOW
Massachusetts Institute of Technology

JUAN-PABLO MONTERO
Catholic University of Chile

CAMBRIDGE
UNIVERSITY PRESS

PUBLISHED BY THE PRESS SYNDICATE OF THE UNIVERSITY OF CAMBRIDGE
The Pitt Building, Trumpington Street, Cambridge, United Kingdom

CAMBRIDGE UNIVERSITY PRESS
The Edinburgh Building, Cambridge CB2 2RU, UK   http://www.cup.cam.ac.uk
40 West 20th Street, New York, NY 10011-4211, USA   http://www.cup.org
10 Stamford Road, Oakleigh, Melbourne 3166, Australia
Ruiz de Alarcón 13, 28014 Madrid, Spain

First published 2000

Printed in the United States of America

Typeface Times Roman 10.5/13pt.   *System* QuarkXPress [BTS]

A catalog record for this book is available from the British Library.

Library of Congress Cataloging in Publication data
Markets for clean air : the U.S. acid rain program / A. Denny Ellerman . . .
[et al.].
      p.   cm.
   Includes bibliographical references and index.
   ISBN 0-521-66083-1 (alk. paper)
   1. Emissions trading – United States.   2. Air quality management –
Government policy – United States.   3. Acid rain – Environmental
aspects – Government policy – United States.   I. Ellerman, A. Denny.
HC110.A4M37   2000
363.738′7 – dc21   99-16913

ISBN   0 521 66083 1   hardback

"If it is feasible to establish a market
to implement a policy, no policy-maker
can afford to do without one."

—J. H. Dales, *Pollution, Property, and Prices*

Contents

Illustrations

xi

Tables

xiii

Preface

This book brings together the results of more than five years of research conducted by the Center for Energy and Environmental Policy Research at the Massachusetts Institute of Technology, with which all of the authors have been affiliated. The Center seeks to provide rigorous, empirically grounded, and accessible economic analysis to inform the public policy debate. It has been the focus of applied economics research on energy and environmental issues at MIT for more than twenty years. The Center historically has concentrated on topics – like emissions trading – that are both interesting to academics and relevant to policymakers and industry analysts. Market-based emissions control instruments are increasingly in vogue, and we are pleased to provide this evaluation of the remarkable public policy experiment with emissions trading that was initiated by Title IV of the 1990 Clean Air Act Amendments, the U.S. Acid Rain Program. We hope that our research will contribute to the consideration of market-based systems as tools for meeting at least some demands for environmental amenities.

As is the case for any major endeavor, there is a long list of people without whose assistance this book would never have appeared. This research has grown out of the inspired suggestion and accompanying funding by the National Acid Precipitation Assessment Program (NAPAP), which initially encouraged us to combine our collective experience to provide an evaluation for NAPAP's Quadrennial Report to the U.S. Congress. Particular thanks for encouragement and support during the early years are due to NAPAP's director,

Michael Uhart, and to Rodney Weiher, chairman of NAPAP's Economics Working Group.

This book also could not have been written without assistance from the Acid Rain Division of the U.S. Environmental Protection Agency (EPA), to which we are indebted in three important ways. First, were it not for the rare vision and dedication of this group of civil servants in making Title IV a successful market-based emissions control system, the subject of this book would not have been nearly as interesting academically, nor as informative for public policy. Second, the cooperation of the Division in providing data and responding to endless questions for clarification and explanation has been extraordinary. Finally, the Division continued the financial support of our work that was begun by NAPAP. We have benefited from interactions with many people in the Division over the years, but three deserve special recognition and thanks: Brian McLean, Joe Kruger, and Larry Montgomery.

The lifeblood of the type of research reported here is data, and three other organizations have been especially helpful in supplying us with this necessity. Carlton Bartels of Cantor Fitzgerald Environmental Brokerage Services has provided data on allowance prices, particularly with respect to future vintages, that are not available anywhere else. Fieldston Publications has provided historical data on coal prices and sulfur premiums, for which thanks are due Peter Ogram. Finally, as with all topics concerning energy, we have relied heavily on the Energy Information Administration for data on coal deliveries and other aspects of power plant operations; thanks are due to Art Fuldner and Kenneth McClevey.

We have also benefited greatly from perspectives provided by a number of industry participants in Title IV abatement and SO_2 allowance trading. In particular, we express our thanks to the electric utilities and unnamed utility employees who took the time to respond to the survey questionnaire on Title IV abatement costs that we circulated in 1996. Their responses were essential to developing the cost estimates reported here. Over the years, we have also engaged in a continuing dialogue with a number of industry participants who invariably have provided interesting hunches, insights, and facts. In particular, we wish to recognize the contributions of Lynda Clemmons and Tom Gros of Enron Capital and Trade Resources Corporation, Richard Chastain and Gary Hart of the Southern

Company, Jerry Golden of the Tennessee Valley Authority, and John McManus of American Electric Power.

A number of our colleagues at other universities and research groups have contributed in ways too complex to explain, and we hope that they will consider this book a further contribution to the ongoing dialogue. Particular thanks are due Robert Stavins of Harvard University, Jeremy Platt of the EPRI, Dallas Burtraw of Resources for the Future, Tom Tietenberg of Colby College, and Richard Morgenstern, now with the U.S. Department of State. Robert Brenner of EPA's Office of Air and Radiation, Robert Hahn of the American Enterprise Institute, and Karl Hausker of the Center for Strategic and International Studies, all of whom helped to create the Acid Rain Program, were also helpful in this research.

The real work in the research effort behind this book was performed by a number of research assistants, two of whom, Montero and Bailey, co-authored this book and a third, Susanne Schennach, contributed the appendix. Amy Ando, Estelle Andrin, Paul Ellickson, Yan Giao, and Sung Kim also made significant contributions, for which we are grateful.

Production of this book would not have been possible without Judith Stitt's meticulous attention to detail and the unflagging and cheerful effort of Heather Mitchell in harnessing recalcitrant computers and assembling text, tables, graphs, and references into one coherent manuscript. Words cannot express our gratitude for being freed from these tasks.

Lastly, our spouses and families have had to be more than usually forbearing during the preparation of this book. To them, as well as to everyone else who has helped us, we express heartfelt thanks and appreciation. The book's flaws are not their fault.

Acknowledgments

The authors gratefully acknowledge the following for permission granted to reprint in the present volume material originally published by their organizations:

Academic Press, Orlando, for:
A. Denny Ellerman and Juan-Pablo Montero. "The Declining Trend in Sulfur Dioxide Emissions: Implications for Allowance Prices." *Journal of Environmental Economics and Management* 36 (1998): 26–45.

American Economic Association, Nashville, for:
Richard Schmalensee, Paul L. Joskow, A. Denny Ellerman, Juan-Pablo Montero, and Elizabeth M. Bailey. "An Interim Evaluation of Sulfur Dioxide Emissions Trading." *Journal of Economic Perspectives* 12 (Summer 1998): 53–68.

Paul L. Joskow, Richard Schmalensee, and Elizabeth M. Bailey. "The Market for Sulfur Dioxide Emissions." *American Economic Review* 88 (4) 1998: 669–85.

The Journal of Law and Economics, University of Chicago Law School, for:
Paul L. Joskow and Richard Schmalensee. "The Political Economy of Market-Based Environmental Policy: The U.S. Acid Rain Program." *Journal of Law and Economics* 41 (April 1998): 37–83.

PART ONE
Background

1 A Market-Based Experiment

A STAR IS BORN (?)

More than thirty years ago, Dales (1968) demonstrated that, in theory, an emissions-trading system, in which rights to emit pollution are available in fixed and limited aggregate amount and are freely tradable, would induce rational firms to reduce pollution at the least possible cost. This basic theoretical argument has been refined and elaborated many times since.[1] Over this same period, the alternative command-and-control approach to environmental policy, in which the design or performance of individual pollution sources is specified, has been applied to a wide variety of problems and has generally performed poorly, with excessive costs and, often, failure to achieve environmental objectives. Nonetheless, until quite recently, emissions trading and related approaches (such as emission taxes) attracted little but hostility from noneconomists and were rarely employed in practice.[2]

Then, with relatively little fanfare, Title IV of the 1990 Clean Air Act Amendments (1990 CAAA, Public Law 101–549), the U.S. Acid Rain Program, passed by the U.S. Congress and signed by President George Bush in 1990, established the first large-scale, long-term U.S. environmental program to rely on tradable emission permits (called

1. Notable works in this tradition include Montgomery (1972), Tietenberg (1985), and Baumol and Oates (1988).
2. For discussions of other environmental programs employing various forms of emissions trading, see Tietenberg (1985), Hahn and Hester (1989), and National Economic Research Associates, Inc. (1994, Chapt. 2). Noll (1989, p. 1275) discusses some of the political reasons such programs are rare; see also Stavins (1998).

3

"allowances" in the legislation) to control emissions. Its target was electric utility emissions of sulfur dioxide (SO_2), the major precursor of acid rain.

Since 1990, policymakers' interest in emissions trading has grown rapidly. This growth accelerated in 1995, when Title IV came into effect. Most observers quickly judged the program to be a great success, largely because the price of emission rights (allowances) was well below expectations.[3] Subsequently, the United States has moved toward implementation of a regional trading program for rights to emit oxides of nitrogen (generally called NO_x, which are important contributors to ozone pollution), and the international community has endorsed, at least in principle, the use of international emissions trading to deal with the threat of global climate change.[4] There seems to be a conference on emissions trading somewhere in the world every day, each accompanied by a raft of papers from universities, think tanks, and government agencies. In less than a decade, emissions trading has gone from being a pariah among policymakers to being a star – everybody's favorite way to deal with pollution problems. As always, when widespread public acclaim for a new approach to an important public policy issue comes so fast and is based on fragments of evidence about performance, at least some will wonder whether such acclaim is truly deserved.

This book provides a comprehensive description, analysis, and evaluation of the source of this widespread public acclaim: the SO_2 emissions-trading program created by Title IV of the 1990 Clean Air Act Amendments. This work is based on the first few years of experience with the program. Our goal is both to deepen understanding of this program in its own right and to make it possible to use experience with Title IV to inform both decisions about the use of emissions trading to control pollution and the design of emissions-trading systems more broadly. We concentrate on political economy, compliance behavior, and abatement cost; an inquiry into the benefits of reduced emissions is beyond the scope of this study.[5] We find that, on

---

3. Ironically, as we show in Chapter 11, the very low allowance prices in 1995 and 1996 reflected the Acid Rain Program's (perhaps inevitable) imperfections more than its virtues.
4. On these and related developments see, for instance, U.S. Council of Economic Advisers (1998, pp. 156–80).
5. NAPAP (1998) provides a discussion of the effects and benefits of the reduction of SO_2 emissions effected so far by Title IV. In general, the pertinent sections state that a

balance, Title IV has indeed performed well and has thereby proven that emissions trading has considerable potential in practice, as well as in theory. But, as we hope subsequent chapters will demonstrate, there is much more to be learned from careful analysis of this complex and important policy experiment than can be inferred from a cursory examination of allowance price levels.

We turn first to a brief description of the structure of the SO_2 allowance-trading program set up by Title IV and of how it was designed to operate. (More details are given in subsequent chapters as needed.) The final section of this chapter provides an overview of the rest of this book.

THE U.S. ACID RAIN PROGRAM

Acid rain (or, more properly, acid deposition) occurs when sulfur dioxide (SO_2) and nitrogen oxides (NO_x) react in the atmosphere to form sulfuric and nitric acids, respectively.[6] These acids then fall to earth, sometimes hundreds of miles downwind from their source, in either wet or dry form. In North America, acid rain is a concern mainly in the northeastern United States, particularly in the Adirondacks and New England, and in southeastern Canada. The motivation for regulatory policies to reduce acid rain is the argument that in this region, acid rain damages aquatic life and harms trees in sensitive forest areas. The dominant precursor of acid rain in the United States is SO_2 from coal-fired and, to a much smaller extent, oil-fired power plants. These emissions are the focus of Title IV of the 1990 Clean Air Act Amendments.[7]

---

statistically significant reduction in sulfur deposition was observed in 1995 by monitors located in the Northeast and the Ohio River Valley, but similarly significant changes in the acidity of waters or other indicia of ecosystem response have not been observed, because of the longer response times of these complex processes.

6. NAPAP (1991).

7. Electric utilities accounted for about 70% of 1985 U.S. SO_2 emissions: Coal-fired units accounted for 96% of this total, and oil-fired units accounted for the remainder (EPA, 1994). The other 30% of emissions is accounted for by a wide variety of industrial, commercial, and residential boilers and process sources (including smelters and paper facilities), as well as by the use of diesel fuel for transportation. Aside from certain voluntary opt-in provisions contained in Title IV, including these other sources in the allowance program was not given serious consideration. These sources are generally individually much smaller than utility sources and are much more diverse. Moreover, there were no systematic baseline emissions data available for these sources

Title IV represents a fundamental change in the regulatory framework governing air pollution in the US. Previous air pollution regulations controlled the emissions rates of individual pollution sources (measured in, for instance, pounds of pollutant per unit of fuel burned) or required that individual sources employ designated control technologies. Aggregate emissions (measured in, for instance, tons of pollutant) were not directly controlled. In contrast, the 1990 acid rain law focuses directly on aggregate SO_2 emissions rather than on emissions by individual sources, their emission rates, or the techniques they use to control emissions. It does so by placing an aggregate cap on SO_2 emissions and gives polluters extensive flexibility to choose whether and how to reduce emissions at specific sources. The introduction of emissions trading goes well beyond trading among utilities. Equally importantly, the 1990 law gives utilities with multiple fossil-fired generating units enormous and unprecedented flexibility in complying with emission limits even if they trade no allowances at all with each other.

Title IV was advertised as requiring a 10-million-tons-per-year reduction in SO_2 emissions from 1980 levels by the year 2000. To achieve this goal, the law created a cap on SO_2 emissions from electric generating plants of roughly 9 million tons per year, effective in the year 2000 and beyond. This emissions cap was to be achieved in two phases. During Phase I (1995–1999), the 263 dirtiest large generating units (located in 110 generating plants and accounting for 88 GW^e of electric generating capacity) were required to reduce their emissions by roughly 3.5 million tons per year, beginning in 1995. In Phase II (2000 and beyond), virtually all fossil-fueled electric generating plants become subject to the national cap on aggregate annual SO_2 emissions. (All states had Phase II units except Alaska and Hawaii, which were simply omitted from the program, and Idaho, which had no fossil-fueled generating units.)

The Phase I reductions and Phase II cap are enforced through the annual issuance of tradable emission allowances, each of which permits its holder to emit one ton of SO_2 in a particular year or any subsequent year.[8] Each unit has thirty days after the end of each year

---

to provide a basis for allocating allowances to incumbents. On this issue, see Kete (1993, pp. 217–21).

8. In fact, these allowances are like checking account deposits, in that they exist only as records in the EPA's computer-based allowance-tracking system. The system, which contains accounts for all affected generating units and for any other parties that want to hold allowances, can be used to transfer allowances from one account to another.

to deliver to the U.S. Environmental Protection Agency (EPA) valid allowances sufficient to cover its emissions during the year. At that time, the EPA cancels the allowances needed to cover emissions. Failure to produce the necessary allowances subjects a utility to substantial financial penalties and requirements to make additional future emission reductions.

Allowances good in any particular year but not needed to cover SO_2 emissions in that year may be "banked" for future use, but allowances can never be borrowed from the future. (As we shall see, this has turned out to be an absolutely critical feature of the program.) Owners of individual units are free to decide what mix of emission reductions and allowance transactions they will employ to meet each year's allowance constraint, and essentially no restrictions are placed on emission reduction techniques. There is also no restriction on who may buy or sell allowances. Brokers have acquired some in hopes of future price increases, for instance, and environmentalists have acquired some in order to reduce emissions more than the law requires.

Phase I (1995–99)

The basic allowance-allocation formula for each unit required to reduce emissions in Phase I (called "Table A units" because they are listed in Table A in the statute) multiplies an emission rate (ER) of 2.5 pounds of SO_2 per million Btus of heat input (2.5 lb/mmBtu, for short) by baseline heat input (generally the unit's 1985–87 average). As discussed in Chapter 3, however, the final bill included significant departures from this formula. The most important of these was designed to favor the use of eastern high-sulfur coal by providing bonus allowances to Phase I units ("extension units") that opted to comply with Title IV via flue-gas desulfurization. This involves installing a relatively expensive facility, generally called a "scrubber," that removes sulfur from the flue gas. The main alternative approach to emission reduction is to switch to coal with a lower sulfur content, which is historically more expensive than high-sulfur coal.

Title IV also contains provisions designed to give utilities additional flexibility in complying with Phase I emission-reduction obligations:

- The "substitution" provision permits utilities to substitute other units for Table A units. Non-Table A units that have been sub-

stituted for Table A units then receive allocations of allowances approximately equal to their historic emissions and, for all intents and purposes, are treated as Table A units.
- The "compensation" provision allows utilities to reduce generation in Table A units in a way that does not simply involve shifting electricity production and the associated SO_2 emissions from a Phase I unit to units not affected by Phase I.

Collectively, these provisions are often referred to as the "voluntary compliance program." As we discuss in Chapter 8, the substitution provision has been much more important than anyone had anticipated, while the compensation provision has been little used.[9]

Phase II (2000 and Beyond)

During Phase II, each fossil-fuel-based generating unit exceeding $25 MW^e$ generating capacity is allocated a specific number of SO_2 allowances per year, and additional reductions in aggregate emissions are required. The Phase II allocation rules for the years 2000–09, which we analyze in detail in Chapter 3, are specified in about thirty statutory provisions. The provisions for 2010 and subsequent years are only slightly less complex. As in Phase I, utilities can cover their emissions with the allowances they were allocated, and buy, sell, or bank allowances for future use. Any individual or firm is free to buy and sell allowances, as well.

Annual EPA Auctions

In addition to allocating allowances to each generating unit, the EPA has been required by Title IV to conduct small annual revenue-neutral allowance auctions since 1993. Auctioned allowances are acquired by the EPA's holding back approximately 2.8% of the allowances issued to each unit; each unit in turn receives a pro rata share of the auction proceeds. The auction is "revenue neutral" in the sense that the EPA takes allowances from each affected source (i.e., each generating unit that must use allowances to cover its emissions) and then pays the source for these allowances based on the market

9. Title IV also established a voluntary program applicable to industrial sources that allowed such sources to "opt in" to the program. However, like the compensation provisions, the voluntary industry-source program has also been little used.

value they fetch at auction. The auction provision was a response to concerns expressed by independent power producers and rapidly growing utilities that an active market for allowances would not emerge, concerns strengthened by assertions during debates on the 1990 Clean Air Act Amendments that utilities would hoard their initial allocations and refuse to sell at any price.[10]

Measuring Emissions

Any effective "cap and trade" system such as that embodied in Title IV requires an accurate method for measuring emissions and tracking allowances. Title IV requires utilities to install continuous emission monitoring (CEM) equipment, and EPA regulations contain powerful financial incentives to ensure that these monitors are operationally accurate. In addition, the EPA created a comprehensive computer database that allows owners of affected units, as well as the EPA and third parties, to track the number of allowances in each unit's "account" at a particular point in time. The system also allows each unit's authorized representative to record transfers of allowances between generating units under common ownership as well as between generating units with different owners. While the terms and conditions of allowance market transactions are not reported to the EPA, any allowances that are bought and sold must eventually appear in the EPA's allowance-tracking system if they are to be used for compliance purposes.

OVERVIEW OF THE BOOK

Like it or not, environmental policies are outputs of political processes. Understanding the political process that drove the design and enactment of Title IV can inform thinking about future uses of emissions trading. Chapter 2 describes the evolution of acid rain control policy in the United States over the last three decades, and the long political process that culminated in the passage of Title IV

---

10. For several years, some allowances were also held back each year for sale at a fixed price (which turned out to be well above market prices); any excess supply was auctioned the following year. Hausker (1992) discusses the political economy of these institutions; see also Joskow, Schmalensee, and Bailey (1998) and Chapter 7 of this book.

in 1990. Since allowances to emit SO_2 are valuable, it should be no surprise that interest groups affected by the program desired to gain title to as many allowances as possible. Moreover, the economic impact on key actors – utilities, coal-mine owners, coal miners, and electricity consumers – of a program designed to reduce SO_2 emissions significantly varied widely from one region of the country to another. There was similar variation in the political influence of the groups affected in each region and of their legislative representatives. In Chapter 3, we examine Congress's ultimate allocation of SO_2 allowances among electric generating units located in different regions of the United States from a political economy perspective, focusing on the role of key interest groups and their supporters in Congress.

With this background, we then turn to a multidimensional analysis of the effects of Title IV on SO_2 emissions, of compliance strategies adopted by the owners of affected generating units, of the behavior and performance of allowance markets, and of the costs incurred by emission sources to comply with the program's requirements. Chapter 4 examines the historical patterns of SO_2 emissions before Title IV took effect in 1995. This is important because SO_2 emissions were declining even before Title IV became effective, due to changes in coal and transportation markets, as well as earlier emission-control regulations aimed at other adverse environmental effects of SO_2 emissions. Chapter 5 presents "counterfactual" estimates of what SO_2 emissions would have been, had there been no Title IV restrictions on them. The level of "counterfactual" emissions then becomes a baseline from which the reduction in emissions attributable to Title IV in the years 1995–97 can be determined. This chapter also discusses abatement techniques used to accomplish that reduction and the way the emission reduction was distributed geographically and among units. In particular, we provide an analysis of why "hot spots" have not appeared. In Chapter 6, we present an analysis of the extent to which operators of Phase I units have made use of the flexibility provided by Title IV to reassign and trade emission rights among units and over time.

Chapter 7 turns to a detailed analysis and evaluation of the development and performance of markets for SO_2 allowances. This analysis examines both the annual EPA auctions as well as the much larger and more complex private markets for allowances and allowance derivatives that have developed in the last few years and the influence of state regulatory commissions. Chapter 8 analyzes why the voluntary compliance program was so heavily utilized and contributed so little to the overall reduction of emissions. In particular, we elucidate an important potential "adverse selection" problem that must be considered in the design of voluntary features of any future emissions-trading program. This problem may be especially important in the design of international CO_2 emissions-trading programs, since in the absence of a world government, all participation is necessarily voluntary. In Chapter 9, we develop estimates of the costs incurred by utilities to comply with Phase I of the program. Some have argued that the low allowance prices observed early in Phase I indicate that the allowance-trading system made large SO_2 emission reductions possible at a small fraction of the anticipated cost. Our estimate of the actual costs of complying with Phase I of Title IV is developed and compared to earlier predictions of the cost to comply with Title IV.

This book concludes with three chapters that identify and discuss a number of questions raised by the experience with the SO_2 trading program. As just noted, Chapter 9 provides an estimate of the cost of complying with Phase I. Of equal interest is the question of how this estimated compliance cost compares with the costs that would have been incurred if a reasonable "command-and-control" system had been employed instead of a cap-and-trade system. That is, how much was saved by turning to a cap-and-trade system instead of an alternative command-and-control system? Chapter 10 provides an estimate of the cost savings achieved by Title IV's emissions-trading provisions when compared to a plausible *alternative* form of SO_2 emission regulation that would achieve the same aggregate reduction in emissions but would not allow for trading of emission rights. Having focused on the benefits resulting from the flexible trading features of Title IV, we turn in Chapter 11 to a discussion of imperfections in certain aspects of emissions trading. We also address the inevitable "errors" (i.e., decisions that 20/20 hindsight reveals to have been suboptimal) made in a world of uncertainty. This discussion necessarily involves an interpretation of the behavior of allowance prices, which have been anything but smoothly rising, as textbook presentations (which generally assume away uncertainty) would suggest. Chapter 12 offers concluding observations and presents some thoughts on the implications of the experience with the SO_2 trading program for the application of similar market-based emission-control approaches to other pollutants, such as air emissions that are thought to contribute to global warming.

2 A Political History of Federal Acid Rain Legislation

The 1970 Clean Air Act Amendments

The 1990 Acid Rain Program and the factors that influenced its structure cannot be understood in isolation from the earlier history of the federal government's efforts to limit SO_2 emissions produced in conjunction with the generation of electricity. The 1970 Clean Air Act Amendments, the first significant U.S. federal air pollution legislation, led to the establishment of national maximum standards for ambient concentrations of SO_2, as for those of carbon monoxide, nitrogen dioxide, particulates, ozone, and lead. The states were largely responsible for meeting these standards in each local area. Each state was required to develop and have approved by EPA a state implementation plan (SIP) specifying actions to be taken to bring the state into compliance with the standards before the deadlines specified in the statute. The motivation for controlling SO_2 emissions at this time was *not* concern about damage caused by acid rain. Rather, it rested on concerns about the effects of ambient SO_2 concentrations on human health (for which "primary standards" were specified in the statute) and on other aspects of human welfare such as visibility (for which "secondary standards" were specified in the statute).

The 1970 Amendments also imposed New Source Performance Standards (NSPS) applicable only to SO_2 emissions from *new* power plants. According to the NSPS, the emissions rate (ER) for new coal

13

plants could not exceed 1.2 lb of sulfur dioxide per million Btu of fuel burned (0.8 lb/mmBtu for oil). These regulations created a significant gap between the SO_2 emission rates of many existing plants and the emission rates permitted for new plants.[1] However, it was assumed that many existing plants that did not meet the NSPS would gradually retire over time, following historical retirement patterns, and that, as older plants retired, the stock of operating plants would gradually become dominated by NSPS plants. This assumption did not take into account strong incentives created by these rules to extend the lives of old, dirty plants, which were relatively expensive to replace with NSPS units.

In addition, to help meet local ambient SO_2 standards, states required some existing and new power plants to have a high smokestack to disperse emissions over a wider area. By keeping SO_2 in the atmosphere longer, however, tall stacks may increase ambient concentrations at distant locations. In addition, tall stacks generally encourage the formation of sulfates and sulfuric acid suspended higher in the atmosphere, increasing both the total amount of acid deposition and the geographic distance over which the acidic deposition spreads.

The 1977 Clean Air Act Amendments

By 1975 it had become clear that many states would not be able to comply with the ambient air quality standards by the deadlines specified for compliance in the statute. In the case of SO_2, this was partly because of utility decisions to continue operating older plants beyond their "normal" retirement dates. In 1977, Congress again amended the Clean Air Act to respond both to the failure of many states to meet their obligations under the 1970 statute and to new concerns raised by environmental groups. At this time, however, acid rain was not yet a policy issue. The 1977 Amendments extended the deadline for meeting ambient standards until 1982, and required EPA to designate areas not meeting the standards by the initial deadlines as "nonattainment" regions, to which tight regulatory controls would be applied. The 1977 Amendments also tightened the NSPS for SO_2 emissions to accelerate the reduction in local ambient SO_2 concentra-

---

1. Pre-1970 plants were still subject to controls under state implementation plans (SIPs) required by the Clean Air Act to ensure that each state came into compliance with national ambient air quality standards. There was wide variation among the states in the aggressiveness of their SIPs and how they affected existing plants.

tions in areas (particularly in the Midwest) still violating national standards.[2] In addition, Congress responded to pressures from environmental and other interest groups to do something to prevent significant deterioration of existing air quality in those regions of the country where ambient air quality currently met the national standards.[3] The latter was perceived by environmentalists to be a significant problem in the West, where (a) rapid economic growth was expected and (b) utilities had access to cheap, low-sulfur coal. Utilities burning this coal could easily meet the 1.2-lb NSPS standard while increasing aggregate SO_2 emissions, and do so without violating national ambient standards because ambient concentrations in the West were far below these limits. Moreover, increased SO_2 concentrations in the West were associated with reduced visibility, sometimes in pristine areas far from the sources of emissions.

Simply reducing the NSPS emissions rate – 0.55 lb/mmBtu was considered – would have accelerated compliance with ambient air quality standards in the East, but would have permitted emissions and ambient concentrations to continue to increase in the West. Moreover, it was effectively argued that a simple reduction below 1.2 lb/mmBtu would have a significant adverse effect on high-sulfur coal production in the East, something that was intolerable to high-sulfur coal producers and the United Mine Workers Union. Midwestern utilities also objected that the costs of meeting a significantly lower emissions rate would be too high. The political solution that emerged from the 1977 legislation and subsequent EPA rule-making satisfied environmentalists, high-sulfur coal interests, and midwestern utilities. It required new coal-fired plants built after 1978 both to meet the ER ≤ 1.2 constraint *and* either (a) to remove 90% of potential SO_2 emissions (as determined by the sulfur content of the fuel burned) or (b) to remove 70% of potential SO_2 emissions and operate with ER < 0.6. This "percent reduction" standard required all new coal plants to operate with flue gas desulfurization facilities – generally referred to as "scrubbers" – even if they burned low-sulfur coal.[4] This provision significantly reduced

---

2. On the material in this paragraph and the next, see Ackerman and Hassler (1981), Cohen (1992, Chapt. 2), and Kete (1993, pp. 158–59).
3. Ackerman and Hassler (1981, pp. 28–33).
4. Oil-fired units built after 1978 also had to meet the 1971 ER constraint (ER ≤ 0.8) and to remove 90% of potential emissions; they faced no percent reduction requirement if ER < 0.2, however. To avoid simply sending SO_2 emissions long distances downwind, the 1977 legislation sharply limited the use of tall smokestacks as a compliance strategy.

the advantage of low-sulfur coal as a means of compliance, making high-sulfur coal interests (coal mine owners and miners) happy, and effectively imposed a lower emissions rate on new sources in the West than in the East. As Ackerman and Hassler (1981) have stressed, this provision gave environmentalists the tighter NSPS they had sought but raised the costs of SO_2 control, and it may well have dirtied the air on balance by encouraging utilities to burn high-sulfur coal and by strengthening incentives to extend the lives of old, dirty plants.

In important respects, the debate over the SO_2 provisions in the 1977 Clean Air Act Amendments was a *regional* dispute involving several blocs: (a) a relatively small number of midwestern states with slow economic growth that relied heavily on dirty coal-burning power plants (i.e., Ohio, Indiana, Illinois, Missouri); (b) an overlapping group of midwestern and Appalachian states that both produced and burned large amounts of high-sulfur coal and exported significant quantities to other states (i.e., Kentucky, West Virginia, Pennsylvania, Illinois)[5]; (c) northeastern states with slowly growing economies that produced relatively little SO_2 (e.g., New York, Vermont, Massachusetts); (d) fast-growing western states with clean generating plants that relied on low-sulfur coal, produced low-sulfur coal, and had abundant reserves to expand production of low-sulfur coal (i.e., Wyoming, Montana, Colorado); and (e) a large number of states with fast-growing economies that relied primarily on oil, gas, nuclear power, and low-sulfur coal and were much less affected by SO_2 emissions or efforts to control them (e.g., California, Texas, Louisiana).[6]

The 1977 legislation was clearly a victory for environmentalists. It is also generally viewed as a victory for high-sulfur coal producers and miners, since the scrubbing provisions reduced what would otherwise have been a very significant economic disadvantage for high-sulfur coal. Conversely, of course, Appalachian and, to a lesser extent, western producers of low-sulfur coal lost. This

---

5. The areas of central and southern Appalachia with low-sulfur coal reserves had interests that diverged from those portions of the region with high-sulfur coal; this resulted in significant intraregional controversy as well.
6. Crandall (1984, p. 27). The 1977 law also contained Prevention of Significant Deterioration (PSD) provisions that required controls in areas that met ambient air quality standards and were a particular concern in the West. Pashigian (1985) finds important regional dimensions in disputes over these provisions.

legislation was viewed as a victory for most midwestern and northeastern coal-burning utilities and their customers, since old plants generally remained relatively lightly controlled,[7] and slow economic growth meant there was little need to build new plants meeting NSPS.[8] The big losers were those states, mainly in the West, that were using low-sulfur coal and growing rapidly. Scrubbing effectively required these states to engage in costly cleanup of what was already clean coal and to bear a disproportionate share of cleanup costs because they were building a disproportionate share of new fossil-fueled capacity. The northeastern states won economically because, like the Midwest, their incremental SO_2 control costs were relatively low. However, environmental interests in the Northeast gradually came to feel that their region had lost environmentally because failure to control emissions from old, dirty midwestern plants effectively meant failure to attack what was increasingly viewed by environmentalists as a serious acid rain problem in the Northeast.

The outcome of the bitter debate over the 1977 Amendments and subsequent EPA rules left the losers, especially in the West and to some extent in the Northeast, very unhappy. These memories, the desire to avoid losing again, and even the desire to "pay back" the midwestern and Appalachian states for the 1977 law's costly percent removal requirement played an important part in the controversies over acid rain that continued during the 1980s.[9]

By 1990, it was clear that total U.S. emissions of SO_2 had peaked in the early 1970s and declined steadily during the early 1980s.[10] The focus of Clean Air Act regulation on new generating units, however, served to extend the economic lives of old, dirty plants that were not burdened with significant control costs. As a consequence of this "new-source bias," by 1985, 83% of power plant SO_2 emissions came

7. Controls had been imposed on some old plants by state environmental agencies in order to meet ambient SO_2 standards. The stringency of these controls varied greatly, however, and they were rarely if ever as strict as the NSPS standard. Nonetheless, in part because of these controls, utility SO_2 emissions declined steadily after the mid-1970s, despite increased coal consumption.
8. In the late 1970s, the technology of choice for meeting incremental generating capacity needs in the East, the South, and portions of the Midwest was nuclear power.
9. See Kriz (1990, especially p. 893) and Stern (1986a, 1986b).
10. GAO (1984, 1994).

from generating units not meeting the 1971 NSPS, and 63% came from units with ER ≥ 2.5.[11]

Table 2.1 shows huge interstate differences in "baseline" (roughly, mid-1980s) aggregate and per capita SO_2 emissions. Differences in per capita emissions reflected differences in the amount of electricity generation per capita (largely reflecting differences in economic and industrial structures), in the use of coal of various types (reflecting accidents of geography and history), and in the vintages of generating plants in use. Per capita emissions tended to be highest in midwestern states that grew relatively little since 1970 and that were located near high-sulfur coal deposits. Emissions tended to be lowest in states that had new power plants and made relatively little use of coal.

Table 2.1 also shows that the correlation between low emissions per capita and classification as a "clean" state under the 1990 law is far from perfect.[12] Oregon and Washington, for instance, had very low emissions per capita because they relied heavily on hydropower, not because their fossil-fueled steam-generating units were unusually clean. At the other extreme, Wyoming had high per capita emissions because it generated a lot of electricity per capita from coal (and sold much of it out of state). Because they are, on average, new and because they burn low-sulfur local coal, however, Wyoming's coal-fired generating units have a low average emissions rate.

Environmentalists and Other Interest Groups Focus on Acid Rain

Acid rain gradually emerged as a serious environmental and political issue only after 1977 because of pressures from environmental groups and northeastern states, and, especially, because the Canadian government objected to transborder flows of acid rain precursors and other pollutants. All expressed concerns about the effects of wet and dry acidic deposition on property, trees, and aquatic life.[13] To help

---

11. These emissions statistics and those discussed subsequently were calculated using the National Allowance Data Base (Pechan, 1995). As noted above, Phase 1 covered only large units with ER ≥ 2.5.
12. While states classified as "clean" tend to have lower than average per capita emissions, the difference is not significant.
13. On the early history of this issue, see Ackerman and Hassler (1981, p. 66), GAO (1984), and Davis (1986).

Table 2.1. *Per capita and aggregate baseline SO$_2$ emissions, by state*

Pounds/ capita	Thousands of tons[a]	State	Pounds/ capita	Thousands of tons[a]	State
1029.5	962.5	West Virginia	53.6	42.7	Utah[b]
550.9	1519.7	Indiana	53.5	82.7	Colorado[b]
548.4	126.7	Wyoming[b]	52.6	151.3	Virginia
439.3	806.6	Kentucky	44.6	396.8	New York
427.8	138.2	North Dakota	41.8	16.6	Montana[b]
425.6	2303.1	Ohio	38.1	60.9	Connecticut
381.7	957.4	Missouri	32.5	68.5	Louisiana[b]
347.4	1037.1	Georgia	27.9	62.8	Washington
341.0	807.2	Tennessee	25.9	97.8	New Jersey
281.0	557.5	Alabama	20.7	12.2	Maine
221.8	69.9	Delaware	6.8	3.3	Rhode Island[b]
197.9	1174.7	Pennsylvania	4.3	1.3	Dist. of Col.
177.3	1013.2	Illinois	0.7	0.9	Oregon
155.5	373.1	Wisconsin	0.6	0.2	Vermont[b]
143.0	72.6	New Hampshire	0.5	6.8	California[b]

Notes: Baseline sulfur dioxide emissions in pounds (from the National Allowance Data Base) divided by the average of 1980 and 1990 populations. Baseline emissions for generating units operating in 1985 are generally the product of each unit's 1985 emission rate and its average 1985–87 fuel consumption.

[a]Baseline generating-unit sulfur dioxide emissions in thousands of tons (from the National Allowance Data Base). All states with emissions of 500,000$^+$ tons are shown except for Florida (635.2) and Texas (641.5). The only state with emissions of 50,000 tons or less not shown is South Dakota (25.8).

[b]Designated a "Clean State" under §406 of the 1990 Clean Air Act Amendments because baseline average emissions rate (ER) from fossil fuel-fired steam generating units did not exceed 0.8 lb per million Btu. "Clean States" not shown, with per-capita emissions in parentheses, are the following: Arizona (70.50), Arkansas (63.55), Nevada (112.92), New Mexico (101.99), Oklahoma (60.66), and Texas (82.21).

Source: Pechan (1995).

resolve scientific disputes about the actual damage caused by acid rain, Congress created the National Acid Precipitation Assessment Program (NAPAP) in 1980. By the end of 1990 NAPAP had spent about $600 million[14] studying scientific issues associated with acid deposition, but its work had no visible effect on the 1990 legislation.[15]

Many acid rain bills were proposed by western and northeastern senators and representatives during the 1980s.[16] This legislation generally called for reductions of 6–12 million tons of SO$_2$ emissions

14. U.S. National Acid Precipitation Assessment Program (1990), p. 7.
15. See Roberts (1991a, b). Observers have argued that among the reasons for NAPAP's lack of impact were its concentration on "good science" instead of policy-relevant analysis and its lack of political support from the environmental community.
16. See Crandall (1984) and the following pages in the indicated annual numbers of *The Congressional Quarterly Almanac* (Washington, DC: Congressional Quarterly, Inc.): *1982,* pp. 425–34; *1983,* pp. 340–41; *1984,* pp. 340–42; *1986,* p. 137; *1987,* pp. 299–301; *1988,* pp. 142–48.

per year from 1980 levels, targeted the dirtiest generating units for cleanup, and often involved some variant of the ER ≤ 1.2 constraint that had been applied to new units since 1971. That is, the proposed acid rain legislation would effectively extend the NSPS emissions requirement contained in the 1970 Clean Air Act to existing sources as well as to new sources. The interest in extending the 1970 Act's NSPS emissions standards to existing sources represents an important policy linkage between the 1970 Act and Title IV of the 1990 Act. In part because the costs of cleanup varied considerably among existing units, these proposals often provided for more flexibility than did traditional command-and-control regulation by, for instance, applying emissions limits at the state level rather than unit by unit.[17] Because the costs of these control strategies would have been heavily concentrated in a few midwestern states, and projections suggested that electricity rates there would have to rise significantly to cover those costs, some proposals included a national electricity tax to help pay cleanup costs and to "share the pain." Some proposals included mandatory scrubbing, while others did not.

During the 1980s, midwestern and Appalachian high-sulfur coal-producing states generally opposed *any* new acid rain controls, while western and northeastern states opposed both a national electricity tax and any additional scrubbing requirements.[18] Acid rain legislation was effectively blocked in the House of Representatives by John Dingell (D–MI), who became chairman of the powerful House Energy and Commerce Committee in 1981. Michigan had relatively little to gain or lose from acid rain legislation; Dingell's main concern was that any legislation amending the Clean Air Act would likely tighten auto emission standards significantly, and he accordingly blocked all such legislation.[19] In the Senate, several acid rain bills were reported out of the Committee on Environment and Public Works, but they were effectively blocked by the majority leader, Robert Byrd (D–WV). West Virginia, with high per capita emissions

17. Pechan (1989) compare six contemporary acid rain proposals.
18. In 1983 a group of six governors from New York and New England, led by then-governor of New Hampshire John Sununu, agreed to an acid rain program that would have reduced annual emissions by about 10 million tons and shared some of the costs through a national electricity tax. They were unable to garner sufficient support for this program, which was aggressively opposed by Pennsylvania, in particular. See Hanley (1983). An acid rain deal involving such a tax was nearly closed in Congress during 1988; see Cohen (1992, pp. 36–44).
19. See, for instance, Cohen (1992, pp. 29–32).

of SO_2 and high production of high-sulfur coal burned in other states, was potentially a big loser from acid rain legislation. Completing the constellation of major "Just Say No!" forces on acid rain was President Ronald Reagan, who opposed environmental regulation generally.[20]

Even if it had been possible, somehow, to pass acid rain legislation during the 1980s, only an extreme optimist would have expected that legislation to reduce emissions efficiently. Writing in 1984, Crandall (p. 27) observed that:

An "efficient" control policy is one that reduces emissions until marginal costs are equal across plants and states. A political optimum policy, in contrast, requires states to reduce emissions by some nationally uniform fraction of their current departure from efficiency. This is indeed the approach taken in [two bills considered between 1982 and 1984]: both would have required proportional rollbacks from current emissions that exceed a threshold level.

LEGISLATIVE HISTORY OF THE 1990 ACID RAIN PROGRAM[21]

Foundations of the Bush Administration's Acid Rain Policy

During the 1980s, the political strength of the environmental movement grew dramatically, fueled in part by the Reagan Administration's apparent intransigence on environmental issues.[22] Population continued to shift to the West and South, and the number of miners of high-sulfur coal dwindled as high-sulfur coal production fell and productivity improved dramatically.[23] The 1988 presidential election was won by George Bush, who had promised to be "the Environ-

---

20. See also Crandall (1984) on other obstacles to assembling a winning pro-control coalition during the 1980s.
21. This section draws heavily on Cohen (1992) and, to a lesser extent, recollections of participants, in addition to the sources cited.
22. The Sierra Club's membership increased more than sixfold between 1980 and 1990 (personal communication with Club officials), and the share of respondents agreeing with the following statement increased from 45% to 80% between 1981 and 1989 (Suro, 1989): Protecting the environment is so important that requirements and standards cannot be too high, and continuing environmental improvements must be made regardless of cost.
23. Between 1980 and 1990, the average daily employment of miners in eastern mines (both high-sulfur and low-sulfur) fell from 202,039 to 115,216. (Source: *Coal Data* [Washington, DC: National Coal Association], various years.)

mental President" and had advocated looking "to the marketplace for innovative solutions" to environmental problems. Bush had a summer home in Maine, where acid rain was perceived to be a problem, and his chief of staff, John Sununu, was a former governor of New Hampshire who had led early efforts to control acid rain. In the Senate, George Mitchell (D–ME) succeeded Robert Byrd as majority leader. Mitchell was an ardent proponent of acid rain controls, having introduced one of the first acid rain control proposals in 1981, and he had chaired the Environmental Protection Subcommittee in the previous Congress. Even with Chairman Dingell still in place in the House, the stage was clearly set for, at the very least, a serious attempt to pass acid rain legislation.

Even before President Bush's inauguration, staff at EPA, in the vice president's office, and elsewhere in the executive branch began work on a set of proposed amendments to the Clean Air Act that would deal with acid rain as well as toxic air pollutants, urban smog, and other air quality issues.[24] Work on acid rain was heavily influenced by an emissions-trading proposal that had been circulated during 1988 by the Environmental Defense Fund (EDF). Though there were concerns about both the workability of the EDF proposal and the size of the emissions reductions it required (12 million tons from 1980 levels), relying on tradable permits to control acid rain would respond to President Bush's call to look "to the marketplace" and could reduce control costs. Moreover, it was hoped that EDF's endorsement would provide protection against knee-jerk antimarket attacks from other environmental groups. Finally, the Project 88 Report (Stavins, 1988), sponsored by Senators Timothy Wirth (D–CO) and John Heinz (R–PA) and conducted at Harvard University's Kennedy School, had engendered widespread discussion of market-based approaches. While some EPA staff clearly preferred traditional command-and-control methods, strong support developed at both staff and political levels within the agency, and the basic idea of using tradable permits to control acid rain was adopted by the Bush Administration without much internal warfare.

The Administration's clean air proposal was announced in general terms on June 12, 1989, and draft legislation was released on July 21.

---

24. For a contemporary view of this process, see Kriz (1989).

The acid rain component of this proposal was structurally very similar to the final bill passed in 1990. The Administration's proposal called for significant reductions in SO_2 emissions to 10 million tons below 1980 levels, comparable to reductions called for by many environmental groups.[25] In Phase I, which was to begin in 1996, 255 large generating units with ER $\geq$ 2.5 in 1985 were granted SO_2 emissions allowances roughly equal to emissions at ER = 2.5 and baseline (average 1985–87) fuel use. The affected units had either to reduce emissions to match their allowance allocations or else to purchase allowances from other affected units that had reduced emissions sufficiently to have allowances to sell. Allowances could be traded, but only within a state or a multistate utility system.

In Phase II, which was originally proposed to begin in 2001, all units with ER $\geq$ 1.2 in 1985 and a capacity of at least 75 megawatts received allowances roughly equal to emissions at ER = 1.2 and baseline fuel use. These allowances could be freely traded within two broad (eastern and western) regions. All other generating units were constrained not to exceed their 1985 emission rates. Only small departures from the Administration's proposed Phase II emissions ceiling were ever seriously considered, so that the allocation of Phase II allowances was essentially a zero-sum game from July 1989 onward.[26] Thus, the Administration's proposed legislation would have effectively gradually extended the 1970 Act's NSPS emission rates to all existing generating units exceeding a minimum size threshold. It could be argued that this had always been the intent of the 1970 Act, but that the generating units operating at that time failed to retire at the rate that originally had been assumed.

25. Reflecting the previous decade's debates, discussion within the Administration focused on reductions of 8, 10, and 12 million tons below 1980 levels, even though emissions had declined significantly between 1980 and 1989. With essentially no information on benefits associated with the different levels of stringency (see the discussion of NAPAP, above), 10 million tons was chosen because it was felt that announcing 8 would provoke strong attacks from environmental groups, while the incremental cost of going from 10 to 12 was estimated to be significantly and unacceptably higher than that of going from 8 to 10.

26. As Kete (1993, pp. 144–55) notes, a "technical" dispute about what Phase 2 emissions level was implied by a 10 million ton reduction, with stakes of between 0.5 and 2.0 million tons per year, persisted until just before the Senate–House conference committee completed its work in October 1990. Debates about allowance allocations had proceeded on the implicit assumption that the Administration's original resolution of that dispute would prevail, however, and that assumption proved correct.

The Policy Debate Moves to Congress

Even with restrictions on interregional trading, which were soon removed in the legislative process in response to fears that regional markets would be too thin, the Administration's nationwide program did not properly reflect the regional nature of the acid rain problem or the role of prevailing winds.[27] In particular, environmentalists and residents in sensitive areas in New York and New England were concerned that acid rain "hot spots" would result from the implicit, but incorrect, assumption embodied in a national trading program that SO_2 emissions anywhere in the country have the same expected environmental impact. Nonetheless, the early *public* debate about this proposal centered instead on its workability,[28] while concerns about regional cost incidence continued to be central to *private* debates behind closed doors on Capitol Hill. The coalition that had defeated acid rain legislation during the 1980s stressed both problems in attempting to defeat the Administration proposal. They offered no alternative legislation, apparently choosing instead to fight the passage of any new acid rain bill rather than offer a compromise. Environmental groups, despite their traditional distaste for market-based policies, did not offer alternative legislation either, perhaps because they feared that a program less flexible or more restrictive than the Administration's would likely be too expensive to pass. The only visible proposal from the environmental community was the EDF emissions-trading initiative discussed above. As already noted, however, the EDF initiative had much in common with the Administration's bill (except that EDF's reduction requirements were larger), and it was never translated into a concrete legislative proposal.

Van Dyke (1991) and others have argued that fairness required that allowances be sold rather than given out for free,[29] but as Cohen (1992) and Kriz (1990) make clear, this alternative was simply not on the table in 1989 and 1990. Instead, the real debate was about whether

---

27. For a general discussion of these sorts of issues, see Tietenberg (1985, Chapt. 4).
28. See, for instance, U.S. House of Representatives (1990, pp. 209–437).
29. The potentially adverse distributional implications of giving to incumbents valuable rights to pollute (see Noll, 1989, p. 1275) are partially attenuated in this case because the recipients are electric utilities subject to economic regulation, so that any associated rents were expected largely to be passed on to consumers as lower electricity prices.

cleanup of the dirtiest generating units should be subsidized by some sort of national electricity tax, an interregional cost-sharing solution that had been seriously discussed through the 1980s. Though it was clear that most costs of such a program would be borne in a relatively few states that produced large quantities of high-sulfur coal and in the states in which that coal was burned in old power plants, President Bush's 1988 election pledge of "no new taxes" required the Administration and most Republicans to oppose any sort of cost-sharing mechanism that could be labeled a tax. Energy producers were, of course, naturally opposed to anything that might lead the way to taxing other energy sources.

Van Dyke (1991) has also suggested that a "zero-revenue auction" of all allowances would have done more to develop the market than did the scheme actually adopted. This essentially would have involved handing out entitlements to the revenues raised from an auction of all the allowances, in much the same way that the allowances themselves were actually allocated. Electric utilities were naturally concerned that the revenue produced from such a large auction would eventually end up retained by the Treasury, so that they would have to pay for *both* abatement costs and allowances to cover their residual emissions. This approach would have at least doubled the program's impact on electricity rates. In addition, many involved parties simply did not believe that the market *could* work on such a large scale, and they feared emerging from a grand auction of all allowances empty-handed and with no sellers on the horizon. As a result, a grand zero-revenue auction was never given serious consideration.[30]

In the House, the Administration's bill went to the Committee on Energy and Commerce, still chaired by John Dingell (D–MI), whose main air-related interest remained minimizing impacts on the auto industry. For some time, Dingell's main antagonist on this and related issues had been Henry Waxman (D–CA) from Los Angeles, chairman of Energy and Commerce's Subcommittee on Health and the Environment. Waxman's subcommittee had jurisdiction over much of the Administration's bill, but the Acid Rain Title was sent to the

---

30. A small annual zero-revenue auction was eventually included in the final bill in response to concerns by independent power producers and rapidly growing utilities that an active market for allowances would not emerge. We analyze these auctions in Chapter 7.

Subcommittee on Energy and Power, chaired by Philip Sharp (D–IN). Indiana had large emissions from old, dirty generating plants, and while Sharp had supported earlier proposals for modest controls on acid rain, he opposed stringent controls targeting existing plants without significant cost sharing with other regions. He had advocated paying for acid rain abatement through a national electricity tax or other cost-sharing mechanism.

Traditionally in the House, ranking minority members of the Committee (Norman Lent, R–NY) and of the two subcommittees just mentioned (Edward Madigan [R–IL] and William Dannemeyer [R–CA], respectively) had played relatively minor roles in the legislative process. However, Madigan's district was supplied with electricity by Illinois Power Company, which operated some of the dirtiest coal units in the country. Illinois also produced a significant quantity of high-sulfur coal, much of which was sold in neighboring states, and one such mine was in Madigan's district. Thus, Madigan likely took a special interest in the Acid Rain Program and, as we shall see, unlike many of the other "dirty" states, Illinois did relatively well in the SO_2 allowance-allocation process.

On the Senate side, the Administration's bill went to the Subcommittee on Environmental Protection, chaired by Max Baucus (D–MT) of the Committee on Environment and Public Works, chaired by Quentin Burdick (D–ND). Fifteen of the sixteen members of the full committee were also members of the Environmental Protection Subcommittee, and Burdick was not much interested in environmental policy, so all the action was in the Baucus subcommittee. Montana, a state that both produces and uses low-sulfur coal, was one of the losers in the 1977 Amendments. Reflecting differences between the two chambers, the ranking member of the subcommittee (and, as it happens, the full committee), John Chafee (R–RI), played a significant role. A "clean" state with low per capita emissions, Rhode Island's main interest was in reducing the acid rain it received from elsewhere, and Chafee had a strong pro-environment record generally.

The (full) committees on the Senate and House sides differed substantially in regional composition. Five of sixteen senators on Environment and Public Works were from New England, where concerns about acid rain were high. On the House side, however, only two of forty-three representatives from New England were on Energy and Commerce. Moreover, the Senate committee had representation from neither the states with the highest SO_2 emissions (Ohio, Indiana, Pennsylvania, Georgia, and Illinois) nor the largest eastern coal-producing states (Kentucky, West Virginia, Pennsylvania, Illinois, and Indiana).[31] On the House side, all but Kentucky and West Virginia were represented on Energy and Commerce. Only 31% of the senators on Environment and Public Works were from states with (old, dirty) Phase I plants, compared with 56% of representatives on Energy and Commerce. Thus the Senate committee with primary responsibility for acid rain legislation had broad representation from states that would favor or be indifferent to tighter controls on SO_2 emissions designed to reduce acid rain, and it had little representation from those states that had traditionally opposed tighter controls. Conversely, the House committee with primary responsibility for acid rain legislation had broad representation from states that would be most heavily impacted by the proposed legislation and little representation from those states favoring tighter controls. Accordingly, the Senate committee's staff had been actively involved in promoting tough acid rain legislation for a decade, while the House committee's staff had been notably more skeptical toward proposed acid rain legislation. The two committees and relevant subcommittees also differed substantially in their attitudes toward environmental protection. The key Senate committees responsible for the Acid Rain Title included members who were more inclined to support environmental legislation generally than were the House committees. This difference is visible in the members' ratings by the League of Conservation Voters (LCV). These ratings were computed as percentages of a select set of "pro-environment" votes. The median 1989 LCV score was 50% for the Senate as a whole and 60% for both the Environment and Public Works Committee (Burdick, chair) and the Environmental Protection subcommittee (Baucus, chair). The median House score was 70%, while the score on the Energy and Commerce Committee (Dingell, chair) was 50%, and on the Energy and Power Subcommittee (Sharp, chair) it was 45%.[32]

31. John Warner (R–VA) was the closest. Virginia is not a particularly high total-emissions or emissions-rate state and relies primarily on low-sulfur coal. It does have a relatively small coal-mining industry in the western part of the state, although much of the coal produced is low in sulfur.
32. As the discussion above might suggest, Waxman's Health and the Environment subcommittee on the other hand had a median LCV score of 70%.

It is not terribly surprising, then, that the Senate committee responded quickly to the Administration's clean air proposal and used it as an opportunity to bring tough new clean air legislation to the floor of the Senate. On November 16, after four days of debate and only one day of markup, the Senate Committee on Environment and Public Works approved clean air legislation by a 15 to 1 vote. This bill reflected a decade of work by the subcommittee's strongly pro-environment staff at least as much as the Administration's proposal.[33] The president threatened to veto the committee's bill unless its costs were reduced substantially, and the bill's reception on the Senate floor, beginning on January 23, 1990, was much less than enthusiastic. In an attempt to avoid continuing stalemate, the majority leader, Senator Mitchell, convened a set of closed-door sessions involving senators and Administration officials. Senator Mitchell or Chairman Baucus chaired these meetings, and key members of the Environmental Protection Subcommittee were in near-constant attendance. But the meetings were open to all senators and their staffs, so that states with large stakes in particular provisions were generally represented when those provisions were discussed. In particular, the Midwest and Appalachia were well represented in discussions of the Acid Rain Title.

On acid rain, the negotiators responded to electric utilities' aversion to unit-specific emissions-rate controls. Essentially all generating units were brought into the allowance system in Phase II, and rules for determining their allowance endowments were adopted. The negotiators also brought forward the starting dates of both phases by a year, thus producing greater emissions reductions in 1995 and 2000 than had the Administration's proposal.[34] In response to

33. At the insistence of Alan Simpson (R–WY), representing a state that both produced and burned large quantities of low-sulfur coal, the committee bill contained a provision purporting to repeal the "percent reduction" provision of the 1977 Amendments. The provision to repeal was retained in the 1990 Amendments, and the EPA was given three years to produce a new NSPS. As of January 1999, EPA had not announced any plans to do anything about NSPS. A major reason is that the repeal provision requires any new standard to allow no unit more emissions than it would have been allowed under the 1978 NSPS. This apparently innocuous language is a Catch-22, since what the 1978 NSPS allows is always less than the sulfur content of the coal burned (the essence of "percent removal"), so that the only way to be sure a unit emits no more than it would have been allowed to emit under the 1978 NSPS is to install a scrubber. In addition, we are told that state regulations effectively require scrubbing in areas where new coal-fired plants have been built, so there has not been strong industry pressure to revise the NSPS.

34. See Kete (1993, p. 210).

efforts by Robert Byrd (D–WV) and other senators from states producing high-sulfur coal, a provision was added to give back the incremental 1995 reductions, a total of 3.5 million tons, as "bonus" allowances for utilities that installed scrubbers rather than switching to low-sulfur coal in Phase I. (This provision is discussed further in Chapter 3.) The incremental reductions in 2000, in turn, were given back at the rate of 540,000 allowances per year over the 2000–09 period through a number of provisions.

A major issue in these negotiations and on the Senate floor, after an agreement between the Administration and the Senate leadership was unveiled in early March, was the so-called Byrd Amendment, which would have provided generous financial aid to high-sulfur-coal miners whose jobs were eliminated by clean air legislation. The Administration and the Senate leadership opposed this amendment, and, after a bitter struggle, prevailed by one vote, 50–49.[35] Clean air legislation finally passed the Senate by a vote of 89–11 on April 3.

Responding to growing pressure to act and to the likely passage of a Senate bill with Administration support, serious work on clean air began in the House in early March. As in the Senate, most important decisions were made behind closed doors. The House process mainly involved Energy and Commerce Committee members and their staffs. The Administration was formally excluded, though there was considerable informal, staff-level communication. Drafting was completed on April 5, and on May 23 the House approved clean air legislation 401–21.

---

35. For discussions of this episode, see Cohen (1990) and Kuntz and Hager (1990). Senator Byrd called on long-standing relationships with his Democratic colleagues and on his power as chairman of the Appropriations Committee, and Democrats voted with him (and against the Senate leadership) 38 to 16. In addition, all Republicans from midwestern and Appalachian coal-producing states voted for the Byrd Amendment, except for Senator Warner (R–VA), despite strong Administration and Republican leadership opposition. Finally, Senators Cochrane (R–MS) and McClure (R–ID) voted for the Byrd Amendment, and thus against both the White House and the Republican Senate leadership, even though they represented no miners of high-sulfur coal. Senator Symms (R–ID) was talked out of doing likewise only in the last minute of voting. Given that these three senators were among the bottom twenty in terms of the AFL–CIO's evaluations of lifetime voting records, it seems unlikely that they were casting pro-labor votes for ideological reasons. Strategic motives are suggested by the facts that these three senators were in the bottom ten in terms of the League of Conservation Voters' ratings of 1989–90 voting records and that the president had threatened to veto any legislation containing the Byrd Amendment. It is most plausible that these senators hoped that passage of the Byrd Amendment would force the president to carry out his veto threat and thus likely kill new clean air legislation.

On acid rain, the House bill retained the original Administration start dates and ceilings for Phase I and Phase II.[36] Like the Senate bill, it brought essentially all generating units into the allowance program and provided incentives for scrubbing. A provision that authorized unemployment and job-training benefits for displaced workers was added on the House floor; it was not restricted to miners and carried a much smaller price tag than did the Byrd Amendment.

The Acid Rain Title produced by the Senate–House conference committee (again behind closed doors, with the Administration formally excluded) was developed from the Senate bill and closely resembled its provisions, while the House prevailed on most of the rest of the legislation.[37] A relatively small provision for aiding displaced workers (Title XI) based on the House bill was added,[38] however, and the provisions for allocating allowances were changed somewhat. In late October the conference bill passed the House by a vote of 401–25 and passed the Senate 89–10; President Bush signed the 1990 Clean Air Act Amendments into law on November 15, 1990.

36. ICF (1990) contains a detailed comparison of the acid rain provisions of the House and Senate bills.
37. See Cohen (1992, Chapt. 10) and Pytte (1990).
38. The Department of Labor received $50 million in specially allocated funds for this program. Approximately $26 million was spent in FY 1992 and FY 1993 to serve about 2,400 participants before the authority to spend this money expired in 1994. After FY 1993, discretionary funds were used to fund further applications for employment and training assistance. As of 1997, $48 million had been spent to serve about 4,000 participants (Greenwald, 1998).

3 The Political Economy of Allowance Allocations

COMPETING THEORIES OF DISTRIBUTIVE POLITICS

In this chapter, we analyze how Congress, influenced by the executive branch and various special interests, distributed SO_2 allowances among electric utilities as an integral part of the process of crafting acid rain legislation that could pass both houses of Congress and be signed by President Bush. The environmental economics and regulation literature contains essentially no empirical work on the economic effects of alternative market-based control mechanisms on different interest groups, largely because the historical record contains few applications of such mechanisms.[1] In particular, little attention has been devoted to how interest-group politics and associated rent-seeking behavior affect the allocation of rights to pollute in the context of a tradable-permit system. Without this type of knowledge it is impossible to understand the political feasibility of alternative control instruments or how they might be structured to have a better chance of gaining acceptance in the political process. The ability to structure market-based mechanisms for internalizing environmental externalities that are acceptable politically will depend heavily on their incidence; that is, on their effects on different interest groups who are represented in one way or another in the branches of

---

1. Distributional and political aspects of other sorts of environmental policies have been examined by, among others, Ackerman and Hassler (1981), Crandall (1984), and Pashigian (1984, 1985).

31

government that ultimately make policy decisions. Whenever valuable property rights[2] are created by legislation, the associated allocation decisions are likely to be highly politicized in much the same way as is tax legislation or appropriations bills.[3] Understanding better how the political process deals with such issues, in which costs and benefits are distributed among the population, can help in designing environmental control programs that are politically acceptable as well as theoretically appealing.

Our analysis is motivated by two related "nonpartisan" distributive politics frameworks for analyzing the political economy of regulatory policy. The first follows Stigler (1971) and Peltzman (1976) and argues that, all else being equal, concentrated interests (e.g., steel producers) should have more political power than dispersed interests (e.g., book lovers). In particular, we examine the impact on the allocation of SO_2 allowances of the fact that mining and burning high-sulfur coal is concentrated in a relatively few states with well-organized interest groups. This is relevant in this context because of the historical influence of these midwestern and Appalachian states (Ackerman and Hassler, 1981; Crandall, 1984) on previous federal environmental legislation affecting SO_2 emissions.

The second framework focuses on the role of constituent interests as they are mediated through legislative institutions. An important branch of this literature emphasizes the role of key committees and subcommittees in the Senate and the House that had various degrees of control over the relevant legislative agenda. Following the extensive political science literature on the organization of Congress and the role of committees (e.g., Shepsle and Weingast, 1984, 1987; Weingast and Marshall, 1988; Weingast and Moran, 1983; Ferejohn and Fiorina, 1975), we examine whether states that had representa-

2. Technically, the SO_2 allowances created by the 1990 CAAA are not property rights. Congress can increase or decrease their quantity or do away with them altogether by changing the law without anyone's having a right to raise a constitutional claim for compensation (see Section 403(f) of the 1990 CAAA). However, for all other intents and purposes, the allowances are treated as property rights. They are freely tradable, there are a variety of market mechanisms that mediate transactions, and the EPA consciously allocated allowances to eligible parties for years beyond 2010 to provide confidence that they would be treated essentially as durable property rights. All this will clearly make it difficult politically to alter allowance allocations in the future.
3. Related research on congressional spending decisions can be found in Kiel and McKenzie (1983), Baron (1989), and Levitt and Poterba (forthcoming).

tion in key committee and leadership positions were able to capture a disproportionate share of the SO_2 allowances. Finally, we also examine the allocation of allowances from a "partisan" distributive politics perspective, by introducing variables that identify states that had competitive races for senator, governor, or the president at about the time allowances were being allocated.[4]

The allocation of SO_2 allowances that emerged during the legislative process that led to the 1990 CAAA represents a particularly interesting case study both of the political economy of economic and regulatory policies in general and of issues that arise in attempts to implement tradable permit schemes in practice. Like many other policy initiatives, the Acid Rain Program did not pass through the legislative process in isolation. It was part of a much larger bill dealing with a wide range of air pollution issues that had been debated for over a decade since the last major amendments to the Clean Air Act were passed in 1977. Title IV accounts for only 51 pages of a very complex and controversial 314-page bill. Moreover, the development of the allowance-allocation provisions is consistent with the observation that informal and ad hoc decision making has become increasingly important in Congress.[5] For example, there were no votes in either house of Congress, on the floor or in any committee or subcommittee, dealing specifically with the statutory provisions governing the initial distribution of allowances. This rules out the use of empirical voting models, which have become an important tool of modern political economic analysis.[6]

On the other hand, since allowances are homogeneous and can be traded and banked, the distributive implications of allowance-allocation rules are easy to quantify. In this case, the allocation of allowances is similar to the allocation of government funds through the legislative appropriations process.[7] The availability of detailed data on the initial allocation of allowances at the generating-unit

4. We do not, however, focus on the role of political parties in Congress, per se. For example, see Cox and McCubbins (1993) and Kiewiet and McCubbins (1991).
5. This development is stressed by Cohen (1992), with the 1990 CAAA as the central example.
6. See Noll (1989, pp. 1270–72) for a discussion of the use of empirical voting models to test interest-group theories of legislative politics and, in particular, Kalt and Zupan (1984), Pashigian (1985), and Peltzman (1990).
7. See, for example, Levitt and Poterba (forthcoming) and the literature they discuss.

level permits analysis of the incidence of individual legislative provisions, as well as analysis of winners and losers under alternative SO_2 allowance-allocation schemes.[8]

As discussed in Chapter 2, it was agreed very early in the legislative process that allowances would simply be given to incumbent producers. Moreover, as discussed further below, a national emissions cap and the timing of the program were also fixed relatively early on, so that the allowance-allocation process itself was, to a good approximation, a zero-sum game. Finally, the direct and indirect costs associated with the Acid Rain Program were highly concentrated in a small number of midwestern and Appalachian coal-mining and coal-burning states, while the benefits associated with reduced emissions were believed to be concentrated in the Northeast. Indeed, the top nine states in terms of SO_2 emissions (all in the Midwest or bordering Appalachia) accounted for 60% of U.S. electric utility SO_2 emissions in 1985 and had the most to gain or lose from allowance-allocation decisions once an aggregate emissions cap was agreed to. All allowance-allocation decisions thus had the prospect of pitting a small number of historically well organized "dirty" states with intense interests in acid rain legislation against the majority of states with relatively low stakes in the issue. And, as noted in Chapter 2, representatives of the "dirty" states organized successfully in 1977 to shift the burdens of SO_2 controls to other states and throughout the 1980s successfully fought off new acid rain control legislation that would target existing generating units. As Noll (1989, p. 1265) observes, "In general, large, heterogeneous groups with relatively small per capita stakes . . . will be disadvantaged relative to small, homogeneous groups with high per capita stakes that are already organized."

The complex process that generated the statutory provisions governing allowance allocations resists simple generalization; however, our analysis of it reveals some interesting features. Most important and least surprising, these provisions clearly show the effects of significant rent seeking by several different interest groups. By

8. Strictly speaking, the data pertain to individual *combustion units*, each of which consists of a combustion device (boiler or turbine) used to power one or more generating units, each of which consists of a single electric generator. Most combustion units power a single generating unit, so our use of the term "unit" for the sake of brevity should cause no confusion. A typical generating *plant* houses several generating units, which may be of different scales, vintages, or types.

comparing actual allowance allocations to plausible alternative benchmarks, we highlight the special-interest effects of various statutory provisions. Hypothetical votes by each house of Congress between alternative Phase II allowance allocations show (under a number of assumptions) that the final allocation chosen could command a majority on the floors of the House and Senate against plausible alternatives. If transaction costs rule out interstate trading, however, as some feared would happen, the final allocation chosen neither minimizes total abatement cost nor equalizes per capita costs across states.

We also endeavor to examine statistically whether political and interest-group variables, which have been commonly associated with the political economy of legislative decision making in general and with that of clean air in particular, can explain the allocation of Phase II allowances. While a few interesting results emerge from this regression analysis, the allocation process does not appear to be consistent with any simple model of distributive politics.

Over all, our results show that, relative to plausible benchmarks, the Phase II allocation process tended to take allowances from the "concentrated" interests in the dirty states and give them to the "diffuse" interests in the clean states. There is some evidence that at least a few high-emissions states gave up Phase II allowances in exchange for more Phase I allowances. There is substantial evidence of narrow special-interest rent seeking, but this can only sometimes be readily associated directly with the power of Senate, House, committee, or subcommittee leadership. During the 1980s, of course, the House and Senate leadership, along with members of key committees and with the support of the Reagan Administration, played important roles in blocking serious consideration of numerous acid rain bills. In this sense, the key committees played their traditional gatekeeper roles (Shepsle and Weingast, 1984, 1987). However, once omnibus clean air legislation was embraced by President Bush and gained support from the Democratic leadership in the Senate, the power of key committees to influence the terms and conditions of the Acid Rain Program, including the allocation of allowances, appears to have been attenuated considerably. Especially in Phase II, the allowance allocations seem to reflect more majoritarian politics (Wilson, 1980; Baron, 1991) than a triumph of concentrated over dispersed interests.

THE ALLOWANCE "PIE"

As Kriz (1990) and others have noted, the acid rain provisions (Title IV) of this legislation were, in the large, a big loss for the coalition that had prevailed in 1977 and "payback time" for those who had lost the "percent reduction" debate then. Old, dirty generating units now had to incur emission-reduction costs that had previously been imposed only on new units. Since utilities were not required to install scrubbers and were given only modest incentives to do so, miners of high-sulfur coal had little job protection and stood to receive limited monetary benefits in the event of job loss.

As it became increasingly likely in early 1990 that some acid rain control program based on tradable allowances would pass, at least some congressional members' attention shifted from broad-brush attack and defense to attempts to shape the final legislative provisions, in particular the allocation of allowances, to extract additional benefits. Of course, other parts of the House and Senate Clean Air Bills were much more important than acid rain to many senators and representatives. Provisions tightening automobile tailpipe standards and regulating gasoline formulations to deal with urban smog and controlling airborne emissions of toxic chemicals were a good deal more controversial than the Acid Rain Title.

Still, contemporary estimates were that Phase I allowances would be worth $250–350 per ton and that Phase II allowances would be worth $500–700 per ton.[9] These estimates implied that distributing roughly 9 million tons of allowances per year for each of the first ten Phase II years would be equivalent to handing out between $45 and $63 billion (undiscounted), and even Phase I would involve around $6 billion. With that sort of rent on the table, one would certainly expect to see serious rent seeking, and Washington did not disappoint.

9. See ICF (1990) and Braine (1991). Though these values were widely discussed at the time, it was clear to most economists that these values of Phase I and Phase II allowances could not obtain in any sort of equilibrium, because Phase I allowances could be banked for use in Phase II. Allowance prices thus cannot increase discontinuously when Phase I ends and Phase II starts. Moreover, at the estimated prices cited in the text, the return on holding an allowance for several years until Phase II begins would be very attractive. Rational response to the opportunity to bank should accordingly lower the ratio of Phase II to Phase I prices well below the 1990 estimates – a prediction confirmed by allowance-market results since 1993.

The process of complicating the allowance-allocation provisions began in earnest in the Administration/Senate negotiations in early February and continued until the Conference Committee completed its work in late October. The parts of the law relating to allocation of allowances in Phase I to generating units in 21 states remained fairly simple, though, as we discuss below, significant changes were made to the original Administration proposal. On the other hand, eight dense pages of about thirty complex and convoluted provisions were developed to govern Phase II allocations of allowances to all fossil-fueled generating units in the continental United States.

Some Phase II provisions appear at first blush to be inconsistent. Some depend on emissions rate, fuel type, and unit size, but there are numerous options open to selected states or utilities, along with an array of "bonus" opportunities and special allocations, many of which are narrowly targeted to benefit specific states or utilities. In order to ensure that the intended constraints on *total* Phase II emissions were satisfied in the face of a rising tide of proposed special-interest provisions, work on the Senate/Administration bill quickly incorporated an overarching "ratchet" provision. This provision, which was not controversial and was retained in the final legislation, in effect said that at the end of the day, total allocations under all other provisions would be scaled down to a specified total. Once the EPA figured out the allocations required by the statute, the ratchet's operation reduced Phase II allowances by about 9.6% from the total implied by strict application of the other allocation provisions in the bill.[10]

At least within the Administration and in the negotiations that led up to the passage of the Senate bill, debates about allowance allocations were conducted primarily in terms of proposed rules for *increasing* particular allocations that were supported by arguments about fairness under autarchy. Thus, it might be argued that units capable of burning both oil and gas deserved more allowances since their emissions were abnormally low in the 1985 baseline data due to unusually low gas prices, so that in a normal year they would burn

10. The "ratchet" had the effect of reducing annual Phase II "basic" allowances from 9.876 to 8.90 million tons and thus, if "bonus" allowances are taken as fixed, of reducing total annual allowances allocated in the first ten years of Phase II from 10.115 to 9.139 million tons (EPA, 1993, p. 5). The large size of the ratchet announced in early 1992 was a great surprise to those involved in the process, most of whom had expected a ratchet of less than 5%.

more oil and thus have higher emissions. Or it might be argued that Florida needed additional allowances to enable it to operate the new power plants that rapid growth would make necessary. On Capitol Hill, these arguments were mainly made by congressional staff; senators and representatives rarely if ever got involved in arguing for narrow special-interest provisions. The persuasiveness of these arguments on equity grounds seemed to reflect, at least in part, a lingering belief that the allowance market would not work well, so that utilities might be forced to cut emissions to below initial allowance endowments. Furthermore, it seemed apparent during the legislative process that participants – members, staff, and utilities – differed significantly in their understanding of how the allowance-trading system would work in practice and what its actual implications would be for affected utilities.[11]

The ratchet also implied that, all else being equal, benefits from rules changes that would *decrease* somebody else's allowances would be widely shared. This, of course, reduced the payoff from advocating such changes, and few if any targeted allowance decreases were even proposed. Thus, for instance, we are unaware of anyone ever having argued that New York, Massachusetts, Minnesota, and Wisconsin utilities should receive fewer allowances because their SO_2 emissions would be constrained below 1985 levels by state acid rain laws.

After the 1990 legislation was passed, the EPA set up an Acid Rain Advisory Committee to assist it in developing the regulations required to implement Title IV and to provide advice on interpreting the statutory language. The EPA also created three internal teams to come to a consensus interpretation of Title IV's complex and interrelated allowance-allocation provisions. In order to record and defend its interpretation, EPA documented the allowance-allocation methods in detail and produced the National Allowance Data Base (NADB) and Supplemental Data File (SDF).[12] The NADB and SDF are essentially large spreadsheets that display the calculations used to allocate allowances to each of 3,842 existing and planned gener-

---

11. One of us (Paul L. Joskow) served on the EPA's Acid Rain Advisory Committee, discussed in Chapter 2. That experience indicated that there was a great deal of misunderstanding about the trading options and flexibility embodied in Title IV, even after it was passed and signed into law.
12. See EPA (1993).

ating units. In order to do this, they provide a good deal of unit-specific information from which allocations under alternative rules can be computed. These spreadsheets are the main source of data for the analysis that follows.

PHASE I ALLOWANCE ALLOCATIONS

Title IV includes a "Table A" that lists the "mandatory" Phase I units and specifies allowances to be allocated to each.[13] Eight of these units were quietly added to Table A before the Senate bill was passed in April. Though these additions were justified by technical corrections to earlier work, it is interesting to note that five of the eight units, accounting for 84% of the allowances allocated to these units, were located in Minnesota, New York, and Wisconsin. The two Wisconsin units had been retired in 1988, so adding them to Phase I clearly made their owners better off by the value of the allowances they were allocated. All three of these states had significant acid rain legislation on the books by 1990. It thus seems likely that adding the Minnesota and New York units to Phase I *and* using their 1985 emission rates to determine their allowance allocations made the owners of these units better off, as well.

Most commentators (e.g., Locke and Harkawik, 1991, p. 24) describe the annual Table A allocations as equal to emissions (in tons) from baseline fuel use and an emission rate (ER) of 2.5 lb per million Btus. As we noted above, however, the EPA's NADB reveals that this formula is only approximately correct. Moreover, Table A does not fully describe the Phase I allocations.

The Table A allocations at the unit level differ by more than 1 percent from those produced by applying this formula to the NADB data, which we will call the *Basic Rule*, in forty-four cases. The sum of all differences is 0.8% of the Basic Rule total. The absolute value

---

13. "Phase I units" include both the units specified in Table A of Title IV and units that have voluntarily become Phase I units under the substitution or compensation provision of the 1990 law. Unless otherwise noted, the information in this and following sections about emissions, generating unit characteristics and locations, and allowance allocations comes from the National Allowance Data Base (NADB) and the Supplemental Data File (SDF). Information about members of Congress, including committee assignments, committee chairmanships, and other leadership positions, comes from standard sources used in studies of American politics.

of the difference exceeded 1,000 allowances per year for 17 units.[14] Fifteen of these accounted for 85% of the positive differences; two accounted for 48% of the negative differences. Most, but not all, of these differences reflect departures from the Administration's original Table A proposal.[15] In large part, at least, these differences reflect the fact that the NADB contains more recent data than were employed in the computations underlying Table A.

Table 3.1 shows that at the state level, the Table A allocations for Wisconsin, Indiana, and Missouri are well above those implied by the 2.5 lb/mmBtu Basic Rule, while Pennsylvania's allocation is noticeably lower. The third data column of Table 3.1 also shows the effects of two "bonus" provisions: Section 404(h), which affected one unit in Iowa, and Section 404(a)(3), which affected all units in Illinois, Indiana, and Ohio, except for three plants that sell mainly to Department of Energy uranium-processing plants.[16] This latter provision was added in response to midwestern pressures for some form of cost sharing – with care taken not to allocate valuable allowances to plants that sold electricity under cost-plus arrangements back to federal facilities. It is worth noting, as well, that representatives from Indiana and Illinois were chairman and ranking member, respectively, of key House subcommittees. Ohio had the highest total emissions of any state in the country and two representatives on the House Energy and Power Subcommittee, one of whom (Thomas Luken, D), had been heavily involved in debates over acid rain legislation proposed earlier in the 1980s.

The next-to-last column in Table 3.1 shows a comparison of the

14. This does not count large, almost exactly offsetting differences for Units 1 and 2 of Georgia Power's Bowen plant. These differences seem almost certain to reflect some sort of error, or the correction of another sort of error.

15. Sixteen percent of the sum of the squared differences between Basic Rule and Table A allocations for the forty-four units for which those differences exceed 1% is accounted for by six units not covered by the Administration's original proposal. The sum of the squared differences between the Table A allocations proposed by the Administration and those passed by Congress equals 76% of the remainder, while the sum of the squared differences between the Administration's Table A and the Basic Rule equals 18%. (The sum of the cross-product terms accounts for the remaining 6%.)

16. Hausker (1992, p. 567) notes that the Midwest bonus provision, added late in conference, was the single breach in the zero-sum barrier imposed by the ratchet provision. A third bonus provision, Section 404(e), provides Phase I allowances to Union Electric in Missouri and Phase II allowances to both Union Electric and Duke Power. About 30,000 allowances have been allocated through 1997 under a final bonus provision, Section 404(f), which rewards using conservation measures or renewable energy to reduce emissions (EPA, 1996b, 1997, 1998).

Table 3.1. *Phase I allowance allocations by state*

State	Basic Rule[a]	Table A difference[b]	Bonuses[c]	Final Allocation	Difference/Pct. from rescaled Basic Rule[d]	Extension allowances[e]
Alabama	230,947	−7	0	230,940	−10,381 / −4.30	3,428
Florida	129,792	3,338	0	133,130	−2,492 / −1.84	33,248
Georgia	581,599	1	0	581,600	−26,123 / −4.30	0
Illinois	353,191	4,709	36,356	394,256	25,201 / 6.83	0
Indiana	640,855	9,485	66,724	717,064	47,424 / 7.08	104,323
Iowa	37,555	2,735	1,350	41,640	2,398 / 6.11	0
Kansas	4,226	−6	0	4,220	−196 / −4.44	0
Kentucky	278,637	−387	0	278,250	−12,903 / −4.43	82,587
Maryland	140,066	−526	0	139,540	−6,818 / −4.66	7,110
Michigan	42,334	6	0	42,340	−1,896 / −4.29	0
Minnesota	4,409	−139	0	4,270	−337 / −7.32	0
Mississippi	54,609	1	0	54,610	−2,452 / −4.30	0
Missouri	345,101	7,889	0	352,990	−7,612 / −2.11	0
New Hampshire	32,207	−17	0	32,190	−1,463 / −4.35	0
New Jersey	20,811	−31	0	20,780	−966 / −4.44	6,242
New York	147,393	3,587	0	150,980	−3,034 / −1.97	11,673
Ohio	863,191	89	96,920	960,200	58,237 / 6.46	167,442
Pennsylvania	536,121	−1,981	0	534,140	−26,063 / −4.65	76,441
Tennessee	386,183	247	0	386,430	−17,100 / −4.24	111,374
West Virginia	496,528	1,342	0	497,870	−20,961 / −4.04	96,131
Wisconsin	130,004	13,376	0	143,380	7,536 / 5.55	0
Total	5,455,761	43,709	201,350	5,700,820	0 / 0.0	700,000

[a]Emissions rate of 2.5 times baseline fuel consumption, in tons.

[b]Difference between Table A and Basic Rule allocations.

[c]From Section 404(h) for the George Neal North Unit 1 in Iowa; from Section 404(a)(3) for units in Illinois, Indiana, and Ohio.

[d]Final Allocation minus (Basic Rule rescaled to same total) / That difference expressed as a percentage of rescaled Basic Rule.

[e]Annual average Phase I extension allowances received, from Section 404(d), after agreed-upon reallocations among utilities.

Source: Joskow and Schmalensee (1998).

Final Allocation in the 1990 law with the Basic Rule allocation scaled up to a total of 5,700,820 tons. None of the differences exceed 10 percent of the Basic Rule benchmark, but at a price of $200/ton, a thousand-ton annual difference corresponds to a million dollars over Phase I. The positive differences (gains) are much more concentrated than the negative differences (losses): The top three gainers (Ohio, Indiana, and Illinois) accounted for 93% of total gains, while the top three losers (Georgia, Pennsylvania, and West Virginia) accounted for 52% of the losses. Only four states have positive differences in excess of 5,000 tons per year, while eight states have negative differences of that magnitude.

One explanation for these differences is that the states that burned more coal than they produced, including Indiana and Ohio, focused their attention on acquiring additional allowances, while the states that produced more than they burned, including Pennsylvania and West Virginia, focused their attention on providing incentives for scrubbing and on direct financial benefits for displaced coal miners. However, Georgia, which produced no coal, and Illinois, which produced about twice as much as it burned in 1990, conspicuously fail to fit this pattern.[17]

The last column in Table 3.1 shows the effects of a final important Phase I provision. In response to pressure from high-sulfur coal states, 3.5 million "extension allowances" (an average of 700,000 per year for the five Phase I years, reflecting the "gain" from moving the start of Phase I from 1996 to 1995) were set aside to encourage the use of "technology" (i.e., scrubbers) as an emissions-reduction technique in preference to fuel switching. On the basis of utility applications, EPA awarded these allowances in September 1994. Because the law was interpreted as requiring the EPA to give utilities either their full request or nothing on a random basis, the utilities involved agreed to reallocate the EPA awards among themselves so that all received rewards very nearly proportional to their requests.[18] The main beneficiaries of this provision were utilities in Ohio, Tennessee, Indiana, and West Virginia, and the high-sulfur coal interests in these and nearby states who benefited from scrubbing high-sulfur coal.[19]

The main point of this section is that even though the Phase I

17. Both states had high total emissions and high emission rates. Georgia had no representation on the Senate Committee on Environment and Public Works or in the Senate leadership. On the House side, it had nobody on the Energy and Power Subcommittee, and only one junior member (J. Roy Rowland, D) on the full Energy and Commerce Committee. It was represented in the House leadership by the minority whip (Newt Gingrich, R). Illinois also had no well-placed representation on the Senate side, but it had the ranking member of the Health and Environment Subcommittee (Edward Madigan, R), a second member on both of the subcommittees involved (Terry Bruce, D), and a third member on the full committee (Cardiss Collins, D). As discussed below, Georgia fared poorly in both Phase I and Phase II, while Illinois fared well in both phases. Illinois would have appeared to have done even better in Phase I, had Illinois Power applied for scrubber extension allowances as had been expected when Title IV was being debated.
18. At the state level, the correlation between extension allowances applied for and those received after reallocation among involved utilities is .9999.
19. Again, Georgia got nothing out of the allowances allocated for scrubber installations, but it also had no high-sulfur coal miners to protect. Illinois miners benefited from the scrubbing incentives, and it was generally expected in 1990 that Illinois utilities would apply for a significant number of extension allowances. Illinois Power eventually

allowance allocations have generally been described as following a simple rule, it is quite clear that the actual allocations were significantly influenced by special interests' rent seeking. In addition to the differences between the Table A allocations and those implied by the Basic Rule, large special allocations of allowances were given to three of the five states with the highest SO_2 emissions (see Table 2.1): Ohio, Indiana, and Illinois. All three also had substantial high-sulfur coal-mining interests. Pennsylvania, West Virginia, and Kentucky, which had both relatively high aggregate emissions and more important high-sulfur mining interests, were not covered by this special provision. However, these six states plus Tennessee (with emissions just above Kentucky's, but few high-sulfur mines) acquired almost all the bonus allowances made available to Phase I units that chose to reduce emissions by scrubbing.[20] Georgia, ranking number 4 in emissions, benefited from neither the special allocation nor the scrubber bonus.

This pattern suggests that Phase I allowances were used partially to compensate three of the high-emissions states (Ohio, Indiana, Illinois) that were well represented on the key committees. Phase I allowances were also used to subsidize scrubbers in response to high-sulfur coal-mining interests. There is some evidence that the states with important coal-mining interests focused more on increasing scrubber allowances than on securing earmarked allowances. Georgia, which was not represented on the relevant committees, did particularly badly overall in the Phase I allowance-allocation process. In order to understand fully what was going on in this process, however, we must relate it to the more complex Phase II process.

PHASE II ALLOWANCES

Calculations of a generating unit's Phase II allowance allocations generally begin with "baseline" emissions, determined by the

decided not to install scrubbers because the Illinois Commerce Commission (which regulates electricity rates) refused to preapprove investments in scrubbers for ratemaking purposes. Illinois Power then became an early and substantial purchaser of allowances.

20. As previously noted, it is likely that utilities in Illinois, particularly Illinois Power, expected to scrub at the time the legislation was being developed, as a consequence of state requirements to continue to burn in-state coal. Eventually, however, Illinois Power chose not to scrub, and sought no bonus allowances.

recorded emissions rate for 1985 and average heat input from fuel burned during 1985–87.[21] The simple allocation rule that is presumed to determine Phase II allocations provides allowances equal to each unit's baseline heat input (fuel use) times the lesser of its actual 1985 emissions rate or 1.2 lb of SO_2 per million Btu, divided by 2,000 to express allowances in tons.[22] However, for the 2000–09 time period with which we are primarily concerned, the statute contains over thirty individual allocation rules that provide for deviations from this simple formula.

These rules fall into three general categories. The first category contains provisions that specify variations from the simple rule based on fuel type, unit age, unit capacity, and capacity utilization during the base period. These allocation rules were generally advertised as dealing with various "technical issues" associated with the fuel and operating attributes of units in these categories during the base period. "Technical considerations" supported widely accepted equity arguments for some of these allocations, such as special provisions for units that operated at low capacity factors during the baseline period due to mechanical problems or unusually low demand. Similarly, plausible "efficiency arguments" supported special allocations for small coal plants, where control options were more limited and costly. Other "technical arguments" supporting, for example, a special allocation for units that happened to burn oil and gas in various ways and at various emission rates during the baseline period because gas prices had been unusually low, are more difficult to accept as being "nonpolitical." As we show explicitly below, the general effect of the allocation rules in this first category is to shift allowances from relatively dirty states to relatively clean states, especially those with oil or gas generating units.

The second category of allocation rules consists of those rules that narrowly focus on special interests – either individual states or individual utilities. Table 3.2 provides the clearest examples. This table was developed by categorizing all Phase II units by applicable allocation rules and then searching for rules that appeared to be narrowly focused on a single state or a small number of generating units. Table 3.2 should remove any doubt that interest-group politics was at work

---

21. As noted above, special provisions were included for units not in operation in 1985 or still under construction in 1990, when the act was passed.
22. Bohi (1994) and Locke and Harkawik (1991, p. 29).

Table 3.2. *Incidence of selected special Phase II (2000–09) provisions*

Section	Coverage	# Units	States (systems) affected
404(h)	Phase I units 1990 ER < 1.0, ≥ 60% ER drop since 1980; system ER < 1.0	1	Iowa (Iowa Public Service)
405(b)(3)	Large lignite units with ER ≥ 1.2 in a state with no nonattainment areas	5	North Dakota
405(b)(4)	State has >30 million kW capacity; unit barred from oil use, switched to coal between 1/1/80 and 12/31/85	4	Florida (Tampa Electric)
405(c)(3)	Small unit, ER ≥ 1.2, on line before 12/31/65; system fossil steam capacity > 250 MW & < 450 MW, fewer than 78,000 customers	2	Missouri (City of Springfield)
405(c)(5)	Small units with ER ≥ 1.2; systems >20% scrubbed rely on small units (large units expensive to scrub)	23	Ohio (Ohio Edison), Pennsylvania (Pennsylvania Power)
405(d)(5)	Oil/gas units awarded a clean coal technology grant as of 1/1/91	1	Florida (City of Tallahassee)
405(f)(2)	Operated by a utility providing electricity, steam, and natural gas to a city and one contiguous county; or state authority serving same area	48	New York (Consolidated Edison, Power Authority of the State of New York)
405(g)(5)	Units converted from gas to coal between 1/1/85 and 12/31/87 with proposed or final prohibition order	3	Arizona (Tucson Electric), New York (Orange & Rockland Utilities)
405(i)(1)	States with >25% population growth 1980–88 and 1988 electric generating capacity >30 million kW	134	Florida
405(i)(2)	Large units with reduced actual or allowable emissions meeting five conditions on emissions and growth	6	Florida (Florida Power Company), Michigan (Detroit Edison)

Source: Joskow and Schmalensee (1998).

in the development of the U.S. Acid Rain Program. Senator Burdick used his chairmanship of the Committee on Environment and Public Works to ensure that his constituents in North Dakota got special allocations for the lignite-fired units that generate electricity there, by inserting Section 405(b)(3).[23] Congressman Dingell seems to have provided regulatory relief for Detroit Edison through Section 405(i)(2). We have been told that Florida Power Company also received benefits under this section, but only because of a drafting error.

It is more difficult to relate some of the other provisions in Table 3.2 directly to well-positioned congressmen from the states that benefited from those provisions. Florida was not represented in the leadership of either House or Senate, and Senator Bob Graham (D–FL) and Congressman Michael Bilirakis (R–FL) were the only Floridians on the relevant committees. Nonetheless, Senator Graham managed to secure thousands of incremental allowances for Florida through Section 405(i)(1).[24] Section 405(c)(3) originated in the House, even though Springfield, Missouri, was represented by a first-term Republican not on the Energy and Commerce Committee. Section 405(g)(5) was broadened in conference to include Tucson Electric, even though Arizona was not represented on the conference committee.[25] Finally, Section 404(h) originated in the House, even though the only Iowan on Energy and Commerce, Tom Tauke (R), was not on the Energy and Power Subcommittee and was campaigning vigorously (though ultimately unsuccessfully) against an incumbent Democratic senator.[26]

These examples make it clear that the ability of a utility or state to obtain favorable Phase II allocation provisions in the statute did not necessarily depend on having one or more members of its state's congressional delegation on a key committee or in the leadership. States like Florida were of "partisan" political importance because of the

23. When an earlier version of Section 405(b)(3) was first proposed at a meeting of Senate and Administration staff, one of us (Richard Schmalensee) laughed. He was forcefully reminded that North Dakota was a relatively poor state with bleak prospects and, more important, that Chairman Burdick was not to be trifled with. Thereafter, no objection was made to Section 405(b)(3).
24. See Kete (1993, pp. 207–10). The impact of this provision is capped in the statute at 40,000 allowances annually. Florida may have been treated well in part because it was a large state with competitive races for both senator and governor in prospect for the fall of 1990. (See Table 3.9 for the definitions of "competitive" used here.) At least one other Florida-specific provision in Table 3.2 was added to the Senate bill at the insistence of the Republican leadership, to give Florida's other senator, Connie Mack (R), something for which he could also claim credit.
25. Morris Udall (D) of Arizona was appointed to the conference, but specifically to deal with issues other than acid rain. *Congressional Record*, June 6, 1990, S–7541.
26. Congressman Tauke, appointed late to the conference as a substitute for another representative. *Congressional Record*, August 3, 1990, H–6908.

presence of close races for senator or governor or their expected importance in the next presidential election. Utilities could also gain influence with influential members of Congress representing other areas through their trade associations, political action committees (PACs), and political contributions. The existence of these alternative pathways through which legislators can be influenced is consistent with the difficulty scholars have had in finding strong empirical linkages between congressional appropriations and the concentration of interest groups in particular states and the seniority and committee assignments of their representatives in Congress.[27] We confront a similar challenge in the regression analysis reported below.

As compared with legislation in other areas, we do not believe that there is anything unusual about the provisions in Table 3.2. The EPA data simply make it easier to identify beneficiaries of these rules than those of functionally equivalent provisions in the tax code. Nor are these necessarily the only "special interest" allocation rules included in Title IV – just the most obvious. For example, Section 405(f)(1) provides special bonuses for oil or gas units with very low emission rates during the baseline period. Units in over thirty states get some benefit from this provision, but the bulk of the benefits are concentrated in California, Florida, and New York. What is clear is that numerous special-interest provisions were inserted to affect the allocation of Phase II allowances. In some cases, these provisions can be easily traced to senators or representatives on key committees or in key leadership positions. But in other cases, utilities or states benefited from special provisions despite the absence of any obvious direct linkages with the presence or absence of their congressional representatives in key gatekeeper positions. More subtle partisan and nonpartisan political linkages were at work here.

The third category of Phase II allocation rules provides for general allocations of bonus allowances to units located in groups of states that fall neatly into the "clean" and "dirty" camps. As discussed above, Section 405(a)(3) allocates 50,000 additional allowances each year to Table A units located in ten "dirty" midwestern states, carefully excluding three plants that sell to the federal government on a cost-plus basis.[28] Section 406 made 125,000 allowances per year

---

27. See Levitt and Poterba (forthcoming) and the references they cite.
28. Technically, these bonus allowances were excluded from the overall emissions cap and were not subject to the ratchet.

available to units in "clean states," which the governor of any of these states could access at his or her option in lieu of accepting other bonus allowances to which the units were entitled. (See Table 2.1 for the definition and list of "clean states.") These allocations clearly reflect efforts to "buy off" two well-organized groups of states with utilities at opposite ends of the dirty–clean spectrum.

ALTERNATIVE PHASE II
ALLOCATION RULES

Given the number and complexity of Phase II allocation rules, inter-actions between them, and the global ratchet, it does not appear either practical or interesting to use the EPA data to try to sort out the effects of each individual provision as we did for Phase I in Table 3.1. Nor is there any simple, systematic way to tie these provisions to specific interest groups or legislators, since there are no votes to observe either on individual provisions or on the Acid Rain Title itself in isolation from the rest of the 1990 Amendments. Instead, we have elected to structure our analysis around the allocation patterns produced by the statute and by the four benchmark alternative allo-cation rules (*PR*, *SR*, *BC*, and *CM*) defined in Table 3.3 and discussed in more detail in the next several paragraphs. We perform a variety of direct comparisons in this section, and then use hypothetical voting and regression techniques for further analysis in later sections of this chapter.

The *Proportional Reduction* (*PR*) rule is a natural starting point for most academic discussions, though it has been found to lack attractive distributional properties in several contexts (Tietenberg, 1985, Chapt. 5). The *PR* allocation implies that in the absence of inter-state trading, all states would reduce their emissions by the same pro-portion to achieve the Phase II emissions cap. This rule implicitly ignores the fact that some states were already clean and generally faced relatively high abatement costs; see, for example, Crandall (1984, p. 27).

The *Simple Rule* (*SR*) resembles the core rule of the initial Admin-istration bill as well as some earlier proposals. Like those bills, it reflects the maximum emissions rate for new coal sources (ignoring the "percent reduction" requirement) in effect since the 1971 NSPS.

Table 3.3. *Alternative Phase II allowance allocation rules*

| Allocation | Code | Correlation with states' final allocations | | Description |
		Total	Per capita	
Proportional reduction	PR	.882	.811	Baseline emissions ratcheted down by 42.3% to equal total Phase II allowances (i.e., the total in the final allocation).
Simple rule	SR	.989	.985	(1) Units on line before 1986 receive (1985 heat input) × max[1985 ER, 1.2], expressed in tons; (2) Units on line in 1986 or later receive unratcheted basic allowances per Section 405(g); (3) Allocations are ratcheted up by 8.5% to equal total Phase II allowances.
Base case	BC	.996	.991	(1) Allowances are allocated using basic provisions in the law that distinguish units by baseline emissions rate, fuel type, and vintage (for units on line in 1986 or later) as described in Footnote 30; (2) Allocations are ratcheted down by 1.4% to equal total Phase II allowances.
Final allocation	FA	—	—	Actual allocation of Phase II allowances, as provided for in the law.
Cost minimization	CM	.956	.887	Allocation of allowances that minimizes estimated total compliance cost in 2005 on the assumption that transaction costs rule out interstate trading; linear state-level marginal cost curves estimated from Table A-16 in ICF (1990) assuming intercepts are $115, as described in the text.

Source: Joskow and Schmalensee (1998).

Each unit operating in 1985 is initially allocated allowances equal to its baseline fuel use times the lesser of its actual emissions rate or 1.2lb/mmBtu, expressed in tons. The basic idea is to bring old coal-fired generating units, which account for the bulk of SO_2 emissions, into conformity with the 1971 NSPS in aggregate.[29] This allocation rule leads to significantly lower aggregate allowances than is provided for by Title IV. Thus, these initial allocations are then ratcheted *up* by 8.5% so total allowances under *SR* will equal the actual Phase II cap. Because of the upward ratchet, this rule makes it possible for units that did not conform to the 1971 NSPS to operate with emission rates somewhat above 1.2 lb per million Btu, on average, and for all other units to receive allowances 8.5% above their baseline emissions.

The *Base Case* (*BC*) was produced by using the six basic provisions in the final law that distinguish units by baseline emissions rate, fuel type, and age – what we referred to in Section 3.4 as the first category of allocation rules.[30] Our original idea was that differences between the *SR* and *BC* allocations would have primarily technical rationales, with political influences affecting primarily the difference between *BC* and the *Final Allocation* (*FA*) actually employed. As we noted above and will demonstrate below, reality was not so tidy. The high pairwise correlations between *FA* and each of *PR*, *SR*, and *BC* shown in Table 3.3 reflect the huge interstate differences in emissions levels and rates in the base period.

29. The original Administration proposal made a distinction between small and large units that is absent here. It also required clean units not to exceed their 1985 emission rates constraint instead of including them in the trading system. See Kete (1993; Chapt. 7, Sect. III) for details.
30. Base Case allowances were allocated as follows before ratcheting down, dividing the results of these formulas by 2,000 to convert to tons. (a) All units that began operation in 1985 or earlier and had ER > 1.2 received baseline fuel use (in Btus) × 1.2, following Section 405(b)(1). (b) All units that began operation in 1985 or earlier and had 0.6 < ER < 1.2 received baseline fuel use × min[actual 1985 ER, maximum allowable 1985 ER] × 1.2, following Section 405(d)(2). (c) All other units (with ER < 0.6) that began operation in 1985 or earlier, except units that derived more than 90% of their total fuel consumption (on a Btu basis) from gas during 1980–89 (the ">90% gas" units), received baseline fuel use × min[0.6, maximum allowable 1985 ER] × 1.2, following Section 405(d)(1). (d) All >90% gas units received baseline fuel use × 1985 ER, following Section 405(h)(1). (e) Units that began operation between 1986 and 1990 received estimated fuel consumption at a 65% operating factor × the unit's maximum allowable 1985 ER, following Section 405(g)(1). Finally, (f) all covered units under construction and expected to begin operation after 1990 received estimated fuel consumption at a 65% operating factor × min[0.3, the unit's maximum allowable ER], following Sections 405(g)(3) and 405(g)(4).

Finally, we used preenactment, state-level compliance cost estimates from ICF Resources (ICF, 1990), an influential report prepared
to inform the legislative process, to estimate the allowance allocation
that would have minimized total compliance costs in the absence of
interstate trading.[31] Comparisons involving this *Cost Minimization*
(CM) allocation are of interest both because of actual and perceived
allowance market imperfections (Stavins, 1995) and because of the
implicit state autarchy assumption made in much of the actual debate
about "fair" allowance allocations. Table 3.3 shows that the *CM*
allocation is also highly correlated with the *(FA)* allowance allocation determined by the 1990 Act, again reflecting the importance of
interstate differences in baseline emissions.[32]

As we noted earlier, many in Congress seemed to believe that there
would be significant obstacles to interstate trading in allowances, or
they did not fully understand how the trading program was supposed
to work, or both. If these beliefs are taken to rule out interstate
trading entirely, our estimated marginal cost functions can be used
along with the uncontrolled emissions in ICF (1990, Table A-16) to
estimate the total expected 2005 compliance costs associated with
various allowance allocations. Table 3.4 reports the results of this
exercise. A comparison across rows shows that our results are not sensitive to reasonable variations in the assumed marginal cost intercept
(see Note 31, cited above). All three rows imply that with no interstate trading, *PR* would involve compliance costs about 30% above
their minimum value. Shifting from *PR* to *SR* reduces total cost signi-

31. Table A-16 in ICF (1990) contains state-by-state estimates of emissions in 2005 (a) with
    no controls and (b) with a common marginal cost of control ($572/ton) that was pro-
    jected to reduce total emissions to near the actual Phase II cap. These data imply a
    point on each state's estimated marginal cost of abatement schedule for 2005. To deter-
    mine those schedules fully, we assume linearity and a common intercept. Table A-16
    of ICF (1990) gives the total cost of control for the case analyzed, including the cost
    of reducing utility NO_x emissions. Comparing the total cost of SO_2 control implied by
    an assumed intercept value with the ICF total cost gives an implied cost per ton of
    NO_x reductions. An intercept value of $115 gives a cost per ton in the center of the
    range discussed by ICF (1990, p. C-12). The *CM* allocation was then computed by
    equating estimated marginal costs across states and setting total emissions equal to the
    Phase II cap. ICF (1990, Table A-16) projected California and Vermont to have zero
    SO_2 emissions in 2005 even with no controls; they received zero allowances under *CM*.
    At the other extreme, Oregon and the District of Columbia were projected to find it
    uneconomic to reduce emissions at all even at an allowance price of $572/ton; their
    CM allocations equal baseline 2005 emissions.
32. The *CM* allocation correlates most closely with *SR* ($\rho = .961$) and *BC* ($\rho = .964$); its
    correlation with *PR* is relatively weak ($\rho = .833$), as Crandall (1984) suggests.

Table 3.4. *Effect of alternative Phase II allowance allocations on cost*

Assumed marginal cost intercept ($)	Implied cost/ton of NOₓ control ($)	Percentage by which total cost exceeds minimum total cost				Coefficient of variation of state per capita cost				
		PR	SR	BC	FA	PR	CM	SR	BC	FA
80	209	35.3	7.0	8.4	9.3	1.01	1.21	1.24	1.31	1.44
115	130	31.2	6.2	7.6	8.4	0.98	1.21	1.24	1.31	1.43
150	51	27.5	5.5	6.9	7.5	0.96	1.21	1.24	1.31	1.42

Note: Total cost and state per capita costs of abatement equal to min[0, ICF (1990, Table A-16) baseline – allowances allocated], based on state-specific linear marginal cost schedules computed using Table A-16 in ICF (1990) and the intercept assumptions indicated; see text for details.

Source: Joskow and Schmalensee (1998).

ficantly, indicating that marginal control costs tend to be lowest at the margin in old, dirty plants. Shifts from *SR* to *BC* or *FA* are estimated to increase costs slightly, though these estimated increases may be small relative to errors of approximation in this exercise. In the presence of transaction costs, there seems at least a plausible *efficiency* case for rejecting *PR* in favor of any of the other allocations.

One often-invoked principle of equity is equality of sacrifice. The last five columns of Table 3.4 report coefficients of variation of states' estimated per capita compliance costs, one measure of inequality of sacrifice. On this measure, *PR* seems the most equitable allocation and *FA* the least equitable. On the other hand, many clean states argued that they had already incurred substantial costs to meet clean air regulations in the previous decade, so that proportional reduction would be unfair. Putting aside *PR* on efficiency grounds, *CM* and *SR* would be preferable to the allocation actually adopted on equity grounds *if* equality of per capita cost were the governing principle of equity. The outcome of the political process suggests that the equity considerations that mattered are not so simply described.

GAINERS AND LOSERS FROM ALTERNATIVE PHASE II ALLOCATION RULES

Gainers and Losers, by Type of Generating Unit

Since utility service areas don't map easily into House districts, and since the Senate had somewhat more influence on the final allowance allocations than did the House, states are the natural units of political economic analysis. As a result, we are ultimately interested in understanding how different allocation rules and movements from one to the other affected different states, and how these effects in turn reflected interest groups and representation in congressional committee and leadership positions. However, most of the Phase II allocation provisions do not relate directly to states, but rather to generating units with different attributes. The distribution of different types of generating units among the states is thus the main determinant (as a matter of arithmetic rather than of causality) of the effects of different allocation rules on individual states. To understand the ultimate effects of alternative allocation rules on the state-level distribution of allowances, we begin with an analysis of how those rules treat generating units with different characteristics.

Table 3.5 summarizes the allowances allocated to generating units of various types in Phase II under *PR, SR, BC,* and *FA.*[33] The table reports the absolute quantity of baseline emissions and the allowance allocations under each of the rules, as well as the percentages of emissions or allowances in each generating unit category. As Table 3.5 indicates, a shift from *PR* to *SR* sharply reduces the allocations of dirty units and ratchets all others above baseline emissions. If the Phase II allowance-allocation process had been used partially to "buy off" the states with many dirty generating units, the main targets of the whole Acid Rain Program, allowances allocated to dirty units would have *increased* from *SR* to *BC* and from *BC* to *FA.* Table 3.5 shows exactly the opposite: Both moves *decrease* the aggregate allowances of dirty units, particularly large, very dirty units. (Table A units fall in this category.) Moreover, all other unit types online by 1985 receive in aggregate allowances under *FA* that exceed their baseline emissions. This pattern is consistent with "We're already clean; don't pick on us!" having been a much more effective equity argument than any notion of equal sacrifice. It is also consistent with a desire of senators from the "clean" western states to pay back the midwestern and Appalachian states for the mandatory scrubbing provision in the 1977 Amendments.[34] Finally, along with the results mentioned earlier in this chapter, it is also broadly consistent with high-emissions states generally being willing to accept fewer Phase II allowances in return for more Phase I allowances.

Clean units do much better under *BC* than under *SR.*[35] The higher allocation to clean units mainly represents a gain by clean oil or gas units. The formula used for allocating allowances to these units in the Base Case (and, for the most part, in the Final Allocation),[36] responded to an argument that these units' baseline emissions were "abnormally" – and thus "unfairly" – low, due to the "unusual" amount of gas burned in the baseline period. It is our understanding

---

33. Since the calculations leading to the *CM* allocation can only be done at the state level, a breakdown of this allocation by unit type is not possible.
34. For an illuminating contemporary account stressing the sort of "payback" considerations mentioned above, see Kriz (1990).
35. The lower allocation to "Other" under *BC* than under *SR* is an artifact; it primarily reflects a legislative decision to exempt some co-generators and other units from the program altogether.
36. See Note 30 supra for the rule.

Table 3.5. *Baseline emissions and effect of Phase II allowance allocation rules, by unit type*

Unit type		Baseline emissions[a]	Implied initial allowance allocations			
			PR	SR	BC	FA
Dirty:	ER ≥ 1.2[b]	13,004 (77.89%)	7,119 (77.89%)	5,375 (58.82%)	4,887 (53.48%)	4,745 (51.92%)
	ER ≥ 2.5, ≥ 75 MW	9,451 (56.61)	5,173 (56.61)	2,910 (31.84)	2,645 (28.94)	2,412 (26.40)
	Other dirty	3,553 (21.29)	1,946 (21.29)	2,465 (26.97)	2,242 (24.53)	2,333 (25.53)
Moderate:	0.6 ≤ ER < 1.2	2,793 (16.73)	1,529 (16.73)	2,881 (31.53)	3,107 (34.00)	3,186 (34.86)
Clean:	ER < 0.6	363 (2.18)	199 (2.18)	394 (4.31)	772 (8.45)	864 (9.47)
	Coal	298 (1.78)	163 (1.78)	323 (3.53)	475 (5.20)	510 (5.58)
	Oil/Gas	61 (0.37)	34 (0.37)	67 (0.73)	292 (3.20)	303 (3.32)
	Gas (>90%)	4 (0.03)	2 (0.03)	5 (0.05)	4 (0.05)	50 (0.55)
New:	On line 1986–90	230 (1.38)	126 (1.38)	250 (2.73)	238 (2.60)	209 (2.29)
Other:	Planned, exempt, etc.	305 (1.83)	167 (1.83)	239 (2.61)	134 (1.47)	135 (1.48)
Total:		16,695 (100.0%)	9,139 (100.00%)	9,139 (100.0%)	9,139 (100.0%)	9,139 (100.0%)

[a]Emissions and allowances expressed in thousands of tons of sulfur. Figures in parentheses are percentages of the corresponding total. Baseline emissions generally equal [1985 emissions rate × 1985–87 average fuel use] for all units on line in 1985.

[b]ER = Baseline emissions rate, in pounds of sulfur emitted per million Btu of fuel burned and percentage of total emissions or allowances.

Source: Joskow and Schmalensee (1998).

that this provision and the "clean states" provision discussed further below were included at the insistence of Senator Bennett Johnston (D–LA). Senator Johnston represented a major gas-producing and gas-consuming state and chaired the Energy and Natural Resources Committee. This Committee has broad oversight authority for federal economic regulation of the electric power industry but did not assert jurisdiction over any part of the 1990 legislation (though it may have threatened to do so). It was logical for gas-burning electric utilities without more direct influence on the relevant committees to turn to Senator Johnston in order to promote such a provision.

Differences between *BC* and *FA* reflect more than a score of other provisions, some of which appear in Table 3.2. Their most striking implication in Table 3.5 is the huge increase in allowances for units burning more than 90% gas. This results mainly from the clean states provision, Section 406, discussed above. The provision allocated a pool of bonus allowances to units in clean states in proportion to generation, not baseline emissions. The big winner from this provision was Texas. It seems hard to find a principle of fairness that rationalizes giving gas plants allowances equal to about 12 times baseline emissions, but the absolute amounts involved are small.

Table 3.5 shows that only the dirtiest large units did less well under *FA* than under *BC*, even though their *FA* endowments were increased by explicit bonuses for Phase I units. Small dirty units (<75 MW) receive more allowances under *FA* than under *BC* because they are explicitly favored in the final legislation. In fact, because of bonuses for low capacity utilization (rationalized, of course, by arguments that the base period was unusual) and the special provisions affecting Florida and North Dakota listed in Table 3.2, allowances were also higher for large units with baseline emission rates between 1.2 and 2.5. Comparing the first and last data columns in Table 3.5 reveals that the dirtiest large units received Phase II allowances equal to 25.5% of their baseline emissions, while all other units, in aggregate, received allowances equal to 92.9% of baseline emissions. In this regard, all of the complex odd and special provisions in the final legislation amplified the impact of a shift from *PR* to *SR* on the dirtiest generating units rather than offsetting it. This indicates that allowances were not used to offset the impact of the acid rain control legislation on the dirty generating units most affected – units that, as we have noted, were concentrated in the midwestern and Appalachian states.

Gainers and Losers, by State

We now consider how the effects of the alternative allocation rules on different types of generating units map into effects on the allowances distributed to different states. Table 3.6 shows the states with the largest gains and losses from a number of hypothetical allocation changes of interest. In percentage terms, these gains and losses tend to be considerably larger than the corresponding differences from the Basic Rule benchmark for Phase I allocations given in Table 3.1. This likely reflects both the greater heterogeneity among Phase II units and the greater incidence of rent seeking in the higher-stakes Phase II allocation process.

In terms of total gains and losses, the shifts from *PR* to *SR* and from *PR* to *CM* are plainly the most important. The incidence of these two shifts is very similar: Old, dirty plants in a few midwestern states lose allowances, and most other plants gain them. The pattern is one of concentrated costs and dispersed benefits – exactly the reverse of the incidence of the scrubber provisions of the 1977 Clean Air Act Amendments.[37]

---

37. The large Texas gain from these shifts reflects its large population of moderate (in the sense of Table 3.5) coal plants.

Table 3.6. *States with largest gains and losses from Phase II allowance allocation changes*

Change	Total shifted	Largest gains			Largest losses		
		State	Gain	% Gain	State	Loss	% Loss
PR→SR	1,535	TX	301	86	OH	506	40
		MI	154	66	IN	297	36
		NC	124	67	MO	225	43
		FL	<u>87</u>	25	IL	<u>143</u>	26
			666 / 43%			1,171 / 76%	
PR→CM	1,975	TX	279	80	OH	686	54
		FL	199	57	IN	278	33
		MI	164	70	MO	269	51
		NC	<u>146</u>	79	IL	<u>256</u>	46
			788 / 40%			1,489 / 75%	
SR→BC	345	CA	77	1034	OH	70	9
		FL	46	10	GA	40	8
		NY	33	14	IN	31	6
		LA	<u>24</u>	32	TN	<u>29</u>	9
			179 / 52%			170 / 49%	
SR→FA	509	CA	85	1143	OH	74	10
		FL	80	18	PA	73	12
		LA	44	59	GA	68	14
		NY	<u>38</u>	16	TN	<u>60</u>	18
			246 / 48%			275 / 54%	
BC→FA	270	FL	34	7	PA	54	9
		NC	29	10	WV	42	9
		ND	26	20	TN	30	10
		IL	<u>25</u>	6	GA	<u>28</u>	6
			115 / 42%			154 / 57%	
CM→FA	893	NY	134	97	WV	185	31
		IL	129	43	PA	137	20
		OH	107	17	KY	76	17
		CA	<u>92</u>	—[a]	TN	<u>60</u>	18
			463 / 52%			458 / 51%	

Notes: States with largest absolute gains and losses (given in thousands of tons) from indicated allowance allocation changes. "% Gain" and "% Loss" are absolute values of changes from indicated bases. Figures in italics give totals of large changes as percentages of all gains (or losses) from the indicated allocation changes.

[a]California receives no allowances in the cost-minimizing allocation.

Source: Joskow and Schmalensee (1998).

In all the other changes shown in Table 3.6, the gains and losses are roughly equally concentrated. In the $SR \to BC$ change, the most important factor affecting state-level gains and losses is the distribution of clean oil/gas units. In the four states with large gains shown in Table 3.6, increases in allowances to clean oil/gas units account for

104% of total gains. Over all, these units account for 64% of the 345,000 tons of total gains associated with this shift. The large losers mainly reflect the operation of the ratchet.

The last three sections in Table 3.6 show the states most affected by shifts from the three most plausible alternative benchmark allocations (SR, BC, CM) to the actual allocation (FA) established in the law. There is a good deal of overlap across these three shifts in the states with the largest gains, even though the statutory provisions primarily responsible differ from state to state. There is also overlap in the states with the largest losses. It is notable, for instance, that Pennsylvania and Tennessee did substantially less well under the actual legislation than under all three benchmark alternatives. This at least suggests that all three shifts may be correlated, at least, with something that can be thought of as the "political" component in allowance allocations.[38]

The one striking exception to this pattern in Table 3.6 is Ohio, which does much better in reality than it would have under CM but much worse than it would have under SR. The key to this difference is that the ICF (1990) estimates on which CM is based imply that at any given percentage abatement, Ohio has the lowest marginal abatement cost in the nation. Thus, in order to minimize total cost in the absence of interstate trading under CM, Ohio receives many fewer allowances than under either SR or FA.

Table 3.7 displays the states with the largest (in absolute value) differences between FA and the average of $SR, BC,$ and CM. In light of the analysis so far, Table 3.7 suggests a few observations and tentative hypotheses. Over all, the passage of an acid rain bill targeted at existing dirty units was a loss for the Appalachian and midwestern coalition that had prevailed in the 1977 debate on SO_2 control. One might have thought that these states, which had the most to lose from this legislation, would have been able to mobilize their well-organized opposition to SO_2 controls and their associated political influence, especially in the House, to obtain a disproportionate share of the allowances to help compensate for their high cleanup costs. However, with the striking exception of Illinois, the opposite generally occurred. Not only did the states that produced and burned dirty

38. Let $\Delta SR, \Delta BC,$ and ΔCM be the vectors of state-specific differences between FA and $SR, BC,$ and $CM,$ respectively. Then the pairwise correlation coefficients are $\rho(\Delta SR, \Delta BC) = .752, \rho(\Delta SR, \Delta CM) = .350,$ and $\rho(\Delta BC, \Delta CM) = .443.$

Table 3.7. *States with largest Phase II gains and losses vs. average benchmark allowance allocation*

Average gain			Average loss		
Absolute	Percent	State	Absolute	Percent	State
61,727	202.03	California[a, b]	93,666	18.17	West Virginia
58,992	27.58	New York[b]	88,052	13.95	Pennsylvania[a]
57,126	15.39	Illinois[a, b]	50,057	15.93	Tennessee
29,839	33.87	Louisiana	31,359	7.65	Kentucky
27,460	5.64	Florida	25,759	16.56	Virginia
27,168	20.65	North Dakota[b]	20,215	34.04	Washington[a]
19,311	16.33	Wyoming[a]	19,943	5.89	Alabama
18,590	35.00	Utah	15,687	4.06	Michigan[b]
18,190	17.26	Minnesota	14,945	2.82	Indiana[b]
15,515	30.75	Connecticut	13,984	17.18	New Jersey
13,383	11.12	Iowa	12,889	8.09	Maryland
12,678	11.07	Oklahoma	11,351	2.68	Georgia[a]
11,880	4.30	Missouri[a]	9,597	5.30	Wisconsin
11,513	18.21	Nebraska	6,194	4.77	Kansas[a]

Notes: Absolute gains and losses are differences between the state's actual (*FA*) allowance allocation and the average of its allocations under the *SR, BC,* and *CM* benchmarks. Percent gains and losses are absolute gains and losses as percentages of the average of the three benchmark allocations.
[a] State represented in Senate or House leadership. (The other state represented was Maine, which had an average gain of 2,597 (28.22%).)
[b] State represented in Senate or House committee leadership. (The other states represented were Montana, which had an average loss of 1,621 (5.24%), and Rhode Island, which had an average gain of 1,117 (47.28%).)
Source: Joskow and Schmalensee 1998.

coal lose in the large when they failed to block the passage of an acid rain law (as they had blocked such laws throughout the 1980s), but also they generally lost in the small in the contest over the allocation of Phase II allowances. This result is consistent with the Phase II allowance-allocation game being one of what Wilson (1980) has called "majoritarian politics," once the 1977 coalition lost its effort to keep the game from being played at all.

Pennsylvania, West Virginia, and Kentucky, which both burn dirty coal and are large net producers of dirty coal, did particularly poorly in terms of Phase II allocations.[39] One hypothesis to explain this is that these states' congressional delegations focused on obtaining benefits for miners, consistent with what we observe for Phase I

39. Recall that they also did poorly in Phase I (see Table 3.1). In Phase I, however, they did benefit significantly from the bonus allowances for scrubbing.

allocations, both as direct financial assistance for coal miners and in the form of incentives to scrub, rather than on obtaining additional Phase II allowances. However, Illinois, which produced more than twice as much high-sulfur coal as it burned, did well in obtaining allowances in both phases, while Georgia, which produced no coal, did poorly in both phases. Ohio and Indiana did much better in Phase I than in Phase II; this may reflect an atypically high valuation of near-term benefits.[40]

Many of the clean states did rather well in Phase II, especially California and Louisiana. These states could focus on Phase II allocations since they had no Phase I units. Similarly, less than 40% of utility SO_2 emissions in New York and Florida, which also did well in Phase II, were from Phase I units – as compared to over 70% in Ohio, Indiana, Illinois, West Virginia, and Georgia. Examination of the Senate and House committee and leadership structures, however, would not suggest that Louisiana or Florida would be winners in this game.[41] Indeed, the two best-positioned congressmen, Chairmen Dingell and Sharp, represented states that wound up doing particularly poorly in Phase II – though Sharp's state, Indiana, did well in Phase I.

It is clear that the distribution of benefits and costs of the 1990 SO_2 regulations were very different from those resulting from the 1977 CAAA. All of the states that had large numbers of old units burning

---

40. Ohio's outcomes may reflect the influence of Congressman Thomas Luken (D), a senior member of the Energy and Power Subcommittee (which had jurisdiction over the Acid Rain Title), who had been very active in the acid rain debates in the 1980s, as well as in the lobbying efforts of American Electric Power (AEP). A large holding company with operations in seven states, AEP accounted for over half of Ohio's 1985 SO_2 emissions. Indiana's results likely reflect the influence of Congressman Philip Sharp (D), chairman of the Energy and Power Subcommittee.

41. New York and California don't really leap out as likely winners, either. New York was represented in the relevant leadership only by the ranking member on Energy and Commerce, Congressman Norman Lent (R), who was not generally thought to be nearly as powerful as Chairman Dingell, and Lent's district is not served by Consolidated Edison. California is represented here by Chairman Waxman, who was primarily concerned with (and only had jurisdiction over) other parts of the 1990 legislation, and the Senate majority whip, Alan Cranston (D), who took no visible part in the Administration–Senate negotiations. California's other senator, Pete Wilson (R), was active in those negotiations, but, like Chairman Waxman, his focus was on vehicle-related provisions. As we noted above, some of Louisiana's success in the Phase II game may reflect the efforts of Senator Bennett Johnston (D), who had some power in this setting as a consequence of his chairmanship of the Energy and Natural Resources Committee. California's significant gain on clean oil/gas units may have been in part a by-product of Senator Johnston's efforts on behalf of similar units in his state of Louisiana.

high-sulfur coal, as well as the states that produced high-sulfur coal, necessarily lost as a consequence of acid rain legislation that tightened controls on existing plants. However, many of these states, especially those that both consumed and produced significant quantities of high-sulfur coal, did worse in Phase II relative to alternative benchmarks than other states, despite the fact that several of these states had senators or representatives in important leadership positions. West Virginia and Pennsylvania, historically among the most aggressive opponents of acid rain legislation, were the biggest losers. In contrast, a broadly distributed set of states that relied primarily on clean coal and gas-fired generation to produce electricity did well relative to these benchmarks. There are important exceptions to these patterns, however, including Ohio and Illinois.[42]

HYPOTHETICAL VOTES ON PHASE II ALLOCATIONS

As is often the case, the details of Title IV were largely worked out behind closed doors. There was never a recorded vote on any aspect of allowance allocations. Since it is very difficult to deny a determined minority, let alone a majority, the right to offer an amendment on the Senate floor, the lack of *any* votes suggests, at least, that *FA* was some sort of majority-rule equilibrium.[43]

One can explore quantitatively the plausibility of this notion by

42. Illinois senators occupied no relevant leadership positions. Illinois was represented in the House by the minority leader, Robert Michel (R), and by the ranking member of the Subcommittee on Health and the Environment, Edward Madigan (R).
43. To be clear, since there is theoretically some alternative allocation with the same total number of allowances that could defeat any proposed allocation, there is no majority-rule equilibrium in a game in which vectors of unit-specific allocations compete for votes. [*Proof:* Let X be a proposed equilibrium vector of unit-specific allocations, and let $W(X)$ be the set of elements of X that correspond to units represented (in whatever sense is relevant) by any arbitrary majority of legislators. Let X' be a vector formed from X by increasing all elements in $W(X)$ by ε and decreasing all other elements by the common amount necessary to equate the sum of the elements of X' to the sum of the elements of X. Then X' defeats X under majority rule, so X is not an equilibrium.] However, any votes would not have been on allowance vectors, but rather on alternative allocation rules. (Similarly, tax legislation is about the rules in the tax code, not the vector of real after-tax household incomes.) As our discussion should have made clear, significant analytical effort would have been required to determine the incidence of alternative systems of rules, putting proposed amendments to a bill on the floor at a significant disadvantage.

making some assumptions about voting behavior and seeing how obvious alternatives would have fared in hypothetical votes.[44] Because it is essentially impossible to define rigorously the relevant set of alternatives or to defend ignoring linkages between allowance allocations and other issues in this and other legislation, this approach cannot provide a rigorous test of any hypothesis.[45] Nonetheless, it is interesting to see what can be learned by a simple analysis of hypothetical votes among the alternative Phase II allocations defined in Table 3.3.

The results of a number of simulated votes are contained in Table 3.8. It is assumed here that senators and representatives vote for the alternative giving their state more allowances – but only if the difference is noticeable. Given the complexity of the Phase II allocation process, states in which actual differences are relatively small could easily have gotten the sign wrong in the heat of debate. Moreover, as others (e.g., Kalt and Zupan, 1984) have observed, if constituents aren't much affected, legislators may be free to indulge their own preferences – which may depend on ideology, logrolling, PAC contributions, or a host of other factors. We have assumed three different thresholds of concern: any change at all, any change above 5% in absolute value, and any change above 10% in absolute value. Those legislators whose states' allowance changes do not pass the relevant threshold are assumed to divide their votes evenly; for the sake of clarity they are simply omitted from the vote counts in Table 3.8. For the sake of completeness we have applied the same calculations to electoral votes (including those of the District of Columbia).

Table 3.8 makes clear that *PR* is a political nonstarter as well as potentially expensive (see Table 3.4): a change from *PR* to *SR* or to *CM* passes overwhelmingly in both Houses under any of our thresholds of concern. There are just too many relatively clean states that would suffer under *PR* for it to gather a majority against any alternative that concentrates the pain in a smaller number of dirty states. This is consistent with *SR* being at the core of most proposals made

44. We are unaware of any previous applications of this technique, though we would not be surprised to learn that some exist.
45. On its face, for instance, dropping the special treatment of North Dakota lignite plants (Sect. 405(b)(3)) would seem to be a clear winner: one small state loses and all others win. But the others don't win much, and Senator Burdick, the powerful chairman of the Environment and Public Works Committee, would have been furious at the amendment's sponsors and supporters.

Table 3.8. Results of simulated votes on Phase II allowance allocation changes

Change	Voting test	States dropped	Senate			House			Electoral votes[a]		
			Yea	Nay	Margin	Yea	Nay	Margin	Yea	Nay	Margin
PR→SR	None	0	70	24	46	303	126	177	379.5	147	232.5
	$|\Delta| \geq 5\%$	3	68	20	48	302	102	200	376.5	120	256.5
	$|\Delta| \geq 10\%$	7	62	18	44	257	99	158	327.5	115	212.5
PR→CM	None	0	62	32	30	235	194	41	300.5	226	74.5
	$|\Delta| \geq 5\%$	1	60	32	28	228	194	34	292	226	66
	$|\Delta| \geq 10\%$	6	54	28	26	199	184	15	258	212	46
SR→BC	None	0	48	46	2	220	209	11	274.5	252	22.5
	$|\Delta| \geq 5\%$	15	40	24	16	178	91	87	223.5	115.5	108
	$|\Delta| \geq 10\%$	31	28	6	22	147	3	144	178.5	9	169.5
SR→FA	None	0	50	44	6	209	220	-11	261	265.5	-4.5
	$|\Delta| \geq 5\%$	15	40	24	16	170	113	57	212.5	139	73.5
	$|\Delta| \geq 10\%$	22	34	18	16	158	75	83	194	92.5	101.5
BC→FA	None	0	42	52	-10	207	222	-15	251	275.5	-24.5
	$|\Delta| \geq 5\%$	19	28	28	0	138	106	32	170	136.5	33.5
	$|\Delta| \geq 10\%$	34	18	8	10	39	24	15	56	35.5	20.5
CM→FA	None	0	48	46	2	242	187	55	290.5	236	54.5
	$|\Delta| \geq 5\%$	7	40	40	0	197	168	29	236.5	210.5	26
	$|\Delta| \geq 10\%$	13	38	30	8	193	111	82	230.5	142.5	88

Note: For each change, congressional delegations or electors of states that gain enough to pass the voting test indicated are assumed to vote yea; delegations/electors of states that lose enough are assumed to vote nay.

[a] Average of 1988 and 1992 electoral votes.

Source: Joskow and Schmalensee (1998).

during the 1980s and with those proposals having been blocked from passage by powerful legislators from states that this change makes worse off, as discussed above. Once these legislators could no longer simply block acid rain legislation, majoritarian politics increased their pain by reducing their allowances below what they would have received under proportional reduction. This is also broadly consistent with the ultimate rejection of efforts to fashion a cost-sharing program built around a national tax on electricity, a possibility that was seriously discussed during the 1980s. Such a tax would, of course, have benefited precisely those states that lose from a shift from PR to SR, BC, or CM.

A change from SR to BC also passes both houses, as well as the Electoral College. Note that its margin increases uniformly as we impose a stricter voting test. The actual allocation of allowances (FA) defeats CM in the House and Electoral College, and generally wins in the Senate, as well. On the other hand, if we assume that every loss of allowances, no matter how relatively or absolutely small, leads to a "Nay" vote, FA fails in the Senate against BC and in the House against both BC and SR. When even a 5% threshold of significance is imposed, however, FA beats both alternatives easily in the House, easily beats SR in the Senate, and needs only a nudge to beat BC in the Senate.

On the whole, Table 3.8 supports the notion that the Phase II allowance-allocation provisions were crafted with sufficient (implicit or explicit) concern for their viability on the floors of both chambers to make them no less attractive than at least some obvious alternatives. If this had not been the case, one would expect to have seen votes involving alternative allocation provisions.

ESTIMATING POLITICAL DETERMINANTS OF ALLOWANCE ALLOCATIONS

Our analysis thus far does not suggest that the Phase II allowance allocations can be explained easily by a small number of "standard" political economy variables. We appear to be dealing with a process of majoritarian politics (once the dam holding back acid rain legislation was broken) combined with a number of special-interest provisions to satisfy narrow constituencies. Committees with jurisdiction were not unimportant in the legislative process, but, particularly in the Senate and in conference, issue-specific groups of legislators played critical roles.[46]

Because an abundance of quantitative information is available, regression analysis can be used to examine whether and how variables measuring the importance of various interest groups, the presence of senators and congressmen in leadership positions, and competitive races for senator, governor, or president in particular states explain the observed allowance allocation in ways consistent with various theories of distributive politics. This analysis is similar in spirit (and results) to the extensive literature that relates congressional appropriations to various political variables (and that fails to find strong support for any simple theories of distributive politics).[47]

As above, our analysis concentrates on the Phase II allocation for the years 2000 through 2009, both because it is more complex and important (in expected dollar terms) than the Phase I allocation, and because it involves a larger sample size. Because of the importance of complex interstate differences in initial conditions, we focus on explaining *differences* between the states' actual allocations (*FA*) and the average of allocations implied by our three benchmarks: *SR*, *BC*, and *CM* (see Table 3.7). This variable is defined as *ΔPHASEII* in Table 3.9.[48]

We focus on differences in numbers of allowances because allowances are homogeneous property rights that should have the same market value no matter to whom they are given. Therefore, the political cost of getting an incremental allowance for one's own constituents should not depend heavily on the state in which they happen to reside. Nonetheless, we performed a number of experiments involving percentage and per capita differences, without obtaining results qualitatively different from those reported below.

As Table 3.9 describes, we employed several exogenous variables intended to capture interstate variations in the importance of interest groups involved in debates about acid rain legislation.

---

46. Cohen (1992) stresses that this bill was typical of recent experience in this last regard.
47. See, for instance, the references cited in Note 3 supra.
48. The differences between the results obtained using this average variable and those obtained for each of the three differences involving individual benchmark allocations are generally small.

Table 3.9. *Variables employed in Phase II regression analysis*

Variable	Mean	Max	Min	Std. dev.	Description
ΔPHASEII	0.00	61.7	–93.7	28.4	Difference between actual (*FA*) Phase II allowances and the average of allocations under *SR*, *BC*, and *CM*, thousands of tons per year from 2000 to 2009.
HSMINERS	1.18	21.6	0	3.64	Estimated number of miners of high-sulfur coal, thousands: product of [fraction of 1992 demonstrated reserves with >1.68 lb sulfur per million Btu (from U.S. Energy Information Admin., *U.S. Coal Reserves: An Update by Heat and Sulfur Content*, DOE/EIA-0529(92), Table C-1)] and [average daily employment of coal miners in 1990 (from National Coal Assn., *Coal Data 1994*, pp. 11–20)].
EMISSIONS	348	2,303	0.16	473	Baseline SO_2 emissions, thousands of tons.
EMRATE	1.49	4.20	0.01	1.03	State average SO_2 emission rate from fossil-fueled electric generating units, pounds per million Btu of fuel burned.
PHIEXT	16.6	190	0	42.1	Phase I extension allowances requested for generating units in the state, average per year from 1995 to 1999, thousands of tons.
SEN	0.27	1	0	0.45	Competitive Senate election dummy variable: equals one if state has a competitive Senate race in 1990 [races labeled "Best Bets" or noncompetitive in 3/17/90 *National Journal* were excluded], zero otherwise.
GOVEV	6.14	50.5	0	9.95	Competitive and important governor's election: product of [a dummy variable for competitive governor's race, constructed like *DSEN*] and [the average of the state's 1988 and 1992 electoral votes].
SWINGEV	10.0	48.2	0.65	8.85	Important swing state: product of {[1 –	*RPCT*–53.4	/50], where *RPCT* is the percentage of the state's popular vote cast for Bush in the 1988 Presidential election, and 53.4 is the sample mean of *RPCT*} and {the average of the state's 1988 and 1992 electoral votes}.
HLEAD	0.10	1	0	0.31	Number of House leadership slots (5 total) filled by the state's delegation.
HCR	0.12	2	0	0.39	Number of House committee (Energy and Commerce) and subcommittee (Energy and Power, Health and Environment) chairmanships and ranking member slots (6) filled by the state's delegation.
HCOMM	1.35	8	0	1.84	Number of House committee (Energy and Commerce) slots (43) plus number of subcommittee (Energy and Power) slots (22) filled by the state's delegation.
SLEAD	0.08	1	0	0.28	Number of Senate leadership slots (4) filled by the state's delegation.
SCR	0.06	1	0	0.24	Number of Senate committee (Environment and Public Works) and subcommittee (Environmental Protection) chairmanships and ranking member slots (4) filled by the state's delegation.
SSUB	0.29	1	0	0.46	Number of Senate subcommittee (Environmental Protection) slots (14) filled by the state's delegation.
ΔPHASEI	0.00	58.2	–26.1	13.7	Actual Phase I allowances minus allocation under rescaled Basic Rule (from Table 3.2), thousands of tons per year.

Notes: Except as noted, data are from EPA (principally the NADB) and standard references on U.S. politics. Sample size = 48: Alaska, Hawaii, and Idaho are excluded from the sample, as from the Acid Rain Program, and the District of Columbia is included.
Source: Joskow and Schmalensee (1998).

These include a variable that measures projected job loss in the coal-mining industry as a result of the legislation (*HSMINERS*),[49] variables that distinguish between clean and dirty states with different levels of SO_2 emissions (*EMISSIONS*) and different emission

49. Two other (conceptually weaker) mining-related variables were computed: (a) Except for Kentucky and West Virginia, which are divided into two regions each, ICF (1990) projections of mining job losses are based on state-level net employment changes,

rates (*EMRATE*),[50] and a variable designed to measure interest in relying on scrubbers by applications for Phase I extension allowances to support scrubber investments (*PHIEXT*).

One might expect that states for which *HSMINERS* is large would be very interested in obtaining allowances as compensation for losses of mining jobs. However, allowances are given to electric utilities, not miners. It is thus at least equally plausible, particularly in light of some of the results mentioned earlier, that representatives of these states would have neglected the pursuit of allowances in favor of seeking aid for displaced miners or attempting to strengthen incentives to scrub. Thus while states with high values of *HSMINERS* cared more than others about the Acid Rain Program, it is unclear whether that concern should be expected to produce more or fewer Phase II allowances.

We would expect *EMISSIONS* or *EMRATE* to have positive coefficients if the "dirty" states were able to use the Phase II allocation process to make up for some of what they lost through passage of acid rain legislation aimed at existing dirty plants. Negative coefficients would be consistent with clean states having been able to use the allocation process to their advantage, which is the pattern suggested in the earlier discussion. Finally, we would expect *PHIEXT* to be negative if the states interested in scrubbing (either because it was the least-cost control option or because of pressures to save high-sulfur coal miners' jobs) gave up Phase II allowances in exchange for greater scrubber incentives during Phase I.

We also computed two sets of more narrowly defined "political" variables. In the spirit of models of partisan distributive politics, variables in the first set are designed to measure states' electoral importance when the 1990 legislation was being considered. These variables include a dummy variable indicating whether there was a competitive election for the Senate expected in 1990 (*SEN*), the national

rather than gross flows out of high-sulfur mining. (b) Aid actually received by May 1995 under the displaced worker provision (Title XI) that was pushed hard by mining-state representatives (discussed in Chapter 2) amounted to less than $29 million and could not have been well anticipated in 1990. Both these variables were highly correlated with *HSMINERS*, and neither outperformed it significantly in regressions.

50. We also considered using emissions from or allowances given to Phase I units as independent variables, but both were almost perfectly correlated with *EMISSIONS* ($\rho = .96$). The share of state emissions accounted for by Phase I plants did not suffer from this infirmity, but its coefficient never approached statistical significance in any experiment.

importance of an upcoming competitive governor's race (*GOVEV*), and a variable that measures the importance of a state as a swing state in the 1988 presidential election (*SWINGEV*). Since 1990 was an election year, it seems plausible that states would have had more clout in the zero-sum allowance-allocation game if they had a competitive senatorial race (*SEN*) or if they were an important state with a competitive gubernatorial race (*GOVEV*). It also seems plausible that important states that were swing states in the 1988 presidential race (*SWINGEV*) would have had extra bargaining strength.[51] If these electoral-importance variables influenced allocations, they should have positive signs. Since the issues in the Acid Rain Program, and in the allowance-allocation process in particular, did not reflect a clear split between Democrats and Republicans, we have not included variables measuring party affiliations or ideological ratings of each state's legislators.

The second set of political variables reflects the nonpartisan distributive politics literature, which implies that the ability of an individual legislator or a group of legislators with similar interests to affect acid rain legislation depends, in part, on whether they occupy positions on key committees or subcommittees or hold leadership positions that provide special influence over the provisions of the bill reported to the Senate or the House floor.[52] The variables in this second set include the number of House and Senate leadership posts (*HLEAD* and *SLEAD*), the number of House and Senate committee and subcommittee chairmanships and ranking member slots filled by a state's representatives (*HCR* and *SCR*), and the number of committee or subcommittee slots filled by a state's representatives in the House and Senate (*HCOMM* and *SSUB*). The leaders of the House (*HLEAD*) and Senate (*SLEAD*) generally have seats at any negotiating table about which they care. Committee membership and, especially, chairmanship or service as the ranking minority member can convey issue-specific influence via agenda control.

As discussed in Chapter 2, on the House side, both the Energy and Commerce Committee (chaired by Congressman Dingell) and two of

---

51. One might also suspect that rich states would have more clout, all else being equal (perhaps because of the presence of campaign contributors), but income per capita had essentially no explanatory power in any equation.
52. See Weingast and Moran (1983), Weingast and Marshall (1988), and Shepsle and Weingast (1984, 1987).

its subcommittees played important roles in the Clean Air process, though only one of the subcommittees (chaired by Congressman Sharp) dealt with the Acid Rain Program explicitly. Thus, *HCR* counts all chairmen and ranking members involved in Clean Air, while *HCOMM* gives extra credit for membership on the subcommittee that dealt with the Acid Rain Program. On the Senate side, the process was very different. The Senate bill was essentially written in negotiations with the Administration in early 1990. While Senator Baucus generally chaired the negotiation sessions, Senator Mitchell assumed the chair at key moments and was heavily involved throughout the process. Similarly, while most senators in the room at any one time were likely to be members of Senator Baucus's Subcommittee on Environmental Protection, the sessions were open to all senators, and many nonmembers participated personally on issues with which they were particularly concerned and had staff in regular attendance. The variables *SCR* and *SSUB* attempt to reflect the essential elements of this process.[53] We would expect all the congressional control variables in this second set to have positive coefficients.

Some of our regressions also included $\Delta PHASEI$, a variable based on Table 3.1 that measures how well or poorly a state did in the Phase I allocation process relative to the ER = 2.5 benchmark.[54] Our idea here is that states that did relatively well in Phase I for reasons not reflected in our Phase II independent variables might also have done well in Phase II, reflecting the same unobserved political forces. This variable is clearly endogenous, and its coefficient cannot be given an unambiguous structural interpretation.[55]

---

53. Idaho, with one subcommittee member, Steve Symms (R), was excluded from our sample because it had no fossil-fueled generating units and was thus not included in the allowance-allocation process.

54. This variable does not reflect actual or anticipated extension (scrubber bonus) allowances; it is from the second-last column in Table 3.1.

55. Several additional variables were employed in a variety of unsuccessful experiments. One might expect that representatives of states with high electricity rates or expecting to need large numbers of allowances to accommodate growth would both be particularly interested in obtaining incremental allowances and particularly able to argue effectively for them, given Florida's ability to obtain Section 405(I)(1), but a range of experiments failed to support either hypothesis. (We used the product of the 1980–90 population growth rates and baseline emissions as a measure of growth-related allowance "needs.") Optimistic economists might expect that states with high baseline average or marginal costs would be both eager and able to obtain incremental allowances, all else being equal, but coefficients of such variables (based on ICF (1990), as above) never approached statistical significance. Finally, we attempted to measure the importance of two other clean air issues, ozone nonattainment and alternative fuels,

Table 3.10 presents illustrative estimation results for six specifications in which *ΔPHASEII* is the dependent variable, and alternative combinations of the three sets of variables discussed above are the independent variables. In the specification represented by the first data column of Table 3.10, as in all the others estimated with a large number of plausible independent variables, most coefficients do not differ significantly from zero.

Several "political" variables in the equation used in the first column never had significant coefficients in any other specification, so we dropped them from further consideration. One of these was *SEN*, even though all of *SEN*'s correlations with the other independent variables were less than .25. In addition, neither *HCOMM* nor *SSUB* ever had significant coefficients, perhaps reflecting the general decline in the importance of committees and the concomitant rise in the importance of other issue-specific groups stressed by Cohen (1992). The coefficient of *SCR* was never significant, even though that of *HCR* was positive and significant in all specifications.

Finally, the coefficient of *HLEAD* was generally negative and sometimes significant. Four of the five House leadership slots were filled by representatives from Georgia, Illinois, Missouri, and Pennsylvania, all states with high levels of SO_2 emissions. (The correlation of *HLEAD* with *EMRATE* is .44.) It seems most likely that there was no real "leadership effect," since a negative effect is implausible and *SLEAD* never had a positive and significant coefficient. The negative *HLEAD* coefficient simply tells us that "dirty" states did poorly in Phase II allocations despite being well represented in the House leadership. Accordingly, we drop both *HLEAD* and *SLEAD* from further consideration.

Dropping the variables just discussed leads us to the second specification in Table 3.10, which has two groups of independent variables, with high intragroup correlations and low intergroup correlations. The first group consists of four variables that we think of as measuring "dirtiness": *HSMINERS, EMISSIONS, EMRATE*, and *PHIEXT*. The lowest of the six pairwise correlations among these variables is .38, and the second lowest is .49. The second group consists of three variables

that might have been involved in cross-Title deals. Specifically, variables measuring the percentage of each state's population in severe or extreme ozone nonattainment areas and each state's production of corn and natural gas (inputs into alternative fuels) never had significant and sensible coefficients in any specification.

Table 3.10. *Phase II regression results*

Independent variable	Dependent variable = $\Delta PHASEII$					
Constant	−4.032	5.142	1.746	4.094	−2.646	−5.412
	(10.550)	(8.770)	(3.618)	(7.810)	(3.983)	(5.386)
HSMINERS	−0.043	−0.814				−2.660[a]
	(1.194)	(1.088)				(0.976)
EMISSIONS	−0.0311	0.023				
	(0.0220)	(0.020)				
EMRATE	1.400	−4.642		−9.054[a]		
	(6.534)	(5.849)		(3.708)		
PHIEXT	−0.604[a]	−0.421[a]	−0.334[a]		−0.466[a]	
	(0.198)	(0.158)	(0.078)		(0.065)	
SEN	−4.594					
	(9.026)					
GOVEV	0.393	0.555				
	(0.593)	(0.530)				
SWINGEV	−1.012	−0.522		0.942[a]	1.039[a]	0.854[a]
	(1.030)	(0.731)		(0.433)	(0.299)	(0.404)
HLEAD	−22.79					
	(15.02)					
HCR	30.67[a]	27.82[a]	30.47[a]			
	(14.24)	(12.68)	(8.328)			
HCOMM	3.923					
	(3.894)					
SLEAD	0.788					
	(13.84)					
SCR	9.549					
	(13.85)					
SSUB	9.481					
	(8.183)					
$\Delta PHASEI$					1.140[a]	0.745[a]
					(0.200)	(0.260)
R^2	.538	.461	.403	.184	.630	.379
Std. error	22.67	22.58	22.40	26.20	17.83	23.11

Note: Standard errors in parentheses.

[a]Denotes significance at 5%. Sample size = 48.

Source: Joskow and Schmalensee (1998).

that we think of as measuring political/electoral "clout": *GOVEV*, *SWINGEV*, and *HCR*. The lowest of the three pairwise correlations among these variables is .58. Within each of these two groups, the different variables are conceptually quite distinct. If their performance in regression experiments could also be clearly distinguished, it might be possible to base a structural story on the results. These data, however, are not so kind.

Note first that in the second data column of Table 3.10, only one variable from each of these two groups has a coefficient that is significant at the 5% level. We ran a number of other regressions with similar results that are not shown here. In the eighteen specifications, which we estimated with two variables from each group, at most one from each group proved significant. In twelve regressions, we estimated with only one variable from each of these groups; however, all "dirtiness" coefficients are negative, all "clout" coefficients are positive, all twenty-four slope coefficients are significant at 5%, and sixteen are significant at 1%. The third and fourth data columns in Table 3.10 show the specifications within this latter set with the highest and lowest values of R^2, respectively.

These results provide strong evidence that dirty states tended to do poorly relative to our benchmarks in Phase II, while states with clout tended to do well. Unfortunately, high correlations within our two groups of independent variables make it impossible to use these data to determine with any confidence what elements or aspects of dirtiness and clout were most important. We are thus unable to discriminate among a large number of plausible structural hypotheses.

We ran the same set of twelve regressions just discussed (and not reported here) using *ΔPHASEI* as the dependent variable and restricting the sample to the twenty-one Phase I states. All coefficients of both dirtiness and clout variables were *positive*, though only one of each was significant at 5%. These results at least suggest that the dirtiest states concentrated on Phase I, where they did relatively well on average, at the expense of Phase II, where they fared less well. These results also suggest that the clout variables are associated with a state's ability to affect the legislative process that led to the allocation of allowances in its favor.

Finally, we reran the twelve regressions with one dirtiness variable and one clout variable on the right, adding *ΔPHASEI* as a third independent variable. All coefficients of dirtiness variables were negative and significant at 5%; all coefficients of clout variables were positive and significant; and all coefficients of $\Delta PHASEI$ were positive and significant. The last two data columns of Table 3.10 show the specifications among these twelve regressions with the highest and lowest R^2 values, respectively. These results suggest that states that managed to do well in Phase I for reasons not correlated with our dirtiness and clout variables also did well in Phase II. Unfortunately, there seems to be no way to use these data to tell us what specific causal forces this effect might reflect, and the complex legislative history summarized above provides no obvious candidates.

This statistical analysis leads to four conclusions. First, and perhaps most important, there does not appear to be any simple, structural theory of distributive politics that is well supported by the data. In particular, the failure of most congressional leadership and committee membership variables seems inconsistent with theories in which power over most legislation is concentrated in the hands of a few people who happen to occupy key positions. This result does not in any sense refute the literature that emphasizes the role of committees, subcommittees, and leadership positions in congressional behavior, however. After all, Congressman Dingell and Senator Byrd managed to block clean air legislation for a decade, with the help of a Republican president opposed to new environmental legislation. But, once acid rain legislation got through the gate, the distribution of influential committee assignment and leadership positions did not help much in predicting allowance allocations. As our discussion of the special Phase II allocation provisions of Title IV (Table 3.2) indicates, some legislators with key committee posts clearly used them to benefit their constituents through the allocation process, but others did not, and several states without obvious influence on the relevant committees or in the leadership did quite well.

Second, there is good evidence that "dirty" states – those with relatively many high-sulfur coal miners, high total emissions and emission rates, and substantial interest in scrubbing as a means to comply with Phase I emissions limits – did relatively poorly in the Phase II allowance-allocation game, all else being equal. There is weak evidence suggesting that the very dirtiest states did relatively well in Phase I, suggesting in turn a willingness to give up Phase II allowances in order to obtain Phase I allowances from states less concerned with Phase I compliance.

Third, there is strong evidence that states with political clout – large swing states in the 1988 presidential election, large states that happened to have competitive gubernatorial campaigns in 1990, or states that had representatives in the House Energy and Commerce Committee leadership – tended to do well in Phase II, and weak evidence that they also did well in Phase I, all else being equal.[56]

Finally, there is strong evidence that states that did well relative to our Phase I benchmark, holding dirtiness and clout constant, also did well in Phase II. In a way, this just reaffirms our first tentative conclusion: something not captured by any of our dirtiness and clout variables produced positive results for both phases. We do not know whether this factor primarily reflects differences in legislators' effectiveness, logrolling on issues outside the Acid Rain Title (or even completely outside the Clean Air Bill), or other effects. Whatever this factor reflects, it appears likely from our earlier work that Illinois had it and Georgia did not.

We do not believe that these regression results should be interpreted as implying that interest-group politics, congressional influence, or considerations of state and federal electoral politics did not play an important role in the allocation of SO_2 allowances. Our earlier discussion shows clear evidence of rent-seeking behavior and congressional influence. However, these effects are apparently too subtle and too complex to be captured in any but the crudest way in this kind of summary regression analysis. This is consistent with the results of related work analyzing congressional appropriations.

56. We also ran a number of regressions using as dependent variables $SUM = D(\Delta PHA\text{-}SEII) + \Delta PHASEI$ and $DIF = D(\Delta PHASEII) - \Delta PHASEI$, where $D = (1.05)^{-5}$ is a discount factor reflecting the five years between the starts of Phases I and II. As before, at most one "dirtiness" and one "clout" variable were significant at the 5% level in any single regression. In both SUM and DIF regressions involving one variable from each group (twelve regressions each), all dirtiness coefficients were negative and all clout coefficients were positive. In the SUM regressions, none of the dirtiness coefficients and eight of the clout coefficients were significant. In the DIF regressions, all of the dirtiness coefficients were significant, along with six of the clout coefficients. These results are consistent, at least, with the notions that the "dirtiest" states gave up Phase II allowances in exchange for Phase I allowances and that clout was valuable. Mechanically, however, these results reflect the high correlations between $\Delta PHASEII$ and both SUM ($\rho = .91$) and DIF ($\rho = .80$).

A MAJORITARIAN EQUILIBRIUM

Environmental regulation is an excellent example of interest-group politics mediated through legislative and regulatory processes. The history of federal regulations governing power plant emissions of SO_2 represents, in many ways, a classic case. Concentrated and well-organized interests in a few states that produced and burned high-sulfur coal were able to shape the Clean Air Act Amendments of 1970 and, particularly, 1977 to protect high-sulfur coal and impose unnecessary costs on large portions of the rest of the country. During most of the 1980s, the midwestern and Appalachian utility and mining elements of this coalition managed to exercise its control over key congressional leadership positions, combining with presidential opposition to new environmental legislation to block acid rain legislation. However, once it became clear that acid rain legislation was likely to be enacted as part of a larger reform of the Clean Air Act, our analysis indicates that this coalition was unable to avoid appreciable control costs by obtaining a disproportionate share of emissions allowances.

With regard to Phase I allowances (apart from scrubber bonuses), three of the states with the greatest emissions and cleanup requirements (Ohio, Indiana, and Illinois) did relatively well compared to other states, while four others (Pennsylvania, West Virginia, Kentucky, and Georgia) did relatively poorly. Aside from Illinois, the utilities and, indirectly, the high-sulfur coal miners in these states benefited from bonus allowances allocated to Phase I units that scrubbed. However, aside from Illinois, these states' traditional coalition of high-sulfur coal producers and high-sulfur coal users was unable to claw back a disproportionate share of Phase II allowances. Indeed, they lost even more during the legislative allocation process than they would have received if several simple alternative allocation rules had been utilized. Specifically, the relatively larger number of clean states with little to gain per capita was more successful in Phase II than was the relatively small number of "dirty" states with much to lose per capita.

If anything, the resulting allocation of Phase II allowances appears to be more of a majoritarian equilibrium than one heavily weighted toward a narrowly defined set of economic or geographical interests.

It is not strongly consistent with the predictions of standard models of interest-group politics or of congressional control. In some cases, influential senators and congressmen managed to capture special benefits for their constituents. In other cases, particular states did much better (or much worse) in the allocation process than might have been predicted by simple theories of distributive politics. On average, relatively dirty states did poorly in Phase II (perhaps because they were more concerned with Phase I and benefits for miners), while states with political "clout" did relatively well in both phases. These results do not have great explanatory power, however, and we can only conclude that the fight to grab allowances, within a range of allocations that could not be easily defeated in the Senate or House, reflects both a more complex and a more idiosyncratic pattern of political forces than one might expect from previous work on the political economy of clean air.

Of course, none of this takes away from the fact that Title IV of the 1990 Clean Air Act Amendments put in place a major long-term program to reduce pollution using an innovative tradable emissions-permit system. At least in theory, the allowance system gives utilities enormous flexibility in meeting aggregate emissions-reduction goals, and thus may allow them to meet those goals at much lower cost than under traditional command-and-control approaches. The rest of this book is devoted to analyzing how well theories about the virtues of pollution permit-trading mechanisms have worked out in practice in the case of the 1990 Acid Rain Program.

4 The Pre-1995 Trend in SO₂ Emissions

4 The Pre-1995 Trend in SO$_2$ Emissions

EXPECTED VERSUS ACTUAL SO$_2$ EMISSIONS

When acid rain legislation was being debated, SO$_2$ emissions were expected to rise throughout the 1990s as a result of the increase in the demand for electricity and continuing reliance on coal-fired generation. For example, in a 1990 analysis of the proposed acid rain legislation, a widely recognized consultant to government and industry predicted that, without acid rain controls, electric utility SO$_2$ emissions would rise by as much as 25% over the 1985 level by the year 2005 (ICF, 1990). Other forecasts, with lower load growth or more gas generation, projected smaller increases in emissions, but none forecast a decrease. In fact, however, 1990 SO$_2$ emissions from electric utilities were 3% below the 1985 level, and 1993 emissions were 7% below 1985 despite continuing growth in coal-fired generation. Even before the emission constraints embodied in Title IV could have affected the trend in SO$_2$ emissions, the historical data indicate that emissions were falling rather than rising.

In this chapter, we discuss why SO$_2$ emissions fell rather than rose after 1985 and develop methods to distinguish the impact of Title IV on SO$_2$ emissions from the impact of other exogenous factors operating during this period. From the standpoint of the environment, any reduction in SO$_2$ emissions, whatever the reason, may be viewed as welcome. However, an accurate estimate of the emission reductions due to Title IV is required for any evaluation of the costs of the

Acid Rain Program. Emission reductions caused by unrelated factors lessen the Title IV abatement requirement and the costs of meeting the fixed cap. Furthermore, if exogenous reductions in emissions are not adequately anticipated, firms will overinvest in abatement, with consequent effects on costs, allowance prices, and the pattern of abatement between Phases I and II.

Aggregate summary data on emissions, heat input, and other variables for 1985 and for the years 1988 through 1993 are provided in Table 4.1 for all fossil fuel-fired generating units in the United States. Two partitions of the data are presented: (a) by designation in Title IV for mandatory control in Phase I (those units listed in Table A of Title IV) and (b) by fuel type. The 1.2 million ton reduction in SO_2 emissions between 1985 and 1993 occurred mostly at Table A units and at coal-fired units. Furthermore, the reduction is due to a decline in the average emission rate at these units, not to a reduction in heat input or generation.[1] Between 1985 and 1993, aggregate SO_2 emissions from all coal-fired plants declined by 7.5% despite a 15.4% increase in heat input at these same plants. In effect, the national average emission rate at coal-fired power plants fell by 20% over these years.

Several possible explanations can be offered for the observed reduction in SO_2 emissions. The fact that almost all of the reduction occurred at Table A units suggests that these units were complying early with the emission reductions mandated by Title IV. Indeed, various studies of compliance plans have noted that utilities were taking actions to reduce emissions well ahead of January 1, 1995, when Phase I became effective.[2] Although competitive firms would not be expected to incur the higher costs implied by early compliance, regulated utilities might well do so when the additional cost of the lower-sulfur coal or a sulfur-reducing retrofit can be passed through to consumers. Moreover, investments necessary to imple-

---

1. The analysis could be performed with any pair of years before or after enactment of the CAAA in 1990. The 1990 data were not available when the legislation was passed, and the last years for which data would have existed during the eighteen-month legislative consideration of the proposal were 1988–89. The beginning year is 1985 because it is a frequent benchmark and is associated with the baseline for the Title IV allocation of allowances. The year 1993 was the last year for which it is possible to argue that fuel choice at Table A units was not affected by the start of Phase 1 on January 1, 1995.
2. Instances are noted in the reviews of compliance plans contained in DOE (1994b), EPRI (1993), and Fieldston (1994). Some of these reductions in emissions were made before April 1989, when the legislation first listing Table A units was proposed.

Table 4.1. *SO₂ emissions by U.S. power plants, 1985–93*

	1985	1988	1989	1990	1991	1992	1993
All units							
SO₂ emissions (thousand tons)		16,243	15,830	15,993	15,820	15,651	15,285	15,065
Heat input (10¹² Btu)		18,579	19,805	20,100	19,791	19,704	19,646	20,259
Emission rate (lb/mmBtu)		1.75	1.60	1.59	1.60	1.59	1.56	1.49
Nameplate capacity (MW)	533,058							
Number of units	2,918							
		Table A vs non-Table A units						
Table A units							
SO₂ emissions (thousand tons)		9,302	8,887	8,862	8,683	8,396	8,140	7,579
Heat input (10¹² Btu)		4,387	4,426	4,427	4,392	4,318	4,351	4,396
Emission rate (lb/mmBtu)		4.24	4.02	4.00	3.95	3.89	3.74	3.45
Nameplate capacity (MW)	88,007							
Number of units	263							
Non-Table A units[a]							
SO₂ emissions (thousand tons)		6,941	6,943	7,132	7,137	7,255	7,145	7,486
Heat input (10¹² Btu)		14,192	15,379	15,673	15,398	15,386	15,295	15,863
Emission rate (lb/mmBtu)		0.98	0.90	0.91	0.93	0.94	0.93	0.94
Nameplate capacity (MW)	445,051							
Number of units	2,655							
		Coal-fired vs Oil/Gas-fired units						
Coal-fired units							
SO₂ emissions (thousand tons)		15,630	15,084	15,208	15,186	15,005	14,742	14,456
Heat input (10¹² Btu)		14,626	15,946	16,039	16,093	16,066	16,224	16,876
Emission rate (lb/mmBtu)		2.14	1.89	1.90	1.89	1.87	1.82	1.71
Nameplate capacity (MW)	347,271							
Number of units	1,417							
Oil/Gas-fired units							
SO₂ emissions (thousand tons)		613	746	785	633	646	542	610
Heat input (10¹² Btu)		3,953	3,860	4,060	3,698	3,638	3,422	3,383
Emission rate (lb/mmBtu)		0.31	0.39	0.39	0.34	0.36	0.32	0.36
Nameplate capacity (MW)	185,787							
Number of units	1,501							

[a]Includes 651 units that are not Phase II units.
Source: Derived from Pechan (1995).

ment compliance plans take time to plan, complete, and bring into service, and early compliance reduces the regulatory and political risks of "just-in-time" compliance.

A related potential explanation is that several states had enacted state laws or amended state implementation plans (SIPs) under the pre-1990 Clean Air Act to require reductions in SO₂ emissions before the effective date of Title IV. These changes in state law and regulation occurred in only a few states, but they could account for some of the reduction in emissions observed as of 1993.

Yet another possible explanation is provided by an examination of the geographic distribution of the reduction in emissions between 1985 and 1993. Virtually all of the 1.2 million ton reduction of SO_2 emissions between 1985 and 1993 was achieved at units in the Midwest, located between 600 and 1,000 miles from the Powder River Basin (PRB). This coal-producing region located in northeastern Wyoming and adjacent counties of Montana is the source of the cheapest and lowest-sulfur coal in America. Rail rates for hauling low-sulfur western coal have fallen significantly since the early 1980s as a result of railroad deregulation, and this reduction in transportation cost could be expected to extend the use of these western, lower-sulfur coals into the Midwest. Thus, the observed reduction in SO_2 emissions and emission rates between 1985 and 1993 might also be explained by the changing economics of coal choice that were unrelated to Title IV.

THE ECONOMICS OF COAL CHOICE

At least as a first approximation, electric utilities minimize the delivered cost of the fuel used to generate electricity. Because coal is a bulky form of energy, transportation costs figure importantly in the delivered price of coal. If all else were equal, distant mines would never provide the least-cost fuel. However, the mine-mouth cost of producing coal varies considerably among regions and even among mines within the same geographic region. Furthermore, transportation rates are typically lower on a per mile basis for longer hauls than for shorter distances. Consequently, if the mine-mouth price and the transportation rate are low enough, distant mines can and often do provide the least-cost coal to a specific plant.

In choosing a particular coal, power plant operators solve the following problem:

$$\text{Min } C_{ij} = MMP_i + r_{ij}d_{ij} \tag{4.1}$$

where

C_{ij} = delivered cost of the ith fuel to the jth plant

MMP_i = mine-mouth price for the ith coal

r_{ij} = transportation rate from the ith mine to the jth plant

d_{ij} = distance from the ith mine to the jth plant

Each competing coal is associated with a certain amount of sulfur dioxide emissions per unit of coal input. Under Clean Air Act regulations antecedent to Title IV, the price of *sulfur* does not figure *directly* in the cost-minimization problem presented by Equation (4.1).[3] These regulations effectively restrict the set of competing coals at any given electric generating unit to those that can meet the source-specific emission rate imposed in the relevant state implementation plan (SIP) or other preexisting requirement.[4] Thus, prior to Title IV, Equation (4.1) was applicable only to the restricted set of coals that complied with the relevant restrictions at each unit. Since virtually all coal-fired units have been in compliance with SIP and other limits, cost-minimizing behavior implies that the sulfur characteristic observed at each generating plant prior to Title IV reflects the choice of the least-cost coal from among the SIP-constrained set of competing coals.[5]

Title IV changes the cost-minimization problem for Table A units by imposing a price on SO₂ emissions that otherwise meet the limits imposed by the preexisting regulation. Two new terms are introduced into Equation (4.1) to reflect the fact that Title IV forces utilities to confront the cost of buying or the revenues from selling allowances and the cost of reducing emissions through fuel switching or scrubbing. This yields Equation (4.2):

$$\text{Min } C_{ij} = MMP_i + r_{ij}d_{ij} + P_a S_i + K_{ij} \tag{4.2}$$

where

3. Electric generating units are subject to a variety of air emission regulations arising from the Clean Air Act of 1970 and subsequent amendments. (See, generally, Tietenberg [1996], pp. 353–64.) Prior to Title IV, emission limits had been imposed by state implementation plans (SIPs) to attain the National Ambient Air Quality Standards (NAAQS), New Source Performance Standard (NSPS), and Prevention of Significant Deterioration (PSD) requirements. Title IV is supplemental to these preexisting requirements, and its provisions do not change or relax any of them.
4. Units that had installed scrubbers to meet the New Source Performance Standard would have a wider range of coals to choose from, but those units are not included in Table A.
5. When long-term contracts are involved, as they often are, currently observed prices for some coal deliveries may be substantially higher than for other currently purchased coals, but the coals delivered under these contracts would have been the least-cost choices when the contract was initiated.

P_a = the price of allowances

S_i = the emission rate associated with the *i*th coal

K_{ij} = the appropriately allocated per unit capital (or other) cost associated with the use of the *i*th coal at the *j*th plant

The last two terms in Equation (4.2) could cause the choice of the least-cost coal to change from what would otherwise be implied by Equation (4.1). Since the price of SO_2 allowances now appears in the cost-minimization equation, the coal user should trade off the cost of buying coal with a lower SO_2 emission rate against the saving in allowance costs (or the increased opportunity to sell allowances) that this would entail. For example, if there were lower-sulfur but higher-cost coals among the SIP-constrained set of competing coals, it is certainly possible that a positive price for allowances would alter the choice of fuel in favor of one of these lower-sulfur coals. In some cases, additional capital or other expenditures may be involved so that the fourth term in Equation (4.2) will be positive and also taken into account in the affected unit's cost-minimizing fuel choice decision. In yet other instances, a positive price for sulfur content may not result in any change in the choice of fuel at a particular plant. Compliance with the newly constraining Title IV limit implies a positive price for allowances, sufficient to ensure that the *aggregate* emission limit is met. This can be, and generally will be, accomplished by reducing emissions at some, and perhaps most, units, but not necessarily by reducing emissions at all affected units.

HISTORICAL PATTERNS IN RAIL AND COAL PRICES

It is a peculiar feature of the American coal economy that the coal with the lowest mine-mouth cost also has the lowest sulfur content but is located farthest from the geographic areas where most coal is used. Because of extraordinary geological conditions, energy from coal is available in the Powder River Basin in northeastern Wyoming at a mine-mouth price of \$0.20 to \$0.30/mmBtu, or the crude oil equivalent of \$1.20 to \$1.80/bbl. Emissions of SO_2 from PRB coals range from 0.5 lb of SO_2 per mmBtu (hereafter lb/mmBtu) to 1.2 lb/mmBtu. This combination of low production cost and low sulfur content is not matched in any other coal-producing region. The two principal competing regions, the Midwest and Appalachia, are less favored with respect to mining cost and sulfur content, but they have the very important advantage of proximity to markets, particularly to coal-fired units between the Mississippi and the Appalachian Mountains. Historically, the substantial cost of transporting PRB coal to the Midwest, typically two-thirds to three-quarters of the delivered price, has diminished the appeal of PRB and other western coals and permitted local, higher-sulfur, and higher(mine-mouth)-cost coals to dominate midwestern markets.

Since PRB coal is carried to market by rail, the deregulation of railroads during the 1980s affected the economics of coal choice. Two effects are particularly important. First, the implementing legislation, the Staggers Rail Act of 1980, effectively introduced competition to the carriage of coal out of the PRB.[6] Second, significant cost-reducing and productivity-enhancing improvements have been achieved by the railroads since the deregulation process began in the early 1980s (USDOE, 1991). The consequence of competition and productivity improvements has been the halving of the rail rate for long-distance shipments of coal out of the PRB. This change in transportation cost reduced the price of PRB coal delivered to midwestern locations, and concomitantly reduced the locational advantage enjoyed by midwestern and Appalachian coals delivered to plants located between the Mississippi River and the Appalachian Mountains, where most Phase I units are located.

The change in rail rates is shown in Table 4.2, which compares the average rate in mills (one-tenth of one cent) per ton-mile for coal shipments from the PRB and from other sources of coal delivered to the Midwest as reported in two studies of coal transportation rates (USDOE, 1991, 1995). The average real transportation cost for coal from the PRB has fallen steadily since 1983 to half of what was charged in 1979, the year before the Staggers Rail Act of 1980 was enacted. In marked contrast, short-haul rail rates for Illinois Basin coal have shown little change in real terms over these same years. Finally, rates for the competing low-sulfur coal from central Appalachia have declined only recently to about three-quarters of

---

6. The Staggers Act ended the Burlington Northern Railroad's monopoly over transportation out of the PRB by removing various obstacles to the Chicago and Northwestern spur that connected the PRB to the Union Pacific Railroad to the south.

Table 4.2. *Rail rates of coal shipments to the Midwest, 1979–93*

Year	Supply Region		
	Powder River Basin	Illinois Basin	Appalachian
1979	2.0	3.1	3.2
1983	2.2	3.5	4.5
1987	1.8	3.2	3.0
1988	1.6	3.8	3.4
1993	1.0	3.4	2.4

Note: Prices are in mills per ton-mile, in 1990 dollars.
Sources: USDOE (1991, 1995).

the pre-deregulation rates. These recent reductions in rail rates may reflect the increased competition from Western coal, as well as railroad productivity improvements and competition from substitute fossil fuels.

The increasing share of PRB coals could also be explained by differing mine-mouth price trends observed for the coals competing to supply power plants located in the midwestern market. Figure 4.1 shows the mine-mouth prices for representative coals from the PRB, the Midwest, and central Appalachia (CAPP) from early 1987 through the second quarter of 1998. The PRB and CAPP coals are both low-sulfur coals, while the midwestern coal is a typical high-sulfur product. As can be seen, the mine-mouth price of the PRB coal is much lower than the price of the other two. Over all, the trend in nominal prices is one of relative constancy for all three coals. Nevertheless, there was about a 10% increase in the mine-mouth price of the midwestern coal from 1987 to 1995 (and a decline thereafter), whereas the price of the PRB coal did not vary by more than a few pennies from $0.28/mmBtu throughout the period. An illustrative calculation of the delivered price of PRB coal in the Midwest compared to the cost of locally produced coal in the Midwest can be made from the data behind this figure and the average rail rates given in Table 4.2. The calculation is made in Table 4.3 for a hypothetical plant located 900 miles from the PRB. This is approximately the distance to the competing Illinois mines and to St. Louis, the major transshipment point for PRB coals. The calculations in Table 4.3 indicate that between 1987 and 1993, the delivered cost of PRB coal fell

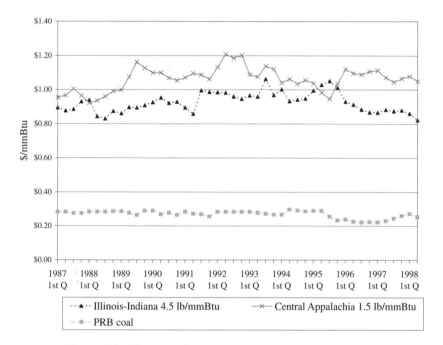

Figure 4.1. Mine-mouth prices for coals competing in the Midwest, 1987–98.

Sources: Coal Markets Priceline and disk update (Fieldston Publications, Inc., 1997).

Table 4.3. *Delivered cost of PRB coal to the Midwest, 1987 and 1993*

(All data in $/mmBtu)	1987	1993	Difference
PRB mine price (8,800 Btu/lb)	0.28	0.28	0
Rail cost[a]	0.92	0.51	–0.41
Delivered cost	1.20	0.79	–0.41
Midwestern mine price	0.90	0.99	+0.09
PRB advantage	–0.30	+0.20	+0.50

[a]Rail rate at 1.8 mills/ton-mile in 1987, 1.0 mills/ton-mile in 1993, both for a distance of 900 miles.
Sources: Mine prices derived from Fieldston (1997). Rail cost derived from USDOE (1991, 1995).

Table 4.4. *Coal price comparisons for plants switching to PRB coal*

Year	Sutherland (IA) Other prices (¢/mmBtu)	PRB prices	% PRB	Contr. exp.	Joppa Steam (IL) Other prices (¢/mmBtu)	PRB prices	% PRB	Contr. exp.[a] (%)
85	143		0.0		171		0.0	
86	140		0.0		176		0.0	
87	134		0.0		162		0.0	
88	146		0.0		136	127	0.4	39.2
89	157		0.0		136	123	1.2	
90	134	91	23.8		117	119	0.9	
91	153	93	78.2		116	89	10.4	
92	162	96	90.5		108	91	24.0	
93	164	79	98.5		106	90	38.5	
94								27.3
%Table A		0%				100%		
Dist. PRB		649				1002		

[a]Percentage of coal, from a region other than PRB, under a contract that is to expire within that year.

Source: Federal Energy Regulatory Commission (FERC) Form 423.

significantly relative to the cost of locally produced coal at the transportation distance used in the example. Indeed, while in 1987 the delivered price of PRB coal was higher than that of locally produced coal, by 1993 the delivered price of PRB coal was lower than the cost of locally produced coal. Accordingly, we would expect to see power plants 900 miles to the east of the PRB switching from locally produced coal to PRB coal imported by rail.

The effect of the declining delivered price of PRB coal on fuel choice is further illustrated in Table 4.4. Two illustrative power plants are chosen: one without any Table A units, located in central Iowa, 650 miles from the PRB (Sutherland), and the other with Table A units, located 1,000 miles from the PRB in southern Illinois on the Ohio River (Joppa). For each plant, the columns show the average nominal delivered price paid for coal from all regions other than the PRB, the price for coal from the PRB, and the share of PRB coal deliveries for the years 1985 through 1993. Neither plant was taking coal from the PRB in 1985; by 1993 the non-Table A Sutherland plant in Iowa had switched almost entirely to PRB coal, while the Table A Joppa plant was taking 40% of its deliveries from the PRB. The Joppa

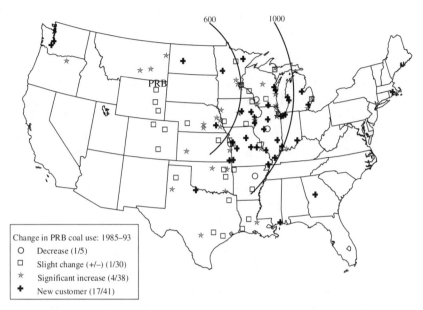

Figure 4.2. Power plants burning Powder River Basin coal, 1985–93.
Source: Ellerman and Montero (1998).

plant started testing PRB coals as early as 1988 and did so for several
years thereafter at not particularly advantageous prices, but with the
delivery of larger quantities the PRB price dropped significantly and
opened up a perceptible advantage over competing coals. The switch
at the plant in Iowa was accomplished later and in much less time,
but the PRB price advantage was also much greater.

Table 4.4 illustrates the economic incentives stimulating the choice
of PRB coal by power plants in the Midwest long before compliance
with Title IV became a constraint. While Table 4.4 presents the calculations for two specific plants, similar results would be obtained for
any number of plants. Figure 4.2 provides additional support for this
conclusion. In this figure, the locations of all plants that purchased
coal from the PRB in either 1985 or 1993 are marked according to
the change in PRB coal use between 1985 and 1993. Four categories
have been defined and depicted in Figure 4.2:

1. Decreased PRB coal use by more than 25% (decrease)
2. Slight increase or decrease in the use of PRB coal (slight change)

3. Significant increase by plants already using PRB coal in 1985 (significant increase)
4. Started to use PRB coal after 1985 (new customers)

Almost all "new PRB coal customers" and most "PRB coal increases" correspond to plants located in the Midwest. Indeed, the largest effects are seen in states such as Missouri, Minnesota, Iowa, Wisconsin, Illinois, Michigan, and Indiana that lie within 600 to 1,000 miles of the PRB, and that also contain a number of Table A units.

The statistics in parentheses in the legend for each of the four categories specified in Figure 4.2 provide additional insights into the nature of the penetration of PRB coal in the Midwest. The first number indicates those plants in each category with Table A units, while the second number is the total number of plants in each category regardless of Title IV designation. Most of the plants that registered "significant increases" or became "new customers" do not have Table A units. Furthermore, plants as far away as Scherer in Georgia and Brayton Point in Massachusetts had already started burning or testing PRB coal in 1993, and neither of these plants have Table A units. These numbers suggest that the penetration of midwestern coal markets by PRB coals has proceeded regardless of the status of the receiving plant under Title IV because lower-sulfur western coals have become cheaper than the predominantly higher-sulfur coals previously consumed in the Midwest. As a result, prior to 1995, utilities were switching to these lower-sulfur coals for largely economic reasons independently of the obligations placed on them by Title IV.

There are other influences operating to reduce sulfur emissions over the long term. For example, under the pre-1990 Clean Air Act, any new generating unit is tightly controlled to new source performance standards, and typically such new units displace power from older sources with higher emission rates. Also, the location of high- and low-sulfur coal deposits in the United States is such that electricity demand was transferred from higher- to lower-sulfur-generating sources by the general shift of economic activity during the 1980s to the South and West, and away from the Midwest. Finally, competition among coal suppliers has led to the virtual elimination of raw (unwashed) coal and the general upgrading of the delivered product that typically entails the removal of some of the pyritic sulfur fraction. These factors were operating during the ten years prior to 1985 when aggregate sulfur emissions also declined despite rising coal use (NCA, 1987). They may have abated in the 1990s, but these factors were likely still present and accounted for some of the observed reduction in SO_2 emissions after 1985 as well.

While declining transportation costs have improved the competitive position of PRB coals in the Midwest, switching to these lower-sulfur and lower-cost coals is often delayed by long-term supply contracts, which are a prominent, albeit diminishing, feature of coal markets.[7] Although every contract is different, some broad generalities are applicable. In the 1970s, when electricity growth seemed assured and high oil and gas prices and problems with nuclear power made coal increasingly the only attractive fuel, many electric utilities signed long-term coal supply contracts for terms typically of twenty years, but often as much as forty years' duration. These contracts effectively dedicated particular coal reserves to the service of the contracting utility at prices that were considered favorable in the 1970s. During the 1980s, market prices fell increasingly far below contract prices, causing the pricing provisions of coal contracts to become the subject of intense renegotiation, buy-out, litigation, and various types of breach.[8] The contracts were usually maintained in some form, however; although the pricing provisions were often amended, the coal contracted for and the associated sulfur attributes continued to be supplied to the buyer's generating units. In effect, the increasingly competitive position of PRB coals manifested itself in lower prices for the contracted coal, but not in lower-sulfur deliveries, at least until the contracts expired, were bought out, or otherwise terminated.

ECONOMETRIC ANALYSIS

Two competing hypotheses incorporating the economics of coal choice can be formulated and tested econometrically. If the reduc-

---

7. Joskow (1985, 1987) provides an analysis of long-term coal supply contracts in effect during these years.
8. Joskow (1988, 1990) discusses the fate of the existing long-term coal contracts during this period.

tion of emissions after 1990 reflects early compliance and related behavior, electric utility operators were incurring additional cost by choosing a higher-cost, lower-sulfur coal and by making some additional compliance expenditure earlier than was necessary for them to respond to their obligations under Title IV. If this type of behavior were observed, it would probably be attributable to distortions caused by the regulation of electricity prices. Alternatively, if the reduction of rail rates prior to 1995 has made distant PRB coals more economically attractive than local, higher-sulfur midwestern coals independently of the need to comply with Title IV, then no additional costs were being incurred by reducing emissions earlier than required by Title IV. The critical difference is that the first hypothesis implies additional cost for the observed emission reduction because of Title IV, while the second does not.

The relevant operating and capital costs at generating units cannot be observed by the analyst, but information about emission rates at the unit level are publicly available. Given the assumption of cost-minimizing fuel choices from within the SIP-constrained set, changes in cost can be inferred from the association of the observed changes in emission rates at generating units with proxies for provisions of Title IV and for declining rail rates. If the hypothesis of early compliance is correct, non-Table A units would not be making the same emission reductions as would Table A units, and the geographic distribution of observed emission reductions would be correlated with a variable indicating whether a unit were listed in Table A. Conversely, if the hypothesis of rail-rate induced economic switching to PRB coals is true, we should observe geographic differentiation in observed emission reductions among Table A units, and there should be little difference observed in fuel-choice behavior between similarly located Table A and non-Table A units. Finally, the effect of state-imposed limits and other factors contributing to the observed reduction in SO_2 emissions can be controlled by the use of appropriate indicator, or "dummy," variables.

The Data

The analysis of fuel-choice behavior is performed with a database provided by the EPA's Acid Rain Division, which contains information on about 3,000 generating units. In addition to providing information concerning boiler number, location, ownership, nameplate capacity, and predominant fuel use, this database provides unit-specific data concerning heat input and SO_2 emissions for 1985 and for 1988 through 1993, summarized in Table 4.1.

The sample is restricted to only those units that are affected by Title IV in Phase I or II and that use coal as the primary fuel.[9] Since the variable of primary interest is the change of emission rates between 1985 and 1993, all units with zero emissions in either 1985 or 1993 are deleted. This last truncation of the sample eliminates some new units and units that may have been retired, but it also removes the effect of units that were active but, for maintenance or other reasons, were not generating electricity in either 1985 or 1993.

Also eliminated from the sample are nine non-Table A units with scrubbers that had relatively low emission rates in 1985 but for which the 1993 emissions, as reported in the database, would be typically associated with nonscrubbed units. It is possible that the scrubbers were not operating in 1993, but it is more likely that the data are in error. In general, the 1985 data were subjected to much more stringent quality control than were data for other years, since emission allocations were dependent on 1985 emission rates.[10] After dropping these units, the sample includes 251 Table A and 788 non-Table A units, which together account for 94% of SO_2 emissions, 77% of heat input, and 57% of capacity for all units in 1985.[11] Table 4.5 provides summary statistics for the sample.

The Model

Two hypotheses – early compliance and rail-rate induced switching to PRB coals – have been advanced to explain the observed reduction in SO_2 emissions. A simple linear specification is used to test the two hypotheses and to disentangle the effect of other factors. We chose 1993 as the terminal year because we expect that Phase I units

9. The primary fuel is defined as that for which heat input is greater than 50% of the total at the generating unit in the baseline period, 1985–87.
10. Personal communication from Larry Montgomery, Acid Rain Division, Environmental Protection Agency. In fact, for units co-located with nonscrubbed units, the rates reported in 1993 for scrubbed units were similar to those reported for nonscrubbed units.
11. The number of Table A units is reduced from the 263 named in the legislation to the 251 used in this sample by the deletion of six coal units that were retired by 1993 and six oil-fired units. Similarly, the sample does not include 374 coal-fired units that are either too small to be subject to Title IV, unutilized, new, or retired. These 374 units account for only 2% of 1985 heat input and SO_2 emissions at coal-fired units.

Table 4.5. *Sample statistics (1,039 units)*

Variable	Mean	Min	Max	Total	Exp. Sign
*RTE*93 (lb/mmBtu)	2.01	0.00	8.08	—	—
*RTE*85 (lb/mmBtu)	2.40	0.08	10.18	—	Positive
TA	0.244	0	1	253	Negative
TAR	1.04	0	10.18	—	Negative
DPRB (mi)	1072	0	1733	—	N.A.[a]
STATELIM	0.071	0	1	74	Negative
LCOAL	0.129	0	1	134	Positive
CCT	0.003	0	1	3	Negative
PHISCRUB	0.023	0	1	24	Positive
EXTREME	0.004	0	1	4	Negative

[a]We have no *priors* for any of the distance variable coefficients.

Source: Ellerman and Montero (1998).

began to implement compliance programs in 1994 to meet the 1995 Phase I compliance deadlines. This specification relates unit-specific emission rates in 1993 (or any previous year) to the 1985 rates plus a set of dummy variables that indicate plant location and other characteristics relevant to fuel choice and emission rates. Emission *rates* are used instead of total tons of SO_2 emitted to normalize for heat input at each unit. The equation for the ith unit is as follows:

$$RTE93_i = b_0 + b_1 RTE85_i + b_2 TA_i + b_3 TAR_i + b_4 DPRB_i + b_5 DPRB2_i + b_6 DPRB3_i + b_7 STATELIM_i + b_8 LCOAL_i + b_9 CCT_i + b_{10} PHISCRUB_i + b_{11} EXTREME_i + u_i$$

for

RTE93	SO_2 emission rate in 1993 (lb/mmBtu)
RTE85	SO_2 emission rate in 1985 (lb/mmBtu)
TA	dummy equal to 1 for all Table A units
TAR	*TA* multiplied by *RTE85*
DPRB	distance from PRB (mi)
DPRB2	squared distance from PRB (mi^2)
DPRB3	cubed distance from PRB (mi^3)

STATELIM   dummy variable equal to 1 if the unit is subject to SO_2 limits imposed since 1985 by state laws or regulations other than Title IV and effective in 1993

LCOAL   dummy variable equal to 1 for Table A units located in states that adopted local coal-protection provisions after 1990

CCT   dummy variable equal to 1 if the unit installed scrubbers in 1993 or before as part of the Clean Coal Technology (CCT) Program of the U.S. Department of Energy (DOE)

PHISCRUB   dummy variable equal to 1 for units planning to install scrubbers in 1994 or later to comply with Phase I requirements

EXTREME   dummy variable equal to 1 for four units that are extreme outliers in that they were burning very-high-sulfur coal in 1985 and very-low-sulfur coal soon thereafter

u error term

The specification attempts to capture many of the unit- and location-specific factors determining fuel choice at a particular unit through the variable *RTE85* (b_1). The year 1985 is both prior to the passage of the 1990 Clean Air Act Amendments and sufficiently close to the enactment of the Staggers Rail Act (1980) that the effects of railroad deregulation had only begun to be felt. If there is no change in emission rates at the unit level, or if the other explanatory variables completely account for observed reductions in emission rates at the unit level, the coefficient on *RTE85* would be unity.

The specification also imposes a common slope coefficient for Table A and non-Table A units across all categories, and it includes three additional sets of independent variables. The first set contains the dummy variables *TA* and *TAR*, used to test for early compliance, or the additional effect that is associated with designation as a Table A unit. A dummy variable for the slope coefficient is introduced for Table A but not for the other categories, to allow for any interaction between the intercept and slope coefficients, since the emission rate is the primary determinant of whether a unit is listed in Table A. If the hypothesis of early compliance is correct, the two coefficients will jointly predict a lower emission rate for Table A units.

A second set of variables, reflecting distance from the PRB, is used to test the second hypothesis, that declining rail rates have reduced emission rates. Ideally, a relative price term that expresses the delivered cost of PRB coal relative to the delivered cost of the local coals would be used. The data exists to construct such an index for some plants and some years, but not for the full sample. Accordingly, the specification tests for evidence of the spatial pattern that would result as cost-minimizing utilities respond to the changing relative prices of competing coals.

A third-degree polynomial is used to control for distance instead of a single continuous variable because of the a priori expectation that distance will not affect coal choice uniformly. For locations closest to and farthest from the PRB, declining rail rates will have little effect on coal choice. For close locations, the low mine-mouth price implies that PRB coals would have been chosen over competing coals in 1985, almost regardless of the ton-mile rate. For distant locations, the lower delivered price in 1993 would still be too high to compete with nearby eastern coals. The principal effect of lower rail rates will be observed in some intermediate region in which PRB coals will have become newly competitive with coals produced at mines located closer to these plants. As suggested by Figure 4.2, this intermediate zone lies between 600 and 1,000 miles from the PRB. If declining rail rates have caused utilities to switch to PRB coals in such a nonuniform pattern, the three distance coefficients will show statistical significance when tested jointly, and they will imply an appropriate pattern of distance effects.

The third set of variables, *STATELIM, LCOAL, CCT, PHIS-CRUB*, and *EXTREME*, accounts for other causal factors not directly related to the two hypotheses, and for a data anomaly. Three states, Wisconsin, Minnesota, and New Hampshire, had enacted acid rain laws or taken regulatory actions to reduce SO_2 emissions that were in effect by 1993; the seventy-four coal-fired units affected by these actions are indicated by *STATELIM*.[12] Next, five states, Kentucky, Illinois, Indiana, Ohio, and Pennsylvania, have enacted

---

12. Other states (e.g., New York, Michigan, and Massachusetts) also had enacted acid rain laws or regulations, but these were not applicable to coal-fired units in 1993.

legislation or taken other measures to alleviate the impact of Title IV on the local high-sulfur coal industry.[13] Since the only units affected currently by such provisions would be those subject to Phase I, the dummy *LCOAL* applies only to the 134 Table A units located in these states. The expected coefficients for *STATELIM* and *LCOAL* are negative and positive, respectively.

Three Table A units had already installed scrubbers by 1993 as part of the DOE's Clean Coal Technology Program, and are designated by *CCT*.[14] The coefficient for this variable should be negative. The possible effect of announced intentions to install scrubbers for Phase I compliance at an additional twenty-four units is represented by the dummy *PHISCRUB*.[15] These scrubbers were not in place in 1993, but utilities that are planning to install scrubbers would not be switching to lower-sulfur coals. Accordingly, the coefficient for this variable would be expected to be positive.

We also include a dummy variable to isolate some unusual data observations. The final variable, *EXTREME*, is associated with four Table A units in Missouri that are distinct outliers in that they burned more higher-sulfur coal than did any other units in 1985 but were among the lowest emitters in 1993.[16] Their behavior reflects a unique situation. These units are located at mine-mouth plants in the coal-producing region with the highest-sulfur coal. By coincidence, this geographic area is also the coal province closest to the PRB from the east (excluding North Dakota, which produces lignite).[17] We hypothesize that the economic advantage of PRB coal over locally produced coal had become so large for plants located in Missouri that the generators were able to overcome pressures to continue to consume locally produced coal and thus to switch to the cheaper PRB alternative.

13. Various issues of *Clean Air Compliance Review* (previously *Compliance Strategy Review*) provide details on attempts to institute local coal-protection measures and the challenges raised in opposition. In particular, see the issues of January 15, 1996; September 25, 1995; May 8, 1995; April 10, 1995; January 16, 1995; September 12, 1994; August 29, 1994; January 17, 1994; and January 3, 1994.
14. These units are Yates #1 and Bailly #7 and #8.
15. These units were selected based on a review of compliance intentions contained in EPRI (1993, 1995) and Fieldston (1994).
16. Three units at the Montrose plant switched to PRB coal prior to 1988, and the remaining unit at the Asbury plant switched to PRB coal in 1990.
17. The Missouri–Kansas seam runs roughly from the northeastern corner of Oklahoma along the Missouri–Kansas border and into central Iowa. Except for a few mine-mouth and small plants, most production from this seam was shut down long ago.

Finally, the effects of long-term contracts on fuel switching have not been addressed. As discussed above, a long-term contract between a generating unit and a coal supplier may make it uneconomical for the generating unit to switch to a cheaper coal because it would be subject to damage payments under the contract if it breached the agreement. Thus, long-term contracts could "lock in" generating units to their existing supply sources for some period of time and delay their switching to another coal that might otherwise be justified for economic or other reasons. It would be extremely difficult to construct a variable that measures the relevant attributes of coal contracts in effect between 1985 and 1993. Accordingly, we have not included such a variable in the analysis. Although including an appropriate variable for long-term contracts might improve the explanatory power of the regression, the omission of this variable should not significantly affect the relative importance of early compliance and declining rail rates. Contracts would delay switching to a lower-sulfur coal equally regardless of whether the reason was early compliance or lower cost, and there is no reason to think that the pattern of contracts is such as to bias estimates of the coefficients of the included variables.

Econometric Results

Results of the ordinary least squares (OLS) regression of Equation (4.3) for the years 1993 back to 1989 are presented in Table 4.6. For the year of primary interest, 1993, the basic intercept, dummy, and slope coefficients have estimated values that are significantly different from both zero and one, the values we would have expected if there were no discernible change in emission rates between 1985 and 1993. With an adjusted R^2 of .77, the equation adequately explains the decline in emission rates between 1985 and 1993 at the unit level, and the t-statistics indicate that most of the estimated coefficients are statistically significant at the 99% level. Since the relevant tests for heteroskedasticity indicate nonuniform variance in the error term, heteroskedastic-consistent (White, 1980) estimates of the standard errors are reported in Table 4.6 and throughout the analysis.[18]

18. White, Goldfield-Quandt, and Breusch-Pagan tests all indicate heteroskedasticity at the 99% significance level. Attempts to remove the heteroskedasticity by several transformations of the data were unsuccessful; hence, for testing joint hypotheses, the OLS estimator with robust variances and the Wald test were used instead of the F test.

Table 4.6. *OLS results for years 1989–93*

	RTE93	RTE92	RTE91	RTE90	RTE89
RTE85[a]	0.7356	0.7851	0.7857	0.8167	0.8261
	(6.6377)	(5.6310)	(5.2312)	(6.2322)	(5.1447)
TA	−0.5290	−0.1046	−0.2394	−0.1831	−0.1683
	(2.9960)	(0.6690)	(1.4880)	(1.2880)	(1.0650)
TAR	0.0660	0.0173	0.0700	0.0650	0.0745
	(1.0690)	(0.3260)	(1.1990)	(1.4030)	(1.4780)
DPRB	−4.43e^{-3}	−3.88e^{-3}	−3.79e^{-3}	−2.15e^{-3}	−7.23e^{-4}
	(5.2340)	(4.9930)	(4.7070)	(3.5840)	(1.2710)
DPRB2	5.86e^{-6}	5.07e^{-6}	5.09e^{-6}	3.13e^{-6}	1.55e^{-6}
	(5.8710)	(5.5520)	(5.4250)	(4.4420)	(2.3100)
DPRB3	−1.99e^{-9}	−1.70e^{-9}	−1.76e^{-9}	−1.11e^{-9}	−6.14e^{-10}
	(5.8200)	(5.4170)	(5.5090)	(4.5720)	(2.6510)
STATELIM	−0.6532	−0.3768	−0.3850	−0.4490	−0.5072
	(5.5240)	(3.4720)	(3.4090)	(3.9960)	(4.4250)
LCOAL	0.5406	0.2510	0.3112	0.2251	0.2036
	(5.1190)	(2.8010)	(3.2380)	(2.7990)	(2.8100)
CCT	−3.7563	−2.8853	−0.0582	−0.0329	−0.3799
	(9.6110)	(2.2770)	(0.8130)	(0.3940)	(2.6590)
PH1SCRUB	0.1403	0.1045	0.1080	0.1618	0.0558
	(0.8240)	(0.6610)	(0.8560)	(1.7360)	(0.7400)
EXTREME	−5.9212	−6.2740	−6.5651	−6.2669	−5.2784
	(18.3120)	(21.3070)	(21.0880)	(18.7890)	(3.9770)
CONSTANT	0.8080	0.6807	0.6733	0.3402	0.0258
	(4.0030)	(3.6330)	(3.3790)	(2.3070)	(0.2020)
Wald-stat. Table A[b]	17.22	0.61	2.22	2.01	2.32
Wald-stat. distance[b]	123.01	112.71	81.61	83.27	57.29
R^2	0.77	0.80	0.80	0.85	0.83
No. observations[c]	1,039	1,037	1,029	1,020	1,010

Note: *t*-statistics, shown in parentheses, were calculated using heteroscedastic-consistent estimates for the standard errors.

[a]*t*-statistics were calculated with H$_0$: β = 1.

[b]For the Wald tests, the critical values for 99% significance are 10.60 and 16.75 for Table A and distance, respectively.

[c]Number of observations differs among years because some non-Table A units produced zero SO$_2$ emissions.

Source: Ellerman and Montero (1998).

As shown in Table 4.6, for the year 1993 the coefficients for Table A (*TA* and *TAR*) fail the 99% significance level when tested individually, but when tested jointly, using a Wald test, the hypothesis that Table A status has no effect upon observed emissions in 1993 is rejected. Distance from the PRB is highly significant. When tested jointly, the three distance variables (*DPRB, DPRB2, DPRB3*) easily exceed the 99% significance level, and individually, all pass the 99% significance level.

The coefficients in year 1993 for variables other than those indicating Table A status or distance from the PRB region have the expected signs and, with one exception, are statistically significant at a level well above 99%. The coefficient of *STATELIM* indicates that state-imposed limits in Wisconsin, Minnesota, and New Hampshire caused an additional 0.65 lb/mmBtu reduction in the emission rate beyond what would otherwise be expected in these states. The coefficient of *LCOAL* suggests that state actions to protect local coal have resulted in 0.54 lb/mmBtu less of a reduction in the emission rate at these Table A units. As expected, the three early scrubbers that are part of the DOE's Clean Coal Technology (CCT) Program show a large reduction in emissions rate over what otherwise would have been expected for these units. The coefficient of *PHISCRUB*, which denotes the twenty-four units that have announced the intent to install a scrubber for Phase I compliance, has the expected positive sign, but the effect is not statistically significant. Finally, no broader meaning can be attached to the highly significant value for the coefficient for *EXTREME* except that it represents units with very special characteristics.

When the regression is run with unit emission rates in 1992, 1991, 1990, and 1989 as the dependent variable, strong support for the importance of declining rail rates is obtained, but no support is found for the importance of Table A status.[19] Distance from the PRB is always significant in these years, and increasingly so with each advancing year (Table 4.6). In contrast, the Table A coefficients do not show any statistical significance in 1989–92. Thus, these regressions suggest that 1993 was the first year in which Table A began to make any difference in SO_2 emissions. Accordingly, it seems safe

19. These results are also obtained with alternative specifications (quadratic and logarithmic) and with an alternative sample in which only units with 1985 emission rates above 2.5 lb/mmBtu are included.

to assume that observed emission rates, and the associated reduction in aggregate SO_2 emissions, for years prior to 1993 do not reflect substantial early compliance responses to Title IV.

Except for the announced intention to install a scrubber, all of the factors expected to influence SO_2 emissions have had the anticipated effects. With respect to the two hypotheses, the reduction in delivered prices of PRB coal associated with declining rail rates clearly provides the better explanation for the reduction in emission rates between 1985 and 1993. Early compliance with Title IV (the Table A effect) is significant only in 1993. In contrast, distance from the PRB, the proxy for declining rail rates, is significant in all years.

Time and Spatial Dynamics

The penetration of midwestern markets by PRB coals can be described as an advancing front resulting from a complex interaction of lower rail rates, transportation and delivery capabilities, contract constraints, and technical limitations on the ability of boilers built for bituminous coals to burn lower-rank, subbituminous coals. As noted previously, the effect will be most evident in some intermediate zone to the east of plant locations where PRB coals already dominate and to the west of plant locations where these distant coals remain noncompetitive, even with lower transportation rates. Figure 4.2 provided one representation of the geographic expansion of this frontier. The polynomial approximation of the effect of distance from the PRB in Equation (4.3) can be used to illustrate and quantify the same effect. The estimated coefficients of Equation (4.3) are used to predict emission rates for each year from 1989 through 1993. The effects of distance from the PRB on emission rates, and by implication the penetration of PRB coal, can be illustrated by selecting a representative unit with an emission rate of 2.5 lb/mmBtu in 1985 and setting all dummy variables equal to zero (including the variable indicating Table A status). Two patterns clearly emerge from the results, presented in Figure 4.3. First, the effect of distance is progressive with time, and it is strongest in a zone extending from 400 to 1,000 miles from the PRB. For instance, at a distance of 600 miles, an expected reduction of 17%, to 2.08 lb/mmBtu, could be observed by 1989, and a further reduction is observed over the next four years, to an expected level of 1.67 lb/mmBtu in 1993. Second, the effect dimin-

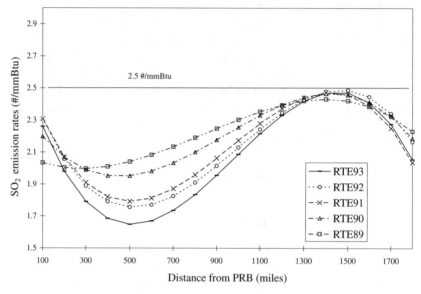

Figure 4.3. Simulated effect of PRB coal expansion on SO₂ emission rates.

Source: Ellerman and Montero (1998).

ishes with increasing distance, so that at 1,000 miles from the PRB, the expected reduction in 1993 is roughly that which was achieved four years earlier for plants located 500 miles closer to the PRB. At a distance of 1,200 miles, the effect largely disappears.[20]

A Quantitative Summary

The effects of early compliance and declining rail rates on SO₂ emissions can be quantified with the help of the econometric analysis presented above. Table 4.7 decomposes the reduction in SO₂ emissions from 1985 levels into constituent elements using the regression coefficients for Equation (4.3) to simulate the two effects. The most

20. Little importance should be attached to the predicted reduction of emissions beyond 1,500 miles and within 400 miles from the PRB. Observations beyond 1,500 miles from the PRB are sparse, so that the indicated reduction in emission rates at these distances reflects little more than an almost out-of-sample extrapolation of the polynomial, dictated by the much greater density of units in the 400–1,500-mile range. A similar out-of-sample effect can be observed for the close-in region within 400 miles, where there are in fact no units with emissions at 2.5 lb/mmBtu or higher.

Table 4.7. *Causes of change in SO₂ emissions, 1985–93*

	(Million tons of SO_2)		
	All units	Table A units	Non-Table A units
Emissions			
Actual 1985	15.27	9.15	6.12
Actual 1993	13.75	7.55	6.20
1993 emissions assuming 1985 emission rates	16.04	9.29	6.75
Estimated 1993	13.87	7.61	6.26
Emissions reduction			
Actual 1985 vs. actual 1993	1.52	1.60	–0.08
1993 emissions assuming 1985 rate vs. estimated 1993 emissions	2.17	1.68	0.49
Decomposition of the reduction in emissions			
(a) Changing sulfur economics	2.00	1.68	0.32
(b) Title IV related factors	0.18	0.00	0.18
Early compliance	0.54	0.54	0.00
Other state limits	0.22	0.04	0.18
Installing scrubbers	–0.06	–0.06	0.00
Clean coal technology	0.07	0.07	0.00
Local coal provisions	–0.59	–0.59	0.00

Source: Ellerman and Montero (1998).

useful measure of the reduction in emissions is the difference between the regression estimate for 1993 emissions, obtained by multiplying actual 1993 heat input by the regression estimates of unit
emission rates, and an alternative estimate formed by multiplying the
1993 heat input for each unit by the unit's 1985 emission rate. The
latter estimate assumes that emission rates remained at 1985 levels
for the entire period up through 1993. When summed across units,
this alternative provides an estimate of what aggregate SO_2 emissions
would have been in 1993 absent any reduction in emission rates but
allowing for the growth of demand for electricity and for changes in
the dispatch of generating units as observed in 1993.

The third and fourth rows of data in Table 4.7 present the two alternative estimates of 1993 emissions. Actual 1985 and 1993 emissions
are also presented, for reference. Note that there is little difference
between "Actual 1993" and "Estimated 1993," the total based on
regression estimates of 1993 emission rates. The second panel reports

the actual reduction in emissions from 1985 to 1993 and a simulated reduction in emissions measured by the difference between estimated emissions using the econometric estimates and what the emissions would have been in 1993 had emission rates not declined after 1985. The reductions in these two cases are further broken down into reductions in Table A units and reductions in non-Table A units. Two sets of factors explain the decline in aggregate SO_2 emissions prior to 1994:

1. Changing sulfur economics, as indicated by the intercept (b_0) in Equation (4.3) and the coefficients for *RTE85* (b_1), the distance variables (b_4, b_5, and b_6), and *EXTREME* (b_{11})
2. Title IV and related regulatory or regulation-response factors, as indicated by early compliance (*TA* and *TAR*), state limits (*STATELIM*), local coal provisions (*LCOAL*), the intended installation of scrubbers (*PHISCRUB*), and the Clean Coal Technology program (*CCT*)

The effect of each is calculated by first setting all the dummy variables in Equation (4.3) equal to 0 for Title IV-related factors, summing emissions across units, classifying the units by Table A status, and calculating the difference from the alternative "no emissions-rate change" estimate for each category. Then, the effect of Title IV-related factors is estimated by setting the respective dummy variables to 1, summing, and calculating the further changes in emissions.

The relative strengths of Title IV-related factors and changing coal-economics factors depends on the distance of generating units from the PRB, of course, but also on whether the state laws to protect local coal producers would have been put in place even without Title IV. With PRB coals invading local high-sulfur markets independently of Title IV, state laws to protect local coal producers might have been proposed even without Title IV (as they were in Oklahoma). The federally imposed Title IV would provide a far more justifiable rationale for protective action than would an underlying loss of competitiveness. If the state laws protecting local coal suppliers were triggered by Title IV, as is usually thought, the 590,000-ton increase in emissions attributable to these provisions almost entirely offsets the 760,000-ton reduction due to early compliance and state limits. In this case, changing coal economics accounts for about 2.0 million tons of the reduction, and the net contribution of Title IV to the pre-Phase I reduction is only 170,000 tons. If it is assumed that the state laws protecting local coal suppliers would have been invoked anyway, the net effect of changing coal economics would be 1.4 million tons of emissions reduction, and 760,000 tons of the pre-Phase I emissions reduction would be attributable to Title IV-related causes. In either case, the effect of changing coal economics is clearly more important in the aggregate than are factors related to early compliance with Title IV. Depending on the interpretation given to state laws protecting local coal suppliers, the effect ranges from 2 times as strong (0.76 vs. 1.41 million tons) to 10 times as strong (0.18 vs. 2.00 million tons).

Of course, what is true for the whole is not necessarily true for each of the parts. The coefficient estimates are not exact predictors, and the specification for distance implies that for any given unit the relative strength of the Title IV effect and changing coal economics depends on plant location. Parameter-restriction tests on the relative strength of the two effects have been undertaken to account for the effects of location and the underlying imprecision of any point estimate. For a Table A unit that burned 3.5 lb/mmBtu of coal in 1995 and that is located 600 miles from the PRB, the distance effect is anywhere from 1.5 to 12.8 times stronger than the Title IV effect in explaining the decline in the emissions rate by 1993. For the same unit 1,000 miles from the PRB, the distance effect ranges from being weaker, 0.6, to 7.5 times stronger than the Title IV effect.

Any interpretation of the two causes of the decline in pre-Phase I SO₂ emissions leads to the conclusion that changing coal economics significantly contributed to the aggregate reduction of SO₂ emissions between 1985 and 1993. Even under the most conservative interpretation, changing coal economics more than offset the effects of load growth (approximately 720,000 tons since 1985) and caused a continuing decline in SO₂ emissions, unlike what was predicted in earlier forecasts of emissions absent Title IV. As a result, these earlier forecasts erred in predicting more emissions and a greater quantity of sulfur that would have to be removed to meet the Phase I and Phase II caps on aggregate SO₂ emissions.

One further feature of Table 4.7 deserves note. We can explain the puzzling occurrence of the largest reductions in emissions at Table A units for reasons largely unrelated to early compliance with Title IV.

Table A units are disproportionately located in the areas most affected by the declining rail rates for PRB coals. Also, by definition, Table A units (a.k.a., the "big dirties") have higher emission rates and larger generating capacity, so that switching to a lower-sulfur coal has more effect on tons emitted at these units.

RAIL-RATE DEREGULATION REDUCES SO$_2$ EMISSIONS

Econometric analysis of the observed changes in unit-level SO$_2$ emission rates at generating plants owned by electric utilities has been used to determine the causes of the reduction of aggregate SO$_2$ emissions that was observed before Title IV became effective in 1995. The analysis indicates that the largest part of the reduction in SO$_2$ emissions between 1985 and 1993 is attributable to changes in the economics of coals of differing sulfur content. Early compliance by Table A units for reasons other than favorable economics of lower-sulfur coal was not an important factor up through 1993.

The principal cause of the change in coal economics appears to be the reduction of rail rates out of the Powder River Basin, based on the distinct geographic pattern of observed emission reductions and the consistently large statistical significance of distance from the PRB. This consequence of the earlier deregulation of rail rates made a very low-sulfur coal economically attractive in areas where local, higher-sulfur coals had previously dominated. It is a geographic coincidence, and a felicitous one, that the market captured by PRB coal encompasses many of the plants designated for early control in Phase I. Long-term contracts and the often limited ability of plants built for midwestern bituminous coals to burn lower-rank, subbituminous coals has delayed switching to lower-cost PRB coals. Nevertheless, these impediments have been reduced over time and by a surprising degree of innovation in blending and adapting existing plants to these cheaper and lower-sulfur coals.

This analysis should of course not be interpreted as suggesting that Title IV has had no effect on aggregate SO$_2$ emissions. The main point of the analysis is rather that it would not be correct to attribute much if any of the pre-1994 emission reductions to early compliance with the provisions of Title IV, since these reductions are largely explained by economic factors independent of Title IV. Moreover, because economic factors led emissions to decrease rather than to increase between 1985 and 1994, the cost of compliance with Title IV should be less than predicted in 1990 since the "no regulation" base case against which reductions must be made is lower than had been expected. In economic terms, railroad deregulation has moved the Powder River Basin closer to the Midwest, and this in turn has reduced the cost of meeting the SO_2 emissions caps specified in Title IV. The effect is the same as if a new PRB had been discovered only half as far away: Both midwestern SO_2 emissions and the cost of Title IV will be less.

PART TWO

Compliance and Trading

5 Title IV Compliance and Emission Reductions, 1995–97

PERFECT COMPLIANCE AND SIGNIFICANT EMISSION REDUCTIONS

Compliance with Title IV has been exemplary. In the first three years of Phase I, every unit subject to Title IV (hereafter referred to as "Phase I" or "affected" units) surrendered the number of allowances required to cover its SO_2 emissions. Moreover, there have been no exemptions, exceptions, or other waivers from Title IV's requirements (EPA, 1996b, 1997, 1998).[1] Phase I units include not only those that were mandated by the legislation to be subject to Phase I but also a large number of units that came into the program under the voluntary compliance provisions of Title IV. These voluntary units have effectively expanded the scope of Phase I to include one-third more generating capacity and one-quarter more heat input than accounted for by the units mandated in Table A to be subject to Title IV in Phase I.

This excellent compliance record is significant and heartening, but it doesn't reveal anything about how the emission reductions required by Title IV were accomplished. Since allowances are readily transferable and no affected unit is required to do more than have enough allowances to cover its emissions, compliance guarantees only that emissions have not exceeded the limited number of allowances

---

1. In fact, slightly more allowances were surrendered in each year than aggregate emissions from Phase I units would have dictated, because of the application of the under-utilization provisions to some units.

issued since the beginning of the program. To understand how operators of Phase I units have responded to Title IV, the purely legalistic concept of compliance must be set aside and attention turned to actual emissions and the changes in emissions at the generating-unit level.

Without a doubt, the most notable feature of the response to Title IV in Phase I is the fact that emissions have been significantly less than the number of allowances issued. Although a total of 23.6 million allowances were allocated to Phase I units for use in 1995–97, effectively permitting that many tons of SO_2 emissions, actual emissions were only 16.2 million tons, approximately one-third less. The resulting 7.4 million tons of aggregate overcompliance has created a bank of an equal number of allowances that can be used in future years.[2]

Two topics concerning the effects of Title IV on emissions at Phase I units are addressed in this chapter. First, an estimate of what emissions would have been without Title IV is developed to provide an appropriate benchmark for gauging the emission reduction attributable to Title IV. We refer to this benchmark as "counterfactual emissions." Second, the change in emissions at Phase I units is described and analyzed in more detail with respect to the distribution of the emission changes among affected units, the geographic distribution of emission reductions, the methods of abatement chosen, and the type of generating unit.

COUNTERFACTUAL EMISSIONS

The reduction in SO_2 emissions caused by Title IV cannot be determined without an estimate of what SO_2 emissions would have been in 1995–97 had Title IV never been passed, or what we call counterfactual emissions. A meaningful counterfactual can be very different from actual emissions in some earlier year. For instance, one measure of the emissions reduction due to Title IV might be the 4.66 million ton difference between 1995 SO_2 emissions at Phase I units and emis-

---

2. The numbers cited in this sentence and the preceding one refer to allowances distributed to Phase I units. Another 450,000 allowances usable during these years were sold at the EPA auction. Thus, the total number of Vintage 1995–97 allowances available for use in later years, the "bank," was 7.85 million allowances at the end of 1997.

sions from those units in 1990, the year Title IV was enacted. While simple, such a measure is inadequate because it does not account for the continuing increase in the generation of electricity at Phase I units. For example, heat input at the 401 continuously affected units rose by 11.6% between 1990 and 1997 so that aggregate SO_2 emissions from these units would have been 1.11 million tons higher, had emission rates remained at 1990 levels. Nor does a simple comparison of aggregate emissions between years recognize the continuing displacement of high-sulfur midwestern coals by low-sulfur western coals that took place for reasons other than compliance with Title IV. As discussed in the preceding chapter, this trend has lessened the reduction in SO_2 emissions required to meet the Title IV cap. Thus, an accurate evaluation of the effect of Title IV on SO_2 emissions requires the development of a counterfactual estimate that accounts both for the effects of the changing demand for electricity and for the effects of the continuing trend toward the increasing use of low-sulfur PRB coal.

Two estimates of counterfactual emissions are presented in the following sections. One is a simple, easily calculated estimate that uses the observed 1993 emission rate and current heat input at all Phase I units. This simple counterfactual was adopted in earlier work addressing only 1995 (Ellerman et al., 1997). With more data from 1996 and 1997 concerning the effect of Title IV, a more sophisticated counterfactual has been developed using a much larger universe of generating units and more powerful statistical techniques to estimate both underlying emission trends and the effect of Title IV on emissions. The aggregate emission reduction attributable to Title IV is approximately the same for the two counterfactuals, about 4 million tons of SO_2 emissions in each of the first three years of Phase I, but the two estimates differ in important details and in the insights provided.

The Simple Counterfactual

A reasonable counterfactual estimate for aggregate emissions in 1995, 1996, or 1997 can be calculated by summing the products of the heat input for the respective Phase I year times the 1993 emission rate at all Phase I units and dividing by 2,000 to express the result in short tons:

$$CF_t = \sum_i \frac{H_{i,t} x R_{i,93}}{2000} \qquad\qquad (5.1)$$

where

> CF_t = aggregate counterfactual emissions in year t,
>
> $H_{i,t}$ = heat input at the ith unit in year t, expressed in million Btu
>
> $R_{i,93}$ = the emission rate at the ith unit in 1993, expressed in pounds of SO_2 per million Btu

The 1993 emission rate reflects the effect of low-sulfur western coals displacing high-sulfur midwestern coals through 1993, while current heat input reflects actual demand for SO_2-emitting fuels by Phase I units in the Phase I year.

Three assumptions are made in the simple counterfactual:

1. None of the emission reduction observed by 1993 was attributable to Title IV.
2. Unit emission rates would not have changed between 1993 and 1995–97 in the absence of Title IV.
3. Heat input is not influenced at the unit level by Title IV.[3]

As with any estimate, the potential for error exists for this simple estimate of counterfactual emissions. To the extent that some units would have switched to PRB coals after 1993 without Title IV, the simple counterfactual will overestimate what emissions would have

---

3. Two exceptions are made to this general rule. The first concerns the seven industrial opt-in units in 1996 and 1997. Since no information is available on the pre-Phase I emission rates at these units, counterfactual emissions are assumed equal to the number of allowances issued to those units. The second exception to the general rule concerns units that had been retired or that were not utilized for the entire year. In 1995, forty-two Phase I units were not used to generate electricity; and this number rose to forty-nine units in both 1996 and 1997. Since the heat input for a retired unit is zero, application of the general rule would result in zero counterfactual emissions, even if there had been positive heat input and emissions at the unit in 1993. In fact, half of the retired units did have positive heat input and emissions in 1993. Although some of these units might have been shut down anyway, for the purpose of calculating the simple counterfactual, units with no heat input in a Phase I year are divided into two groups, depending on their heat input in 1993. For units with no heat input in 1993, both the counterfactual and the reduction attributable to Title IV are considered to be zero. For units with heat input in 1993, we assume that the subsequent retirement was attributable to Title IV, and assign counterfactual emissions equal to 1993 emissions. The counterfactual emissions and consequent Title IV emissions reductions attributable to retirements are small: 23,000 tons in 1995, 39,000 in 1996, and 50,000 in 1997.

been without Title IV and therefore, the emissions reduction attributable to it. Conversely, to the extent that any pre-1995 emission reduction can be attributed to Title IV, the simple counterfactual will provide an underestimate of what emissions would have been and of the Title IV emission reduction. The potential error involved in the heat-input assumption for the simple counterfactual is ambiguous, as will become clear in the discussion of the econometric model used to estimate the second counterfactual.

The Econometrically Estimated Counterfactual

The alternative to the simple counterfactual relies upon panel data regression techniques to provide an estimate based upon a much larger universe of generating units and a longer time series on emissions and heat input. This counterfactual, developed by Susanne Schennach, is discussed in more detail in the Appendix to this book. Here, we provide a general overview of this approach along with the results and some comparisons with the simple counterfactual.

The sample used for these estimates includes non-Phase I units as well as Phase I units, and pre-1993 emissions as well as post-1993 emissions. Phase I units are placed in the context of the larger electrical systems in which they operate, and trends in heat input and emissions unrelated to Title IV can be identified. The sample includes all fossil-fired generating units in states with Phase I units and in certain adjacent states, namely, all units located in states east of the Mississippi River, less Maine, Vermont, North Carolina, and South Carolina, plus Minnesota, Iowa, Kansas, and Missouri.[4] Observations for these units were taken over a ten-year period, from 1988 through 1997. In all, the database consists of 13,640 observations at 1,364 generating units in 26 states, of which 457 units have been subject to Title IV for at least one year.

---

4. Connecticut and Rhode Island are included, despite having no Phase I units, because of the tight integration of the electrical systems in these states with Massachusetts and New York, both of which have Phase I units. Delaware and Virginia are included because of similar relations with New Jersey, Maryland, and West Virginia. Two western states, Utah and Wyoming, are not included, despite having five Phase I units in 1995 or 1996, because these units are small in relation to the total generation in the two states and in relation to the rest of the Phase I units. Their inclusion would have introduced too much "noise" for the additional information they could have provided. The seven industrial opt-in units are also not included because they are not part of any electrical system and no emissions data is available for the years before they became Phase I units.

The econometric technique employed to estimate the second counterfactual is fixed effects linear regression with abundant use of "dummy" variables to capture the effects of Title IV. A particularly noteworthy feature of this technique is that it allows unit-specific, time-invariant "fixed effects" to be estimated to capture unit-specific effects, like a unit's size or its position in the dispatch order of the electrical system to which it belongs, which do not vary over time.

Aggregate emissions are predicted by the following equation, in which the coefficients are estimated by the regression, and the counterfactual is predicted by setting D^{TIV} to 0.[5]

$$SO_{2_t} = \sum_i \left\{ \alpha_i + SO_{2_{i,88}} \left[\frac{\sum_j (H_{j,t} - H_{j,88})}{\sum_j H_{j,88}} \right. \right.$$
$$\left. \left. + \sum_k b_k D_k^{TIV} + t \sum_m c_m D_m^T \right] \right\} \qquad (5.2)$$

Thus, the counterfactual for the tth year depends on a time-invariant, "fixed effects" variable specific to the ith unit and the effect of three factors represented by the three terms within square brackets. These three factors are, respectively, the heat-input trend of the jth group to which that unit belongs, the effect of Title IV as expressed by a set of dummy variables, and two time trends in emission rates that are independent of Title IV. The predicted change in emissions is given by the sum of the terms within square brackets, as the percentage increase of SO_2 emissions for the ith unit in the tth year relative to emissions in the base year, 1988.

All generating units in the sample are assigned to one of four heat-input groups, according to Phase I status and geographic location. The first partition sets apart the units that did not become Phase I units in 1995–97 from those that did, in order to provide a control group for estimating the effects of Title IV. The second partition distinguishes between units located within 1,200 miles of the PRB and units located elsewhere. This geographic partition is required to obtain a good estimate of the effect on counterfactual emissions of the substitution of PRB coals for high-sulfur midwestern coals within the 600- to 1,200-mile zone of influence. Fossil-fired generation of electricity grew at a much faster rate for units located within 1,200 miles

5. The complete specification of this equation and the definition of variables is given in the Appendix at Equation (A.1).

of the PRB than for those located farther east.[6] If we did not control for the differing rates of increase in heat input this way, the change in emission rates due to the non-Title IV-related expansion of PRB coals in the Midwest would not be properly identified.

The second term within square brackets in Equation (5.2) includes a number of categorical variables that could be expected to reflect the effect of Title IV on emissions. Separate dummies are specified for Phase I units with retrofitted scrubbers, all other Table A units, and substitution units. The effect of Title IV on emissions can be expected to differ for units in each of these categories, and whether an affected unit belongs in one category or another can be readily established based on its legal status and abatement technique. For instance, units with retrofitted scrubbers reduce emissions more than do nonscrubbed units. Substitution units are similar to nonscrubbed Table A units but differ markedly from Table A units in size, utilization, and pre-Phase I emission rates. The effect of Phase I is estimated separately for 1995, 1996, and 1997 for retrofitted scrubbers and other Table A units to allow for the possibility of differing abatement from year to year. Two more dummy variables are employed to capture anticipatory abatement actions. One applies to three Title IV scrubbers that were retrofitted in 1992 and 1993 under the Clean Coal Technology Program. The other is employed for nonscrubbed Table A units in 1993 and 1994 to identify any early action undertaken by these units, such as pre-1995 switching to lower-sulfur coals beyond what would be indicated by the PRB trend.

A key issue in establishing a counterfactual for Title IV is estimating the effect of the expansion of PRB coals into the Midwest that is unrelated to Title IV, as well as any other time trends that would affect SO_2 emissions. The larger database allows estimation of emissions trends that began in the mid-1980s and continued through 1997 for the entire sample. Two such trends are captured by the emission-trend variables that constitute the third term within square

6. The reasons for the difference in load growth are not entirely clear, but two possible explanations can be offered. The 1,200-mile outer limit of the PRB zone of expansion generally divides the Midwest from the East Coast and the Southeast. Bulk power transfers generally flow from the Midwest to the East Coast, and between 1988 and 1997 these flows were increasing. Also, the increased utilization of nuclear plants during this period may be relevant. Nuclear facilities constitute a larger share of generating capacity on the East Coast and in the Southeast than in the Midwest. Their use increased over these years, and that increase would have had a greater effect on reducing heat input into fossil-fired units outside the Midwest.

brackets in Equation (5.2). The first variable applies to all coal-fired units within what we have called the PRB zone of expansion, 600 to 1,200 miles of the Powder River Basin. This variable simulates the effect of continuing displacement of high-sulfur midwestern coals by western, predominantly PRB, coals due to changes in rail rates, as discussed in Chapter 4. The second emission-trend variable applies to oil- and gas-fired units, wherever located. Heat input at oil and gas units east of the Mississippi has diminished over this time period in response to (a) the lower price of coal relative to that for oil and gas, (b) increasing bulk power transfers to the East Coast, and (c) higher utilization of nuclear plants. All of these factors reduced the utilization of oil and gas units during these years. Isolating this trend is important, not so much because of the emissions from oil and gas units, but because a failure to differentiate these units would obscure the effect of Title IV on SO_2 emissions from coal-fired units.

The first and third terms within square brackets in Equation (5.2) capture the elements common across all units with respect to heat input and emission trends. The second term, the set of Title IV dummies, describes the observed effect of Title IV on Phase I units. Setting each of these terms to zero permits the counterfactual to be estimated. The underlying assumption of this counterfactual is that, absent Title IV, emissions would change with the heat-input aggregates, modified only by the preexisting trends toward greater use of PRB coals in the Midwest and less use of oil- and gas-fired units. A second assumption, underlying the heat-input categories, is that Title IV does not affect the distribution of generation between PRB and non-PRB regions, or between Phase I and Phase II units.

This alternative counterfactual differs from the simple counterfactual in three important respects. First, and perhaps most importantly, the counterfactual does not depend on the observed 1993 emission rates at Phase I units as a proxy for counterfactual emission rates in 1995–97. The richer specification and the larger database allow for the identification of emissions trends unrelated to Title IV that could be expected to affect emission rates during 1995–97.

A second and related difference is that pre-1995 emission reductions attributable to Title IV can be identified. Just as the simple counterfactual's dependence on the 1993 emission rate implicitly assigns all post-1993 emission reductions to Title IV, so it also implicitly assumes that none of the emissions reductions observed in 1993 could be attributed to Title IV. The econometrically estimated counterfactual indicates that Title IV can be credited with almost 1 million tons of SO_2 emissions abatement prior to 1995: 50,000 tons in 1992, 398,000 tons in 1993, and 537,000 tons in 1994.

The third difference concerns the treatment of Title IV-induced shifts in heat input among units. Two features are used to capture the effects of heat-input shifts in the econometrically estimated counterfactual. The first is the use of observed emissions to estimate the effect of Title IV, instead of relying on observed changes in emission rates, as is done in estimating emission reductions using the simple counterfactual. To the extent that heat input is shifted among units *within* any of the four heat-input groups, the heat-input shift is taken into account in the coefficients for the Title IV dummies.

The shift of heat input from nonscrubbed Table A units to Table A units retrofitted with scrubbers can be used as an illustration. As explained more fully in the appendix, Title IV had the effect of reducing emissions by about 90% at Table A units retrofitted with scrubbers, and by about 30% at all other Table A units. At the same time, there was a shift of heat input from nonscrubbed to scrubbed units that resulted in an average 10% decrease in heat input at the former and a 12% increase at the latter. The estimated coefficients for these two types of Phase I units take this heat-input shift into account. Had there been no shift of heat input, the coefficient for scrubbed units would have been slightly greater (e.g., –0.91) and that for nonscrubbed units, somewhat less (e.g., –0.23).

The second feature used to capture the effects of heat-input shifts in the econometrically estimated counterfactual is the partitioning of the heat-input groups between Phase I and Phase II units. As discussed in the appendix, an additional regression is used to test for heat-input shifts between Phase I and Phase II units both before and after 1995. This "auxiliary" regression indicates no discernible evidence of any shift from or to what were to become Phase I and Phase II units prior to 1995, but very strong evidence of such a shift once Phase I became effective, as would be predicted. That shift in heat input between groups is captured, however, by the heat-group variable in Equation (5.2), so that heat input is higher in 1995–97 for the two Phase II groups (PRB and non-PRB) and lower for the two Phase I groups. So long as the heat-input shift does not affect emission rates at the unit level, the estimated coefficients properly measure the effect of Title IV. They are measuring what appears (after heat-input shifts within the groups) to be the average change in emission rate attributable to the Title IV dummy, after controlling for the effects of the PRB and oil/gas time trends. When the auxiliary regression detects a heat-input shift from Phase I to Phase II, the only issue from the standpoint of the aggregate emission reduction is the difference between the average emission rates for the two groups. If the average emission rate for the Phase I and Phase II groups is the same, then the heat-input shift has no aggregate emission effect. If the average Phase II unit emission rate is lower, then the heat-input shift has an aggregate emission-reducing effect. If the average Phase II rate is higher, the heat-input shift has an aggregate emission-increasing effect. In fact, the average Phase II emission rate is lower than the average Phase I emission rate, and therefore the observed heat-input shift has a slight emission-reducing effect, on the order of 3–4% of the estimated Title IV emission reduction.

The estimated effect of Phase I on heat-input trends at Table A units in the non-PRB region is illustrated by Figure 5.1, which shows the evolution of aggregate heat input for Table A units prior to 1995, normalized to 1988, and the divergence thereafter. For the years 1995–97, the second line from the bottom represents the average heat-input level for all units without Title IV. The other three lines show the heat input levels for Title IV scrubbers, Phase II units, and nonscrubbed Phase I units, from top to bottom, after the Title IV-induced heat-input shifts. By 1997, the heat-input levels for Phase II units and Phase I units retrofitted with scrubbers was about the same, 19–20% above their 1988 levels and the post-Title IV heat-input level for unscrubbed units.

EMISSIONS REDUCTIONS RESULTING FROM TITLE IV

The difference between aggregate estimated counterfactual emissions and actual emissions is the reduction of SO_2 emissions attributable to Title IV. The difference as measured using each counterfactual is presented in Table 5.1 for the first three years of Phase I and for the immediately preceding two years. Both estimates indicate an aggregate reduction of SO_2 emissions attributable to Title IV of about 4 million tons in each of the first three years of Phase I. The

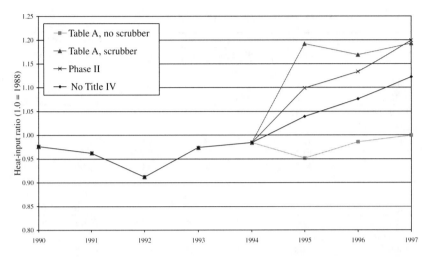

Figure 5.1. Estimated Phase I effect on heat input (coal units, non-PRB zone).

Sources: Derived from Pechan (1995), EPA (1996b, 1997, 1998), and Appendix to this book.

Table 5.1. *Title IV emission reduction, 1993–97*

	Simple counterfactual	Econometric counterfactual	Difference
1993	0	398	+398
1994	0	537	+537
1995	3,961	4,153	+192
1996	4,076	3,791	−285
1997	4,257	3,955	−302
Total	12,294	12,834	+540
Average 1995–97	4,098	3,966	−132

Sources: Derived from Pechan (1995), EPA (1996b, 1997, 1998), and Appendix to this book.

second counterfactual suggests slightly lower abatement during these three years but slightly higher abatement overall because of almost 1 million tons of pre-Phase I abatement in 1993 and 1994.

Table 5.2 presents more detailed data on Title IV compliance for two sets of Phase I units. The first set comprises all affected units in each of the first three years of Phase I. The number of Phase I units

Table 5.2. *Title IV SO$_2$ compliance statistics, 1995–97*

	All affected units in each year			Affected units in all three years		
	1995	1996	1997	1995	1996	1997
Units						
Table A	263	263	263	263	263	263
Voluntary	182	168	160	138	138	138
Total	445	431	423	401	401	401
Capacity (MW^e)						
Table A	88,036	88,036	88,036	88,036	88,036	88,036
Voluntary	41,643	37,179	32,815	28,854	28,854	28,854
Total	129,679	125,215	120,851	116,890	116,890	116,890
Heat input (10^{12} Btu)						
Table A	4,708	4,897	5,048	4,708	4,897	5,048
Voluntary	1,932	1,504	1,360	1,122	1,130	1,185
Total	6,640	6,401	6,408	5,830	6,027	6,233
Emissions (thousand tons)						
Table A	4,451	4,765	4,775	4,451	4,765	4,775
Voluntary	847	668	699	497	502	537
Total	5,298	5,433	5,474	4,948	5,267	5,312
Average rate (lb/mmBtu)						
Table A	1.89	1.94	1.89	1.89	1.94	1.89
Voluntary	0.88	0.90	1.03	0.89	0.89	0.91
All units	1.60	1.70	1.71	1.70	1.75	1.71
Counterfactual (thousand tons)						
Table A	8,172	8,607	8,787	8,172	8,607	8,787
Voluntary	1,088	903	945	703	710	750
Total	9,260	9,510	9,732	8,875	9,317	9,537
Reduction (thousand tons)						
Table A	3,721	3,842	4,012	3,721	3,842	4,012
Voluntary	240	234	245	206	208	213
Total	3,961	4,076	4,257	3,927	4,050	4,225
Allowances (thousands)						
Table A	7,215	6,888	5,822	7,215	6,888	5,822
Voluntary	1,329	1,234	1,136	959	950	895
Total	8,544	8,122	6,958	8,174	7,838	6,717
Banking (thousands)						
Table A	2,764	2,123	1,047	2,764	2,123	1,047
Voluntary	482	565	437	462	449	358
Total	3,246	2,688	1,484	3,226	2,572	1,405

Sources: Derived from Pechan (1995) and EPA (1996b, 1997, 1998).

in any single year varies because units in the voluntary compliance program can enter and exit in any year of Phase I, as they choose. Since the changing composition of units can create problems of comparability in subsequent analysis, data is provided for a second set of

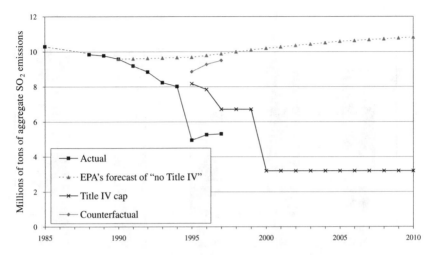

Figure 5.2. Title IV in historical perspective.
Sources: Derived from Pechan (1995) and EPA (1996b, 1997, 1998).

units: those that have been subject to Phase I for all three years examined here. There have been 401 such units, including 138 substitution
units, and they account for at least 95% of emissions from all Phase
I units in any given year.

In Figure 5.2, the Title IV emission reduction is placed in historical perspective, namely, in relation to past emissions, expectations of
emissions growth at the time Title IV was enacted, and the allowances
distribution to these units since 1995 and into Phase II. To ensure
complete comparability of the data over time, the aggregates for
emissions and allowances represent the 401 units that were affected
in all three years of Phase I.[7] This figure shows at once the pre-Phase
I decline in emissions, the sharp reduction of emissions in 1995, the
significant overcompliance in 1995–97 and consequent banking, and
the further reduction that will be required in Phase II. The aggregate
reduction is the difference between the simple counterfactual for
these units and actual emissions, and the amount of banking is the
diminishing difference between the allowance allocation and actual

7. Obviously, no prior forecast of SO_2 emissions for these 401 Phase I units exists. The fore-
    cast in Figure 5.2 was obtained by scaling an earlier EPA forecast of SO_2 emissions from
    all electric utility generating sources (Pechan, 1995) to the proportion of emissions
    attributable to the 401 units in 1990.

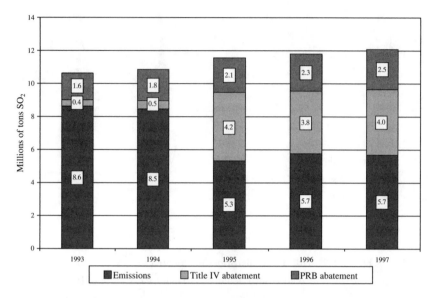

Figure 5.3. Emissions, Title IV and PRB abatement according to econometrically estimated counterfactual, 1993–97.

Sources: Derived from Pechan (1995), EPA (1996b, 1997, 1998), and
Appendix to this book.

emissions. A further approximately 40% reduction of emissions will
be eventually required in Phase II. It is widely expected that the
allowances being banked by these units in Phase I will be used over
the first five to ten years of Phase II to avoid what otherwise would
be a further sharp reduction of emissions in the year 2000.

The emissions reduction attributable to Title IV and the emissions
reduction associated with the independent economic shift to PRB
coal is displayed in Figure 5.3, using the second counterfactual as our
benchmark. The bottom segment of each column represents actual
emissions from all units affected in any one year of Phase I.[8] The
middle segment is the abatement attributable to Title IV, and the top
segment represents abatement resulting from the independent economic expansion of PRB coals into the Midwest. Economic penetration of PRB coal has made a significant contribution to reducing SO_2
emissions, but its effect has not been as great as that of Title IV. Even

8. The numbers given for actual emissions are as predicted by the simulation. The error
   for the aggregate is always within 2.5 percentage points of observed emissions.

though the economic penetration of PRB coal can be expected to continue to increase, it will be overshadowed even more by Title IV once Phase II begins.

The econometrically estimated counterfactual also reveals a slightly different evolution of abatement from 1995 through 1997 compared to the simple counterfactual. Whereas the simple counterfactual shows Title IV abatement increasing steadily from year to year, the alternative counterfactual indicates less abatement in both 1996 and 1997 relative to 1995. As will be explained presently, this pattern is not implausible, since it appears that there was overinvestment in abatement in Phase I, which led to lower allowance prices in 1996 and 1997 than in 1995. The simple counterfactual indicates increasing abatement in 1996 and 1997, because an annual increment of 200,000 tons of abatement, identified by the alternative counterfactual as resulting from the additional economic penetration of PRB coal, is attributed to Title IV.

Whichever counterfactual one chooses to rely upon, Title IV can be credited with a significant reduction in annual SO_2 emissions. The econometrically estimated counterfactual does a better job of taking into account all the various factors operating in these years that affect emissions. For that reason, we favor it as providing the best estimate of the aggregate reduction of emissions attributable to Title IV. Nevertheless, we will often rely on the simple counterfactual because of its ease of use and the distortions that can occur with small subsets of generating units when some of the constituent units are not well predicted by the more elaborate counterfactual.

The Distribution of Abatement among Phase I Units

One of the most striking features of Title IV abatement at the level of the generating unit is the concentration of the aggregate emission reduction at relatively few units. As shown by Figure 5.4, 21 units (on the far left of the figure) account for 50% of the entire 1997 emissions reduction by the 401 continuously affected units. Ninety percent is accounted for by 100 units, only one-quarter of the total number of Phase I generating units. A handful of units (depicted on the far right of Figure 5.4) actually increased emissions, but the vast majority of the Phase I units made very little change in emissions.

Part of the explanation for the extreme skew in the distribution of

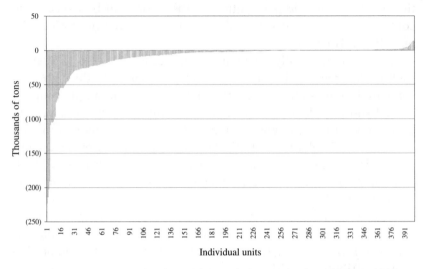

Figure 5.4. Distribution of SO$_2$ emissions reductions, by unit, 1997.
Sources: Derived from Pechan (1995) and EPA (1996b, 1997, 1998).

emissions reductions lies in the differing size of the generating units. For an equal reduction in emission rates, expressed as pounds of SO$_2$ per million Btu of heat input (lb/mmBtu), a larger unit or a more heavily utilized unit will produce a larger reduction in tons of SO$_2$. For instance, the 25% of the units that account for 90% of the aggregate emissions reduction also account for 48% of total heat input. Nevertheless, when the same units are arrayed by their reduction in emission *rate*, which normalizes for unit size and utilization, as in Figure 5.5, the skew is still pronounced, although not as extreme. The division of units into those reducing emissions and those increasing emissions is the same in Figures 5.4 and 5.5. However, the ordering of units is different, since the units making the greatest emission-rate reductions are not necessarily the units making the largest tonnage reductions. For instance, the largest emission-rate reduction, 6.57 lb/mmBtu, was observed at a little-utilized and now retired thirty-five-year-old, 500 MW^e coal-fired unit in Indiana. Because the unit was little utilized, however, it reduced emissions by only 1,234 tons, which places it about 225th in the tonnage size of reduction. Still, the number of units making really large rate reductions, more than 4.0 lb/mmBtu, is small, while the number of units making no

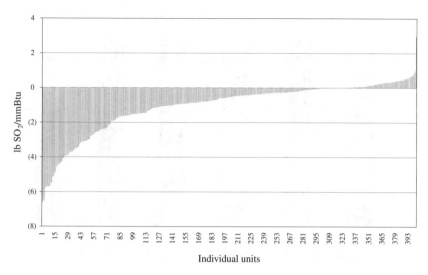

Figure 5.5. Distribution of emission-rate reductions, by unit, 1997.
Sources: Derived from Pechan (1995) and EPA (1996b, 1997, 1998).

significant reduction in emission rates is large. If we take a variation of 0.5 lb/mmBtu as an outer bound for the normal variability in average annual sulfur content for any coal, only 203 units made rate reductions greater than this amount. By this measure, half the Phase I units made no significant reduction in emission rates.

These two figures show a distinct tendency for larger and more heavily utilized units to make a greater reduction in their emission rates than units with less heat input. To illustrate, for the 401 continuously affected Phase I units, the correlation coefficient between heat input and the reduction in the SO_2 emission *rate* is +.54, not much less than the correlation coefficient between heat input and the reduction in emissions, +.69.

The highly skewed distribution of 1997 emission-rate reductions by unit is typical for 1995 and 1996, as well. There has been some change in emission rates among affected units since 1995, but the division of units and heat input into low-, mid-, and high-emission-rate units has remained very stable over these three years. Figure 5.6 shows the number of units with emission rates below 2.0 lb/mmBtu (low-sulfur coal), between 2.0 and 3.5 lb/mmBtu (mid-sulfur coal), and above 3.5 lb/mmBtu (high-sulfur coal) for the first three years of Phase I, as

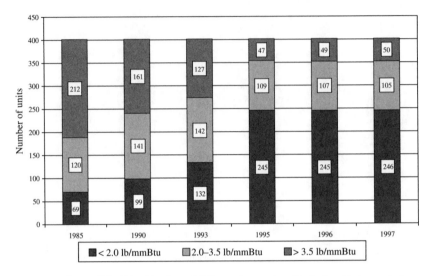

Figure 5.6. Distribution of 401 continuously affected units, by emission-rate category, 1985–97.

Sources: Derived from Pechan (1995) and EPA (1996b, 1997, 1998).

well as for three earlier years. The pre-Phase I trend toward lower-sulfur coal is clearly illustrated, as well as the significant shift in distribution of units between 1993 and 1995. Since 1995, a slight shift to higher emission-rate units has occurred, but it is small compared to the change due to Title IV. The heat-input shifts among these categories has been even larger because of the tendency for larger, more utilized units to make large emission-rate reductions. For instance, among these 401 units, the number of units with emission rates below 2.0 lb/mmBtu has almost doubled since 1993, while the heat input into units in this low-emitting category has increased by two-and-a-half-fold.

The Emission Reduction by Abatement Technique

Broadly speaking, SO_2 emission rates can be reduced by two methods: scrubbing and fuel switching.[9] "Scrubbing" is the short

---

9. Emissions can also be reduced by increased efficiency in generating electricity, retirements, or shifting load to lower-emitting units. Improvements in generation efficiency cannot be evaluated from heat-input data alone, but there is little to suggest that increased efficiency made a significant contribution to the emission reduction attributable to Title IV. As previously noted, retirements and load shifting made very small contributions.

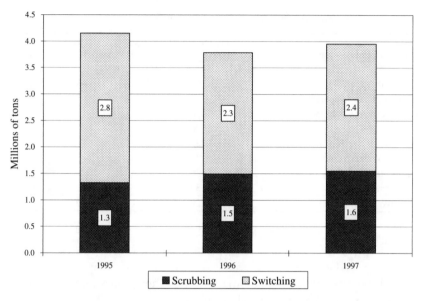

Figure 5.7. Title IV emissions reductions, by abatement technique.
Sources: Derived from Pechan (1995), EPA (1996b, 1997, 1998), and Appendix to this book.

name for flue-gas desulfurization, a process by which the postcombustion flue gas is cleaned of most of its SO_2 content (usually around 95%) by a chemical reaction with limestone or other base reagents as the combustion exhaust passes up the stack. Scrubbers are costly because they require a large up-front capital investment, but once in place, their operating costs are relatively low.

Fuel switching refers to the substitution of a lower-sulfur fuel, typically a lower-sulfur coal, but also natural gas, for the higher-sulfur coal previously used. The amount of the reduction depends on the sulfur content of the lower-sulfur fuel, which can be below 1.0lb/mmBtu for many coals and is zero for natural gas. Although some retooling of a generating unit designed to burn a higher-sulfur coal is typically required for switching, the initial investment is not large, so that most of the cost of switching is the premium paid for the lower-sulfur fuel.

Almost 37% of the total Title IV emission reduction in 1995–97 came from scrubbing, as shown in Figure 5.7. Units that were retrofitted with scrubbers were responsible for 32% of the total emission reduction attributable to Title IV in 1995, and for 39% in

Table 5.3. *SO₂ emission reductions from fuel switching, 1995*

Source of lower-sulfur fuel	SO₂ abatement (thousand tons)	Fuel-switching share (%)
Central Appalachia	1,241	43.9
Southern Appalachia	98	3.5
Northern Appalachia	336	11.9
Midwest	666	23.6
Powder River Basin	325	11.5
Other Western coal	92	3.2
Imported coal	36	1.3
Natural gas	33	1.2
Fuel-switching total	2,828	100.0

Sources: Derived from FERC Forms 423, Pechan (1995), EPA (1996b, 1997, 1998), and Appendix to this book.

both 1996 and 1997.[10] The contribution of these units explains much of the extreme skew observed in Figures 5.4 and 5.5. Moreover, nine of these twenty-seven units are located at four large plants – Cumberland, Gavin, Harrison, and Conemaugh – that account for 1.0 million tons, or 70% of the reduction from retrofitted scrubbers.[11] These few units, totaling 9,125 MW^e, or 7.5% of total affected capacity in 1997, account for one-quarter of the Title IV emissions reduction in Phase I from all sources throughout the country.

Table 5.3 shows the production sources of the lower-sulfur fuel used by units reducing emissions by fuel switching, the alternative to scrubbing. The single largest source of lower-sulfur coal for units that switched fuels to reduce emissions was central Appalachia, the traditional source of high-quality, low-sulfur coal, which accounted for 44% of the reduction in emissions by coal switching. Title IV also prompted units to switch to Powder River Basin and other western

10. Only twenty-one retrofitted scrubbers were operating for all or most of 1995. The remaining six were on line by the end of 1996, as was required for any retrofitted unit qualifying for Phase I extension allowances. In addition, a number of substitution units had already installed scrubbers to meet New Source Performance Standards (NSPS). Their number was 26 in 1995, 20 in 1996, and 16 in 1997, and their contribution to the total emissions reduction declined from 43,000 tons in 1995 to 35,000 tons in 1997, 1% or less of the total.
11. These plants, located in Tennessee, Ohio, West Virginia, and Pennsylvania, are operated by the Tennessee Valley Authority, American Electric Power, Allegheny Power, and General Public Utilities, respectively.

sources of low-sulfur coals over and above what is indicated by the econometrically estimated counterfactual as increases in non-Title IV-related conversions to these coals. In 1995, western coals accounted for 15% of the emission reduction from coal switching attributable to Title IV.

These low-sulfur coal-producing regions had competition from some surprising sources: the predominantly high-sulfur coal-producing regions of the Midwest and northern Appalachia. Lower-sulfur coals from these two regions contributed 35% of the 1995 emission reduction from switching, only eight percentage points less than central Appalachia. The coals providing these emission reductions were not the 1.2 lb/mmBtu coals available from such regions as central Appalachia or the PRB, but local mid- or even high-sulfur coals that contained less sulfur than the coal previously used by customer generating units. Some of the mid-sulfur coals had not been produced in these regions previously; however, with the premium for lower-sulfur content, these coals were now worth producing, and were cheaper than competing low-sulfur coals from Central Appalachia and even from the PRB.

A good example of this phenomenon is provided by the Coleman plant in Kentucky. This plant purchases virtually all of its coal on a spot basis, and has reduced its emissions by 25%. The share of its low- to mid-sulfur central Appalachian coals increased slightly from 4% in 1993 to 10% in 1995. The remaining 90% of its coal continued to be purchased from the Midwest and northern Appalachia. The key difference was that the SO_2 content of that coal was reduced from 4.1 lb/mmBtu to 3.1 lb/mmBtu at an added cost of about $0.10/mmBtu.

The surprisingly large contribution to the Title IV emission reduction from traditionally high-sulfur coal-producing regions reflects several features of allowance trading and coal markets. First, under Title IV, all SO_2 emission reductions are equally valuable. Reducing emissions from a rate of 4 lb/mmBtu to 3 lb/mmBtu has the same value as moving from 2 lb/mmBtu to 1 lb/mmBtu. Thus, many mid- and even high-sulfur coals benefited from switches away from even higher-sulfur coals. Second, location is always an important consideration in the choice of coals. A nearby coal that would incur low transportation costs for delivery to a power plant will always have an advantage over more distant coals. Thus, nearby, lower-sulfur-content coals had an advantage. Finally, utilities had the flexibility to reduce emissions by a little, a lot, or not at all. How much of a reduction would be effected and how many allowances would be surrendered depended on the comparison between allowance prices and the premiums at which lower-sulfur coals were available. With compliance defined simply as having sufficient allowances to cover emissions, there was no need to reduce emissions as much as would have occurred by switching at every location to a truly low-sulfur coal. The results were a significant reduction of SO_2 emissions by switching within the traditionally high-sulfur coal regions, and commensurately less demand for conventionally defined low-sulfur coals.

The last notable feature about the fuel switching observed at Phase I units in 1995 is the insignificant share associated with natural gas. Prior to 1995, it had been expected that up to 500 billion cubic feet of natural gas annually (equivalent to about 20 million tons of coal) would find a new market as a substitute for coal as a result of Title IV (GRI, 1991). In fact, the only natural gas that found a home in a Phase I unit was along the East Coast, where it displaced higher-sulfur oil.[12] For most other Phase I units, which were burning coal to start with, the penalty for sulfur content was not high enough to compensate for the higher delivered price of natural gas and the costs of retrofitting units to burn natural gas. Several Phase I coal-fired units in the Midwest were hooked up to natural gas pipelines (e.g., Vermillion in Illinois and Conesville in Ohio), but the reduction in emissions at these units either has been small or has been accomplished by switching to lower-sulfur coal.

Geographic Distribution of Title IV Abatement

Acid rain is a regional problem for which the source of emissions and the patterns of atmospheric transport matter. The region most damaged in the United States has been the Northeast, and the primary source of precursor emissions is perceived to be the heavily coal-burning states in the Ohio River Valley. Since Title IV sanctioned unrestricted emissions trading and allowances were valued equally whether the emissions occurred in Florida or Ohio, there

---

12. Six oil-burning units reduced emissions by increasing the share of natural gas. Three of these units were located on Long Island, two in Maryland, and one in Massachusetts.

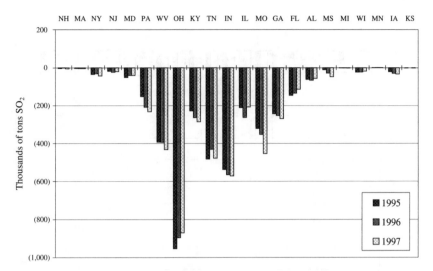

Figure 5.8. Title IV emissions reductions, by state and year.
Sources: Derived from Pechan (1995) and EPA (1996b, 1997, 1998).

was no assurance that reductions would be made in the Ohio River Valley and the Midwest generally, where they mattered the most from an environmental standpoint. As a result, concerns about "hot spots" were often expressed, and some states addressed these by making local attempts to restrict the scope of Title IV allowance trading.[13]

The concerns proved to be unfounded. As shown by Figure 5.8, in which the 22 states with the 401 continuously affected units are arrayed from northeast to west, most of the reduction occurred in the upwind midwestern states. The eight midwestern states of greatest concern, arrayed from Pennsylvania to Missouri on Figure 5.8, contributed 84% of the emission reduction for the three years as a whole. There were slight shifts among these core states, but the shifts were compensating. For instance, the 83,000-ton decrease in reduction in Ohio between 1995 and 1997 was compensated by increased emission reductions of 119,000 tons in Pennsylvania and West Virginia.

13. For instance, various attempts were made to prevent utilities in New York from selling allowances out of state, based on the argument that such sales would lead to more emissions in upwind states.

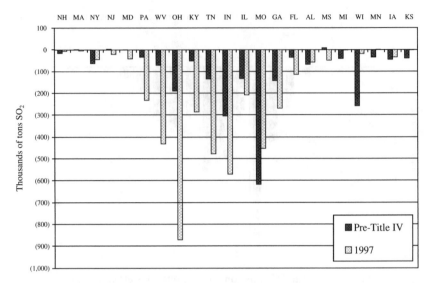

Figure 5.9. Comparison of 1997 Title IV emissions reductions with pre-Title IV emissions reductions, by state.

Sources: Derived from Pechan (1995) and EPA (1996b, 1997, 1998).

There is also a decidedly more eastern cast to the emission reductions made in response to Title IV than to the reductions that occurred prior to 1993. Figure 5.9 compares the 1997 reduction with the pre-Phase I reduction, with the states ordered from east to west as before. The three easternmost of the eight core states – Ohio, West Virginia, and Pennsylvania – accounted for only 13% of the pre-Phase I reduction of 2.3 million tons but 37% of the Title IV emission reduction.[14] In effect, Title IV moved the emission reductions farther east and closer to the Northeast.

Still, there is a puzzle. Why, with unfettered emissions trading, did so much of the emissions reduction occur where it was most desired from an environmental standpoint? One explanation is the interaction between the nonproportional emission reduction implied by the Title IV allowance allocation and the distinctly autarkic approach that utilities adopted in making compliance decisions for Phase I. In

14. For the purposes of this comparison, the pre-Phase I emission reduction is determined by the difference between 1985 and 1993 emission rates multiplied by 1997 heat input.

the absence of trading, the allocation of Phase I allowances would have required utilities to reduce emission rates at Phase I units to an average of about 2.5 lb/mmBtu. This requirement, in contrast to a proportional rule, implied a greater reduction by units with high pre-Phase I emission rates, most of which were located in the eight core states. Although utilities were free to trade, the evidence is overwhelming that few were willing to base decisions in preparation for Phase I compliance entirely on purchases of allowances in a nascent and uncertain allowance market. As a result, nearly all utilities with Phase I units reduced emissions within their service territory as necessary to ensure that emissions were within the allowances allocated to the utility. In fact, there was only one significant exception: Illinois Power. Others may have intended to rely partially upon allowance purchases, but most of the reductions necessary to ensure compliance were performed internally. Given the locations of the high-emission-rate units, this tendency toward autarkic compliance ensured that most of the emission reduction occurred within the eight-state area.

Even so, autarkic compliance is not a complete explanation. The actual reduction of emissions within this core eight-state area was greater than would have been required if each utility had operated under a state cap. Figure 5.10 compares the "required" emission reduction of each state in 1997 with the actual reduction in emissions.[15] The first column indicates the emissions reduction that would have been required by the allowances distributed to Phase I units within the state. The second column indicates the actual reduction in 1997, which includes all the effects of allowance trading, whether for banking or trading among utilities and states. For six of the eight core midwestern states, the actual reduction was greater than what was required, sometimes significantly so. For only two states, Kentucky and Illinois, did emissions trading lead to less emissions reduction.[16] On balance, the eight core states reduced emissions about 25% more than would have been required without trading: 3.5 million tons compared with a 2.8-million ton requirement. The greater-than-required

15. Using the year 1997 imposes a more stringent test since fewer allowances were distributed in this year than in 1995 and 1996.
16. Illinois Power's explicit compliance strategy of depending on external allowance purchases explains Illinois's case. In the case of Kentucky, one unit operated by the Tennessee Valley Authority was the beneficiary of allowances produced by overcompliance at a TVA unit located in Tennessee.

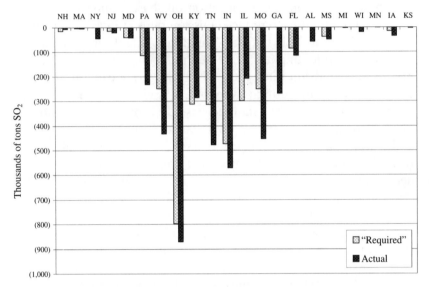

Figure 5.10. Effect of emissions trading on emissions reductions, by state, 1997.

Sources: Derived from Pechan (1995) and EPA (1996b, 1997, 1998).

emission reduction in these states is consistent with the prediction of lower abatement cost in these states by some early studies of Title IV (ICF, 1990).[17]

The favorable economics of SO_2 emission reduction in these core states is also indicated by the choice of abatement technique, shown by Figure 5.11. A clear regional pattern emerges in the choice of scrubbing and fuel switching, with one telling exception. Abatement by switching occurred more to the West and the Southeast, where PRB coals figure more prominently, while most of the reduction from scrubbing took place in the six easternmost of the eight midwestern states. The exception was Ohio, which alone among the more eastern of these states resorted equally to switching and scrubbing. Ohio is close to the low-sulfur coal-producing region of central Appalachia, which is located in West Virginia and Kentucky. More importantly, the rivers that drain central Appalachia, the Kanawha and Big Sandy, flow into the Ohio River, along which many of Ohio's Phase I units

17. See the discussion of the cost-minimizing allocation of allowances in Chapter 3.

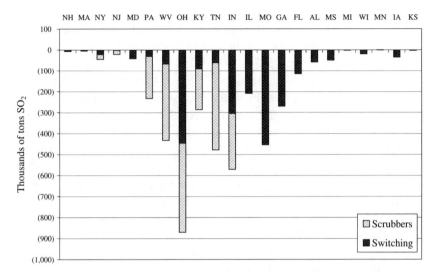

Figure 5.11. 1997 emissions reductions, by state and abatement technique.

Sources: Derived from Pechan (1995) and EPA (1996b, 1997, 1998).

are located. Consequently, coal can be transported to these units more cheaply than to Phase I units in West Virginia or Kentucky, which may be closer geographically but across many ridges and valleys of the Appalachian Mountains.

The location of scrubbers in these core states is due to a combination of explicit incentive in Title IV, favorable economics where the sulfur content of the coal and the utilization of generating units are high, and local inducement through favorable cost-recovery rulings by the state public utility commission. Phase I extension allowances provided a clear incentive to advance the construction of scrubbers into Phase I, and that incentive was augmented in some cases by favorable treatment by the local regulatory commission. Nevertheless, eight of the twenty-seven retrofitted units did not receive any extension allowances, and four retrofitted units were located in non-coal-producing states.[18] More importantly, scrubbers are most

18. The retrofitted units that did not receive extension allowances were located at Petersburg (IN), Culley (IN), Smith (KY), and Milliken (NY) plants. Although the units in Indiana and Kentucky may have benefited from local coal provisions, these considerations did not apply in New York. Scrubbers were also retrofitted in New Jersey and Georgia.

economic when located at large, heavily utilized units close to cheap, high-sulfur coal supplies.[19] Generating facilities having these characteristics are far more likely to be found in the eight core midwestern states than elsewhere.

In summary, the concentration of Phase I emission reductions in these eight Ohio River Valley and midwestern states is due to several closely intertwined factors. The nonproportional emission reduction required by Title IV and the autarkic approach to compliance adopted by almost all utilities with a large number of Phase I units implied a larger emission reduction for utilities in this area. That outcome was not altered by emissions trading, and was even strengthened, because the economics were favorable to abating more in these states. Most of the large, heavily utilized, high-sulfur coal-burning generating units in Phase I were located in these states, and scrubbing can be very attractive when conditions are right. In addition, many Phase I units are located along the Ohio River, where low-sulfur coal from central Appalachia is an economically attractive abatement alternative. Finally, the incentives to scrub, whether built into Title IV or local in origin, also contributed to the concentration of emission reduction in these states.

Role of Voluntary Units

The number of units that voluntarily became subject to Title IV is surprising. However, two qualifications need to be noted. First, the emission reduction accomplished by these voluntary units has been relatively small. Second, the response from nonutility industrial sources was much smaller than expected. The reasons for the small emission reduction from voluntary units and for the very different response from electric utilities and industrial sources reveal some important limitations to voluntary programs.

As of the end of 1997, 206 units had decided voluntarily to be affected in at least one of the first three years of Phase I, as detailed in Table 5.4. Electric utility generating units constituted 199 of these

19. The number of tons abated over which the considerable, fixed capital costs of a scrubber can be spread largely determine the economics of scrubbing. Hence, the higher the sulfur content of the coal and the higher the utilization of the generating unit, the lower the unit cost of abatement. The units retrofitted with scrubbers had an average pre-retrofit emission rate of 4.10 lb/mmBtu, well above the average of 3.02 lb/mmBtu for all Phase I units.

Table 5.4. *Voluntarily affected units, 1995–97*

	Units	Generating capacity (MW^e)	Coal-fired units	Oil/Gas units	Units with scrubbers
All years	138	28,854	113	25	15
1995 & 1996	12	3,599	11	1	4
1995 & 1997	3	391	3	0	0
1996 & 1997	6	3,150	4	2	0
1995 only	29	8,799	27	2	6
1996 only	5	1,577	3	2	0
1997 only	6	420	6	0	0
Electric utility units	199	46,790	167	32	25
Industrial opt-in units	7	NA	7	0	0

Sources: Derived from Pechan (1995) and EPA (1996b, 1997, 1998).

units, and they comprised 46.8 MW^e of electric generating capacity, about half again as much capacity as that associated with the 263 Table A units that were legally obligated to participate in Phase I. A large majority of these electric utility units (70%) have remained in the voluntary program for all three years.

The small aggregate emissions reduction from the voluntary units, about 5–7% of the annual total, reflects two features of the program. First, as will be discussed more extensively in Chapter 8, many units entered Phase I not because they could reduce emissions at lower cost than Table A units, but because their emissions had evolved in a manner that caused them to receive more allowances than their counterfactual emissions. That is, by opting into Phase I, these units received more allowances than they needed to cover their "unregulated" emissions. These "excess allowances" had value to them – either through sale, use in other generating units they owned, or banking for use in Phase II – and this value induced them to participate voluntarily in Phase I. A second and more subtle reason for the voluntary units' minor contribution to the aggregate emission reduction is the effect of the size and emission-limit thresholds that determined which units would be mandated to participate in Phase I. By definition, the voluntary units are either relatively low-emission units, those that fall below either the 2.5 lb/mmBtu 1985 emission-rate threshold, or small units, those below the 100 MW^e size threshold. A number of voluntary units did have high emission rates and did reduce emissions, but they were small and much less heavily utilized.

Table 5.5. *Characteristics of 1995–97 voluntarily affected units*

	Units	Generating capacity (MW^e)	Average size (MW^e)	1993 utilization (%)	1993 emission rate	Emission rate reduction (%)	Average annual Phase I emission reduction[a]
High-emission-rate coal units	50	3,077	62	32	2.73	38	51,576
NSPS scrubbers	15	7,904	527	58	0.49	35	44,802
Other coal units	48	10,719	223	50	1.66	22	92,813
Old oil/gas units	14	756	54	1	0.82	100	275
1970s oil/gas units	11	6,398	582	17	1.00	58	19,444
All units	138	28,854	209	42	1.24	29	208,910

[a]Using the simple counterfactual.
Sources: Derived from Pechan (1995) and EPA (1996b, 1997, 1998).

Similarly, a number of big units volunteered to be subject to Phase I, but they had low emission rates to begin with. In both cases, the result has been a small reduction in tons, even for large-percentage reductions in the emission rate.

The generating units voluntarily participating in Phase I fall into several clearly distinguishable categories, listed in Table 5.5. The first category consists of fifty coal units with a 1985 emission rate above Table A's 2.5 lb/mmBtu threshold but a capacity below the 100 MW^e size threshold. The average age of these units was forty-five years in 1995, and the oldest unit in this group was put in service in 1923. Five of these units were retired before Phase I began, another nine were retired between 1995 and 1997, and the remaining thirty-six units continue in use at about the same utilization rate as before 1995. Their heat-input-weighted average emission rate is 32% lower during Phase I than it was before (1.86 lb/mmBtu in 1997 vs. 2.73 lb/mmBtu in 1993).

The second category comprises large coal units with pre-Title IV scrubbers that were required to meet the New Source Performance Standard (NSPS) or local air regulations, typically 1.2 lb/mmBtu or lower. These units reduced emissions by 35% on average, but their average pre-Phase I emission rate was only 0.49 lb/mmBtu.

The third category consists of forty-eight other coal units. These units vary greatly in age and size, but all had a 1985 emission rate below 2.5 lb/mmBtu, and none had a scrubber. Five of these units were retired prior to 1993, and another three have been taken off line since then. Almost half of the aggregate emission reduction from voluntary units comes from these units, which are more heavily utilized and not particularly small, and for which the pre-Phase I emission rate is not extremely low. Even so, the total reduction of emissions from these units is small in absolute amount.

A sizable number of oil-fired generating facilities voluntarily became subject to Phase I regulations. These units fall into two categories: fourteen small, old units and eleven large units that came on line in the 1970s. Both types of units are characterized by low utilization compared even to the old coal-fired units. Four of the old oil units had been retired by 1993; and the remaining ten units, as well as one 1970s oil unit, were retired when Phase I began.

Unlike the response to the substitution and compensation provisions under which electric utility generating units volunteered, the response to Title IV's industrial source opt-in provisions was meager. As of 1997, only seven units at two plants had entered, and no others are anticipated. The units that successfully entered the industrial opt-in program illustrate what appears to be the primary impediment to a greater participation rate by industrial sources: the cost of monitoring emissions.[20] Industrial opt-in units must have the capability of continuously monitoring emissions, typically by installing a continuous emissions monitoring system (CEMS). In contrast to industrial sources, all electric utility generating units subject to Title IV in either Phase I or Phase II were required to install a CEMS by January 1, 1995. Consequently, electric utility units entering the voluntary compliance program did not face the same impediment as the industrial opt-in units.

As if to prove the point, none of the seven industrial opt-in units needed to install a CEMS. Four of the seven units were industrial steam plants owned by Du Pont that were retired under an arrangement whereby the replacement steam was provided by the Johnsonville plant, owned by the Tennessee Valley Authority. The Thermal Energy Exception, which governed this application, allocated allowances to the replacement source in an amount equal to the increased emissions by that source. Since the units at the Johnsonville plant are listed in Table A, no incremental monitoring costs were involved. The other three units were electric generating units owned by Alcoa and used to supply electricity to an aluminum smelter located in Indiana. As a part of prior state permitting, these three units had already been required to install CEMS equipment. Finally, two other applicants, Union Camp and the City of Dover (Del.), withdrew, citing as reasons the cost of CEMS equipment in relation

20. This discussion paraphrases Atkeson (1997), to which the interested reader is referred for more details.

to the expected value of the allowances generated by the proposed emissions reductions.

In summary, utility units were much more likely to volunteer to be covered by Phase I in part because they were already required to have the monitoring equipment that presented such an obstacle to industrial opt-in sources. Moreover, the aggregate emission reduction attributable to these Phase I opt-in units was not large in part because of the adverse selection problems to be discussed in Chapter 8, but also because the very characteristics that made them eligible to be voluntary units meant that they didn't have much to contribute. As a result, the aggregate emission reduction in Phase I was accomplished almost entirely by the mandated Table A units.

6   Emissions Trading: The Effect on Abatement Behavior

UNIT-LEVEL EMISSIONS TRADING

The primary objective of most environmental measures is to reduce emissions of pollutants. As the preceding chapter has shown, Title IV has been very successful on this score. In fact, it has been more successful in reducing emissions than any other regulatory program initiated during the long history of the Clean Air Act. As if this were not enough, Title IV has another almost equally important objective that distinguishes it from previous environmental legislation: the reduction of compliance cost. Economists have long argued that, in theory, a tradable permit approach to pollution control should involve significantly lower costs than the traditional command-and-control approach of specifying source-specific standards.[1] Title IV provides as good a test of this proposition as any that is likely to be encountered, and that test involves, as a first step, determining whether allowances have been traded among units.

The effect of trading on abatement behavior at the unit level during Phase I has been considerable, as illustrated by Figure 6.1. The solid black line represents the level of SO_2 emissions control that would have been required of each Phase I unit in 1997, given the allocation of allowances to units and their 1997 heat input, with no re-allocation of allowances.[2] This "no-trading" emission rate will vary

---

1. Tietenberg (1985) develops this argument.
2. For units at which the allowance allocation was not binding, the counterfactual (1993) emission rate is shown.

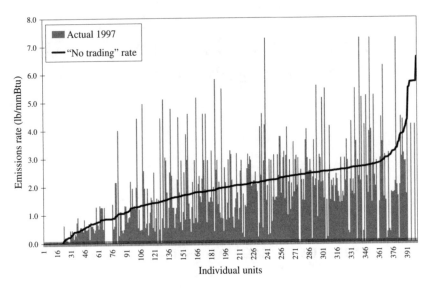

Figure 6.1. Unit-level emissions trading, 1997.
Sources: Derived from Pechan (1995) and EPA (1996b, 1997, 1998).

widely from the 2.5 lb/mmBtu "basic rule" because heat input will
have changed considerably for most units from the 1985–87 baseline
that was used for allocating allowances. Units with increased heat
input will face a lower no-trading emission rate, and less utilized units
will face a less stringent rate or, when not constrained at all, the counterfactual rate. Finally, units retired before 1993 are assigned a no-
trading emission rate of zero. Each vertical column in the figure
indicates the emission rate observed for the same units in 1997. The
distance between the black line and the vertical columns indicates
the effect of emissions trading on abatement at these units. When a
vertical column is below the solid black line, operators reduced emissions beyond what was required to free up allowances for use elsewhere or later. Conversely, when a vertical column is above the solid
black line, operators used allowances for other units or from earlier
compliance to avoid what must be presumed to have been more
costly abatement. In the absence of emissions trading, observed emission rates would follow or cluster around the solid black line.

The departures from the no-trading line are numerous and frequently large. In 1997, more units are below the line (219) than are

above it (162), and most units have departed from the no-trading emission rate considerably, some by as much as 5.0 lb/mmBtu, on both the upside and the downside. The departure from the no-trading rate provides a measure of the extent to which operators resorted to emissions trading in complying with Title IV. Taking this measure to be the square root of the average of the squared deviations, the average departure in 1997 was 1.51 lb/mmBtu. Although there is no single benchmark against which to compare this indicator, it is a large number when viewed against two informative standards. With no trading, units would have actual rates equal to or slightly below the no-trading emission rate, which is clearly not the case. The average deviation can also be compared to the range of observed emission rates, which is 7.27 lb/mmBtu in 1997. By either standard, the resort to emissions trading by utilities with Phase I-affected units has been substantial. All of this indicates that the operators of Phase I units have not taken allowance allocations at the unit level as given and they have made abundant use of the flexibility provided by emissions trading, which suggests in turn that the cost-reducing objective of Title IV is being achieved.

SOME CLASSIFICATIONS AND DEFINITIONS

The response of the operators of Phase I units to emissions trading can be analyzed by classifying Phase I units based on three characteristics: (a) whether the unit is constrained by the allowance allocation, (b) whether it is a supplier or demander of allowances, and (c) whether it has reduced emissions. As shown in Table 6.1, every Phase I unit falls into one of six mutually exclusive categories, determined by these characteristics, depending on the relationship between three data points: the annual allowance allocation, A; annual emissions, E; and counterfactual emissions, CF.[3] The relationship between A and CF determines whether a Phase I unit is constrained ($A < CF$) or not ($A \geq CF$). The relationship between A and E determines whether a unit is a supplier of allowances ($E < A$) or a demander of allowances ($E > A$). Finally, the relationship between E and CF determines whether a

---

3. The simple counterfactual is used for each unit and year, namely, the product of the unit's emissions rate in 1993 and its heat input in 1995, 1996, or 1997.

Table 6.1. *Classification of Phase I units*[a]

Class	Definition	1995	1996	1997
1	$CF > A \geq E$	107	107	127
2	$CF > E > A$	52	71	82
3	$E > CF > A$	24	29	39
4	$A > CF \geq E$	166	144	112
5	$A > E > CF$	49	45	33
6	$E > A > CF$	3	5	8
Total	All units	401	401	401
1,2,3	Constrained ($A < CF$)	183	207	248
1,4,5	Suppliers ($E < A$)	322	296	272
2,3,6	Demanders ($E > A$)	79	105	129
1,2,4	Reducers ($E < CF$)	325	322	321

[a]Includes units affected in all years, 1995–97.

Sources: Derived from Pechan (1995) and EPA (1996b, 1997, 1998).

unit has reduced emissions ($E < CF$) or not ($E \geq CF$). The population of each category varies from year to year as the allowance allocation, counterfactual emissions, and abatement actions change.

Constrained units are not necessarily demanders of allowances, nor are unconstrained units necessarily suppliers. The supply and demand position is determined by the relationship between allowances and actual emissions, which is not the same as the relationship between allowances and counterfactual emissions that determines whether a unit is constrained. For example, the first three categories in Table 6.1 are composed of units that were constrained by the annual allowance allocations ($A < CF$), while Categories 4 through 6 include the unconstrained units, those with counterfactual emissions less than the allowances allocated to them for the year ($A > CF$). Many constrained units have overcomplied, or reduced emissions below the allowance allocation ($E < A$), as indicated for Category 1, and thereby have become suppliers of allowances, like the unconstrained units populating Categories 4 and 5. Similarly, nothing prevents an unconstrained Phase I unit from increasing emissions even beyond its allocation of allowances and thereby becoming a demander of allowances ($E > A$), as did the few units in Category 6. As such, these unconstrained units joined the constrained units in Categories 2 and 3 in being demanders of allowances.

Finally, the relation of emissions to the counterfactual indicates whether emissions have been reduced. Categories 1, 2, and 4 consist of units that reduced emissions relative to the counterfactual ($E < CF$), while Categories 3, 5, and 6 include units with actual emissions higher than the counterfactual emissions ($E > CF$).[4] Although there is a definite tendency for units reducing emissions to be constrained by the allowance allocation and to be suppliers of allowances, this is far from always being the case. For instance, Category 4, the second most numerous one in all three years, consists of units that reduced emissions even though they were unconstrained by the allowance allocation. By the same token, Category 2 indicates constrained units that reduced emissions but not all the way to the allowance allocation so that they were demanders of allowances from other units. As noted in Chapter 5, emissions and abatement actions have been relatively stable over this three-year period. As a consequence, the number of units that reduced emissions relative to the counterfactual has been virtually unchanged from year to year.

There was a clear trend between 1995 and 1997 for more units to become constrained by the allowance allocation, and for more units to become demanders of allowances. This trend reflects two circumstances. First, the number of allowances allocated to Phase I units declined steadily from 1995 to 1997, since most Phase I extension and early reduction credit allowances were distributed in the first two years of Phase I.[5] Second, counterfactual emissions increased by about 0.7 million tons between 1995 and 1997. With relatively unchanging abatement levels, these two factors moved sixty-five units from the unconstrained categories to the constrained ones, and fifty units from a supplying category to a demand category.[6]

---

4. Eighty percent of the units were "reducers" by this classification, whereas Chapter 5 noted that a relatively small number of units accounted for most of the reduction in emissions. The classification adopted here is a precise one, categorizing every unit as either reducing or increasing emissions, even if by only one ton. Most of these 300+ reducing units made very small reductions. For this reason, no significance should be placed on the decline in the number of these units from 325 in 1995 to 321 in 1997.

5. In addition to approximately 1.3 million Phase I extension allowances distributed in each of 1995 and 1996, about 350,000 early reduction credits were issued in 1995.

6. In balance, fewer units moved to the demand side than became constrained because much of the movement was from Category 4, the category with the largest number of generating units in 1995, which is a supplying as well as an unconstrained category. As the allowance allocation fell below counterfactual emissions, units in this category continued to supply allowances for emissions trading, albeit fewer. Units moved from being suppliers to demanders only when the allowance allocation fell below actual emissions.

"Banking" of allowances introduces yet another important consideration. In an economic sense, banking is the means by which the operators of Phase I units can conduct arbitrage between actual marginal abatement costs in Phase I and expected marginal abatement costs in Phase II in order to reduce the overall costs of compliance with Title IV.[7] In an accounting sense, banking simply equates current supply and demand. During Phase I, the excess of current supply over current demand is banked for later use, and in Phase II, drawing down the bank will permit current demand for allowances to exceed current supply for awhile. Thus, the active arbitrage of costs between Phases 1 and 2 becomes a source of demand for allowances in Phase I and a source of supply in Phase II. The relationship for any given year can be illustrated by the following equation, in which entries for the *i*th units are all nonnegative.

$$\Delta B_t = \left(\sum_i OC_{i,t} + \sum_i X_{i,t} \right) - \sum_i CD_{i,t} \tag{6.1}$$

where

ΔB_t = change in the allowance bank in year *t*

$OC_{i,t}$ = allowances available from overcompliance, that is, by the reduction of emissions below the lesser of allowances or the counterfactual for the *i*th unit in year *t*

$X_{i,t}$ = allowances distributed in excess of the greater of the counterfactual or actual emissions for the *i*th unit in year *t*

$CD_{i,t}$ = current demand in year *t* for "extra" allowances to cover emissions in excess of the allowance allocation at the *i*th unit

The two terms in parentheses on the right-hand side of Equation (6.1) represent the sources of current allowance supplies, namely, (a) allowances "produced" by overcompliance and (b) "excess"

7. Since allowance allocations are lower in Phase II than in Phase I, diminishing returns implies that the marginal cost of abatement will be higher in Phase II. Therefore, it will always be economical to overcomply by some amount in Phase I, depending on the discount rate and the time between the production of the banked allowance in Phase I and its use in Phase II.

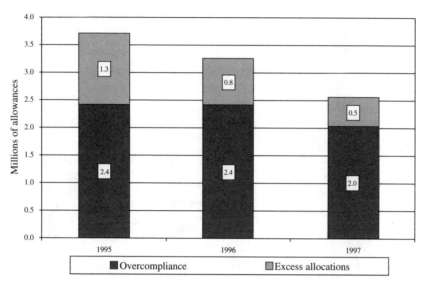

Figure 6.2. Sources of supply for emissions trading, 1995–97.
Sources: Derived from Pechan (1995) and EPA (1996b, 1997, 1998).

allowances available to units without any abatement action. The relative importance of these two sources of supply in the first three years
of Phase I is shown in Figure 6.2. The total supply of allowances available for emissions trading is shown by the height of the columns.
Recall that the total supply of allowances is equal to those allowances
not used to cover emissions at Phase I units in the current year. The
figure indicates that the supply of allowances declined from
3.69 million allowances in 1995 to 2.56 million allowances in 1997.
The top segment of each column represents the number of excess
allowances supplied in each year $[A - \max (CF, E)]$.[8] This amount
dropped significantly, from 1.27 million in 1995 to 0.52 million in 1997.
The remaining source of supply, represented by the bottom segment,
is overcompliance $[\min (CF, A) - E]$, that is, allowances made available by abatement action beyond what would have been required
to reduce emissions to the allowance allocation. Overcompliance

8. Some units with excess allowances increased emissions from the counterfactual and
   thereby consumed some of the potentially available supply of allowances. Although
   these instances technically represent a source of both supply and demand, we ignore
   them, since there are so few.

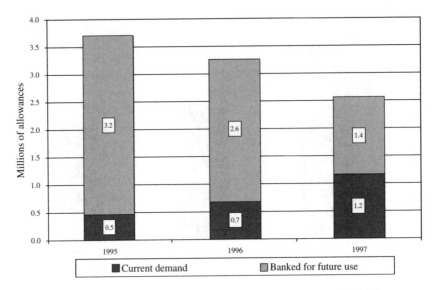

Figure 6.3. Sources of demand for emissions trading, 1995–97.
Sources: Derived from Pechan (1995) and EPA (1996b, 1997, 1998).

was the major source of supply of allowances for emissions trading during the years 1995–97, but it too has declined over time as the reduced allocation of allowances has increased the abatement that would have been required of these units without any emissions trading.

As a matter of accounting, demand must equal supply, and Figure 6.3 indicates the corresponding demand for traded allowances during the first three years of Phase I. The bottom segment of each column shows the demand for allowances to cover emissions in excess of the allowance allocations at various units in the current period. Recall that this quantity is what is represented by the third term on the right-hand side of Equation (6.1). This use of allowances increased significantly, from 0.46 million in 1995 to 1.15 million in 1997. Nevertheless, the main source of demand for allowances in the first three years of Phase I was banking, as represented by the top segment of each column. The number of allowances banked has diminished quite rapidly during Phase I, from 3.23 million allowances in 1995 to 1.41 million allowances in 1997, as a result of both the reduction in the supply of allowances available for emissions trading and the increase in current demand.[9]

The changes observed in these components of allowance supply reflect the same trends that caused Phase I units to move among the various categories in Table 6.1. With abatement action relatively unchanged between 1995 and 1997, the reduction in the aggregate number of allowances issued and the increase in counterfactual emissions reduced the current supply of allowances available for emissions trading, increased current demand for allowances, and reduced the number of allowances banked.

OVERCOMPLIANCE

The principal source of allowances for emissions trading has been abatement action to reduce emissions at constrained units below their allowance allocation (or below the counterfactual at unconstrained units). Sixty-five percent of the 1995 vintage allowances available for trading resulted from 1995 abatement and overcompliance, and the percentage rose to 80% in 1997. Since the allowance supply from overcompliance is determined in part by abatement actions, many of the same observations that apply to emissions reductions also hold true for overcompliance. For instance, as shown in Figure 6.4, the few units with scrubbers account for a significant proportion of overcompliance. These units contribute a greater proportion of overcompliance than they do of abatement because scrubbers make deeper cuts in emissions than is typically the case for switching to low-sulfur coals.

As was also the case with emission reductions, the suppliers of allowances resulting from overcompliance are highly concentrated. Table 6.2 shows the sources of overcompliance for the entire three-year period, by abatement technique, and for the ten utilities that overcomplied most. Five utilities account for 60% of all allowances produced by overcompliance. With the notable exception of the Southern Company, scrubbing was the principal source of

---

9. These numbers do not include allowances sold at public auction each year, nor do they include the contributions from substitution units that entered and exited in different years. The slightly higher numbers for allowances banked when all Phase I units are considered are shown in Table 5.2.

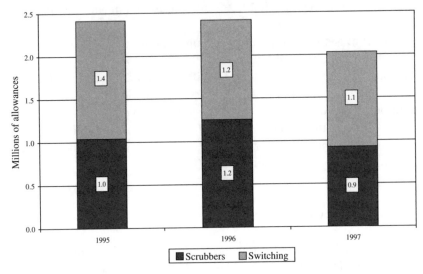

Figure 6.4. Sources of overcompliance, 1995–97.

Sources: Derived from Pechan (1995), EPA (1996b, 1997, 1998), and Appendix to this book.

Table 6.2. *Principal sources of overcompliance, 1995–97*

	Total over-compliance	From scrubbers	Other abatement	% by scrubbers
All utilities	6,858	3,727	3,131	54%
Ten largest utilities	5,275	3,144	2,131	60%
All others (39 utilities)	1,583	583	1,000	37%
Ten largest utilities				
American Electric Power	1,112	864	248	78%
Tennessee Valley Authority	957	846	111	88%
Southern Company	948	15	933	2%
Allegheny Power	694	687	7	99%
General Public Utilities	441	441	0	100%
Cinergy	235	114	121	49%
Union Electric	232	0	232	0%
Ohio Edison	230	14	216	6%
No. Indiana Public Service	227	163	64	72%
Associated Electric Coop	199	0	199	0%

Sources: Derived from Pechan (1995) and EPA (1996b, 1997, 1998).

overcompliance among the top five, ranging from 78% for American Electric Power (AEP) to 100% for General Public Utilities Company (GPU). The Southern Company relied almost entirely on switching to lower-sulfur coals, although it did retrofit a scrubber on one small unit; it alone accounts for 30% of the allowances produced by over-compliance by fuel switching. Significant overcompliance by fuel switching can also be observed among the big midwestern utilities, AEP and Ohio Edison, at units located mostly in Ohio. Finally, switching to PRB coals produced almost as much overcompliance as did scrubbing, and those utilities able to switch to PRB coals, such as Union Electric and Associated Electric Cooperative, both in Missouri, emerged among the top ten suppliers of allowances through overcompliance.

EXCESS ALLOWANCES

In theory, every Phase I unit is constrained by its allowance alloca-tion, so that there are no unit-specific excess allowances. In practice, there are many exceptions. When the basis of the allocation is his-toric emissions, as is the case for Title IV, an initially constraining allowance allocation may become nonbinding for some units as uti-lization or emission rates change subsequent to the historic baseline – that is, as a result of a changing counterfactual. In addition, affected units may receive additional allowances as an incentive or special consideration, such as the Phase I extension allowances and early reduction credits in Title IV. These "special allowances" can convert what would have been a constraining allocation into a nonbinding one.

From the perspective of emissions trading, the reason for excess allowances, whether a changing counterfactual or special allowances, is unimportant; they are just one more source of allowance supply, distinguished only by the circumstance that no abatement cost is required to produce it. Yet, because excess allowances require no abatement expenditure, they tend to be controversial, and because special allowances are sometimes perceived as a gift or payoff of some sort, the two tend to be equated. In fact, excess allowances and special allowances are quite distinct. Special allowances do not necessarily become excess allowances, and they are no less valuable when the effect is only to require the recipient to buy fewer allowances externally to cover emissions. Moreover, because change is not uniformly beneficial to all parties, changing counterfactuals create excess allowances for some units at the same time that compliance is made more costly for other units. In the case of Title IV, changing counterfactual emissions has been a far more important source of excess allowances than has been the creation of special allowances.

The relative contributions of these two sources of excess allowances can be determined from a comparison of the actual allowance allocation to the "Basic Rule" allocation described in Chapter 3. For Table A units, the basic rule is 2.5 lb/mmBtu times baseline (average 1985–87) heat input. For voluntary Phase I units, the basic rule is whatever emissions would be if the units did not volunteer, but in actual implementation, the rules are more complicated: baseline heat input times the least of three alternative emission rates.[10] Special allowances are defined as the difference between the actual allocation and the Basic Rule allocation. The number of such allowances was quite large in 1995 and 1996, 1.87 million and 1.55 million, respectively, as compared with 1997, 0.38 million. As will now be shown, most special allowances did not become excess allowances; they simply reduced the implied abatement requirement at constrained units.

Figure 6.5 shows the total amount of excess allowances supplied for emissions trading and the relative importance of special allowances and changing counterfactuals as sources of allowance supply in the first three years of Phase I. The height of each column represents the number of allowances issued in excess of counterfactual emissions in each year. The top segment indicates the number of special allowances

10. Allowances are issued to substitution units according to complicated and heavily litigated rules whereby average 1985–87 heat input for a unit is multiplied by the least of
three emission rates for the unit. These three rates are (a) the lower of the actual or
allowable 1985 SO_2 emissions rate, (b) the greater of the 1989 or 1990 actual emission
rate, or (c) the most stringent federal- or state-allowable SO_2 emissions rate applicable in 1995–99, as of November 15, 1990. Originally, substitution units were to receive
allowances based only on the 1985 emissions rate; however, environmental groups
brought suit against EPA to prevent issuance of "excess" allowances. This litigation led
to the addition of the references to 1989–90 emission rates and other pre-Title IV limitations on 1995–99 emission rates. The resulting redefinition of the baseline emissions
rate effectively prevented issuance of allowances for reductions in the emissions rate
achieved between 1985 and 1989–90, as well as for any 1995–99 reductions otherwise
required.

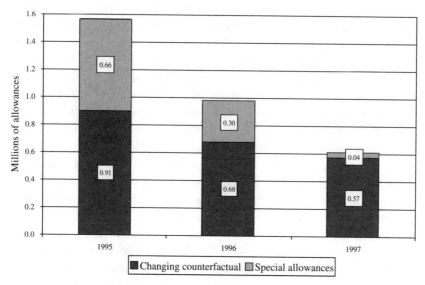

Figure 6.5. Sources of excess allowances, 1995–97.
Sources: Derived from Pechan (1995) and EPA (1996b, 1997, 1998).

that were also excess allowances, while the remainder, the bottom segment, shows the number of excess allowances resulting from changes in the counterfactual.[11] Special allowance allocations have never been the principal source of excess allowances, and their importance has diminished greatly from 1995 to 1997. In 1997, fewer than 10% of all excess allowances can be traced to departures from the basic allocation rules. In contrast, the changing counterfactual has always been the principal source of excess emissions, and by 1997 it had become virtually the only source.

Excess allowances are the inevitable and largely unpredictable result of changing fuel and operational characteristics at affected units. A typical example is a Phase I unit burning a 4.0 lb/mmBtu midwestern coal in 1985 – which was therefore included in Phase I

11. The total number of excess allowances in Figure 6.5 is slightly larger than the supply attributed to excess allowances in Figure 6.2 because about 10% of the allowances issued in excess of the counterfactuals were used by units that had increased their emission rates over the counterfactual (1993) rate. These allowances were "excess," as here defined, and an opportunity cost was incurred by each unit increasing its emission rate, but the allowances were not available for use at other units during the year they were issued or later.

and allocated allowances based on the 2.5 lb/mmBtu rate – that switched to a 1.2 lb/mmBtu PRB coal for reasons other than Title IV. Another frequent example is a Phase I unit that, for one reason or another, is being utilized much less intensively than it was during the baseline period. Since electricity demand has been growing in most generating systems, most of these instances reflect shifts in the generation of electricity supplied by these generating systems to other units, such as nuclear facilities and Phase II units. The number of retired units has not been particularly large: 33 of 423 Phase I units in 1997, which account for 84,000 allowances, or 1.2% of all allowances and 14% of excess allowances in that year.

The total number of excess allowances has diminished over time, as also shown on Figure 6.5. Most of the decline is due to the phasing out of the two largest Phase I sources of special allowances, the Phase I extension allowances and early reduction credits; however, continuing load growth also contributes to this trend. As the increase in aggregate electricity demand has placed greater demand on all units, what had earlier been excess allowances are progressively eliminated.

CURRENT DEMAND FOR ALLOWANCES

A cap-and-trade system makes it possible for a Phase I unit to emit more SO_2 than the allowances allocated to it. However, to do so, it must acquire additional allowances initially allocated to other generating units. It may do so by making transfers among Phase I units operated by the same utility ("internal," or "intrautility," trading), by making purchases of allowances from other utilities ("external," or "interutility," trading), or by using banked allowances from earlier years.

The share of Phase I units acquiring extra allowances increased from about 20% of the total in 1995 to about 30% in 1997, whether the proportion is measured in terms of the number of units, their generating capacity, or their heat input, as given in Table 6.3. Not only did the number of units requiring extra allowances increase, but so too did the proportion of their emissions covered by acquired allowances. This trend is shown in Figure 6.6, where the aggregate counterfactual emissions for all units requiring additional allowances

Table 6.3. *Units acquiring additional allowances, 1995–97*

	1995	1996	1997
Number of units	79	105	129
Capacity (GW^e)	23.50	27.58	35.34
Heat input (10^{12} Btu)	1,265	1,507	1,920
Counterfactual emissions	2,339	2,868	3,468
Actual emissions	2,026	2,515	3,112
Allowance allocation	1,562	1,831	1,961
Reduction	314	353	356
Acquired allowances	463	684	1,150

Sources: Derived from Pechan (1995) and EPA (1996b, 1997, 1998).

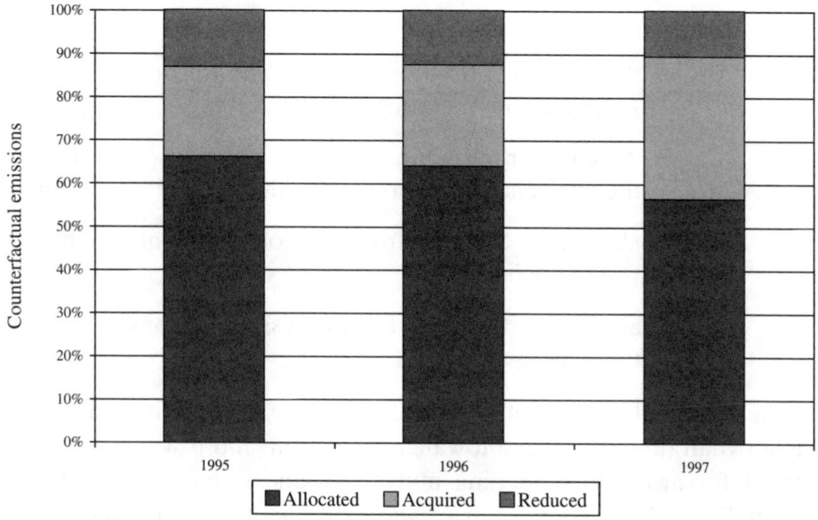

Figure 6.6. Emissions at units acquiring extra allowances, 1995–97.
Sources: Derived from Pechan (1995) and EPA (1996b, 1997, 1998).

are divided into shares of emissions covered by allocated allowances, emissions covered by acquired allowances, and emission reductions at those units. For those units acquiring allowances, the fraction of counterfactual emissions covered by the statutory allocation declined from 66% in 1995 to 57% in 1997. At the same time, the proportion of their emissions accounted for by acquired allowances increased from 21% to 33% of counterfactual emissions.

Although current demand for extra allowances is significant and increasing in the aggregate, its incidence among utilities with Phase I affected units has been far from uniform. A few utilities have relied almost entirely upon acquired allowances to allow them to sustain emissions at levels greater than their allowance allocations, while other utilities have had no demand for extra allowances in the current period. The extent to which utilities depend upon emissions trading to cover emissions in the current period can be indicated by the following internal trading ratio.

$$TR = \frac{\sum_i D_i}{\sum_i OC_i + \sum_i X_i} \qquad (6.2)$$

where

> TR = the ratio of current internal demand to current internal supply for an operating utility
>
> D_i = demand for allowances to cover emissions greater than the allowance allocation at the ith unit, where applicable
>
> OC_i = allowances available from overcompliance at the ith unit where applicable
>
> X_i = allowances available from excess allocations at the ith unit where applicable

The ratio will be 0 for utilities with no Phase I units with emissions higher than the unit-level allowance allocation, and it will be greater than 1 for any utility needing more allowances than are available internally in the current year. At the extreme, if there is no current internal supply, the ratio is undefined.[12] Any ratio less than 1 indicates that the utility is banking allowances for use in future periods.

Table 6.4 divides the forty-nine holding companies and operating utilities with Phase I units, as of the end of 1997, into three groups according to their current demand for allowances during 1995–97.[13]

---

12. This possibility occurs only in a few instances of utilities having one or two affected units. For instance, Duquesne Lighting has a single Phase I unit, for which it acquired additional allowances externally for all three years.
13. As the result of recently consummated mergers, several of these utilities are now single companies. In the last quarter of 1997, Union Electric and Central Illinois Public Service became Ameren, and Ohio Edison and Centerior became First Energy.

Table 6.4. *Phase I affected utilities ranked by 1997 internal trading ratio*

	Units	MW^e	Internal trading ratio				Current demand (allowances)			
			1995 (%)	1996 (%)	1997 (%)	1995–97 (%)	1995	1996	1997	1995–97
Utilities with high current demand										
Duquesne Lighting	1	565	NA	NA	NA	NA	4,720	1,841	9,371	15,932
Baltimore Gas & Electric	2	400	0.0	NA	NA	193.3	0	7,265	10,745	18,010
Illinois Power	15	2,724	648.1	678.8	913.8	734.5	131,992	152,107	153,340	437,439
Northeastern Utilities	3	595	192.6	97.2	860.2	239.5	4,785	3,300	8,310	16,395
Central Illinois Public Service	15	3,354	29.4	170.9	555.9	126.3	10,810	25,875	37,308	73,992
Tampa Electric	4	1,823	136.5	170.5	231.9	178.7	17,372	22,769	28,142	68,283
American Electric Power	35	12,720	16.5	40.0	126.1	49.7	90,027	171,001	366,739	627,768
Cinergy	22	7,489	27.4	48.0	116.1	55.0	34,499	41,803	77,482	153,783
Centerior	25	4,123	54.2	122.9	115.5	96.5	29,964	57,267	67,274	154,505
Mid-American Energy	2	283	60.3	75.7	109.6	78.5	1,241	1,211	1,469	3,921
Tennessee Valley Authority	26	9,006	15.5	18.0	74.2	32.2	59,462	70,718	210,318	340,498
So. Mississippi Elec Pwr Assn	2	400	0.0	22.0	67.1	15.4	0	276	501	777
So. Indiana Gas & Electric	3	692	39.0	140.8	56.7	77.4	8,105	26,052	10,287	44,444
Atlantic City Electric	2	299	25.3	25.3	50.9	32.9	3,736	4,203	6,663	14,602
Niagara Mohawk Power	5	2,112	45.6	35.9	50.2	43.9	8,663	5,909	8,114	22,686
15 Utilities	162	46,585	32.4	55.7	126.9	64.4	405,376	591,597	996,062	1,993,035
Utilities with modest current demand										
Big Rivers Electric	7	1,413	5.9	8.8	39.0	18.4	1,808	3,839	15,151	20,798
Potomac Electric Power	6	3,298	0.0	0.0	33.2	6.0	0	0	5,318	5,318
Northern States Power	6	1,697	0.0	0.0	31.7	1.9	0	0	712	712
Virginia Electric & Power	3	1,662	8.8	28.0	29.5	21.9	4,485	12,527	15,502	32,514
Pennsylvania Power & Light	7	2,131	3.2	7.1	21.2	7.7	1,250	2,098	2,990	6,338
Utilicorp United	3	524	0.0	0.0	20.3	2.5	0	0	367	367
Allegheny Power	19	6,218	4.3	0.2	18.9	6.4	13,422	630	37,157	51,209
General Public Utilities	8	2,924	11.3	5.4	17.8	11.4	12,477	9,656	29,553	51,686
Ohio Edison	25	4,859	0.3	13.1	17.3	9.6	412	16,648	18,466	35,526
Kentucky Utilities	5	1,410	0.0	0.0	14.6	2.4	0	0	4,795	4,795
Union Electric	12	5,652	0.9	34.7	11.9	8.6	3,100	30,225	15,369	48,694
Indianapolis Power & Light	7	1,605	683.2	10.7	11.4	26.8	12,646	2,987	5,649	21,282
New York State Elec & Gas	3	435	18.3	0.0	4.5	6.6	2,482	0	784	3,266
Hoosier Energy R.E.C.	2	233	NA	0.0	0.0	31.9	2,215	0	0	2,215
Springfield, City of (MO)	4	403	0.0	89.1	0.0	16.7	0	3,791	0	3,791
15 Utilities	117	34,464	4.5	8.3	18.3	9.5	54,296	82,401	151,813	288,510
Utilities with negligible current demand										
Kansas City Power & Light	5	1,971	0.0	0.0	7.4	1.7	0	0	2,370	2,370
Dairyland Power Coop	4	869	0.0	0.0	1.3	0.3	0	0	147	147
Wisconsin Electric Power	8	1,692	0.0	0.0	0.3	0.1	0	0	87	87
Southern Company	47	13,774	0.6	1.9	0.0	0.9	3,448	10,042	1	13,491
Other Iowa Utilities	4	693	0.0	0.0	0.0	0.0	0	0	0	0
No. Indiana Public Service	3	1,156	0.0	0.0	0.0	0.0	0	0	0	0
Owensboro, City of (KY)	2	416	0.0	0.0	0.0	0.0	0	0	0	0
Long Island Lighting	6	1,923	0.0	0.0	0.0	0.0	0	0	0	0
Associated Electric Coop	5	2,335	0.0	0.0	0.0	0.0	0	0	0	0
Dayton Power & Light	4	2,441	0.0	0.0	0.0	0.0	0	0	0	0
Commonwealth Edison	5	2,928	0.0	0.0	0.0	0.0	0	0	0	0
Electric Energy	6	1,100	0.0	0.0	0.0	0.0	0	0	0	0
Wisconsin Power & Light	6	784	0.0	0.0	0.0	0.0	0	0	0	0
Central Hudson Gas & Electric	2	1,242	0.0	0.0	0.0	0.0	0	0	0	0
Consumers Power	4	1,040	0.0	0.0	0.0	0.0	0	0	0	0
Wisconsin Public Service	6	469	0.0	0.0	0.0	0.0	0	0	0	0
East Kentucky Power Coop	3	626	0.0	0.0	0.0	0.0	0	0	0	0
Empire District Electric	1	213	0.0	0.0	0.0	0.0	0	0	0	0
Kansas City, City of (KS)	1	158	0.0	0.0	0.0	0.0	0	0	0	0
19 Utilities	122	35,829	0.3	0.8	0.3	0.5	3,448	10,042	2,605	16,095
High current demand (> 50%)	162	46,585	32.4	55.7	126.9	64.4	405,376	591,597	996,062	1,993,035
Modest current demand (10% to 50%)	117	34,464	4.5	8.3	18.3	9.5	54,296	82,401	151,813	288,510
Negligible current demand	122	35,829	0.3	0.8	0.3	0.5	3,448	10,042	2,605	16,095
Total	401	116,878	12.6	21.0	45.0	24.2	463,120	684,040	1,150,480	2,297,641

Sources: Derived from Pechan (1995) and EPA (1996b, 1997, 1998).

The list is ranked by the ratio of current demand to internal supply in 1997. The first group in Table 6.4 consists of utilities exhibiting relatively high current demand for allowances, those with an internal trading ratio greater than 50%. In 1997, these fifteen utilities accounted for 87% of the current demand for allowances by all utilities with Phase I units. Ten of the fifteen had trading ratios higher than 100%, indicating that they were either purchasing allowances externally or drawing down allowances banked in 1995 or 1996. Six of these utilities – Duquesne Lighting, Baltimore Gas and Electric, Illinois Power, Northeastern Utilities, Central Illinois Public Service, and Tampa Electric – have been external acquirers of allowances over the three years as a whole, but not necessarily in each of those years. The other four with internal trading ratios over 100% in 1977 – AEP, Cinergy, Centerior, and Mid-American Energy – are net bankers over the three years, but they ceased accumulating allowances by internal abatement actions and were drawing down their allowance banks in 1997. The other five utilities in this group were net bankers in 1997, but by less than half of what was available internally from overcompliance or excess allocations. A typical example is the Tennessee Valley Authority, for which three-quarters of the allowances produced by the two scrubbed units at the Cumberland plant supplied extra allowances for between thirteen and sixteen other affected units, depending on the year.

The middle group in Table 6.4, another fifteen utilities characterized as having modest demand, are those that used less than half of the allowances supplied internally to meet current demand but at least 10% in at least one year. Eight of these utilities became more significant users of extra allowances in 1997, four for the first time that year. Two of these utilities – Indianapolis Power and Light and Hoosier Energy Rural Electric Cooperative – acquired allowances from external sources in 1995, but became significant bankers thereafter.[14] In this group, as well as in the first group, there is a distinct tendency for utilities with retrofitted scrubbers to use the allowances freed up by overcompliance at these units to cover emissions at

14. In the case of Indianapolis P&L, two scrubbers were installed at the Petersburg units in 1996, but they were not in place in 1995. Also, Indianapolis P&L was one of the four utilities installing scrubbers that did not receive Phase I extension allowances. Hoosier Energy REC required additional allowances in 1995, despite a reduction in emission rates, because of an unexpectedly large demand for generation from the Phase I units.

nonscrubbed units owned by the same utility. Of the sixteen utilities with retrofitted scrubbers, fourteen relied upon scrubbers to produce most and often all the emission reductions made by these utilities.[15] Only two, Northern Indiana Public Service (NIPSCO) and the City of Owensboro (Kentucky), did not use allowances produced by the scrubbers at other units. For Owensboro, there were no other Phase I units, and the third Phase I unit at NIPSCO switched to PRB coal and has had emissions well below the allowance allocation.

The last group in Table 6.4 includes nineteen utilities with negligible or no current demand for allowances. A prominent feature of this group is that most of the utilities are located either in states that had enacted local acid rain laws (e.g., Wisconsin, New York) or in areas that have been most affected by PRB coal displacements (e.g., Iowa, Missouri, Kansas, Illinois). The counterfactual was lower than the unit allowance allocations for two-thirds of the units in this group, and nine of the utilities had no units at all where extra allowances might have been used. Thus, many of the utilities in this group had no need for extra allowances. Neither of these explanations – state laws or low counterfactuals – apply to seven utilities in this group, which might be expected to have at least some units for which it would be cheaper to use allowances than to reduce emissions. It is possible that these utilities ignored the cost-savings opportunities offered by internal trading from 1995 to 1997; however, an equally plausible explanation is that all of the affected units at these utilities are sources of cheap abatement.

The Southern Company is a particularly prominent member of this third group. Of the 1.5 million allowances available to this utility through overcompliance and excess allowances, less than 1% were used internally. In large part, the slight internal demand reflects the circumstance that three-quarters of Southern's nearly fifty Phase I units were unconstrained by the Phase I allowance allocation. Nevertheless, in addition to receiving about 500,000 excess allowances over the 1995–97 period, this utility also supplied another 1.0 million allowances by overcompliance. As a result, on only five occasions were allowances used to cover emissions above the allowance allocation.

---

15. The two exceptions were the Southern Company and Ohio Edison, both of which installed scrubbers at relatively small units and undertook extensive abatement at non-scrubbed units.

Table 6.5. *Current external demand for allowances, 1995–97*

Utility name	Allowances			
	1995	1996	1997	1995–97
Illinois Power	111,627	129,698	136,560	377,885
Tampa Electric	4,647	9,414	16,009	30,070
Duquesne Lighting	4,720	1,841	9,371	15,932
Central Illinois Public Service		10,734	30,596	41,330
Baltimore Gas & Electric		7,265	10,745	18,010
Northeastern Utilities	2,300		7,344	9,644
Centerior		10,672	9,020	19,692
Indianapolis Power & Light	10,795			10,795
Hoosier Energy R.E.C.	2,215			2,215
So. Indiana Gas & Electric		7,546		7,546
American Electric Power			75,922	75,922
Cinergy			10,727	10,727
Mid-American Energy			129	129
Total external demand	136,304	177,170	306,423	619,897
Total current demand for allowances	463,120	684,040	1,150,480	2,297,641
% Acquired externally	29	26	27	27

Sources: Derived from Pechan (1995) and EPA (1996b, 1997, 1998).

In discussing emissions trading under Title IV, a distinction has often been made between internal and external trading. Prior to implementation, it was generally expected that utilities would trade internally but that there would be little external trading with consequent loss of some of the cost savings available from emissions trading. The number of allowances acquired externally for compliance with Title IV is given in Table 6.5, by utility and year. In all, thirteen utilities required allowances in at least one year beyond what was available internally in the current year. The aggregate number of allowances so acquired increased steadily from 136,000 in 1995 to 306,000 in 1997; however, as a percentage of the current demand for allowances, the share of external acquisitions remained relatively constant, between 25% and 30%.

Illinois Power is the only example of a large utility that relied almost entirely on external acquisitions of allowances as a means of complying with Title IV requirements. Over the first three years of

Phase I, Illinois Power surrendered 378,000 allowances more than had been issued to its Phase I units, and these allowances constituted 86% of the total current demand for allowances by this utility. Illinois Power alone accounts for 61% of all the allowances acquired externally by the thirteen utilities that acquired allowances externally during these first three years of Phase I.

Among the other twelve utilities, there was great variation in circumstance and resort to external sources. Tampa Electric and Duquesne Lighting were, like Illinois Power, net acquirers of allowances from external sources in all three years. Central Illinois Public Service, Baltimore Gas & Electric, and Northeastern Utilities were net external acquirers over the three years as a whole, although each banked allowances in at least one of the three years. The remaining seven utilities were positive bankers over the three years as a whole, but drew down the accumulated bank or acquired externally in at least one year.

In summary, the predominant model is that of internal trading in which overcompliance or excess allowance allocations at some units provide allowances to cover emissions at other units, all within the same year. Well over half the utilities with Phase I units have used a generally diminishing internal supply of allowances to meet generally rising current demand to cover emissions. About 75% of the current demand for allowances has been met by internal supply, and the balance has been obtained externally from other utilities or by drawing down the utility's bank.

BANKING OF ALLOWANCES

Although the current demand for allowances has increased steadily, banking of allowances remains the predominant form of emissions trading in Phase I. As shown by Figure 6.3, nearly three-quarters of the 9.5 million allowances freed up for emissions trading in the first three years of Phase I were banked for later use in Phase II. Since utilities are the agents making decisions about allowance use, banking is best understood by aggregating data to the operating-utility or holding-company level.

Following the accounting structure presented in Equation (6.1), banking can be seen as the net result of the abatement actions and

Table 6.6. *Sources and uses of retained allowances, 1995–97*

Thousands of allowances/tons	1995	1996	1997	1995–97
Total retained at unit level	3,689 / 100%	3,256 / 100%	2,555 / 100%	9,500 / 100%
Sources				
Overcompliance	2,415 / 67%	2,410 / 74%	2,032 / 80%	6,858 / 72%
Excess allocations	1,214 / 33%	845 / 26%	523 / 20%	2,642 / 28%
Users				
Current demand at other units	463 / 13%	684 / 21%	1,150 / 45%	2,298 / 24%
Banking	3,226 / 87%	2,571 / 79%	1,405 / 55%	7,202 / 76%

Sources: Derived from Pechan (1995) and EPA (1996b, 1997, 1998).

allowance allocations that mostly determine overcompliance, current demand, and excess allocations. The number of allowances falling into each category during 1995–97 and the resulting amount of banking are given in Table 6.6 in aggregate, and in Table 6.7 individually for the forty-nine operating utilities and holding companies with Phase I units, ranked in order of cumulative banking. In this table, the totals are summed across all of the 401 continuously affected Phase I units. Internal supply is the sum of the first two columns, and banking equals internal supply minus current demand. The amounts shown as "banked" do not necessarily represent allowances held by these utilities in their accounts at the end of 1997, but the net supply of or demand for allowances by these agents as a result of abatement actions and allowance allocations in 1995–97. The allowance stocks actually held by these entities may vary considerably from the numbers shown here as a result of purchases or sales in the external allowance market.

Each utility's sources and uses of allowances varied considerably. All utilities but one, Duquesne Lighting, had some sources of internal supply. Nearly all produced some allowances by overcompliance, and most utilities, but far from all, received excess allowances. Twenty-eight utilities used allowances available from overcompliance and excess allocations both to meet current demand and for banking. Fifteen utilities had no current demand for extra allowances and were therefore bankers only. As noted above, only six utilities required allowances from other utilities to cover their emissions during these first three years and therefore did not accumulate any allowances for sale or later use. Among individual companies, the Southern

Table 6.7. *Sources and uses of allowances by utility, 1995–97*

Utility name	Over-compliance	Excess allocations	Internal supply	Current demand	Banking
Southern Company	947,804	524,671	1,472,475	13,491	1,458,984
Allegheny Power	693,569	107,578	801,147	51,209	749,938
Tennessee Valley Authority	956,805	101,156	1,057,961	340,498	717,463
American Electric Power	1,111,930	151,218	1,263,148	627,768	635,380
Union Electric	231,941	332,612	564,553	48,694	515,859
General Public Utilities	441,039	13,604	454,643	51,686	402,957
Ohio Edison	230,245	141,376	371,622	35,526	336,096
No. Indiana Public Service	227,332	16,618	243,950	0	243,950
Long Island Lighting	30,129	202,427	232,556	0	232,556
Associated Electric Coop	198,995	0	198,995	0	198,995
Kentucky Utilities	170,059	26,989	197,048	4,795	192,253
Dayton Power & Light	89,028	78,943	167,971	0	167,971
Commonwealth Edison	147,512	5,199	152,711	0	152,711
Kansas City Power & Light	60	140,072	140,132	2,370	137,762
Cinergy	235,358	44,232	279,590	153,783	125,806
Electric Energy	124,206	0	124,206	0	124,206
Wisconsin Electric Power	0	118,988	118,988	87	118,901
Virginia Electric Power	138,128	10,407	148,535	32,514	116,021
Wisconsin Power & Light	57,629	44,227	101,856	0	101,856
Big Rivers Electric Corp	105,142	8,172	113,314	20,798	92,516
Central Hudson Gas & Elec	10,592	75,041	85,633	0	85,633
Potomac Electric Power	63,906	25,211	89,117	5,318	83,799
Pennsylvania Power & Light	45,756	36,409	82,165	6,338	75,828
Consumers Power	4,258	69,523	73,781	0	73,781
Indianapolis Power & Light	77,133	2,160	79,293	21,282	58,011
Dairyland Power Coop	14,449	38,335	52,784	147	52,637
Other Iowa Utilities	38,434	12,846	51,281	0	51,281
Wisconsin Public Service Corp	12,343	36,629	48,972	0	48,972
New York State Elec & Gas	49,608	0	49,608	3,266	46,342
City of Owensboro (KY)	39,314	0	39,314	0	39,314
East Kentucky Power Coop	37,897	0	37,897	0	37,897
Northern States Power	417	36,613	37,030	712	36,318
Atlantic City Electric	44,442	0	44,442	14,602	29,840
Niagara Mohawk Power	22,668	28,968	51,636	22,686	28,950
Empire District Electric	0	23,571	23,571	0	23,571
City of Springfield (MO)	13,955	8,771	22,726	3,791	18,935
Utilicorp	8,210	6,221	14,431	367	14,064
So. Indiana Gas & Elec	57,417	0	57,417	44,444	12,973
Centerior	56,514	103,658	160,172	154,505	5,667
Hoosier Energy R.E.C.	6,949	0	6,949	2,215	4,734
So. Mississippi Electric Power	4,976	65	5,041	777	4,264
City of Kansas City (KS)	1,273	2,394	3,667	0	3,667
Mid-American Energy	4,997	0	4,997	3,921	1,076
Baltimore Gas & Electric	9,317	0	9,317	18,010	(8,693)
Northeastern Utilities	6,845	0	6,845	16,395	(9,550)
Central Illinois Public Service	43,558	15,036	58,594	73,992	(15,398)
Duquesne Lighting	0	0	0	15,932	(15,932)
Tampa Electric	38,213	0	38,213	68,283	(30,070)
Illinois Power	7,918	51,636	59,554	437,439	(377,885)
Totals	6,858,270	2,641,577	9,499,846	2,297,641	7,202,206

Sources: Derived from Pechan (1995) and EPA (1996b, 1997, 1998).

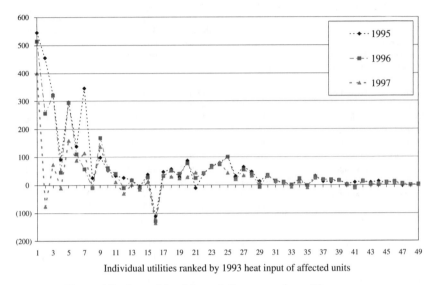

Figure 6.7. Annual banking of allowances, by utility.
Sources: Derived from Pechan (1995) and EPA (1996b, 1997, 1998).

Company was by far the largest contributor to the cumulative bank. American Electric Power (AEP) created the most allowances by overcompliance. However, its contribution to the cumulative bank was less than half that of the Southern Company, because AEP was also the largest user of allowances to cover extra emissions and it received considerably fewer excess allowances.

Most utilities did not greatly change their net banking behavior during the first three years of Phase I, but there have been a few notable changes in net banking posture from 1995 to 1997. These changes can be seen graphically in Figure 6.7, where the 1995, 1996, and 1997 banking positions are shown for the 49 utilities, listed from largest to smallest in order of 1993 heat input at affected units. With a few exceptions, the 1997 line is lower than the 1995 or 1996 lines. The most dramatic change is for American Electric Power, ranked as the second utility from the left-hand-side of the figure, which went from banking 455,000 allowances in 1995 to a draw-down of that bank by 76,000 allowances in 1997. Changes are also particularly apparent for the Tennessee Valley Authority and Union Electric, ranked as the third and seventh utilities, respectively, from the left of Figure 6.7.

Each reduced its number of allowances banked by about 200,000 between 1995 and 1997.

Although there is a tendency for the bigger utilities to be bigger bankers, this is not always so. Neither Cinergy nor Centerior, ranked as the fourth and eighth utilities from the left of Figure 6.7, has been a large banker in any year, and both are now drawing down their allowance banks. Conversely, much smaller entities, such as Kentucky Utilities and Northern Indiana Public Service, ranked twentieth and twenty-fifth by heat input, banked nearly 100,000 allowances each in the earlier years, and made significant contributions to their banks (respectively, they were the seventeenth- and tenth-ranked bankers in 1997). Illinois Power, ranked sixteenth by heat input, was a net buyer of extra allowances from other utilities in all years.

FROM INTERNAL TO EXTERNAL TRADING

As shown by Figure 6.1 at the beginning of this chapter, emissions trading has changed abatement behavior at the unit level. The abatement actions undertaken by the operators of Phase I units have remained relatively constant over the first three years of Phase I, but the use of allowances has changed considerably as various bonus allowance provisions have expired and as load growth has caused counterfactual emissions to increase. On the supply side of the allowances available for trading, excess allowances have virtually disappeared. Therefore, the nearly exclusive source of allowances to meet the demand for use in the current year and for banking is the significant overcompliance at a number of Phase I units. On the demand side, the use of allowances to cover emissions greater than allowance allocations at a number of Phase I units has increased, with a concomitant decrease in the number of allowances available for banking. Finally, with a few notable exceptions, most of the demand for allowances to cover unit-level emissions above Phase I allowance allocations has been met internally.

Although utilities have clearly taken advantage of the flexibility afforded by emissions trading, an observer looking only at allowance allocations and emissions at Phase I units might reasonably conclude that nearly all the trading has been conducted among units owned by the same utility and that little external trading of allowances among utilities has occurred. As will be made clear in the next chapter, this has not been the case. First of all, the external market comprises more than electric utilities operating Phase I units. Utilities with Phase II but no Phase I units can defer high abatement costs at some units by purchasing allowances in Phase I. Similarly, utilities with excess Phase II allowances need not wait until Phase II to turn these into cash. They can sell them in the Phase I market.

Moreover, there is no reason to believe that the only utilities with Phase I units participating in the external market would be those, like Illinois Power, that need allowances to cover emissions greater than the Phase I allowance allocations. The data and analysis presented in this chapter do not address whether allowances not used at a utility's Phase I units have been banked internally or sold into the external market, nor whether those banking might also be buying in the external market. Whether an overcomplying utility would be buying or selling would depend upon the comparison of the market price with the marginal cost of current abatement and the expected, discounted cost of Phase II abatement. Although some utilities with Phase I units may be trading emissions only internally, it would not be surprising that many (and perhaps most) are trading emissions both internally and externally.

The next chapter addresses the development and performance of the external allowance market. The perspectives offered by this chapter and the next one are related, of course. Buyers in the allowance market are a larger group than the small number of utilities needing allowances for Phase I compliance, just as sellers are a larger group than those having more allowances than needed for Phase I or Phase II compliance. As a consequence, the development of an allowance market is not limited by the relatively small external demand for allowances to cover emissions above Phase I allowance allocations at Phase I units.

7 Emissions Trading: Development of the Allowance Market

The argument for the cost-minimizing properties of emissions trading rests, of course, on the assumption that an external market for permits exists and that it is reasonably efficient. By "efficient" we mean that the prices for permits are transparent to buyers and sellers, transaction costs are low, arbitrage opportunities are quickly exploited, and buyers and sellers take full advantage of the opportunities to reduce compliance costs by engaging in trading activity. The limited experience with emissions trading prior to 1990 was not particularly encouraging in this regard (Hahn, 1989; Hahn and Hester, 1989), and there was considerable doubt whether the tradable permit feature of Title IV would meet with any greater success than did earlier programs involving emissions trading.[1]

Unlike previous tradable permit programs, Title IV embraces emissions trading among utilities with remarkably few restrictions. First, allowances can be traded nationally.[2] Second, no review or prior approval of trades is necessary. Third, the purchase and holding of allowances is not restricted to utilities for which these permits would become a necessary input for the coal- or oil-fired generation of electricity. All sources receiving allowance allocations as well as third parties, such as brokerage firms and individuals, are free to buy allowances from or sell them to any other party. Fourth, neither

1. Smaller-scale programs employing tradable permits to phase out leaded gasoline and CFCs have met with somewhat more success (NERA, 1994).
2. As noted in Chapter 5, the concern that regional patterns of emission reductions would result in hot spots has not been realized (EPA, 1996a).

the frequency nor the mechanisms for trading allowances is limited. Finally, allowances that are good for use in one year may be saved and used in future years.

Despite the lack of restrictions governing allowance trades, however, several sources suggested early on that electric utilities would be reluctant to engage in allowance-trading activity for a variety of reasons including regulatory, industry, and market factors.[3] Particularly in the early years of the Acid Rain Program, many market observers considered allowance prices to be too low and quantities of allowance transactions to be too few. The design of the mandatory EPA auction mechanism and state regulatory behavior were two institutional features that received a large amount of critical attention for supposedly inhibiting the development of an efficient allowance market.

In this chapter, we examine the development of the allowance market with a focus on price transparency, price revelation, price dispersion, transaction costs, and allowance-trading activity. In particular, we make three arguments. First, a robust and efficient allowance market has emerged, as evidenced by the convergence of spot, or current, allowance prices quoted by several independent sources, the narrowing of the dispersion of bid prices in the EPA auctions, the flat term structure of allowances prices, and the growth of trading activity.[4] Second, the somewhat unusual auction design adopted by the EPA could not have had any significant long-term adverse effect on the performance of the allowance market as a whole. Rather, to the extent that the auctions brought parties to the market and helped to establish a range of market valuations, the auctions fulfilled their primary objective of stimulating the development of private market trading activity. Third, the available evidence concerning state public

3. See Bohi (1994), Bohi and Burtraw (1992), Burtraw (1996), Cason (1993), Cason and Plott (1996), GAO (1994), and Solomon (1994).
4. It is important to note that there is no specific threshold numerical volume of allowance trading that would be indicative of a well-functioning allowance market. That is to say, a large amount of trading, as measured in terms of volume of allowances traded, number of allowance trades occurring, or simply the number of states with utilities trading allowances, is not in and of itself necessarily an indication of how well the market is functioning. More allowance trading, or less for that matter, relative to what has been observed, without additional information about market behavior and performance, says very little about the success of the allowance-trading program. For example, if by chance permits had been allocated "perfectly" among generating units such that the marginal costs of compliance at all units were equal when emissions were reduced to the number of allowances allocated to each unit, then no trading should be expected. The more allowance allocations depart from such a perfect distribution, the greater the cost savings from trading, and the more allowance trading is desirable.

utility commission rulings does not indicate that state regulatory behavior inhibited the development of allowance-trading activity. In view of this evidence and analysis, we believe that the market for allowances had become reasonably efficient by as early as mid-1994, a full year and a half before utilities had to surrender allowances to EPA to cover their emissions in the first year of the program.

ANNUAL EPA AUCTIONS

Although Title IV encourages the development of a robust private allowance market through relatively nonrestrictive rules on allowance trading, Title IV also mandated a set of small, annual revenue-neutral allowance auctions. These auctions, administered by the EPA, were designed to stimulate the development of a private market by providing early price signals and to provide a source of allowances to new entrants in the event that no allowances were made available through private transactions.[5] The auctions occur only once a year, in late March, and cover only two or three vintages of allowances at a time. Each year, roughly 2.8% of the allowances that have been allocated to utilities are held back and auctioned in annual "spot" and "seven-year advance" auctions.[6] Allowances sold in the seven-year advance

5. The initial version of Title IV as proposed by the Bush Administration did not contain provisions for the mandatory EPA auctions nor for the "Direct Sales Reserve," which was established to provide a source of allowances for independent power producers. These provisions were added to the bill as it worked its way through Congress in response to fears that market imperfections, such as irrational hoarding by utilities or antimarket behavior by state public utility regulators, might make it impossible for new entrants to acquire the allowances necessary to construct and operate new generating capacity. It was the intention of the Bush Administration, the proponents of the legislation in Congress, and the EPA in drafting the regulations implementing the CAAA that private trading arrangements, not the EPA auctions, would be the primary mechanisms through which allowances would be traded.
6. In the 1993, 1994, and 1995 spot auctions, 50,000 vintage 1995 allowances were offered for sale. In 1996, 150,000 vintage 1996 allowances were sold. In 1997, 1998, and 1999, 150,000 spot allowances will be sold. In the year 2000 and later years, 100,000 spot allowances will be sold. From 1993 through 1996, 100,000 allowances were offered for sale in the seven-year advance auction. Allowances sold in the advance auction are first usable seven years after the auction. In addition, because of the Direct Sales Reserve provision of the law, 25,000 vintage 2000 allowances were auctioned in a "six-year advance" auction in 1994, 25,000 vintage 2001 allowances were auctioned in 1995, and 25,000 vintage 2002 allowances were auctioned in 1996. Because EPA closed down the Direct Sales Reserve beginning with the 1997 auctions, the 25,000 allowances involved will be included in the seven-year advance auction, which accordingly involves 125,000 allowances per year from 1997 onward.

auction are first usable seven years after the auction. For example, in the 1993 seven-year advance auction, vintage 2000 allowances were sold; in the 1994 seven-year advance auction, vintage 2001 allowances were sold, and so on. The revenues from all these auctions are returned to utilities in proportion to their share of the allowances that were held back for the auctions. Private parties may voluntarily offer allowances for sale in any of the annual EPA auctions. Each voluntary offer to sell allowances in the EPA auctions involves both a quantity and a minimum acceptable (i.e., reservation) price.

The EPA has interpreted the statutory language[7] of Title IV as requiring it to implement a "discriminatory" auction, in which the winning bidders must pay the price they bid rather than a uniform market-clearing price.[8] Allowances that private parties submit voluntarily for sale in the EPA auction are put up for sale after the supply of withheld allowances has been fully allocated. The seller with the lowest reservation price is matched with the highest remaining bid, the seller with the second lowest reservation price is matched with the second highest remaining bid, etc., until there are no more bids that exceed the reservation prices submitted by sellers.[9] When private allowances are sold according to a discriminatory auction mechanism, the buyer pays and seller receives the bid price, not the clearing price.

The discriminatory auction mechanism implemented by the EPA's regulations has received much critical attention in the trade press as well as in the academic literature. Critics of the EPA auction mechanism argue that, in the absence of an effective private market, the discriminatory price feature of the annual EPA auction generates a lower market-clearing price than would a standard uniform-price auction (Cason, 1993, 1995; Cason and Plott, 1996). This downward bias occurs because voluntary sellers in the EPA auctions have incen-

7. "The auctioned allowances shall be allocated and sold on the basis of bid price, starting with the highest-priced bid and continuing until all allowances for sale at auction have been allocated" (Section 416(d)(2) of Title IV of the 1990 CAAA).

8. The EPA has solicited comments on whether it has the statutory authority to switch to single-price auctions and whether such a switch would be desirable (*Federal Register*, June 6, 1996, vol. 61, no. 110, pp. 28, 996–97). Despite the generally negative evaluation of EPA's discriminatory auctions in the economics literature, all comments received were in favor of retaining the existing structure. As a result, EPA has decided not to switch to a single-price auction. (Personal communication, Acid Rain Division, U.S. Environmental Protection Agency, December 1996.)

9. Note that the allowances withheld by EPA are effectively sold at a reservation price of zero.

tives to set reservation prices too low. The central argument for the downward bias is that, in the EPA auction, lowering one's reservation price both increases the likelihood of a sale and, conditional on a sale occurring, increases the expected price received (as long as buyers' bids are not all identical). Thus, all else being equal, lower reservation prices will be set by rational sellers in the EPA auctions than in a single-price auction.[10]

It is crucial to the downward-bias argument that trade *only* occur at auction. If other venues for allowance trading interact with the EPA auctions, then these additional trading opportunities place opportunity-cost bounds on the allowance values for EPA-auction participants. In the extreme case in which the outside market is perfectly competitive and a universally known market price of allowances exists for which no buyer will pay more and no seller will accept less, the opportunity-cost bounds transform the EPA auction into a common-value auction. Only if the nonauction part of the market is seriously imperfect – or, in the limiting case, nonexistent – can auction prices depart substantially from competitive market prices. As will be discussed shortly, the outside market for allowances that has developed is best characterized as a competitive one with a uniform transparent price. Moreover, there is no evidence that the discriminatory price auction mechanism has inhibited the development of an active and efficient private allowance market with transparent prices and low transaction costs.

It has also been suggested that if the EPA had used a single-price auction, many more allowance transactions would have taken place in the auction rather than having been "pushed" into the "inefficient" bilateral private market. This is highly unlikely, because the EPA auctions provide a very restricted subset of the contractual arrangements and "products" that buyers and sellers regularly use in the private market. For instance, utilities with excess vintage 1995 allowances typically also have excess allowances of several adjacent vintages. Similarly, utilities seeking allowances to support investments in long-term compliance strategies frequently seek streams of allowances involving many consecutive vintages. Streams of allowances can easily be bought and sold in the private market, but it is impossible

---

10. It may even be optimal for sellers to set a reservation price below the marginal cost of emission reduction, even though this creates a positive probability of an unprofitable trade.

to do this in the EPA auctions. In addition, utilities seeking allowances to respond to short-term changes in emissions value the flexibility to buy or sell allowances at any time, rather than being restricted to a single trading day per year. The March auction date is particularly inconvenient given that utilities must settle their accounts by January 31 for the previous year. Thus, even if the EPA auctions were perfectly efficient, they would not supply important product and trading options available in the private market.

EMERGENCE OF THE PRIVATE ALLOWANCE MARKET

This section uses the evolution of market prices and quantities, bidding behavior in the EPA auctions over time, and relationships between spot and futures prices for allowances to understand the development of the allowance market as a whole.

Prices and Quantities

At the time Title IV was passed and subsequently, a number of projections of future allowance prices were made available to the EPA and published in the trade press. Early predictions placed allowance prices during Phase I in the $290–410 range, and prices for allowances during Phase II in the $580–815 range, all in 1995 dollars.[11] Later predictions, for instance by EPRI (1993), were a little lower: $205 to $350 for a 1995 Phase I price.[12] Prices turned out to be even lower during the first three years of Phase I, and only in 1998 did allowance prices

---

11. See, for instance, ICF (1990) and Braine (1991). The original estimates, in 1990 dollars, ranged from $250–350 for Phase I and $500–700 for Phase II. We have used the Consumer Price Index to inflate these to the numbers given in the text. (All other numbers in this paragraph are in current [i.e., nominal] dollars.) The large difference in price projections for Phase I and Phase II does not make a lot of economic sense, since Phase I allowances can be banked for use in Phase II. However, the models used to make these projections did not take intertemporal arbitrage opportunities into account.
12. The prices given in EPRI (1993) were $190, $250, and $320 for "estimated floor," "expected price," and "estimated ceiling," respectively, stated in 1992 dollars. This study also predicted Phase II prices assuming intertemporal arbitrage at a real discount rate of 6%. The predicted expected prices for the years 2000, 2003, and 2007 were $340, $400, and $480, all in 1992 dollars. The predicted ceiling and floor prices for 2007, after exhaustion of the bank, were $650 and $200; however, the latter reflected a scenario in which coal-fired power plants were being replaced by natural gas.

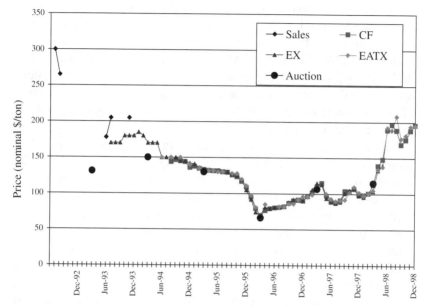

Figure 7.1. Allowance prices, 1992–98 (1995 or current vintage).

Sources: *Allowance Price Indications*, Cantor Fitzgerald Environmental Brokerage (1993–97*); *Compliance Strategy Review*, Fieldston
Publications (1992–97*); *Exchange Value*, Emission Exchange Corp.
(1993–97*). *Selected issues.

reach the lower bounds of the EPRI estimate. In fact, the most salient
feature of the first year of Title IV, 1995, was the steady decline in
allowance prices, from an average of around $150 in the third quarter
of 1994 to an all-time low of about $65 in early 1996. After early 1996,
allowance prices began to rise. The March 1998 spot auction cleared
at $115, the highest price observed since mid-1995, and then, in the
next three months, the price rose to almost $200 and remained
trading in a range between $170 and $210 for the remainder of 1998.
Figure 7.1 displays the evolution of allowance prices from mid-1992
through December 1998.

As the allowance market has developed, three public sources of
price data have emerged. These three sources are indicated in Figure
7.1. First, trade press reports provide information on the prices at
which some private trades take place. The primary drawback of trade
press data is that it is scarce, since buyers and sellers tend to keep the
details of their allowance transactions confidential.

The second source of price data is cash, spot-market allowance-price indices published by three private organizations: Cantor Fitzgerald (CF), the Emission Exchange Corporation (EX), and Fieldston Publications (EATX).[13] The first two of these are market makers that accept bids to buy and sell allowances on behalf of clients and sometimes trade for their own account. All three publish allowance-price information for clients without identifying specific parties to the transactions.

Finally, extensive allowance-price data is reported from EPA's annual March auctions from 1993 through 1998. This information includes bid prices and quantities submitted by each buyer, the prices and associated quantities at which allowances were offered voluntarily for sale by individual sellers, and the bid prices that cleared the EPA's auctions. Bidding data along with data on the voluntary sales component of the EPA's annual auctions are examined in the next section. In the present section, only the market-clearing price in the EPA's annual spot auction is of interest.

Figure 7.1 displays these three sources of price information for current allowance prices from May 1992, when the first bilateral allowance trade was reported, through December 1998. Few trades occurred before the first EPA auction. Although reports of electric utilities and financial intermediaries actively seeking buyers and sellers for allowances appeared in the trade press as early as 1991,[14] the first reports of bilateral trades appeared in the press in May and July 1992 at prices of $288 and $326, respectively, in 1995 dollars.[15] Not surprisingly, allowance prices in both of the first two trades were

13. The indices published by these three independent organizations are an average cash, spot-market price of a current vintage allowance expressed in current dollars. Each is determined from private information available to the organization on recent and pending transactions, market activity from previous weeks, offers to buy and sell, and prices that buyers and sellers have indicated a willingness to accept. The current vintage includes not only allowances issued for the current year but also those issued for prior years that have not yet been used. Prior to January 1995, the current vintage was the 1995 vintage.

14. *Energy Daily*, May 15, 1991. Early reports of trades can be found in the *Wall Street Journal* (May 11, 1992, and July 1, 1992), the *New York Times* (May 11, 1992), *Energy Daily* (May 13, 1992, and July 1, 1992) and various issues of *Compliance Strategy Review*.

15. The first announced trade was a sale of 10,000 allowances (vintage information was not revealed) by Wisconsin Power and Light Company to the Tennessee Valley Authority at $265 per allowance (then-current dollars). The second was a purchase of 25,000 allowances by Ohio Edison from the ALCOA Corporation, a joint owner of a Phase I-affected plant, for $300 per allowance (then-current dollars).

close to the initial estimates of Phase I allowance prices referred to above, since these projections were the primary source of information available to buyers and sellers when allowances first began to be traded. Although trade press reports indicated that other bilateral trading activity was taking place, no additional information on prices in private transactions appeared before the EPA's first auction in March 1993.

The market-clearing price in the March 1993 spot auction was $131, substantially below both the earlier allowance-price estimates and the transaction prices reported from private bilateral trades that occurred in 1992.[16] Trade press reports at the time suggested that utilities and intermediaries were surprised by the low prices that emerged in the auction, and generally concurred that allowance purchases in the 1993 EPA auction were "quite a bargain."[17]

It was at this time that critics began to assert that shortcomings in the EPA's auction design, namely the discriminatory price auction mechanism, were biasing allowance prices downward and inhibiting the development of an effective allowance market. Subsequent private-market transactions reported in 1993 in the trade press as well as early price-index quotes reported by EX in 1993 appeared to support this downward-bias hypothesis, as they were substantially above the price that cleared the 1993 spot auction. Moreover, the market-clearing price of $150 in the 1994 EPA spot auction – which was higher than the 1993 auction price, a bit more than 10% lower than the prevailing EX price, and still quite far below earlier projections of Phase I allowance prices – seemed to lend further support to the downward-bias hypothesis.

Nevertheless, by mid-1994 various independent indicators of the market price for allowances converged. Following the EPA's second auction in March 1994, EATX and then CF also began to publish information on allowance prices associated with confidential private transactions and offers to buy and sell. As is evident from Figure 7.1, by August 1994 the prices reported by the three trade sources for allowances sold and offered for sale or purchase in the private market were almost identical. In addition, by late 1994 all three of these price indices had fallen to the level established by the 1994 spot auction.

16. The market-clearing price in the 1993 advance auction (for vintage 2000 allowances) was $122.

17. *Electric Power and Light*, May 1993, p. 1.

Table 7.1. *Allowances sold in EPA auctions and in the private market*

	Number of allowances sold in EPA auction	Number of allowances transferred in private market[a]	Allowance swaps/loans
Through March 1993	150,010	130,000	0
April 1993–March 1994	176,200	226,384	38,750
April 1994–March 1995	176,400	1,466,996	71,616
April 1995–March 1996	275,000	4,917,560	419,129
April 1996–March 1997	300,000	5,105,924	2,266,972
April 1997–March 1998	225,000	8,452,358	3,923,793
Total	1,302,610	20,299,222	6,720,260

[a]The number of allowances sold in the private market includes interutility trades, trades between utilities and third parties, and trades between two non-utility parties. This number excludes intrautility trades (including intra-holding company trades), reallocations, and options to trade which have not been exercised.
Sources: Derived from EPA auction data and EPA's allowance tracking system.

Moreover, the March 1995, 1996, 1997, and 1998 spot auctions yielded market-clearing prices virtually identical to the contemporaneous prices reported by the three industry sources of allowance-price information. The close alignment of prices quoted by several independent sources strongly suggests the emergence of a relatively efficient allowance market by mid-1994.

At the same time allowance-price indicators were converging, allowance-trading activity was increasing. Table 7.1 reports the number of allowances that appear to have been traded through both the EPA's auctions and in private, arm's length transactions from March 1993 through March 1998. The first column reports the total number of allowances, withheld and privately offered, sold in each of the EPA's annual auctions. In total, just over 1.3 million allowances have been traded through the EPA's mandatory and voluntary private auctions. The volume of private-market transactions is more difficult to determine since no source reports the precise quantity of allowances covered by purchase-and-sale agreements.

Data contained in the EPA's "allowance-tracking system" can be used to make an estimate of the volume of arm's length trades that took place annually from 1992 when the first trades took place through the March 1998 EPA auction.[18] We have used the EPA's

18. The allowance-tracking system (EPA, 1995c) is a publicly available, computerized program used by the EPA to keep track of allowance allocations, record reallocations of allowances between generating units, and make withdrawals of allowances equal to SO_2 emissions in each compliance year. All affected generating units were given an

allowance-tracking system to identify arm's length trades based on the recorded movement of allowances between accounts in the following way. First, all movements of allowances between accounts are identified. Then, all movements associated with special EPA allocations (e.g., bonus allowances made available for scrubbers), with the EPA auctions, and with noncommercial exchanges are eliminated.[19] The remaining allowance movements can be considered private, arm's length allowance transactions, as indicated by the second column of Table 7.1.

This measure of private, arm's length transactions is only approximate in that it does not include all relevant allowance sales and purchases, and it also includes some transactions that may not directly influence the current market price. First, there is no obligation to record allowance transactions with the EPA until the holder desires to use the allowances for compliance purposes, although it is our understanding that prompt recording of private trades was the rule rather than the exception through at least mid-1996.[20] Nonetheless, since there is no doubt some lag between the time a deal is struck and the time allowances are moved between accounts in the EPA's allowance-tracking system, the recorded data must lag behind actual commercial transactions to some extent. Second, forward transactions are not included (by definition), and trades pursuant to option agreements are not recorded until (and unless) options are actually exercised.[21] Increased use of such derivatives beginning in 1996 may result in a substantial gap between recorded and actual trades in the later years (Bartels, 1997). Finally, the ATS also includes arm's length transactions that may not directly influence the current market price.

individual allowance account (called a "unit account") in the EPA's computer system, and any third party (including utilities and holding companies) desiring to trade allowances must establish an account (called a "general account"), as well.

19. "Noncommercial" activities are classified as all movements of allowances involving unit or general accounts with common operating utility or holding company ownership. Noncommercial transactions include both reallocations due to prior contractual or joint ownership agreements as well as intrautility allowance transactions.

20. Personal communication, Acid Rain Division, U.S. Environmental Protection Agency, June 1996, and personal communication, Cantor Fitzgerald Environmental Brokerage Services, November 1996.

21. In June 1993, for instance, *Compliance Strategies Review* reported that AMAX Energy purchased from Long Island Lighting Company an option to purchase Phase I allowances (quantity and prices were not disclosed). Until (and unless) the option is exercised and the allowances are recorded by the parties in the allowance-tracking system, this trading activity will not appear in the EPA's allowance-tracking system.

For instance, many utilities "swap" allowances of one vintage against allowances of another vintage, in which cases the only price determined is the discount for the far vintages. Similarly, utilities with large allowance banks may "loan" allowances to third parties, typically to provide liquidity to market makers, in which cases the only price determined is the "interest" or the number of additional allowances returned to the lender. Moreover, the allowances loaned out and returned are often of different vintages so that combined swaps and loans are often found. As indicated by the third data column in Table 7.1, the number of swaps and loans has increased greatly since early 1996.[22]

Altogether, by March 1998, about 20.3 million allowances changed hands through private transactions between unrelated parties, compared to 1.3 million through the EPA auctions. It is also evident from Table 7.1 that there was very little private trading activity prior to the second quarter of 1994: Through March 1994, the EPA auctions represented at least half of the allowance-trading activity occurring as of those dates. Most of the 20.3 million allowances that were exchanged among private parties through March 1998 were traded after March 1994. Taken together, Figure 7.1 and Table 7.1 suggest that in the early stages of the development of the allowance market, buyers and sellers had little information about market-clearing allowance prices. Initial transaction prices appear to have been influenced by earlier allowance-price projections, and there appears to be no single market price guiding all traders. The lack of a single visible market price is likely to have led to the lack of private market transactions, while the lack of private market transactions is likely to have reinforced the lack of a visible and well-defined market price.

Beginning around May 1994, however, Figure 7.1 shows that private-market prices came almost exactly into line with the results of the March 1994 EPA auction. By the March 1995 auction, market values in all trading venues were essentially the same, and it seems clear that a single visible market price had emerged. Moreover, as

---

22. Swaps and loans are determined by an algorithm that identifies all matched exchanges occurring within 200 days of each other and where the quantities exchanged are within 8% of the other. A pure loan would involve Party A transferring x allowances to Party B and Party B returning $x + 3\%$ (for instance) allowances 180 days later. Pure swaps are contemporaneous exchanges across vintages when Party A transfers x near-term allowances to Party B in return for $x + y\%$ far-term allowances. See Andrin (1999) for a more complete explanation.

uncertainty about allowance market values was resolved and the date when 1995 emissions had to be covered with allowances neared, allowance-trading activity increased.

The fact that private-market prices came almost exactly into line with the results of the March 1994 EPA auction casts significant doubt on the hypothesis that the EPA's discriminatory price mechanism biased allowance prices downward. It seems at least as plausible that nonauction prices had been held up artificially by the earlier projections of higher prices. The early auctions suggested, correctly as it turned out, that those projections were too high. To the extent that the auctions brought parties to the market and helped to establish a range of market valuations, they fulfilled their primary objective of stimulating the development of private market-trading activity.

Interaction of the Private Market and the Annual Auctions

The development of an effective private market for allowances can also be seen in the dispersion of bid and offer prices in the EPA auctions held since 1993. In the limiting case in which the allowance market is perfectly competitive and without friction, there would exist a single, universally known market price of allowances, P^*. In this case, there would be essentially no dispersion of bid and offer prices in the EPA auction, since no buyer would pay more than P^* and no seller would accept less than P^*.

Figure 7.2 illustrates buyers' offer curves and sellers' offer curves for the 1993 through 1998 spot auctions.[23] The intersection of the buyers' offer curve and the sellers' offer curve defines the market-clearing price, the price of the lowest bid at which allowances were purchased.[24] Figure 7.2 demonstrates that the buyers' offer curve

---

23. Similar curves can be constructed for the six-year and seven-year advance auctions, and they illustrate the same point, as shown in Joskow, Schmalensee, Bailey (1998).

24. The buyers' offer curve is constructed by drawing, at a height corresponding to each bid price, a horizontal line with length corresponding to the associated bid quantity. These lines are then joined end-to-end, starting with the highest bid price and working down to the lowest. On the supply side of the market, the number of allowances offered for sale in the mandatory (as required by Title IV) auction is represented by a vertical line at the relevant quantity on the horizontal axis. The sellers' offer curve is completed by drawing horizontal lines at heights corresponding to the associated

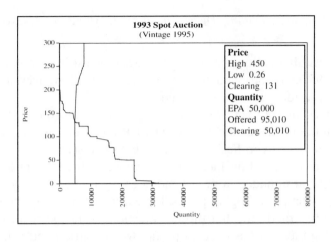

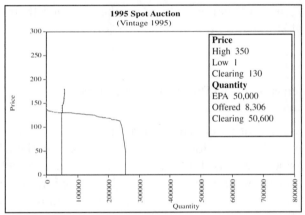

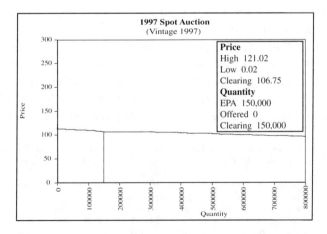

Figure 7.2. Evolution of bids and offers at EPA spot auctions, 1993–98.
Source: EPA auction data.

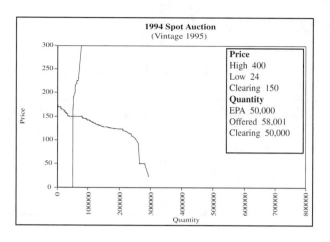

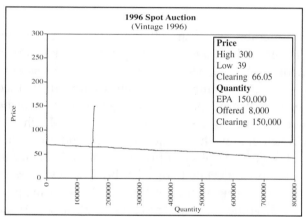

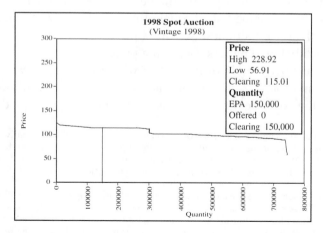

Figure 7.2. *(cont.)*

Table 7.2. *Percentage differences between average winning bids and lowest winning bids in EPA auctions*

Year	Spot auction (%)	6-Year advance auction (%)	7-Year advance auction (%)
1993	20.6	—	11.5
1994	6.0	5.7	6.4
1995	1.5	2.3	1.6
1996	3.2	1.9	1.9
1997	3.4	0.3	2.0
1998	1.6	—	2.5

Source: EPA auction data.

flattened considerably between 1993 and 1998, consistent with the development of a robust and efficient private market. The buyers' offer curve for the March 1993 spot auction shows considerable dispersion. A significant volume of allowances traded at prices well above the market-clearing price, and a large number of lowball bids can be observed. The buyers' offer curve for the March 1994 spot auction is much flatter than that for 1993, and the number of allowance sales that took place at prices significantly higher than the market-clearing price declined considerably. The few sales that did take place in 1994 at prices far above the market-clearing price were to individuals or groups typically purchasing a single allowance for noncommercial reasons. By 1995, the buyers' offer curve had become quite flat, and remained so through 1998: Few bids were made at prices much above the market-clearing price, and few were made at prices much below the market-clearing price.[25]

The same narrowing in dispersion of winning bids is shown quantitatively in Table 7.2. The table shows the percentage difference between the average price paid and the lowest price paid (the

reservation prices and with lengths corresponding to the quantities voluntarily offered by sellers at those prices. These are joined to the top of the vertical line just discussed, beginning with the lowest reservation price and working up to the highest, since voluntary offers to sell do not get matched with buyers' offers to buy until the EPA's mandatory sales offering is fully subscribed.

25. A few individual buyers have continued to pay high prices up through the 1998 EPA auctions. These purchases have by and large been by environmental groups, law student associations, and other nonstandard commercial transactions that have been made by groups attempting to make a statement. If one wants to purchase a small quantity of allowances for whatever reason, the EPA's auction is the place to do so, because utilities and intermediaries will not deal in such small quantities.

market-clearing price) in each auction. The smaller the differences shown in Table 7.2, the more closely does buyer behavior in the EPA auction conform to the perfectly competitive, frictionless ideal.

The flattening of the buyers' offer curve between 1993 and 1998 is consistent with the evidence given in the previous sections. The development of a robust and efficient outside market significantly tightened the opportunity-cost bounds on the behavior of auction participants. In the 1995, 1996, 1997, and 1998 auctions, it is clear that the frictionless, perfectly competitive ideal is a good approximation to reality, despite the continued presence of a few noncommercial high bidders.

Although the number of allowance sales that took place at prices significantly higher than the market-clearing price declined considerably after the 1994 auction, there remained a long tail of offers to buy at prices that were up to 10% below the best available information about market prices.[26] At first blush, this long tail of lowball bids may seem irrational since, if the outside market is efficient, no serious bidder should expect that such bids would be successful.

Putting in bids slightly below the expected market price makes sense, however, for a regulated electric utility seeking to purchase allowances. First, the price that will clear the market is never known with certainty. In an auction with essentially no transaction costs, there is nothing to lose by submitting bids at prices slightly lower than those being quoted in the private market, especially when transaction costs are associated with equivalent private-market sales. Second, regulated electric utilities may prefer to acquire allowances through confidential private market transactions that provide flexibility to arrange the ideal portfolio of allowance quantities and vintages rather than through the EPA auction. However, the prices a utility negotiates in the private market may be subject to scrutiny by its state regulatory commission. By submitting bids to the EPA auctions at prices slightly below the prevailing private market values, a utility can justify to regulators that it paid the lowest reasonable price for the allowances purchased.

The EPA auction data also can be used to further address the

26. Since there is no fee required to submit a bid and minimal requirements to do so, there is little to lose from submitting a low bid; this was especially the case in 1993 when relatively little information was available to predict the market-clearing price for allowances.

Table 7.3. *Allowances privately offered for sale in EPA auctions*

Year	Allowances offered	Allowances offered that sold	Percentage offered that sold	Total allowances sold	Percentage of total sales offered
1993	125,510	10	0.01	150,010	0.01
1994	155,001	1,200	0.77	176,200	0.68
1995	22,306	1,400	6.28	176,400	0.79
1996	22,000	0	0.00	275,000	0.00
1997	0	—	—	300,000	—
1998	0	—	—	275,000	—
Total	324,817	2,610	0.80	1,352,610	0.002

Source: EPA auction data.

criticism that the discriminatory price auction mechanism biased the price of allowances downward. As noted above, the theory put forth by Cason (1993, 1995) and Cason and Plott (1996) implies that voluntary sellers in the EPA auctions have incentives to set reservation prices too low, resulting in a downward-biased market-clearing price. This theory does not harmonize well with the facts, however. Table 7.3 demonstrates that, particularly after 1994, relatively few allowances were voluntarily offered for sale in the EPA auctions, and none at all were offered in 1997 or 1998. In fact, those allowances that were voluntarily offered for sale were typically offered at prices significantly *higher* than the market-clearing price.[27] As a result, less than 1% of the private allowances offered for sale were sold, and less than one-quarter of 1% of the allowances sold in the EPA auctions were voluntarily offered (as opposed to the allowances withheld by law by EPA). In all, only 2,610 allowances have been sold using the private seller mechanism, out of just over 1.3 million that have been sold in EPA auctions and almost 21.6 million that had been traded overall through March 1998. Table 7.3 makes clear that, if the EPA auctions have become a sideshow to the private allowance market, the private sale component of those auctions has always been a very minor act in that sideshow. However serious the flaws in the auctions' provisions for voluntary allowance sales, they clearly cannot have had a discernible effect on the performance of the allowance market as a whole.

27. The most plausible explanation for this seller behavior seems to be that some utilities use the EPA auction process to demonstrate to regulators that they could not sell their allowances at prices above those prevailing in the private market. In addition, as noted above in connection with the persistence of "lowball" bids, there is no cost to offer to sell at a high reservation price.

The Intertemporal Allowance Market

Since SO_2 abatement strategies commonly involve long-term investment and contracting decisions that affect emissions for many years, a futures market for allowances should be expected to emerge if utilities take advantage of opportunities for intertemporal cost savings made possible by the banking provisions of Title IV. A robust private market for forward allowances has in fact developed, and readily available forward prices are obtainable from intermediaries and other third-party brokers. Forward-market characteristics provide additional evidence of the development of a relatively efficient allowance market.[28]

The simple economics of banking behavior implies that, in a world of certainty without transaction costs and with banking across all relevant periods, arbitrage between current and expected future compliance costs will cause the immediate settlement prices for allowances of different vintages to be equal.[29] For example, the immediate settlement price (the price payable today) for a vintage 1996 allowance in 1996 should equal the immediate settlement price of a vintage 1997 allowance in 1996 if allowances are carried over from 1996 into 1997.

Put another way, over the time period in which banking occurs, the allowance price will increase at the rate of interest. For example,

---

28. In addition to active options and futures markets, an active market for "swaps" has developed. A utility that needs allowances today but expects to have excess allowances in, say, 2004 will often find it more tax efficient to swap allowances with another entity than to buy allowances today and sell allowances in 2004. The other party to the transaction must be compensated for giving up the convenience yield from holding excess allowances over time to deal with unforeseen events. The necessary compensation has declined over time, consistent with a general rise in utilities' confidence that allowances can easily be acquired on the private market as needed.

29. In all periods, an individual holder of allowances chooses a level of SO_2 abatement such that the current marginal cost of abating in that period equals the current price of a spot-market allowance ($MC_t = P_t$). With no uncertainty, across any two periods with banking, the spot price of allowances must rise at the rate of interest. If it rose less rapidly, nobody would hold allowances over time. If the spot price rose more rapidly, it would make sense to abate more today to generate more allowances to hold. But doing so would raise today's marginal cost and, thus, today's spot price – lowering the difference between today's and tomorrow's spot prices. If the spot price rises at the rate of interest, the discounted price of different vintages – the immediate settlement price – must be constant. Schennach (1998) provides a detailed theoretical analysis of collective banking behavior of affected units, incorporating electricity demand, the number of affected units, environmental regulations, and technological innovations. The theoretical model illustrates both the time path of allowance prices and abatement over time.

assuming banking between 1996 and 1997 and an interest rate of 5%, if the spot price of a vintage 1996 allowance in 1996 is $100, then the spot price of a vintage 1996 allowance in 1997 will be $105. The discounted forward price of a vintage 1997 allowance will also be $100 in 1996, and the spot price will be $105 in 1997.

The real allowance market, of course, operates in a world with uncertainty, so the analysis must be modified. The possibility of unexpected changes in electricity demand, in the number of affected units, in technology, and in environmental regulations all impart some uncertainty to the allowance market. As a result, an affected unit (or its operating or holding company) benefits from holding a stock of allowances on hand to buffer itself against unexpected changes in SO_2 emissions. The benefit that accrues from holding a stock of allowances (or any other traded commodity) on hand is called a *convenience yield*.[30] Because of the convenience yield, and to the extent that the allowance market is marked by uncertainty, the immediate settlement prices of allowances of different vintages will not be equal.

In fact, it is easy to show that immediate settlement prices for future dates (i.e., discounted forward prices) should be less than the current spot price and should decline as more distant dates are considered. This condition is described as *weak backwardation* in the term structure of allowance prices.[31] Suppose one buys an allowance today and simultaneously sells it forward, for delivery in T periods at a fixed price to be paid then. The return on this risk-free portfolio is the forward price (F_T) to be received in T periods less the spot-market price today (P_1) plus the convenience yield (CY_T):

$$(F_T - P_1) + CY_T. \tag{7.1}$$

Since this portfolio is risk free, its return must equal the risk-free return. The risk-free return is the return from selling the allowance on the spot market today and subsequently investing that money in an asset with a certain return, such as a Treasury bill, until period T:

$$r_T P_1, \tag{7.2}$$

where r_T is the rate of interest between today and period T. Equating (7.1) and (7.2) and rearranging gives:

---

30. Williams and Wright (1991).   31. See Bailey (1998b).

$$\frac{F_T}{(1+r_T)} + \frac{CY_T}{(1+r_T)} = P_1 \tag{7.3}$$

Rewriting Equation (7.3) in terms of the discounted forward price f_T, the discounted convenience yield cy_T, and the spot price gives:

$$f_T + cy_T = P_1 \tag{7.4}$$

Note that f_T is the immediate settlement price for T periods in the future: it is the price that must be paid today to purchase one allowance usable in T periods.

For any positive convenience yield, it follows from Equation (7.4) that allowance prices will be weakly backwardated: $f_T < P_1$. For example, a positive convenience yield will cause the spot price for a vintage 1996 allowance at some date in 1996 to be greater than the immediate settlement price for a vintage 1997 allowance at the same date. Moreover, it is easy to extend this argument to show that f_{T+k} $< f_T$ for any positive T and k. (Imagine simultaneously buying forward in period T and selling forward in period $T + k$.) As can be seen from Equation (7.4), the less uncertainty in the market and thus the smaller the convenience yield, the smaller will be the differences between immediate settlement prices of different vintage allowances.

The actual term structure of allowance prices is virtually flat and weakly backwardated. This is illustrated by Figure 7.3, which shows immediate settlement prices for current and future vintage allowances. Each horizontal line on this figure represents, at six-month intervals since July 1995, a single month of immediate settlement data for successive allowance vintages.[32] The consistent, overall flatness of the term structure indicates that allowances of different vintages are regarded as virtually interchangeable and that intertemporal arbitrage is occurring. Without arbitrage, the steadily increasing number of current vintage allowances in Phase I (i.e., the current year's vintage plus banked allowances from prior vintages) would create a glut that would depress the current price of Phase I vintage allowances well below the current price for Phase II vintage allowances. Instead, the immediate settlement prices of near (Phase I) and far (Phase II) vintages have remained nearly equal to one

32. Prices for every month of the year are not illustrated in Figure 7.3 so as not to clutter the graph. Including data from all months of the year does not qualitatively change the trend illustrated by Figure 7.3.

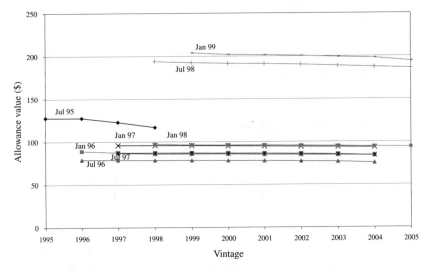

Figure 7.3. Term structure of allowance prices.
Source: Cantor Fitzgerald Environmental Brokerage Services.

another, despite significant changes in the value of allowances. Perceptions of current and (more likely) future demand and supply will affect the price of allowances, just as they affect the prices of crude oil and wheat, but intertemporal arbitrage and the ready substitutability of allowances of different vintages keep the term structure flat. This serves to keep the incentives for abatement in Phases I and II aligned, as required by intertemporal efficiency.

Two notable features of the term structure of allowance prices are the greater degree of flatness after 1995 and the increase in the horizon of the term structure. The flatter the term structure, the lower are convenience yields, from Equation (7.4). An increase in the horizon of the term structure, in turn, reflects a deepening of the market, as participants find it efficient to develop and trade new instruments. Both features are depicted clearly in Figure 7.4, which shows the percentage discount from the current vintage (spot) value of immediate settlement prices for future vintages, plotted against the number of years until the future vintage can be used to cover emissions.[33] In July 1995, the discount for allowances first usable two

33. From Equation (7.4), the percentage discount is the total convenience yield over the relevant period as a percentage of the spot price.

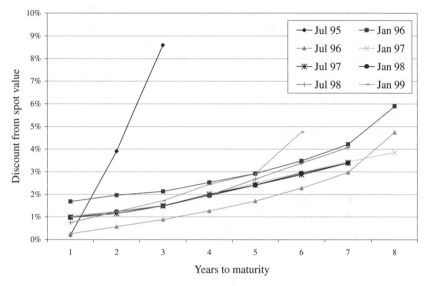

Figure 7.4. Convenience yields for SO_2 allowances.
Source: Cantor Fitzgerald Environmental Brokerage Services.

or three years in the future was high compared to what it would become as the allowance market matured. The subsequent lowering of the discount by January 1996, the tight clustering thereafter, and the extension of the horizon indicate that a robust futures market had developed by 1996. The futures market was slower in getting organized than the spot market, but the latter is a prerequisite for the former.

Several explanations can be offered for the decline in convenience yields after 1995. First, the flattening of the term structure may reflect a reduction in transaction costs.[34] A decline in transaction costs would reduce the convenience yield because it would decrease the penalty paid by an operator that sells current-vintage allowances for cash only to find later that more allowances need to be purchased. Second, since a decline in uncertainty directly reduces the convenience yield, the flattening of the term structure of allowance prices is consistent with the resolution of uncertainty about the value of allowances,

34. Commissions per allowance averaged $1.75 in mid-1994, $1.00 in late 1995, $0.75 in September 1996, and $0.50 in early 1997.

which would have occurred as participants gained confidence in the spot allowance market and in increased market liquidity. One further contributing factor may have been the resolution of uncertainties about how emissions would be measured by continuous emissions monitoring systems and increasing confidence in the operation of these systems. The flattening of the term structure after 1995 likely reflects some combination of these factors, but it also provides compelling evidence that a robust and efficient allowance market has emerged.

INFLUENCE OF STATE ELECTRIC UTILITY REGULATION ON ALLOWANCE TRADING

When a tradable permit program to reduce sulfur dioxide emissions from electric utilities was first proposed, concerns were voiced about whether utilities would participate in allowance trading and whether the regulatory framework within which electric utilities operate would discourage their participation. Regulation, it was feared, would not provide utility managers the incentive or even the ability to pursue cost-saving opportunities made available by emissions trading.[35] Despite these fears, however, there is little evidence to suggest that state public utility commission regulation – or the lack thereof – adversely affected electric utilities' decisions to trade allowances in the critical 1993–95 period during which the allowance market was developing.

To understand how certain features of electric utility regulation could adversely affect utilities' incentives to trade allowances, a short review of traditional electric utility regulation is required.[36] Traditionally, the electric utility industry has been subject to extensive price and entry regulation by state and federal regulatory agencies. At the state level, state public utility commissions (PUC) regulate both entry and retail pricing of electric utilities. In particular, a state PUC grants one or more (usually private and investor-owned)

35. See, for example, Bohi and Burtraw (1992). Fullerton, McDermott, and Caulkins (1996) argue that the potential cost-increasing impact of adverse state regulatory behavior could be substantial.
36. For more on the regulatory process, see Joskow (1989).

electric utilities a legal monopoly to provide service to retail consumers in that state in return for assuming an obligation to serve all consumers in their territory with reliable service at regulated rates. In exchange, the electric utility is provided a "fair rate of return" on capital.

Because the typical electric utility receives almost all of its revenues from retail sales, and because most of a utility's assets are wholly owned by the same corporation, most of the utility's costs are subject to state, rather than federal, regulatory authority. Retail electricity prices are set at the state level through formal hearing processes and are designed to reflect the cost of providing service. A utility must submit to its state PUC any proposed changes in the level or structure of its existing rates. Proposed rate changes are evaluated in a formal administrative proceeding called a rate case. In a rate case, a state PUC is not bound to set rates that cover all the operating and capital costs incurred by the electric utility. A PUC may disallow, entirely or in part, any costs that are deemed to be imprudent or any costs for services it believes the utility could have obtained more cheaply or did not require at all. Moreover, regulatory lag and other incentive mechanisms (Joskow and Schmalensee, 1986) provide utilities with some additional incentives to control costs.

As a result of the regulatory process, the nature and behavior of a utility's PUC has the potential to be an important factor affecting the utility's decision to trade allowances. Because emission allowances are a relatively new operating cost for a PUC to assess, utilities may have perceived an added risk when trading allowances. In particular, utilities might have worried that because of inexperience, their commissions would too frequently declare allowance trades imprudent and disallow some costs. For example, a utility may perceive an added risk that during a rate case, the commission might question whether allowances were sold for the best possible price. A utility might also face political pressures to adopt control strategies that protect local coal-mining interests (as discussed in Chapters 2 and 3), and state regulators might reinforce these pressures by providing cost recovery for those strategies (but not for allowance-based strategies) in regulated utility prices.

On the other hand, the implementation of Title IV happens to have coincided with growing competitive pressures being placed on utilities as a consequence of incentive regulatory schemes, industry restructuring, and deregulation (Joskow, 1997). These pressures intensified after 1994, when the California commission issued its "Blue Book" on industry restructuring and on wholesale and retail competition. As industry restructuring and competition pressures increased, utilities could no longer count on passing inefficiently high costs along to retail customers, whom they might no longer serve exclusively in the future. While the implementation of an SO_2 emissions-trading system at the same time competition was rapidly being introduced to the electric utility industry may have been a fortuitous coincidence, the incentive structure faced by electric utilities during this time period is likely to have changed significantly from what it might have been, had the traditional regulated monopoly industry structure been sustained.

These competitive pressures do not imply that regulatory incentives were no longer relevant as Title IV was being implemented. The formative period that we focus on here, through the end of 1995, must be viewed as a transition period: Utilities had to respond to incentives created by regulatory institutions, by the expected evolution of competitive electricity markets, and by the interactions between them. By 1997, however, the pressures of industry restructuring and competition had become a dominant theme in the electricity sector. Formal PUC regulations, called generic orders, as well as informal PUC rulings, called guidelines, may still have affected utilities' incentives to trade emission allowances. If nothing else, an affirmative PUC order or guideline would have given utilities some assurance that the costs they incurred to comply with Title IV would not become "stranded costs" when competitive pressures intensified. Although a guideline does not carry the same force as an order, guidelines nevertheless convey a commission's attitude and intent. Generic orders as well as guidelines on allowance trading indicate the state PUC's expected treatment of emission allowances in rate-making cases, thereby reducing the likelihood that a utility's allowance-trading activity would be ruled imprudent. It is possible that utilities in states with no formal rulings engaged in informal conversations with their state commission regarding the rate-making treatment of allowances, but this type of guidance is much less certain and certainly less secure than that provided by generic orders.

As of the close of 1995, fifteen state public utility commissions had explicitly addressed allowance trading through the issuance of a

Table 7.4. *States with PUC guidelines or generic orders*

Guidelines issued	Generic order issued
Florida (1993)	Connecticut[a] (1993)
Illinois (1993)	Georgia (1994)
Maryland (1993)	Indiana (1993)
New Hampshire (1995)	Iowa (1994)
New York (1993)	Mississippi (1993)
Ohio (1993)	Missouri (1993)
	North Carolina[a] (1994)
	Pennsylvania (1993)
	Wisconsin (1994)

Note: To date, issuances of guidelines and generic orders have been mutually exclusive.
[a]States with no Phase I-affected units.

formal generic order or an informal guideline. Table 7.4 identifies the states whose PUC had issued a guideline or generic order on the regulatory treatment of allowances.[37] The number of states issuing regulatory statements on allowance trading grew sharply over time, from zero in 1992 to ten in 1993, to fifteen by the close of 1995. In most cases, regulation was prompted by a request from one of the utilities in the commission's jurisdiction for a ruling, prior to the appearance of any trading activity in that state.[38]

Four general observations about the regulatory treatment of allowances that have been issued, formally or informally, by state public utility commissions emerge from reading the guidelines and generic orders and from conversations with commission staff. First, none of the guidelines and formal orders prohibit or substantially restrict allowance-trading activity. Second, across all states issuing regulations, PUC regulations on allowance-trading activity largely require 100% of both expenses and revenues to be returned to the ratepayers. Third, in terms of accounting practices, the net gain (or loss) incurred from allowance transactions are used to offset (or

37. See Bailey (1998a) for a summary of the orders issued in each state.
38. The New York State Department of Public Service, however, took the initiative in 1992, prior to any trading activity or requests from utilities for guidelines on allowance treatment, to issue a notice to utilities under its jurisdiction soliciting comments on basic questions regarding the rate-making treatment of allowances and the role the New York state commission should have in shaping utility emission compliance actions.

increase) fuel costs. Fourth, a few states have taken an incentive-based approach to allowances, allowing their utilities to retain a portion of any gains from allowance sales beyond those sales that are "below the line."[39]

Bailey (1998a) describes and presents the empirical methodology used to assess the effect of these early state PUC regulations on allowance-trading activity in 1993, 1994, and 1995. Briefly, a reduced form model was used to assess the direct and indirect effects of regulatory and nonregulatory activity on allowance-trading behavior. Because regulatory rulings may have been endogenous, a simultaneous equations (logit) model was used to analyze the effect of state regulatory rulings on allowance-trading activity.[40]

This assessment indicates that explicit state regulation has encouraged rather than discouraged allowance-trading activity.[41] Controlling for the effect of nonregulatory factors, the presence of a regulation on allowance-trading activity has a positive and statistically significant effect on the probability that utilities in that state engage in allowance-trading activity. Additional empirical analysis in Bailey (1998a) suggests that state PUC regulations on allowance-trading activity had some effect on the number of allowance trades taking place, but not on the volume of allowances transacted. All else being equal, a state with a regulation may be expected to have made more allowance transactions to acquire the same volume of allowances as a state without a regulation on allowance-trading activity.

More significant, perhaps, than the econometric result that PUC regulations appear to have encouraged rather than discouraged

39. A "below-the-line" transaction is one that only involves shareholder monies. All gains or losses from below-the-line transactions are absorbed by the electric utility shareholders, not by the ratepayers. All rulings issued by the end of 1995 permit utilities to retain 100% of the gains and losses from below-the-line transactions.

40. It is likely that a state PUC's decision to issue a regulation on allowance-trading activity and the electric utility's decision to trade allowances are jointly determined. A state PUC regulation on allowance-trading activity is expected to increase observed trading activity in that state by minimizing risk born by utilities in that state. Increased allowance-trading activity by utilities in a state is expected to increase the likelihood that the state PUC will issue a regulation on allowance-trading activity so as to address the issue of allowance trading comprehensively rather than on a continuing case-by-case basis.

41. The likelihood of trading appeared to be affected by how favorable the PUC was to shareholder interests and to an increase in trading over time. Trading increased the likelihood of a PUC ruling, as did the presence of a large number of Phase I-affected units.

trading is that, of the thirty-four states that had seen allowance-trading activity by January 1996, nineteen had yet to concern themselves with rate-making treatment of allowances. That is to say, allowance transactions had not been deterred in nineteen states despite the lack of specific guidance. Conversations with PUC commission staff in these states indicate that the reason a ruling had not been issued was typically that the commission had not received any requests for formal or informal guidance from utilities under their jurisdiction. While this is an imperfect, and perhaps biased, measure of the need for regulatory rulings, it does suggest that some utilities have been comfortable trading without a formal ruling on how allowances will be treated for rate-making purposes. The incentive to control costs to prepare for industry restructuring and competition, as well as the growing prevalence of rate-freeze schemes, no doubt provided strong incentives for utilities to take advantage of the opportunities to reduce costs created by the allowance market.

THE ALLOWANCE MARKET WORKS

Our analysis indicates that an efficient market for sulfur dioxide allowances emerged a few years after enactment of Title IV, certainly by mid-1994. Not only did futures markets develop, but, by early 1996, prices in those markets indicated a relatively low convenience yield – suggesting, in turn, relatively little fear of being caught short without sufficient allowances to meet regulatory requirements. Despite widespread fears, state public utility commissions did not act to inhibit allowance trading in the critical early years of the market's development, and many utilities were willing to trade allowances despite having received no formal guidance about the treatment of such trades from their regulators. If the historically staid, conservative electric utility industry can so rapidly engender the allowance market described in this chapter, it is plausible to expect efficient markets for emissions rights to be the norm, as long as the legal and institutional framework defines those rights clearly and does not restrict when or how they can be traded on the private market.

While it is interesting to ask whether the particular auction mechanism specified in Title IV led the allowance market to develop more slowly than it would have under some alternative mechanism, we do not think it is possible to provide a definitive answer. The auctions did provide potentially valuable price information early. In particular, the auctions first revealed that allowance prices would be (at least for a time) well below initial expectations. It is hard to dispute the notion that alternative auction designs might have provided that information earlier and stimulated earlier development of the private market. It appears equally hard to support that notion, however.

8 Title IV's Voluntary Compliance Program

As noted in Chapter 1, Title IV includes a voluntary compliance program intended to enable owners of the 263 Table A units subject to Phase I to make some of the required emission reductions at other units, which then become Phase I-affected units. As we have also noted, the response to this program has been much greater than expected. More than half the electric utilities with Table A units have voluntarily brought units into Phase I in each of its first three years: 182 units in 1995, 161 in 1996, and 153 in 1997. One hundred thirty-eight units – more than half of these units – were subject to Phase I in all three years.

Yet, as encouraging as this response has been, on closer examination it serves to illustrate a general problem with such voluntary provisions. In principle, allowances should be allocated to voluntary units equal to what the emissions of these units would be if they were not part of the program (i.e., counterfactual emissions). If this could be done exactly, participation would be attractive only to units with particularly low abatement costs. In practice, however, allowance allocations generally differ from counterfactual emissions. Units with relatively low control costs that would receive an allocation below their counterfactual emissions are thereby discouraged from participation, while units with relatively high control costs are encouraged to participate by an allocation above their counterfactual emissions. All else being equal, since participation is voluntary, operators will tend to introduce units with expected emissions less than the allowance allocation (as well as those with lower control costs), while keeping units with higher emissions out of the program, even if control costs are relatively low.

This problem of "adverse selection" poses an unavoidable dilemma in the design of voluntary features in tradable-permit programs. In setting a rule for allocating allowances to voluntary units, the regulator faces the classic regulatory trade-off between production efficiency (minimization of total SO_2 control costs) and information rent extraction (reduction of excess allowances).[1] If the allocation rule is generous, participation by units with lower control costs will be greater, but the cap will be loosened by the issuance of more excess allowances. If the rule is less generous, there will be fewer excess allowances, but participation by units with lower control costs will be less.

In this chapter, we use the ample response to the substitution provisions in Title IV as a case study to determine the seriousness of the adverse-selection problem. In particular, we examine the reasons for the high participation rate in Phase I and the balance between additional lower-cost abatement and excess allowances. We also discuss several implications for the design of cap-and-trade mechanisms and the incorporation of voluntary participation opportunities based on the experience from Title IV.[2]

PATTERNS OF VOLUNTARY COMPLIANCE

The Applicable Rules

As noted in Chapter 1, Title IV includes three distinct voluntary compliance provisions. Two of these, for "substitution units" and for "compensation units," apply to electric utility generating units that would

---

1. See Laffont and Tirole (1993).
2. Virtually no literature addresses the welfare implications and instrument design problems of voluntary opt-in provisions in phased-in emission-trading programs, perhaps because few such programs have been implemented. In a slightly different context, Hartman (1988) and Malm (1996) found strong evidence of adverse selection in voluntary energy-conservation programs and concluded that the net benefits of such programs are significantly lower than had been traditionally believed. Conversely, Arora and Cason (1996) found no evidence of adverse selection (or free ride) in the EPA's 33/50 voluntary program, which aims to encourage companies to report to the EPA their release of chemicals covered by the Toxic Release Inventory. In a recent work, Montero (2000) discusses the optimal design of a phase-in program with opt-in possibilities.

not be affected by Title IV until Phase II. The substitution provision enables utilities to designate one or more non-Table A units to make reductions in place of a commonly owned or operated Table A unit. The substitution units thus designated receive allowance allocations approximately equal to their historic emissions, and are treated as if they had been Table A units. The compensation provision allows utilities to reduce generation in a given Table A unit below its baseline level. The source of any compensating generation must be designated, however, and when that compensating unit is sulfur-emitting, it receives allowances approximately equal to its historic emissions and is brought into Phase I.

The third voluntary compliance provision, the industrial opt-in provision, applies to industrial boilers that would not otherwise be subject to Title IV at all. The response to the industrial opt-in provision has been small – seven boilers at two locations – and those units are not further considered in this chapter.[3]

Among the non-Table A electric utility units brought voluntarily into Phase I, nearly all entered the program under the substitution provision.[4] Since the few compensating units' essential function was to substitute for Table A units, subsequent references to "substitution units" should be understood to include the compensating units.

The process of allocating allowances to substitution units has been controversial from the beginning. Allowances are issued to substitution units according to complicated and heavily litigated rules whereby average 1985–87 heat input for a unit is multiplied by the least of three emission rates for the unit. These three rates are (a) the lower of the actual or allowable 1985 SO_2 emission rate, (b) the greater of the 1989 or 1990 actual emission rate, or (c) the most stringent federal- or state-allowable SO_2 emission rate applicable in

---

3. Monitoring costs and the transaction costs associated with establishing the baseline appear to have exceeded the gains from selling or banking allowances (Atkeson, 1997). Only three industrial plants have found it worthwhile to apply under the industrial sources opt-in provisions, two of which have obtained approval and received allowances. Monitoring costs are not an issue for electric utility units, since all Phase II units were to have installed a continuous emission monitor by the start of Phase I.

4. The response to the compensating unit provisions was slight for several reasons. First, relatively robust load growth during the early years of Phase I increased the demand on all units. Second, operators also had the option either to prove that the compensating power was shifted to other Table A units or to sulfur-free generating units (i.e., nuclear or hydro), or to have allowances equal to the amount of underutilization deducted from unit accounts.

1995–99 as of November 15, 1990.[5] Thus, all the information used for establishing allowance allocations to substitution units dates from at least five years prior to the start of Phase I. Such old information is unlikely to produce accurate estimates of counterfactual emissions for substitution units in Phase I.

Several other factors have been important in conditioning the response to Title IV's voluntary compliance program. First, as a practical matter, substitution units must be owned or operated by electric utilities that own or operate a Table A unit.[6]

Second, non-Table A generating units may participate in the program for all, part, or none of Phase I. Moreover, the choice of whether to enter or exit the program in any particular year need not be made until the end of November of that year, at which point it should be possible accurately to estimate emissions for the year. Nevertheless, more than half the units that have been substitution units for at least one year have remained in the program for all three years for which we have data.

A third relevant factor is the complex interaction with Title IV's NO_x emissions program. Depending on the type of boiler, all Phase II units will be subject to NO_x emission *rate* limitations in Phase II, and some Phase I units (those with Group 1 boilers)[7] became subject to a less stringent Phase I NO_x emission-rate limitation, beginning January 1, 1996. Units that are subject to Title IV in Phase I must meet both the SO_2 and NO_x requirements, so that a substitution unit with a Group 1 boiler also has to meet the Phase I NO_x emission-rate limit. If the unit was declared a substitution unit prior to January 1, 1995, however, and if it meets the Phase I NO_x requirements for

5. Originally, substitution units were to receive allowances based only on the 1985 emission rate; however, environmental groups brought suit against EPA to prevent issuance of "excess" allowances. This litigation led to the addition of the references to 1989–90 emission rates and other non-Title IV limitations on 1995–99 emission rates. The resulting redefinition of the baseline emission rate effectively prevented issuance of allowances for reductions in the emission rate achieved between 1985 and 1989–90, as well as for any 1995–99 reductions otherwise required.
6. Substitution-by-contract provisions were developed to facilitate participation by Phase II units operated by utilities without Table A units, but they provide for substantially lower allowance allocations and have been little utilized.
7. Boilers of coal-fired units are classified in either Group 1 or Group 2. Group 1 includes tangentially fired boilers and dry-bottom, wall-fired boilers other than units applying cell-burner technology. Group 2 includes wet-bottom, wall-fired boilers; cyclone boilers; boilers applying cell-burner technologies; vertically fired boilers; arch-fired boilers; and any other type of utility boiler (e.g., fluidized-bed or stoker boilers) that is not a Group 1 boiler.

all years of Phase I (even if it subsequently exits the SO_2 voluntary compliance program), it qualifies for "NO_x grandfathering."[8] Grandfathered units are *permanently* exempted from the more stringent Phase II NO_x limits. Thus, the NO_x emission-rate limit is a consideration for any Group 1 boiler that enters the voluntary program, both as an inducement for those qualifying for the NO_x grandfathering provision and as a potential additional cost for those that did not become substitution units in 1995.

Evidence on Voluntary Compliance

The existence of an adverse-selection problem in Phase I is strongly suggested by Table 8.1, which compares aggregate heat input and SO_2 emissions for units that entered the voluntary compliance program and for units that did not do so. The first column of this table provides data for Table A units, for reference. The middle column covers the 138 units that remained in the voluntary compliance program for all of the first three years of Phase I. The last column provides data for units that were eligible to become substitution units but did not do so.[9] Units that participated in the voluntary compliance program for one or two years are not included in either of these last two columns in order to exhibit contrasting trends in heat input and SO_2 emissions.

The most notable comparison concerns heat-input trends. By 1993, heat input at what were to become substitution units had fallen by about 9% relative to average 1985–87 heat input, while it had remained about the same for Table A units and risen by 24% for eligible units that did not become substitution units. Since then, heat input at substitution units has risen apace with Table A units (both were 15% above 1993 levels in 1997), and heat input at the eligible, nonparticipating units has risen even more (24%). Thus, among the non-Table A units that were eligible to become substitution

8. The NO_x grandfathering provision is distinct from the "early-election" provision of the NO_x program, which operates independently of the SO_2 program. The early-election provision permits any Phase II unit with a Group 1 boiler to defer the applicability of the Phase II NO_x limit until 2008 by electing to meet the Phase I NO_x rate limitation beginning in 1997.
9. The entire universe of eligible units – those that share a common owner or operator with a Table A unit – includes 620 units that can be identified with parent utilities and holding companies listed in Pechan (1995), FERC Form 423, and the *U.S. Electric Utility Industry Directory*. See Montero (1999) for more details.

Table 8.1. *Statistics of Table A, substitution, and eligible units for selected years*

Variable	Table A units	Substitution units[a]	Other eligible units[b]
No. of units	263	138	421
Total capacity (MW)	88,007	28,845	92,666
No. of coal-fired units	257	113	286
No. of units with NSPS scrubbers (before '90)	1	15	34
No. of units with Title IV scrubbers	26	0	0
Total baseline 1985–87 ($\times 10^{12}$ Btu)[c]	4,363	1,156	3,035
Total heat input 1990 ($\times 10^{12}$ Btu)	4,391	1,195	3,446
Total heat input 1993 ($\times 10^{12}$ Btu)	4,395	1,057	3,749
Total heat input 1995 ($\times 10^{12}$ Btu)	4,707	1,121	4,404
Total heat input 1996 ($\times 10^{12}$ Btu)	4,897	1,130	4,568
Total heat input 1997 ($\times 10^{12}$ Btu)	5,048	1,213	4,667
Total SO_2 emissions 1985 ($\times 10^3$ ton)	9,302	994	1,967
Total SO_2 emissions 1990 ($\times 10^3$ ton)	8,683	899	2,288
Total SO_2 emissions 1993 ($\times 10^3$ ton)	7,579	655	2,409
Total SO_2 emissions 1995 ($\times 10^3$ ton)	4,445	503	2,753
Total SO_2 emissions 1996 ($\times 10^3$ ton)	4,759	507	2,851
Total SO_2 emissions 1997 ($\times 10^3$ ton)	4,769	543	2,993
Average SO_2 rate 1985 (#/mmBtu)	4.24	2.44	1.24
Average SO_2 rate 1990 (#/mmBtu)	3.76	2.13	1.12
Average SO_2 rate 1993 (#/mmBtu)	3.30	1.76	1.06
Average SO_2 rate 1995 (#/mmBtu)	2.10	1.19	1.02
Average SO_2 rate 1996 (#/mmBtu)	2.14	1.10	1.03
Average SO_2 rate 1997 (#/mmBtu)	2.10	1.07	1.07
Total 1995 allowances ($\times 10^3$)[d]	7,215	959	—
Total 1996 allowances ($\times 10^3$)	6,888	950	—
Total 1997 allowances ($\times 10^3$)	5,822	895	—

[a]Substitution units in 1995, 1996, and 1997.
[b]Eligible units that never have opted in.
[c]Average fuel use during the baseline period, 1985–87.
[d]Does not include auction allowances in any year.
Sources: Derived from Pechan (1995) and EPA (1996b, 1997, 1998).
Forthcoming in *Journal of Political Economy*.

units, those that did so on average experienced decreased utilization as Phase I approached, while utilization of the others rose, on average.

Emission rates exhibit the same pattern. In 1993, on the eve of Phase I, the heat-input-weighted average emission rate among units that became substitution units was 28% below what it had been in

1985. Table A units were 22% below, while other eligible units were 15% below the respective 1985 levels. Since 1993, the average emission rate has been reduced comparably for Table A and substitution units, 36% and 39%, respectively, while the average rate for eligible units has remained about the same.

As a result of changes in both utilization and emission rates before Phase I, total SO_2 emissions from the 138 substitution units were 34% below their historic levels in 1993. In comparison, 1993 SO_2 emissions from Table A units were 19% below historic levels, and emissions for the other eligible units were 22% *above* historic levels. These aggregate data indicate that substitution units were those eligible units that, because of trends in heat input or pre-Phase I changes in emission rates, had reduced emissions in advance of Phase I.

In fact, as Table 8.1 shows, the substitution units in aggregate were issued allowances (based on historical data) that were above 1993 emissions and, except for 1997, above even 1990 emissions. (In contrast, the allowance issuance to Table A units, which was fixed in the statute, was always lower than the 1993 level, even in 1995 when the largest number of bonus allowances was issued.) Despite strong evidence that allowances above counterfactual emissions – excess allowances – were issued, Table 8.1 also indicates that substitution units reduced emissions below 1993 levels once they became subject to Phase I. Thus, both elements of the dilemma that must be faced in designing voluntary compliance programs – excess allowances and lower-cost abatement – appear to exist in Phase I. A more rigorous econometric analysis of the reasons for opting in is in order, and we describe such an analysis in the next section.

THE DECISION TO VOLUNTEER

At least three economic reasons why a Phase II unit might choose to opt into Phase I can be identified from the discussion thus far: to claim excess allowances, to take advantage of low marginal control costs (i.e., below allowance prices), and to qualify for NO_x grandfathering. Because the NO_x grandfathering provision applies only to substitution units in 1995, the analysis focuses on that year. A discrete choice econometric model is employed to disentangle the relative importance of these three factors in a decision to opt in, and to see whether these and other "economic" variables successfully explain electric utilities' behavioral responses to the voluntary compliance program.

Model Specification

The discrete dependent variable, *SUB*, is 1 if the corresponding unit was designated a substitution unit in 1995, and 0 otherwise. We assume that a unit is volunteered if and only if the corresponding net benefit, which we cannot observe directly, is positive. This leads to the following basic model:

$$SUB = 1 \qquad \text{if } SUB^* > 0, \text{ and}$$
$$SUB = 0 \qquad \text{if } SUB^* \leq 0,$$

where *SUB** is an index function that can be written as

$$SUB^* = a_0 + \Sigma a_k x_k + u \tag{8.1}$$

and x_k represents the k unit's characteristics that affect the decision to opt in. The error term, u, has a standard logistic distribution. The model predicts that an eligible unit will be a substitution unit if the index function $a_0 + \Sigma a_k x_k$ is greater than 0 or if $\Lambda(SUB^*) > 0.5$, where $\Lambda(\cdot)$ is the logistic cumulative distribution function.

The k variables in the index function are chosen to capture the benefits and costs of opting an eligible Phase II unit into Phase I. The variable *EXALLOW* captures the benefits associated with excess allowances. It is the difference between the allowance allocation and counterfactual emissions for the year (i.e., the unit's emissions if it had not opted in), normalized by the unit's generating capacity. Since substitution units are allowed to withdraw from Phase I until the last month of the year, *EXALLOW* can be considered a good approximation of operators' expected excess allowances. Allowance allocations were determined by using either the actual allowance allocation for eligible units that did opt in or the allowances that would have been issued according to the previously described final allocation rules for eligible units that did not opt in.

For units that did not opt in, counterfactual emissions as defined above are equal to actual emissions. For substitution units, counterfactual emissions in any particular year are estimated using three approaches. The first two are the counterfactuals already explained in Chapter 5: the "econometrically estimated counterfactual" and the "simple counterfactual." The third is the "special counterfactual" described in Montero (1999), which is based on separate estimation of counterfactual heat inputs and emission rates using models focusing on the voluntary compliance program.[10] To simplify the exposition, this section presents results only from the special counterfactual; Montero (1998a) shows that results based on the first two counterfactuals are quite similar to those based on the special counterfactual.

When a Phase I unit (which may or may not be a Table A unit) and a Phase II unit share a common stack, either the Phase II unit must be designated as a substitution unit or an additional continuous emissions monitoring (CEM) system must be installed. In part because the latter option is expensive, all twelve Phase II units sharing stacks with Table A units were opted in as substitution units in 1995. However, some eligible Phase II units sharing a common stack with a Phase I substitution unit did not opt in. To take account of this situation, we included an additional variable, *COMSTACK*. This variable takes on the value of 0 for single-stack units. For eligible units sharing a stack, *COMSTACK* is defined as the aggregate excess allowances at the common-stack level divided by aggregate generating capacity at the common-stack level.[11] The basic argument is that a unit for which *EXALLOW* is negative would nonetheless participate if *COMSTACK* is sufficiently positive that the additional monitoring costs exceed the allowance costs associated with the negative *EXALLOW*. We expect the coefficient of *COMSTACK* to be positive.

Capturing the effects of unit-specific SO_2 control costs in Equation (8.1) is difficult because we lack good estimates of these costs for most eligible units. We follow two approaches. First, we include variables that measure both the unit's emission rate in 1993 (*RTE93*) and its distance from the Powder River Basin (*DPRB*). We would expect

10. Montero (1999) finds that designation as a substitution unit did not affect the heat input, so actual heat input is used to calculate the special counterfactual. Designation as a substitution unit did significantly affect the emission rate, however, as did location in the same plant as a Table A unit and several other variables (appropriately) excluded from the econometrically estimated counterfactual. On balance, the special counterfactual shows some additional abatement unrelated to Title IV by substitution units that is not picked up by the other two counterfactuals.
11. For eligible units sharing a common stack with a Table A unit, only data from eligible units were used to compute *COMSTACK*.

lower compliance costs for units with higher emission rates, since the probability of finding nearby suppliers of lower-sulfur coals is higher, and control technology options are greater. Accordingly, the coefficient of *RTE93* is expected to be positive. We also believe that the closer a unit is to the PRB (or any other western coals), the lower will be its cost of compliance. Note that including *RTE93* and *DPRB* simultaneously controls for those units near the Powder River Basin that had already switched to low-sulfur coal for economic reasons and thus have low initial emission rates. It would generally be prohibitively expensive for such units to make further reductions. Second, we restrict attention to a subsample of coal-fired units for which we can employ a (marginal) cost variable for coal switching and cleaning, *MGCOST*. This variable is based on EPA's (1991) average control cost estimates.[12]

For both approaches, a variable to control for coal-contract constraints is included. A contract-constrained unit has fewer possibilities for coal switching, with consequently higher control costs and fewer opportunities to opt in. Based on data from FERC Form 423, the dummy variable *CONTRACT* is formed, equal to the ratio of the amount of coal delivered under contract to the total coal deliveries to the unit's power plant in 1993 or 1995, whichever is lower. The coefficient of *CONTRACT* should be negative. Finally, a dummy variable, *SCRUB*, serves as a proxy for further control costs of units with New Source Performance Standard (NSPS) scrubbers.

To estimate the effects of the NO_x grandfathering provision, it is important to note that only coal-fired units with Group 1 boilers are required to adhere to NO_x emission-control requirements during Phase I.[13] Consequently, we first create the dummy *GROUP1*, equal to 1 for eligible units with Group 1 boilers only, and equal to 0 otherwise. To estimate the *costs* of meeting Phase I NO_x control requirements that would be incurred by eligible units that opt in, we use the variable *NOXPH1*: the difference between the unit's 1993 NO_x emission rate and the Phase I required rate (restricted to be nonnegative),

---

12. Fixed costs of fuel switching are generally minimal, so average and marginal abatement costs are almost the same and equal to the sulfur premium.

13. The importance of NO_x grandfathering is suggested by the fact that, of the 124 substitution units in 1995 with Group 1 boilers, 104 filed applications to opt in before January 1, 1995, and were thus eligible for NO_x grandfathering. The other 20 units filed during 1995, when, presumably, their total emissions for that year could be more accurately forecast.

multiplied by *GROUP1*. To estimate potential *benefits* from NO_x grandfathering, however, we need a proxy for the costs of compliance with NO_x requirements in Phase II. *GROUP1* contains information on these costs, as does *MCNOXG1*, which is the estimated marginal cost of compliance with NO_x requirements in Phase II for Group 1 boilers. This variable was created only for those units about which EPA (1991) supplies control-cost data. In addition, to test whether NO_x grandfathering becomes important only if marginal control costs are high, we use a dummy variable, *MCNOXHG*, which is equal to 1 if and only if estimated marginal control costs are above the mean *MCNOXG1* – \$711/ton of NO_x. The coefficients of *GROUP1*, *MCNOXG1*, and *MCNOXHG* are expected to be positive.

Depending on relations between allowance prices and fuel costs, there may be incentives ex post to shift generation to or away from Phase I-affected units. The larger the fraction of capacity that is Phase I affected, the greater the loss in dispatch flexibility from volunteering additional units for Phase I regulation. Thus, the more of a plant's capacity that is in Table A units, the less likely the plant would be to bring an eligible unit into Phase I, ceteris paribus. To capture this potential loss in generation flexibility at the plant level if an eligible unit is opted in, we include *GENCOST*, calculated as the ratio between total capacity of the Table A units in an eligible unit's plant and total plant capacity. Based on the argument above, its coefficient should be negative.[14]

Finally, some electric utility staff have told us that uncertainty about the actual utilization level of generating units can be an important factor in a decision to bring an eligible unit into Phase I.[15] If a unit's utilization level proves to be greater than that projected at the time the unit was opted in, its operator will need additional allowances to cover the extra emissions. If the operator instead withdraws the unit from the voluntary compliance program at the end of the year, utility regulators generally impose administrative costs. Thus, the greater the uncertainty about future utilization, the less likely a unit will be opted in. Since uncertainty is higher for cycling and peaking units, and these tend to be relatively small compared to base-load units, we measure uncertainty by *UNCERT*: the inverse

---

14. Note that *GENCOST* must be less than 1.0, since by definition no eligible unit can be in a plant consisting entirely of Table A units.
15. Telephone interviews with various electric utilities' operators (August 1996).

Table 8.2. *Summary statistics for "eligible" and "reduced" samples for 1995*

Variable	Eligible sample (620)				Reduced sample (316)			
	Mean	Std. dev.	Min	Max	Mean	Std. dev.	Min	Max
SUB	0.29	0.46	0.00	1.00	0.36	0.48	0.00	1.00
EXALLOW	−0.39	37.32	−383.94	234.83	0.04	37.50	−123.15	234.83
COMSTACK	−1.24	14.30	−76.35	151.41	−2.78	18.41	−76.35	151.41
RTE93	1.27	1.19	0.00	5.70	1.70	1.26	0.00	5.70
DPRB ($\times 10^3$)	1.17	0.32	0.00	1.73	1.15	0.26	0.55	1.73
MGCOST					883.43	707.06	188.00	5,000.00
SCRUB	0.10	0.29	0.00	1.00	0.12	0.33	0.00	1.00
CONTRACT	0.44	0.37	0.00	1.00	0.56	0.33	0.00	1.00
GROUP1	0.56	0.50	0.00	1.00	0.66	0.47	0.00	1.00
MCNOXG1					711.44	2,011.52	0.00	25,580.80
MCNOXHG					0.24	0.43	0.00	1.00
NOXPH1	0.15	0.17	0.00	1.05	0.17	0.16	0.00	0.78
GENCOST	0.10	0.22	0.00	0.89	0.12	0.23	0.00	0.89
UNCERT	13.10	13.83	0.77	100.00	9.25	9.41	0.77	66.67

Sources: Derived from Pechan (1995) and EPA (1996b, 1997, 1998).
Forthcoming in *Journal of Political Economy*.

of each unit's installed generating capacity multiplied by a scalar such that *UNCERT* is 100.0 for the smallest unit in the sample. The coefficient of *UNCERT* is expected to be negative.

Econometric Results

As noted above, two samples are used because EPA's (1991) estimates of SO_2 and NO_x control costs for Group 1 boilers cover only a subset of eligible units. The first sample includes all 620 eligible units ("eligible sample"); the second sample includes only the 316 eligible coal-fired units for which cost data are available ("reduced sample"). Table 8.2 displays the summary statistics for the two samples.

Table 8.3 shows the maximum likelihood (ML) logit estimates of the coefficients for each variable for the two samples. The estimating results show that almost all relevant coefficients differ significantly from zero and have the expected signs. Furthermore, the results are quite consistent across alternative samples and model specifications.

The coefficient estimates for *EXALLOW* and *COMSTACK*, which are intended to capture the effects of excess allowances, are positive

Table 8.3. *ML logit estimates for participation in the substitution provision equation*

Variable	Model 1	Model 2	Model 3	Model 4
EXALLOW	0.0617	0.0745	0.0894	0.0940
	(7.841)	(6.016)	(6.411)	(6.346)
COMSTACK	0.1111	0.1325	0.1282	0.1334
	(4.136)	(3.530)	(3.568)	(3.642)
RTE93	0.7378		1.2666	1.2980
	(5.273)		(4.922)	(4.813)
DPRB (x 10^3)	−1.4003		−0.5837	−0.3122
	(3.581)		(0.855)	(0.431)
MGCOST (x 10^3)		0.2639		
		(1.080)		
SCRUB	0.9812	0.5940	1.7153	1.5228
	(2.670)	(1.251)	(3.035)	(2.591)
CONTRACT	−0.6534	0.6232	−0.3858	−0.4692
	(1.847)	(1.166)	(0.649)	(0.778)
GROUP1	0.6845			
	(1.800)			
MCNOXG1 (x 10^3)		0.2932	0.2670	
		(2.386)	(2.249)	
MCNOXHG				1.8117
				(3.868)
NOXPH1	−1.9444	2.5088	1.8168	0.6755
	(1.820)	(2.206)	(1.493)	(0.515)
GENCOST	−0.8595	−1.8795	−3.4880	−4.1301
	(1.310)	(2.101)	(3.020)	(3.354)
UNCERT	−0.0793	−0.0842	−0.1611	−0.1508
	(5.007)	(2.775)	(3.815)	(3.706)
Constant	0.7025	−1.0956	−0.9101	−1.3321
	(1.219)	(2.092)	(0.904)	(1.272)

Table 8.3. *(cont.)*

Variable	Model 1	Model 2	Model 3	Model 4
Log-likelihood	−234.90	−115.20	−99.57	−94.93
Correctly classified (%)	84.35	85.13	87.66	88.92
Test statistics (χ^2)				
H_0: (i)	92.85(2)	57.18(2)	56.69(2)	54.29(2)
H_0: (ii)	35.08(4)	3.97(3)	26.04(4)	24.66(4)
H_0: (iii)	3.84(2)	13.35(2)	8.25(2)	17.91(2)
No. Observations	620	316	316	316

Notes: Asymptotic normal test statistics are in parentheses; 10%/5%/1% critical levels are 1.645/1.960/2.576. The three null hypotheses for which χ^2 statistics are presented are for (i) excess allowances, (ii) low control costs, and (iii) NO_x grandfathering. Figures in parentheses give degrees of freedom for each statistic. The corresponding 10%/5%/1% critical levels are as follows: (2) 5.99/7.38/10.60, (3) 7.82/9.35/12.84, and (4) 9.49/11.14/14.86.
Forthcoming in *Journal of Political Economy*.

and significantly different from zero at the 99% level in all cases. The coefficient estimates for the variables included to control for SO_2 marginal control cost (*RTE93, DPRB, MGCOST, SCRUB,* and *CONTRACT*) are less consistent, but still significant in most cases. In Model 1, all these coefficients have the expected signs and are highly significant except for *CONTRACT*, which differs significantly from zero only at the 90% level. In Model 2, however, which employs EPA's control-cost estimates and is fitted to the reduced sample, these coefficients tend to be insignificant and sometimes have the opposite sign from Model 1. In fact, *MGCOST* proved to be a poor proxy for actual marginal costs, mainly because changes in coal markets made 1990 estimates unreliable indicators of the situation in 1995. Models 3 and 4 replaced *MGCOST* with its proxies *RTE93* and *DPRB*, and produced better results. Although not significant, *CONTRACT* and *DPRB* at least have the expected signs in these models.

The variables *MCNOXG1* and *MCNOXHG*, intended to measure the benefits of NO_x grandfathering, perform well in the reduced sample in Models 2, 3, and 4. (*GROUP1* does less well in Model 1, as one would expect.) The costs of early compliance with NO_x regulations, on the other hand, are either generally unimportant to the opt-in decision, or are not well captured by *NOXPH1*. Only for Model 1 does the *NOXPH1* coefficient have the expected sign, and it is significant at only the 90% level.

Coefficients intended to capture the effects of loss in generation flexibility (*GENCOST*) and uncertainty about utilization (*UNCERT*) always have the expected sign. And, except for *GENCOST* in Model 1, they are significant at below the 5% level.

The goodness of fit of our logit models can be evaluated by computing the number of eligible units whose status is successfully predicted. The predicted value for *SUB* takes the value of 1 if $P(SUB^* > 0) = \Lambda(\hat{SUB}) > 0.5$, and 0 otherwise. As shown in Table 8.3, the rate of correct classifications varies between 84% and 89% for the different models. Electric utilities' response to Title IV's voluntary compliance program can thus be well explained using economic variables, suggesting at least that administrative requirements and other transaction costs were relatively unimportant.

Competing Reasons for Opting In

In order to estimate the importance of various factors affecting the decision to opt in, we first tested null hypotheses for group coefficients related to (i) excess allowances, (ii) low control costs, and (iii) NO$_x$ grandfathering, separately. For all three models, the first of these is (i) $a_{EXALLOW} = a_{COMSTACK} = 0$. In Models 1, 3, and 4, the second null hypothesis is (ii) $a_{RTE93} = a_{DPRB} = a_{CONTRACT} = a_{SCRUB} = 0$, while in Model 2 it is (ii) $a_{MGCOST} = a_{CONTRACT} = a_{SCRUB} = 0$. The NO$_x$ grandfathering null hypotheses are as follows: for Model 1, (iii) $a_{GROUP1} = a_{NOXPH1} = 0$; for Models 2 and 3, (iii) $a_{MCNOXG1} = a_{NOXPH1} = 0$; and for Model 4, (iii) $a_{MCNOXHG} = a_{NOXPH1} = 0$. The χ^2 statistics at the bottom of Table 8.3 indicate that all three hypotheses are rejected at well beyond the 1% level except for (iii) for Model 1 and (ii) for Model 2. These χ^2 statistics indicate that variables related to all three factors (i.e., excess allowances, low SO$_2$ abatement costs, and NO$_x$ grandfathering) are important in the decision to bring an eligible Phase II unit into Phase I, but the statistics are silent about the relative importance of these factors in producing the substantial participation observed.

Following Arora and Cason (1996), we developed a more intuitive approach to interpret parameter estimates. Based on results for

Table 8.4. *Estimated impacts of statistically significant coefficients on opting-in probability*

Row	Example eligible unit (in "reduced" sample) with:	Estimated participation probability (%)	Increase (%)
1	All characteristics at sample means	22	—
2	Sample means +1 std. dev. *EXALLOW*	90	314
3	Sample means +1 std. dev. *COMSTACK*	77	250
4	Sample means +1 std. dev. ea. *EXALLOW* and *COMSTACK*	99	354
5	Sample means +1 std. dev. *RTE93*	59	170
6	Sample means +1 std. dev. *SCRUB*	31	44
7	Sample means +1 std. dev. ea. *RTE93* and *SCRUB*	70	221
8	Sample means +1 std. dev. *MCNOXHG*	38	73
9	Sample means −1 std. dev. *GENCOST*	42	94
10	Sample means −1 std. dev. *UNCERT*	54	145

Forthcoming in *Journal of Political Economy*.

Model 4, Table 8.4 shows the relative impact of different factors on the probability of an eligible unit's opting in. Each row shows the increase in the predicted opt-in probability caused by increasing the indicated explanatory variable or variables by one standard deviation. The first row indicates that when all variables are at their sample mean values, Model 4 predicts a unit's probability of opting in to be 22%, which is below the actual participation rate for the reduced sample (114/316 = 0.36) and for the eligible sample (182/620 = 0.29). The second row indicates that if a unit's excess allowance measure, *EXALLOW*, increases by one standard deviation from its sample mean, with all other variables remaining at their sample mean values, the probability that the unit will opt in increases from 22% to 90%. *COMSTACK* has also a great impact, increasing the opting-in probability to 77%, as shown by row 3. The enormous impact of *EXALLOW* and *COMSTACK* combined is shown in row 4.

As shown in rows 5, 6, and 7, SO_2 control-cost considerations also appear to be important. Row 8 suggests, though, that the benefits of NO_x grandfathering are relatively less important. It is important to recognize, however, that these estimates relate to the sample as a whole. A number of units with large and negative *EXALLOW* opted in during 1995 to benefit from NO_x grandfathering. Because a substitution unit need only be under Phase I in 1995 to benefit from NO_x grandfathering, it is not surprising that almost all substitution units in this situation dropped from Phase I in 1996.

EFFECTS ON THE SO$_2$ MARKET

The foregoing analysis reveals the usual mixture of motives. A comparison of rows 2, 5, and 8 in Table 8.4 indicates that having counterfactual emissions below the allowance allocation appears to be the most influential factor explaining units' high participation in the voluntary compliance program.[16] Thus, there is ample evidence that adverse selection was important. At the same time, the results above indicate that lower SO$_2$ control costs were also a motivating factor, especially for units with high emission rates and units already equipped with scrubbers. A critical issue in assessing this aspect of Title IV is the net effect of these two factors, both of which will likely be present in any voluntary compliance program.

The balance between these two factors in the first three years of Phase I depends on something that can only be estimated: counterfactual emissions. Table 8.5 presents the three different counterfactual estimates discussed in the preceding section and the balances each implies between these two factors.

For every year, the difference between allowance allocations and actual emissions is known exactly. Depending on the year, from 420,000 to 554,000 allowances issued to substitution units were either banked or used at other units during the year. This difference can always be split between excess allowances (allowance allocation minus counterfactual emissions) and emission reductions (counterfactual emissions minus actual emissions). Unfortunately, our estimates of counterfactual emissions from substitution units vary by as much as 237,000 tons. Accordingly, the share of the difference between allowance allocations and emissions attributed to excess allowances in Table 8.5 varies from 44% to 100%.

Based on the numbers from the first two counterfactuals in Table 8.5, the effect of the voluntary compliance program on the SO$_2$ market seems to be small. For example, if we focus on the simple counterfactual, at the end of the first year of compliance, emission reductions from substitution units represented 5% of the total emission reduction observed in 1995. This suggests a measurable but small reduction in abatement costs. This same counterfactual implies that

---

16. The same conclusion can be drawn from the other three models in Table 8.3, and for years 1996 and 1997.

Table 8.5. *Accounting for allowances from the voluntary compliance program*

	1995	1996	1997
Number of units	182	161[a]	153[a]
Total capacity (MW^e)	41,643	37,179	32,815
Heat input (million mmBtu)	1,932	1,487	1,323
Allowances (thousands)	1,329	1,185	1,040
SO$_2$ emissions (thousands of tons)	847	631	620
Allowances not used in year (thousands)	482	554	420
Counterfactual estimates			
Econometrically estimated counterfactual	1,112	783	910
Simple counterfactual	1,088	854	849
Special counterfactual	921	707	620
Excess allowances and allowances from emission reductions			
Econometrically estimated counterfactual			
Excess allowances	217 (45%)	325 (59%)	183 (44%)
Allowances for emission reductions	265 (55%)	229 (41%)	237 (56%)
Simple counterfactual			
Excess allowances	241 (50%)	331 (60%)	191 (45%)
Allowances for emission reductions	241 (50%)	223 (40%)	229 (55%)
Special counterfactual			
Excess allowances	408 (85%)	478 (86%)	420 (100%)
Allowances for emission reductions	74 (15%)	76 (14%)	0 (0%)

[a]Excludes seven units under industrial opt-in provision

Sources: Derived from Pechan (1995), EPA (1996b, 1997, 1998), and Appendix to this book.

excess allowances represented about 6% of the total allowances banked at the end of 1995. Even in the likely event that excess allowances were not anticipated, this estimate implies that they represented only 12% of the almost 1.7 million tons of unanticipated reduction from Table A units by 1993 (see Chapter 4). The picture implied by the simple and econometrically estimated counterfactuals is accordingly one of small impact on both control costs (through low-cost emission reductions) and aggregate emissions (through excess allowances).

The much larger excess allowance estimates for the special counterfactual imply a more substantial increase in aggregate emissions,
however, and essentially no offsetting reduction in control costs. At
this stage in our work, we cannot choose confidently between these
two pictures, though we can rule out any notion that substantial
savings in control costs were obtained with only a tiny effect on
aggregate emissions. Multiplying the estimates of total excess
allowances in Table 8.5 by 5/3 as a rough and ready way to scale up
to all of Phase I, these estimates imply increases in the allowance
bank at the end of Phase I (and thus in total SO_2 emissions over time)
of 1.2–2.2 million tons.

The voluntary compliance program would in general be expected
to have some depressing effect on allowance prices. Lower reduction
costs in at least some substitution units shift the aggregate marginal
abatement cost curve downward, and excess allowances, anticipated
or not, loosen Title IV's constraint on SO_2 emissions. A rough comparison of the numbers in Table 8.5 with observed transactions
volumes (Chapter 7) and with emission reductions and banking from
Table A units (Chapters 5 and 6) suggests that the effect on prices
should be small. In a simulation exercise, Montero and Ellerman
(1998) confirm this suggestion.

IMPLICATIONS FOR PROGRAM DESIGN

The fact that excess allowances were handed out under Title IV and
emissions were thereby increased raises interesting issues about how
to design phased emission-trading programs with voluntary opt-in
possibilities for nonaffected sources. Like many other regulatory
design problems, this one is afflicted by asymmetric information: the
regulator has less information on individual sources' counterfactual
emissions and control costs than do the owners and operators of
those sources.

In a world with perfect information and no transaction costs, a
regulator would issue allowances to potential opt-in sources (eligible
sources under Title IV) equal to their counterfactual emissions in
each period (Montero, 2000). In practice, however, the regulator
cannot estimate counterfactual emissions precisely and yet must
establish a permit allocation rule in advance that cannot be changed

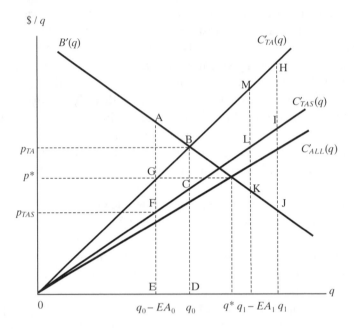

Figure 8.1. Costs and benefits from voluntary compliance.

easily even if new information arrives. Thus, in deciding how to set the allocation rules for affected and opt-in sources, the regulator faces the classical trade-off in regulatory economics between production efficiency and information rent extraction (Laffont and Tirole, 1993). For instance, a too-restrictive allocation rule for opt-in sources may inefficiently leave too many low-cost sources outside the program.

The trade-off between production efficiency and information rent extraction is illustrated in the one-period model of Figure 8.1, depicting the costs and benefits of voluntary compliance. The horizontal axis indicates the amount q by which total emissions are reduced below their counterfactual level, $B'(q)$ represents the marginal social benefit of emission reduction, and $C'_{TA}(q)$ represents the marginal control cost of emission reduction from emission sources that must be covered by the program – Table A units, for short. As usual, we assume that $B'(q) > 0$, $B''(q) < 0$, $C'(q) > 0$, $C''(q) > 0$, $B'(0) > C'(0)$, and $B'(q) < C'(q)$, for q sufficiently large.

Suppose that q_0 is the emission-reduction target chosen by the authority to be imposed upon Table A units.[17] Aggregate control costs would be the area under $C'_{TA}(q)$ from 0 to q_0, and the equilibrium allowance price would be p_{TA}. If the regulator now implements a voluntary opt-in provision covering an additional set of sources – substitution units, for short – and establishes an opt-in allowance-allocation rule for these units equal to historic emissions, the new marginal control-cost curve shifts downward due to the inclusion of some units with low marginal control costs. Let $C'_{TAS}(q)$ be the aggregate marginal control costs from Table A and substitution units. If individual counterfactual emissions from substitution units have not changed from their historic levels, and the reduction target q_0 remains the same, aggregate control costs reduce to the area under $C'_{TAS}(q)$ from 0 to q_0, and savings from the voluntary opt-in provision are given by $A(OBC)$, where $A(\cdot)$ denotes area.

Realistically, however, some substitution units will have reduced their counterfactual emissions below historic levels so that total allowances distributed to substitution units will be above total counterfactual emissions by some amount EA_0 of excess allowances. This reduces the required emission reduction from q_0 to $q_0 - EA_0$. The adverse-selection effect is represented by this reduction in the original reduction target. Aggregate control costs are now the area under $C'_{TAS}(q)$, from 0 to $q_0 - EA_0$, and the equilibrium allowance price is p_{TAS}. While savings from lower-cost reductions are given by $A(OGF)$, savings from avoided reductions are given by $A(EGBD)$. On the other hand, emissions will be larger than otherwise by an amount equal to EA_0. The social cost of additional emissions is given by the area under $B'(q)$ from $q_0 - EA_0$ to q_0, which is $A(EABD)$.

The total savings or net benefits associated with this illustrative voluntary opt-in program are given by $A(OGF) - A(GAB)$, which can be positive or negative, depending on the slope of the $B'(q)$ and $C'(q)$ curves, how much reduction substitution between affected and opt-in sources is economically available (i.e., the distance between C'_{TA} and C'_{ALL}), and where the original reduction target is located. As we raise the initial reduction target, marginal costs increase while marginal benefits decrease, along with the negative effect of excess allowances.

17. Note that when reductions are imposed only upon Table A units, the optimum reduction solves $B'(q) = C'_{TA}(q)$.

For instance, if the reduction target is raised to q_1, the excess allowances produced by adverse selection may actually increase welfare. For simplicity, let us say that in Figure 8.1, $C'_{TAS}(q)$ is still the aggregate marginal control costs from Table A units and substitution units when q_1 is the original reduction target and the allowance allocation rule is, again, historic emissions.[18] By the reasoning above, it is not difficult to see that, given the new reduction level $q_1 - EA_1$ (where EA_1 is the new level of excess allowances), total benefits from the voluntary opt-in program are equal to $A(OML) + A(MHJK)$, which is obviously positive.

This analysis has important instrument design implications. Abstracting from the political economy of how the target for Table A sources is decided, let $C'_{ALL}(q)$ in Figure 8.1 be the marginal cost curve when all relevant units are considered (in this case, Table A and all eligible units). Note that $C'_{TAS}(q)$ can never be below $C'_{ALL}(q)$ because some low-cost non-Table A units may not opt in if the allowance allocation is below their counterfactual emissions. The "first-best" outcome when all sources are considered is the pair p^* and q^*. Now, if the original target imposed upon Table A units is q_1, the opt-in program comes closer to the first-best. This is because the target reduces from q_1 to $q_1 - EA_1$, and the marginal cost shifts downward from $C'_{TA}(q)$ to $C'_{TAS}(q)$. Furthermore, if the target is high enough, the regulator can find an opt-in allocation rule that can restore the first-best, in which case $C'_{TAS}(q)$ is just $C'_{ALL}(q)$.

However, if the reduction target is below the first-best, like q_0, the regulator cannot restore the first-best and faces a general trade-off between shifting the marginal cost downward and reducing emission reductions.[19] This is simply the trade-off between production efficiency and information rent extraction described above. The optimal opt-in rule would exactly offset, at the margin, cost-efficiency gains with the information rent losses (allocation of excess allowances). At this point, the regulator does not want to increase the

---

18. In fact, an increase in the abatement target will lower the C'_{TAS} curve somewhat. A higher target implies higher allowance prices, which in turn make it optimal for more units with low control costs but unfavorable allowance allocations to opt in.
19. This trade-off is present unless all eligible units that would opt in the first-best equilibrium have marginal costs so low relative to expected allowance prices that a stringent allowance-allocation rule (in particular, one that would always provide allowances below counterfactual emissions) would not prevent any of them from opting in. One can hardly expect to encounter this case often in practice.

opt-in allocation rule because the gains in cost efficiency from letting new low-cost nonaffected sources to opt in – $C'_{TAS}(q)$ gets closer to $C'_{ALL}(q)$ – are lower than the losses from having more excess allowances.[20]

ADVERSE SELECTION IS A PROBLEM

The adverse-selection problem cannot be avoided in the design of voluntary features in emission-trading programs. An "opt-in" provision that is attractive to sources with lower control costs is almost certain to involve the allocation of excess allowances (i.e., allowances in excess of the unit's true counterfactual emissions) to sources that are reducing emissions for other reasons.

In setting a rule for allocating allowances to voluntary units, the regulator faces the classic regulatory trade-off between production efficiency (minimization of total control costs) and information rent extraction (reduction of excess allowances). A strict rule for allocating allowances will reduce the number of excess allowances given out, but, by distributing allowances below counterfactual emissions, it will also discourage some sources with low control costs from opting in.

In this chapter, we used the ample response to the substitution provisions in Title IV as a case study to determine the seriousness of the adverse-selection problem. In particular, we examined the reasons for the high participation rate in Phase I and the balance between additional lower-cost abatement and excess allowances.

We found that the total number of allowances distributed to substitution units in each of the first three years of Phase I was above what the total emissions from these units would have been in the absence of the voluntary compliance program. Therefore, this voluntary provision has increased emissions beyond what they otherwise would have been under Title IV. Our rough calculations earlier in this chapter suggest that this increase is somewhere between 1 million and 2 million tons of sulfur dioxide. Though the intent of the volun-

20. This framework can be used to estimate the ex post net benefits from the voluntary compliance program. Doing so requires expanding the one-period model of Figure 8.1 to a multiperiod setting and adding banking. For a numerical exercise along these lines using marginal benefit estimates from unrelated studies (e.g., EPA, 1995b), see Montero (1999).

tary program was to attract units with low control costs, our analysis indicates that the most powerful inducement to participate was an allocation of allowances above counterfactual emissions. Nonetheless, two of our three estimates of counterfactual emissions indicate that the voluntary program also led to appreciable incremental Phase I emission reductions from non-Table A units. It does not appear that the voluntary compliance program has had an appreciable effect on allowance prices.

9 Cost of Compliance with Title IV in Phase I

CONFUSION ABOUT CONTROL COSTS

The initially low price of allowances in Phase I led to some misunderstanding and controversy about the cost of compliance with Title IV. Specifically, the initially low and declining allowance prices were interpreted as an indication that the costs of complying with Title IV were dramatically less than had been anticipated. For instance, prominent representatives of President Clinton's Administration asserted that:

> during the 1990 debates on the Clean Air Act's Acid Rain Program, industry initially projected the costs of an emission allowance ... to be approximately $1,500. ... Today those allowances are selling for less than $100.[1]

and

> We've reduced the emissions that cause acid rain for less than a tenth of the price that was predicted. ...[2]

These statements err both in the interpretation of allowance prices and in the recollection of what earlier studies had estimated Title IV's costs to be. Our interpretation of the low allowance prices early in

---

1. Carol M. Browner, Administrator, U.S. Environmental Protection Agency, in testimony before the U.S. Senate Committee on Environment and Public Works, February 12, 1997.
2. Kathleen McGinty, Chair of the Council on Environmental Quality, Executive Office of the President, from transcript of Climate Brief by Sperling, Terullo et al., U.S. Newswire via Individual Inc., Washington, DC, October 22, 1997.

221

Phase I and of the subsequent doubling of allowance prices in 1998 is provided in Chapter 11. In this chapter we develop an estimate of the cost of complying with Title IV in Phase I and compare it with the predictions of the same cost made in earlier studies of Title IV. The objective in this chapter is not to estimate the cost *savings* attributable to emissions trading when compared to some hypothetical alternative emissions control mechanism. That more difficult analytic task will be addressed in Chapter 10. For now, we seek only to establish what the SO_2 emission reduction in Phase I did cost, as best we can determine it.

Our approach is a bottom-up, cost-engineering one in which we seek to identify the incremental costs incurred by Phase I units in response to the requirements placed on them by Title IV. Our cost estimates are based on data collected from a variety of sources, supplemented and extended by economic reasoning. Data on investment and fuel costs are available in the public domain from trade press reports and industry studies, such as those conducted by EPRI. We also conducted a survey of the operators of affected units in which confidentiality of the reported data was promised.[3] With few exceptions, this survey information confirms data that are available in the public domain. We also rely on interviews with utility and plant compliance managers to resolve ambiguities in the publicly available data and to explain the intricacies of compliance at particular plants.

The cost estimate presented in this chapter is the same as that from our earlier study (Ellerman et al., 1997), and thus it strictly applies to 1995 only. Updating the cost estimates for fuel switching would have required a more detailed analysis of coal deliveries to Phase I power plants in 1996 and 1997 than seemed worth the effort, given the small changes in aggregate abatement observed in these first three years of Phase I. In contrast, the cost data for scrubbing can be easily updated for 1996 and 1997, and we provide updated data as appropriate in the following discussion.

Estimation of the Phase I cost of compliance is greatly simplified by the relatively small number of units that made significant reductions of emissions in Phase I; we were able to confine our attention

---

3. Utilities that responded to our survey operated 130 Phase I units (29% of the 1995 total) with 48,256 MW^c of capacity (37% of 1995 Phase I capacity), which accounted for 43% of aggregate 1995 SO_2 emissions from affected units.

to about half of the Phase I units.[4] As noted in Chapter 5, 20 units account for about 50% of the total Phase I emission reduction, and one-quarter of the Phase I units account for 90% of it. Between the units that did not reduce emissions at all and those that made small reductions indistinguishable from normal variations in emissions levels, half of the Phase I units can be set aside for the purposes of estimating abatement cost. In the end, we examine the costs of reducing emissions at 70 plants with 206 Phase I units that account for 3.89 tons of SO_2 emission reduction in 1995.[5]

As with any estimate of costs, even an ex post one, a number of assumptions must be made. The next section explains the assumptions we made here. Readers less interested in methodology may wish to skip to the subsequent section, which presents our cost estimate and compares it with earlier predictions of Phase I compliance cost. Following that, we discuss the costs of scrubbing and fuel switching in more detail, concentrating on how those costs have changed and how the differing structure of fixed and variable costs between scrubbing and switching have affected abatement in Phase I. The final section of the chapter addresses an important but often neglected component of compliance cost: monitoring.

ASSUMPTIONS AND DATA SOURCES

The cost of compliance is the additional cost incurred to comply with some environmental or other legal requirement. In the case of Title IV, the cost of compliance is the additional cost of generating electricity at Phase I units, and it consists of both capital and operating cost. The capital cost takes the form of an appropriate annual amortization of the initial investment in scrubbers and in equipment required to switch to coals other than those for which a boiler was originally designed. The incremental operating costs are typically the extra cost for lower-sulfur fuels and the operating costs for running scrubbers.

---

4. Some of the excluded units may have incurred costs equal to the value of the additional allowances required to cover emissions above their allowance allocation. This cost is, however, a transfer payment to those that did not incur cost in reducing emissions.
5. Since fuel-delivery data are available only at the plant level, we examine *all* Phase I units at any plant where a Phase I unit reduced emissions by 5,000 tons or more.

Capital Costs

The largest single category of expenditure for complying with Title IV is the $3.5 billion investment in retrofitted scrubbers at twenty-seven Table A units at sixteen electricity-generating plants. Because of the cost and the implications for coal choice, electric utility decisions to retrofit scrubbers have been extensively reported in the trade press and in earlier studies of Phase I compliance strategies, particularly EPRI (1995). In addition, a number of utilities with Phase I scrubbers responded to the MIT/CEEPR questionnaire (1996), and the data they reported for scrubber capital costs were nearly identical to the figures reported for investment in retrofitted scrubbers in EPRI (1995). Accordingly, we rely on the latter source for the initial capital costs for all Phase I scrubbers.

Much less information is available publicly on the capital investment required for fuel switching, probably because it is not nearly as significant as the investment required for scrubbing. As a result, to estimate this component of cost we have placed greater reliance on responses to the MIT/CEEPR questionnaire, on inferences based on changes observed in emissions, and in the sulfur content of fuel deliveries in 1995. The questionnaire responses indicate that the capital cost associated with switching to a subbituminous PRB coal ranges from $15 to $75 per kilowatt of electrical generating capacity (kW^e), depending on the plant, and that the capital cost of a switch to other bituminous coals ranges from zero to $15/$kW^e$. Where a questionnaire response or other sources have provided the initial capital investment for switching at a Phase I unit, that reported figure is used. In all other cases, default values have been adopted based on responses to the MIT/CEEPR questionnaire: $50/$kW^e$ for switching to PRB coal, and $10/$kW^e$ for switching to lower-sulfur bituminous coals. These default values were used for all Phase I units observed switching to PRB coals and for all those switching to lower-sulfur bituminous coals, if the reduction in emission rate was greater than 0.5 lb/mmBtu.

The initial capital investments in scrubbing and switching are amortized using a simple formula that recognizes interest cost, an allowance for depreciation, and inflation:

$$F_t = \left(\frac{K_0}{T} + rK_t\right)(1+i)^t,$$

where F is the annual fixed or capital cost charge for year t, K_0 is the initial investment cost, T is the life of the capital equipment, r is a *real* interest rate, K_t is the nondepreciated investment at the beginning of each year, and i is the inflation rate. All capital is assumed to have a life of twenty years, the real interest rate is assumed to be 6.0%, and the inflation rate 3.0%. Based on this formula, we applied an annual capital charge of 11.33% to the reported or inferred capital investment at the seventy plants that noticeably reduced SO_2 emissions in 1995.[6]

Operating Cost

The operating costs for scrubbing consist of a charge and, in some cases, a credit. The charge is the nonfuel operating expense: limestone or other absorbent material, sludge disposal, and the "parasitic" loss of power to run the scrubber. Based on questionnaire responses and further inquiry, we estimate this cost to be $65 for every ton of SO_2 removed by scrubbing.[7] A credit is recognized where units retrofitted with scrubbers switched in 1995 to a higher-sulfur coal than was used in prior years. This credit reflects the savings in fuel cost that is the mirror image of the additional cost for units switching to lower-sulfur coals. As is the case with the charge for switching to a lower-sulfur coal, this credit depends on the spot-market coal sulfur premium and the observed change in the sulfur content of the coal delivered to the Phase I plant.

For switching, the principal operating cost is the premium for the lower-sulfur fuel that is chosen in response to Title IV. Despite the ready availability of monthly data on the cost of coal delivered to power plants (FERC Form 423), the premiums paid for lower-sulfur coals are not easily observed. Not only do delivered prices include

---

6. The nominal interest rate is often applied in such calculations. However, use of the nominal interest rate when inflation is positive leads to different rental rates for different vintages of capital that provide identical services. This problem is avoided by recognizing that real capital services are properly discounted by the real interest rate, and the payment or rental rate for those services is then inflated. Our 6% real interest rate was obtained by subtracting an estimate of 3.0% for inflation from a nominal weighted average cost of capital for electric utilities in 1995 of 9.0%.

7. The variable cost of scrubbing is usually given as so many mills per kWh, depending on the sulfur content of the coal being scrubbed. The relationship between the mills/kWh charge and sulfur content is approximately linear and slightly declining as sulfur content increases. See Table C-2 in ICF (1989).

transportation costs unrelated to sulfur premiums, but changes in contract terms and conditions further confound the interpretation of delivered prices. Even when contract and transportation factors can be held constant, interyear comparisons can mislead. The sulfur premium is at best 20% of the price of a coal (usually less), and the more significant value of heat content not only varies from year to year, but also has declined secularly.

Fortunately, in most cases it is not necessary to look at delivered prices. Most *bituminous* (non-PRB) coal switching has involved coals from the same coal supply region. Therefore, if mine-mouth prices can be observed in the coal-supplying regions, the confounding influence of transportation charges and contract terms can be avoided. The trade press regularly reports mine-mouth prices for coals of differing sulfur content in all coal-supplying regions, so that the premiums for lower-sulfur coals at the mine can be determined.

For the calculation of these premiums, we relied on spot-market prices reported by *Coal Outlook* since late 1991. Where switching among bituminous coals from the same supplying region was observed, the prevailing sulfur premium in that region was assigned. For 1995 contract deliveries, the average spot-market sulfur premium in 1993 or 1994 was used, since most of the contracts would have been negotiated prior to 1995. For 1995 spot deliveries, the spot-market premium prevailing for the region in 1995 was used. When the switch to lower-sulfur coal also involved a change of supply region, there was no alternative to looking at delivered prices. In those cases, a premium was assigned based on differences observed in the 1995 prices for coals of differing sulfur content delivered to the plant in question and to nearby plants.

Special Considerations for PRB Coal Switching and Coal Contracts

Two special cases of switching deserve further comment. The first involves plants with Phase I units switching to PRB coals. Unlike the case for low-sulfur bituminous coals, the delivered cost of PRB coals to a Phase I plant will always be less than the delivered cost of the higher-sulfur coal being replaced. This is because the conversion of a generating unit initially built for bituminous coals involves a significant investment in upgraded precipitators and coal and ash-handling equipment. The conversion will not be made unless the savings in fuel cost is sufficient to amortize the initial investment in retrofitting cost.[8] The twelve plants containing thirty-one Phase I units switching to or increasing the blend of PRB coal in 1995 were handled on a case-by-case basis. If a unit's observed savings in fuel cost exceeded its annualized capital cost, no compliance cost was recorded; otherwise, the positive difference represented compliance cost. For most units switching to PRB coals in 1995, as for those that switched earlier, no net cost of compliance is apparent.[9] Nevertheless, several plants on the eastern frontier for PRB coals did record positive costs for switching to PRB coals in 1995, and those costs are included in our estimates.

The second special case involves long-term supply contracts. A number of Phase I-affected units have been supplied with coal under twenty-, thirty-, and even forty-year contracts, signed mostly before the 1980s, that linked mine to power plant for the term of the contract.[10] Like all contracts, these are enforceable in the courts, and Title IV provided no grounds to renege on such agreements.[11] The pricing provisions of these contracts reflect energy price expectations at the time of signature, and current contract prices are often higher than the current market prices for new contracts, or for spot coal, of the same quality. The increasing disparity between contract and market prices since the mid-1980s has led not only to considerable dispute – judicial and otherwise – but also to accommodations with respect to Title IV. Specifically, several electric utilities with Phase I units encumbered by such contracts appear to have prevailed upon their suppliers to provide lower-sulfur coal at the contract price. The utility pays no fuel

8. In principle, the same argument applies for switching to a lower-sulfur bituminous coal. However, the additional capital investment is sufficiently small so that the compensating difference in delivered fuel cost lies within the usual variation of delivered fuel prices.

9. Contract expirations or amendments to accommodate Title IV determine the timing for most switches to PRB coals. In some cases, contracts for high-sulfur coal may have been terminated. Any payments associated with termination because of Title IV are not included as part of the cost of compliance with Title IV. Contract law would require damages approximately equal to the present value of the difference between contract and market price if the contract were breached. We assume that suppliers extract such payments or equivalent value from the buyer when contracts are reformed voluntarily.

10. See Joskow (1987) for a discussion of these contracts.

11. However, a number of contracts signed since the mid-1980s specifically included provisions that allowed termination or appropriate modification, if and when proposed acid rain legislation became effective.

premium in these cases, but there is a resource cost to society: the additional cost of supplying the lower-sulfur coal. In effect, the supplier forgoes the coal sulfur premium in exchange for a reduced chance of litigation and an improved prospect of continuing to supply the buyer when the current contract expires. From a societal standpoint, the extra costs incurred by the supplier are resources devoted to compliance, just as surely as if the utility had paid the producer more explicitly. To reflect this cost, the sulfur premium obtained in the supplying region is assigned in those instances where a lower-sulfur coal has been observed being delivered under an existing contract at little or no additional cost.

ESTIMATES OF PHASE I COSTS OF COMPLIANCE

MIT/CEEPR Estimate for 1995

Using these assumptions, Table 9.1 presents the summary components of total annualized compliance cost for the 3.9-million-ton reduction of SO_2 emissions from the counterfactual in 1995. The total cost of abatement was $726 million, and the average total cost of compliance is between $187 and $210 per ton, depending on whether or not one includes reductions made by switching to lower-sulfur fuels that were also lower cost fuels. These reductions are denoted in Table 9.1 as "No-cost PRB." The 425,000 tons of SO_2 emission reductions in this category reflect reductions made at units that switched to a lower-sulfur fuel, usually PRB coal, that was cheaper, on a total cost basis, than the formerly used higher-sulfur coal.[12]

The difference in total annualized cost between scrubbing and switching is significant. On an average total cost basis (including both capital and variable cost), scrubbing has been considerably more expensive than switching: about $265 per ton of SO_2 removed, as compared to $153 per ton for fuel switching. Moreover, while 80% of

12. Almost all of this coal came from the Powder River Basin (PRB); less than 3% originated in Colorado and Utah. Also, 4% of the "No-cost PRB" reduction is due to switching from oil to natural gas. Some of the switching to cheaper PRB coals in 1995 was due to contract expirations; in other cases, however, the contract remained in place but appears to have been modified in response to Title IV, changing the coal source to the same company's PRB mine.

Table 9.1. *1995 cost of compliance with Title IV*

Method	Reduction ($\times 10^3$ tons)	Total cost of compliance (million $)			Average cost ($/ton SO$_2$)
		Fixed	Variable	Total	
Scrubbing	1,754	375.0	89.3	464.4	265
Switching	1,709	57.2	204.1	261.3	153
Subtotal	3,462	432.2	293.5	725.7	210
No-cost PRB	425	0	0	0	0
Total	3,888	432.2	293.5	725.7	187

Sources: Derived from MIT/CEEPR Title IV Questionnaire (1996), FERC Form 423, EPRI (1993 and 1995; hereafter, EPRI93 and EPRI95, respectively), EPA Emissions Monitoring System (ongoing reports), EPA (1996b), Pechan (1995), Fieldston (1994), and Pasha (1993 and 1995).

the total cost of removing a ton of SO$_2$ by scrubbing in 1995 is tied up in the annual capital charge (interest, depreciation, and return on equity investment), almost 80% of the total cost of switching to lower-sulfur coals is variable, virtually all in the form of the premium paid for the lower-sulfur coal. As will be explained later, this difference in the structure of cost between the two abatement techniques is important in understanding the patterns of abatement in Phase I.

Although we make no attempt to produce a comprehensive estimate of abatement costs in 1996 and 1997, it is clear that the total and average costs are slightly higher in both years, for two reasons. First, not all the Phase I scrubbers were on line in 1995 and included in the 1995 cost estimate.[13] Second, because of this, the share of abatement provided by scrubbing has increased. Because scrubbing is relatively more expensive, even though aggregate abatement is relatively unchanged, the average cost could be expected to be slightly higher. The only offsetting factor is the decline in the coal sulfur premium, corresponding to lower allowance prices, and therefore in the average cost of fuel switching.

Another way of illustrating the cost of compliance in 1995 is given by Figure 9.1, in which each unit's contribution to the aggregate 3.9-million-ton reduction in SO$_2$ emissions is arrayed in ascending order by that unit's average total abatement cost. The schedule of

13. Two units each at Petersburg and Henderson came on line in mid-1995, and one unit at Conemaugh and one at Niles came on line in 1996. The total initial investment corresponding to the annual capital charge in Table 9.1 is $3.15 billion. Total investment for all twenty-seven scrubbers is about $3.5 billion and the corresponding annual capital charge is approximately $400 million.

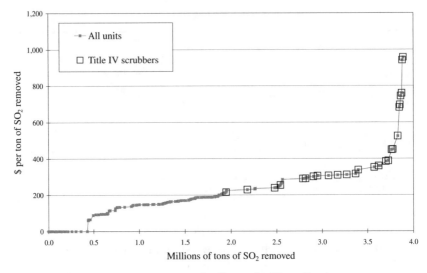

Figure 9.1. Long-run "marginal" cost for Phase I units.

costs in this figure represents a sort of long-run marginal abatement cost curve for the Phase I units, based on ex post costs and utilization rates. Since many generating units are not included in Phase I, this schedule is not the national marginal abatement cost curve. Moreover, many of the costs shown for particular units may not be the least-cost abatement choices at those units, because of either poor decisions ex ante or ex post departures of abatement costs or utilization rates from ex ante expectations. Nevertheless, the curve does show the great disparity in cost among units that are summed together for the aggregates in Table 9.1.

Scrubbed units and switched units are distinguished from one another in Figure 9.1. Although there is some overlap, the scrubbed units are found at the higher end of the curve, whereas the switching units tend to the lower cost end of the curve. The cost of SO_2 abatement for the scrubbed units ranges from a low $189/ton to a high of nearly $800/ton, while the corresponding range for the switched units is from zero to $300/ton. About 17% of the switched units had costs higher than the cheapest scrubbed unit; and thirteen of the twenty-seven scrubbed units had unit abatement costs lower than the highest cost switching unit.

When all costs are considered, it is reasonable to think of the long-run marginal cost for Phase I compliance as falling somewhere between $300 and $350 per ton. The units above $350/ton are few and exceptional, and all installed scrubbers. They constitute a very high-cost tail, and their number drops from nine in 1995 to six in 1997 as a result of improved utilization rates at the corresponding generating units. A few units move in and out of this high-cost category because of annual variations in utilization, but five units have remained in this category for the entire three years because of a combination of relatively high initial capital costs, relatively low utilization, and use of relatively low-sulfur coal.[14]

Estimates of Phase I Costs before Implementation

Meaningful comparisons with earlier estimates of the costs of complying with Phase I are difficult under the best of circumstances. Not only must adjustments be made for inflation, but care must be taken to ensure that the underlying assumptions about economic growth and demand for electricity are comparable. This latter concern is particularly important where the environmental limit is a fixed cap, as in Title IV, because small variations in aggregate growth will cause much larger variations in required abatement and costs. Also, many of the early studies from the 1980s do not provide appropriate comparisons because they concerned proposals that differed substantially from the legislation that was enacted in 1990. In addition, many studies concerned with Title IV ignored the Phase I transition and provided estimates only for Phase II, when the Title IV limitations would be fully phased in. Finally, not all studies were done with comparable care or documented well enough to permit reliable comparisons with other work.

Fortunately, there are two sets of studies that can be used. The first set includes studies conducted by ICF Resources Incorporated in 1989 and 1990 for EPA to predict the effects and costs of the implementation of Title IV. The second set of studies are associated with EPRI, then the Electric Power Research Institute, which commissioned studies in 1992 and 1995 for the benefit of its members. Yet

14. A basic property of this technology, discussed below, is that the higher the sulfur content of the coal that is burned, the more sulfur is removed by the operation of a given scrubber, all else equal. This translates directly into a lower cost per ton of sulfur removed.

Table 9.2. *Estimates of Phase I compliance costs*

Source	'95 emissions w/o CAAA (million tons)	Title IV reduction (million tons)	Total cost (million '95$)	Average cost ($/ton)
ICF89L (constrained)	16.64	3.56	871	245
ICF89L (flexible)	16.64	3.32	599	180
ICF90L (flexible)	16.64	3.12	573	184
EPRI93	16.29	4.36	1338	307
GAO94	9.37[a]	3.90	1163	298
EPRI95	14.65	3.18	894	281
Actual '95 (MIT)	15.70	3.46–3.89	726	187–210

[a]Table A only

Sources: ICF (1989, Tables B1 and B5), ICF (1990, Tables B1 and B5), EPRI (1993, Table C-1), GAO (1994, pp. 26 and 74), and EPRI (1995, Table A-3).

another study was prepared in late 1994 for the General Accounting Office by the same contractor that did the earlier EPRI study. All of these studies are well documented with respect to both assumptions and results. The ICF studies are earlier and more model-dependent in method, while the EPRI studies were done after enactment of the legislation and with the benefit of the considerable compliance planning that electric utilities were then conducting.

The estimates of emission reduction and compliance cost provided by these before-the-fact studies are displayed in Table 9.2, as well as our cost estimates discussed above. As should be expected of studies predicting the future, alternative scenarios were selected that allowed growth in the demand for electricity to vary. There was also considerable doubt about the extent of emissions trading, so that alternative estimates were made for assumptions corresponding to more or less trading. For example, in the ICF studies, only the low-load-growth scenarios are included in this comparison, since they correspond more closely to actual load growth since 1990. With respect to trading, scenarios that anticipated more trading are more appropriate for any comparison with actual abatement and costs, since that assumption more nearly approximates what actually happened.[15] The assumption about the extent of emissions trading can

15. There are also slight differences between the 1989 and 1990 estimates with respect to the provisions of the legislation. The ICF (1989) estimate was based upon the initial Bush Administration proposal, whereas the ICF (1990) estimate was based on nearly

make a considerable difference in the estimate, as shown by the comparison between the 1989 ICF scenarios labeled "constrained" (no interutility trading) and "flexible" (with interutility trading). In this early projection, which did not include any banking of allowances, emissions trading accounted for a difference in cost of nearly $300 million, or almost one-third the more costly estimate.

Even using only these careful and well-informed studies, comparisons must be made with caution. The cost estimates provided by these studies have been converted to 1995 dollars in Table 9.2 using the GDP deflator, but other incomparable features are not so easily remedied. For instance, these studies took an approach to amortizing capital investments that followed regulatory accounting rather than the approach rooted in financial theory that we adopted.[16] In addition, we used a uniform lifetime of twenty years for all capital equipment in computing the depreciation component of the capital charge, while others, such as EPRI (1993), used a fifteen-year lifetime for scrubbers. Estimates of what SO_2 emissions would have been without the constraints imposed by the Clean Air Act Amendments also varied considerably, with consequent differences in the amount of abatement that would be required to meet the fixed cap. Moreover, studies differed in their predictions of the amount of additional emission reduction that would be performed in Phase I to bank allowances for use in Phase II. As a result, the total cost of the predicted Phase I emission reduction from one study cannot be directly compared to the total cost from another study.

One way of making the comparison is to plot the estimates for total cost and corresponding abatement as is done in Figure 9.2. In this figure, the diamonds indicate our estimates of actual cost in 1995 (with and without the no-cost PRB switches), and the labeled dots indicate the estimates from these earlier studies. EPRI's 1993 estimate of nearly $1.4 billion in compliance cost in early Phase I was higher than that in any of the other studies, but so was their estimate of the amount of abatement that would be provided in response to Title IV. Conversely, ICF's 1990 estimate predicted total cost of only

final legislation. In the comparison made here, we use the ICF (1990) estimate for the Senate bill, which more closely approximated the final legislation than did the House bill.

16. All of the earlier studies appear to have used a fixed annual capital charge based on a nominal interest rate, instead of a capital rental price based on the real interest rate that escalates with inflation, as we have. See Note 6 supra.

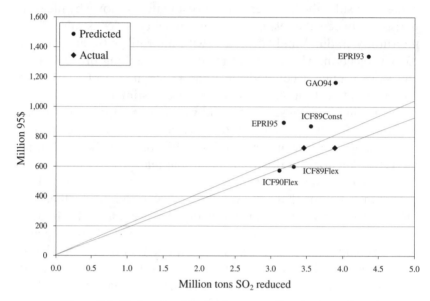

Figure 9.2. Estimates of Phase I cost, predicted vs. actual.
Source: ICF (1989, 1990), EPRI (1993, 1995), and GAO (1994).

$500 million, but it also anticipated less abatement. The statistic that provides the best index for comparison is average total cost per ton of SO_2 emissions reduced: total abatement cost divided by the reduction in emissions. Average cost is given in the last column of Table 9.2; and the average cost lines for our estimates of actual cost in 1995, with and without the no-cost PRB switches, are indicated by the plot lines. Estimates above these lines predicted higher average cost, and those below predicted lower average cost.

Table 9.2 and Figure 9.2 show that the actual cost of compliance with Title IV in Phase I is not dramatically lower than what had been predicted, particularly for those scenarios that assumed relatively widespread emissions trading and load growth close to what actually occurred. Earlier estimates of expected average cost range from a high of $307 per ton of SO_2 removed (EPRI93) to $180 per ton (ICF89Flex). Our estimate, at $187 to $210, is closer to the low side than the high side of this wide range. The "industry" estimates, i.e., EPRI, are on the high side, around $300, although notably GAO94 endorsed this view on the eve of Phase I's implementation, while the

EPA estimates, i.e., ICF, are on the low side, somewhat below $200. The difference between $200 and $300 per ton is significant, particularly when multiplied by 3–4 million tons of abatement, but it does not come close to a factor of 10; and it may well be within the range of reasonable differences in opinion among careful and responsible analysts. What we take from this comparison is that the actual costs of compliance with Phase I have been on the low side of what was expected and that the earlier estimates, by both government and industry, were reasonable predictions of the cost of compliance in Phase I.

THE COST OF ABATEMENT BY SCRUBBING

Although scrubbers were few in number and represented a costly choice for abating SO_2, the actual cost incurred for scrubbing in Phase I has been considerably less than expected. The average total cost of scrubbing in Phase I has been about half of what was expected, and the costs in Phase II appear likely to be lower still.

Evidence of Lower than Expected Cost

Both ICF90 and EPRI93 provide sufficient data to compute *expected* average total cost for scrubbing at the time that the planning for Phase I compliance was in progress. Table 9.3 compares *expected* SO_2 removal cost, based on data from EPRI and ICF, with our estimate of actual SO_2 removal cost. The ICF90 and EPRI93 estimates for scrubbing costs are calculated for a representative retrofitted unit based on specifications provided in EPRI93.[17] The MIT/CEEPR estimate is based on actual cost data and the actual performance of the twenty-seven retrofitted scrubbers during Phase I. By this comparison, Phase I scrubbers were removing sulfur at an average total cost of $286 per ton in Phase I – almost 40% less, or $180

17. The representative retrofitted unit in EPRI (1993) is a 300MW^c unit with retrofit difficulty factor of 1.27. The unit is assumed to remove 90% of the sulfur from a 3.97lb coal and to operate at a 65% capacity factor and gross heat rate of 9,722 Btu/kWh. ICF (1989) provides more complete cost data for scrubbing. The ICF data shown here correspond to the representative retrofitted unit in the EPRI study.

Table 9.3. *Expected and actual cost and performance data for Phase I scrubbers*

('94$)	ICF90	EPRI93	Actual
Basic cost data			
Initial capital ($/kW^e)	$249.00	$229.00	$249.00
Fixed O&M ($/kW-yr)	$6.55	$8.19	$2.00
Variable O&M (mills/kWh)	1.81	2.24	1.26
Performance data			
Removal efficiency (%)	90	90	95
Utilization (%)	65	65	82
Coal SO_2 (lb SO_2/mmBtu)	3.97	3.97	4.10
Gross heat rate (Btu/kWh)	9,722	9,722	9,800
Tons SO_2/MW^e	99	99	137
Cost per ton SO_2			
Capital charge (@ 11.33%)	$285	$262	$206
Fixed O&M	$66	$83	$15
Variable O&M	$104	$129	$65
Average total cost	$455	$474	$286

Sources: Derived from EPRI (1993), ICF (1990), MIT/CEEPR Title IV Questionnaire (1996), EPRI (1995).

per ton of SO_2 removed, than what had been predicted by earlier estimates.[18] The cost savings arise from two factors: more intensive utilization of scrubbed units and lower operating and maintenance (O&M) costs.

Capital Investment and Utilization

The largest cost component for scrubbing is the annualized amortization charge for the initial capital investment. When this cost component is expressed as dollars per ton of SO_2 emissions abated, the denominator, tons abated, is as important as the numerator, the annual capital charge. The number of tons abated depends both on the utilization of the unit and, with 95% removal, on the

18. This computation of average total cost is higher than that shown in Table 9.1 for two reasons. First, Table 9.1 excludes two scrubbers that were not brought on line until 1996 and includes only a half year's capital charge for four scrubbers brought on line in the latter part of 1995. These six units cost more on average than the twenty-one units that were on line for all of 1995, so that the average in Table 9.3 is increased by the full weighting of these six units in 1996 and 1997. Second, Table 9.1 includes savings in fuel cost where shifts to cheaper, higher-sulfur coals by some retrofitted units have been observed. Since these savings were not included in the estimates with which the comparison is being made, they are not included in Table 9.3.

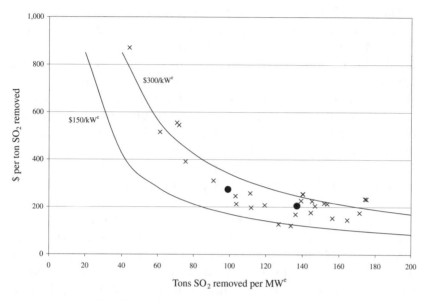

Figure 9.3. The fixed costs of scrubbing.

sulfur content of the coal burned at the unit.[19] The higher the sulfur content of the coal and the greater the utilization of the unit, the more tons of SO_2 removed over which the annual capital charge can be spread, and the lower the fixed cost of abatement per ton of SO_2 removed.

The effect of variations in the number of tons of SO_2 removed is illustrated in Figure 9.3, in which the per ton fixed cost of scrubbing is plotted against the number of tons of SO_2 removed. The two lines in Figure 9.3 can be thought of as iso-investment curves, which show how the fixed annual capital charge, expressed on a per ton of SO_2 removed, falls as the number of tons removed annually per MW^e of electric generating capacity is increased. These two lines represent initial investments of $150/kW^e$ and $300/kW^e$ bearing an annual capital charge of 11%.

19. Since the coal used in a generating unit after a scrubber is retrofitted may have a higher sulfur content than the coal formerly used, the difference of emissions attributable to Title IV is always calculated by reference to the sulfur content of the pre-1995 coal. If the unit moves to a higher-sulfur coal after the retrofit, a credit for the fuel cost savings would be appropriate.

The x's in Figure 9.3 position the twenty-seven retrofitted scrubbers according to the capital investment cost and tons of SO_2 removed in 1997, which is the first year that all were operating for the full year. Most of the Phase I scrubbers incurred capital costs between the two approximate iso-investment curves. Only two units came in at less than $150/kW^e, and six units had capital costs exceeding $300/kW^e. For these relatively more costly units, the unit fixed cost of abating SO_2 varied from $871 a ton to $234 a ton, depending entirely on the tons of SO_2 reduced per MW^e of generating capacity. For instance, the initial investment cost for the two units with per ton fixed costs of $234 is almost identical to that for the unit with per ton fixed cost of $871, but the utilization of the two low-cost units was 93% against 30% for the other unit. These two units were also removing 1 pound more SO_2 per million Btu than the high-cost unit. The three units with SO_2 removal costs between $500/ton and $600/ton have experienced relatively high utilization, about 80%, but the initial capital costs were relatively high, and the sulfur content of the coal used before scrubbing was not particularly high, around 2.5 lb SO_2 per mmBtu.

The effect of the difference between expected and actual utilization is illustrated by the large black dots in Figure 9.3, which are based upon the figures in Table 9.3. The dot to the left is the average of the numbers for the ICF and EPRI studies, while the dot to the right reflects the average characteristics for the actual experience of the twenty-seven retrofitted units. The two dots are on virtually the same iso-investment curve, and the average sulfur content of the coal is the same, but the better than expected utilization, 82% versus 65%, shaved about $70 off the average per ton cost for SO_2 abatement.

Operating Expense

The second factor causing lower than expected scrubbing costs is operating expense, which is conventionally split into two components in utility accounting: fixed operations and maintenance cost (O&M) and variable O&M. The former includes the annual personnel costs associated with operating the scrubber, which, like the annual capital charge, is reduced on a per ton basis by removing more tons. Variable O&M cost depends on the tons removed, and it consists principally of the power needed to run the scrubber and the limestone and sorbents used to capture the SO_2 in the flue gas.

Reliable and consistent data on scrubber operating expenses are hard to obtain, but what can be pieced together points to scrubber operating costs that are half of those implied by the earlier EPRI and ICF estimates. The MIT/Actual estimates for fixed and variable O&M cost in Table 9.3 are based upon the responses to the MIT/CEEPR questionnaire, supplemented by further queries and other data. These data indicate fixed O&M cost ranging from $1.45 per kW^e-year to $2.44 kW^e-year, and variable costs ranging from below a mill per kilowatt ($50/ton SO_2) to as high as 1.65 mills/kWh ($90/ton SO_2). These numbers for variable O&M cost are broadly consistent with the continued operation of all Title IV scrubbers during late 1995 and early 1996, when allowance prices dipped below $70. Furthermore, several operators of scrubbed units indicated in response to questions that they were close to the point where they would cut back on operations if allowance prices got any lower. Accordingly, we settled on 1.2 mills/kWh ($65/ton) as a representative average for the variable O&M cost of scrubbing. The only other estimate of operating expense for Phase I scrubbers is provided by the Energy Information Administration in its study of Phase I compliance cost (DOE, 1997). This study, which was based on data from six utilities – several of which retrofitted scrubbers – cites an estimate of 1.42 mills/kWh for "average operating and maintenance costs, exclusive of capital recovery." This figure works out to $75/ton, using the same assumptions as in Table 9.3.

While trade press discussions of scrubbers frequently cite capital costs or scrubber costs in general, they do not specifically distinguish the reasons for lower than expected operating costs. Nevertheless, changes that would affect operating expense are frequently cited, and our queries to operators have corroborated these reports. The most often mentioned source of cost reduction in operating expense is improved instrumentation and control, which reduces personnel requirements and results in general improvements in reliability, less parasitic power consumption, reduced chemical requirements, and improved by-product management. Other frequently cited improvements are the elimination of flue gas reheat, simpler designs, the use of additives, and reduced reagent preparation costs.

Implications

A common theme in current articles and discussions about scrubbers is that Phase I scrubbers are different from the earlier "NSPS" scrubbers, and that Phase II scrubbers will be better still.[20] For instance, scrubber manufacturers have asserted that Phase II scrubbers could be built with initial investment costs of $100–150/kW^e of capacity, about half of the average capital cost of the Phase I scrubbers.[21] With initial investment cost this low, scrubbers could be easily justified on an ex ante basis at allowance prices of $200, as can be seen by reference to the $150 iso-investment cost curve in Figure 9.3. Vendor claims about lower scrubber capital and operating costs have been met with some skepticism and a general attitude of "show me,"[22] but utility announcements of new scrubber investments since mid-1998, when allowance prices rose to $200, provide further support for the belief that scrubbing costs have fallen considerably. Tampa Electric announced the first Phase II scrubber in July 1998 on two Phase I units at its Big Bend plant in Florida for a cost of $100 per kW^e of capacity.[23] Several months later, Mission Energy announced, without any details on cost, that it would retrofit a scrubber at its newly purchased Homer City plant in Pennsylvania. Then, in February 1999, Dominion Resources announced a decision to retrofit scrubbers on two Phase I units at its Mt. Storm plant in West Virginia for a cost of $107 per kW^e of capacity.[24] The capital costs reported for these new scrubbers confirm that the cost of new scrubbers in Phase II will be much lower than predicted as recently as 1990 or as experienced with the Phase I scrubbers.[25]

20. An article in one trade journal carried a title that said it all: "Scrubber myths and realities: Don't let common misperceptions about flue gas desulfurization bias a realistic appraisal of this capable control technology," *Power Engineering*, January 1995.
21. "Scrubber Costs Vary, Still Down, Vendors Say," *Clean Air Compliance Review*, April 7, 1997.
22. One utility executive's response to vendor claims about scrubbers at $100/kW^e was: "Where can I get one?" (Rick Collins of TVA, quoted in ibid.)
23. See *Clean Air Compliance Review*, July 27, 1998.
24. See *Clean Air Compliance Review*, February 24, 1999.
25. The existence of a NSPS scrubber at another unit at Big Bend and of a Phase I scrubber at the third Mt. Storm unit may have offered some economies in cost. A significant reduction in the cost of scrubbing is also indicated by the coals that these units have been burning: between 2.5 and 3.0 lb of SO_2 per mmBtu. If the capital costs were not significantly below the capital cost of the Phase I scrubbers, it would not be economic to scrub such mid-sulfur coals with allowance prices at $200.

Two major implications flow out of this experience. The first concerns the cost of compliance in Phase II. The reductions of scrubber cost observed in Phase I, as well as those claimed and being acted upon for Phase II, indicate that the costs of complying with Title IV in Phase II will be less than expected, perhaps by a larger margin than was true in Phase I. Recent estimates of the cost of compliance with Phase II are already significantly lower than earlier studies, although some of the difference may be due to recognition of the trend to increased use of PRB coal. Estimates of the cost of Phase II, when the SO_2 allowance bank is exhausted, range from $1.1 to $1.9 billion,[26] significantly below earlier, pre-1995 estimates, which ranged from $1.6 billion to $6.0 billion in 1995 dollars. (An important implication of lower Phase II costs is a lower price for allowances in Phase I, as we discuss further in Chapter 11.)

The second implication of the reduction in scrubber cost concerns the potential influence of the type of regulatory regime on innovation, or what is sometimes called dynamic efficiency. The experience with Title IV scrubbers stands in marked contrast with the more than two decades of experience with scrubbing mandated by the NSPS. A recent study of the advances in scrubber technology in the United States through 1992 found "no significant progress ... in abatement technology" and attributes this result to the "small incentives for innovation [associated with] the form of regulation typically used in the U.S." (Bellas, 1998). There are other factors at play, such as concomitant changes in information technology and electric utility regulation, which have nothing to do with Title IV and could explain this difference in technological advance. Moreover, the requirements placed upon the scrubber are not identical with respect to reliability and the percentage of sulfur removed, so the scrubbers being compared are not necessarily identical in terms of performance.[27] Still,

---

26. Since Phase II costs will be less while the bank is being drawn down, Phase II "equilibrium" is commonly described as the year after the bank has been exhausted. More recent estimates of expected Phase II cost can be found in Carlson et al. (1998) and EPRI (1997). A convenient summary of early predictions of cost and abatement is found in Smith, Platt, and Ellerman (1998).

27. For instance, NSPS regulations would require that the associated generating unit be shut down if the scrubber malfunctioned, whereas Title IV would require only that more allowances be used to cover the additional emissions. As a result, spare modules and other costly features aimed at achieving near 100% reliability are not required. NSPS scrubbers are also required to remove between 70% and 90% of the in-coal sulfur, depending on the coal.

the striking contrast between technological stagnation in scrubber technology before 1992, under a regulatory regime of direct emission controls, and technological progress since then, under a regulatory regime with tradable permits, is hard to ignore. If subsequent research is able to confirm the suggested relation between regulatory regime and innovation, the implications will extend far beyond Phase II and Title IV.

THE COST OF ABATEMENT BY SWITCHING TO LOWER-SULFUR COAL

Most Phase I units have elected to reduce emissions by switching to lower-sulfur coal, and fuel switching has generally been the lower-cost abatement option. Despite this cost advantage, the share of fuel switching in abatement attributable to Title IV has not increased since 1995, because of the differing structure of cost between scrubbing and switching. Most of the scrubbing cost is fixed, and therefore sunk, while the cost of switching to lower-sulfur fuels is mostly variable. Furthermore, the operating costs for scrubbing, about $65 per ton of SO_2 removed, are lower than the premium paid for lower-sulfur coals, which tends to be equal to the value of allowances. As a result, Phase I scrubbers are inframarginal suppliers of abatement: It is economical to operate them for all allowance prices thus far experienced. In contrast, switching to lower-sulfur coal is the form of abatement that is on the margin in the short run and is thus responsive to changes in allowance prices.

Sulfur content is only one of many characteristics by which coals may differ, and these other characteristics are relevant in discussing abatement accomplished through coal switching. In particular, a distinction must be drawn between switching to subbituminous coals, such as those from the PRB, and switching to bituminous coals. This distinction is required because the retrofit investment requirements differ significantly depending on whether the lower sulfur coal to which the Phase I unit is being switched is bituminous or subbituminous. In turn, this difference leads to the same sort of inframarginal/marginal distinction that has just been noted for scrubbing and switching.

Switching to PRB Coals

The high-sulfur Phase I units that are candidates for switching to lower-sulfur coals were all built to handle bituminous coals that were available locally. By definition, subbituminous coals are inferior quality coals in what counts most, Btu content. That is, they have more water and ash content per ton than bituminous coals. Consequently, units that were not built for PRB coals must make a sizable capital investment to adapt the generating unit and associated facilities to burn these coals. Boilers must be modified to perform adequately with the very different combustion characteristics of PRB coals, coal-handling facilities must be enlarged to handle the greater volumes of lower Btu content coal, and precipitators must be upgraded to deal with the greater ash throughput. The magnitude of the expenditure depends on the plant, but typically the cost ranges from \$15 to \$75 per kilowatt of generating capacity (kW^e).

As noted previously, the up-front capital investment for switching to a PRB coal requires that the price of the PRB coal must be lower than the price of the competing bituminous coal to justify the conversion. As discussed in Chapter 4, most of the switches to PRB coals have not been caused by Title IV, but by the increasingly advantageous price comparison with the local coal. However, with the beginning of Phase I, allowance values have provided an additional incentive for Phase I units to switch to PRB coals.[28] Once the conversion has been made, these retrofitted PRB units become inframarginal suppliers of abatement, like units retrofitted with scrubbers, because the variable cost comparison after conversion will be consistently favorable to the PRB coal, assuming that the Btu price relations do not change dramatically. Thus, as with scrubbing, this abatement choice contains an irreversible element that makes it relatively immune to subsequent fluctuations in allowance prices.

The high degree of innovation in adapting boilers built for bituminous coals to burn PRB coals has been one of the major surprises

---

28. The extra boost from allowance value is significant. With allowance prices at \$100, each pound of SO_2 per million Btu emission-rate reduction would be worth \$0.05/mmBtu. Assuming a 2.0lb/mmBtu reduction from switching, the added incentive is \$0.10/mmBtu for coals that are being delivered to power plants in the Midwest at prices of about \$1.00/mmBtu. When appropriately amortized the initial capital investment for switching to PRB coals works out to be about \$0.15/mmBtu.

in Phase I. Fifteen years ago, conventional wisdom held that boilers in the Midwest could not be adapted to burn subbituminous coals without a significant derating, or loss of generating capacity. Thus, early studies of Phase I compliance typically found that when the derating was taken into account, it would be cheaper to abate by scrubbing or switching to more costly low-sulfur bituminous coals from central Appalachia. An implicit assumption in these early studies was that switching to a PRB coal was an all or nothing matter. As rail rates fell during the 1980s and PRB coals became cheaper, operators began to experiment with blending small quantities of these increasingly attractive coals. Not surprisingly, they found that as long as the fraction of coal from the PRB was small, boiler performance was not adversely affected, but cost and emissions were reduced. Eventually, in what must be considered a triumph of tinkering and continuous thinking, it was found that the subbituminous coal could be blended with the local bituminous coal up to a point without incurring a significant derating. The point at which the loss of generating capacity made the switch uneconomical depended on the boiler and the coals being blended, but continuing innovation and lower PRB coal prices have increased the blend over the years. Blends of 40–60% PRB coals were common by the time Phase I began, and even 100% PRB "blends" can be observed.

No generating plant symbolizes this evolution better than Illinois Power's Baldwin plant, for which a 100% conversion to PRB coal was announced in late 1998. Baldwin is a large ($1.9\,GW^e$) plant consisting of three Table A units located adjacent to two high-sulfur coal mines in southern Illinois. These mines have supplied the plant under long-term contracts running through 1999 in one case and to 2010 in the other. Illinois Power had initially decided to retrofit a scrubber at these three units, but it suspended construction in August 1992 (DOE, 1997). In 1993 it decided to rely upon the purchase of allowances to cover emissions at these units, and it has been notable as the only electric utility, with a significant number of Phase I units, to depend heavily on the external purchase of allowances. Nevertheless, in November 1998, Illinois Power announced that it had renegotiated the 2010 contract to switch the source of coal at the end of 1999 from the nearby high-sulfur mine (about $5.0\,lb\ SO_2$ per mmBtu) to coal from PRB mines owned by the same company. It also announced that it would be conducting a solicitation for a second source of PRB coal to replace the contract expiring in 1999. Thus, the conversion to PRB coals will be 100%, and the company stated that the units will suffer no derating of electric generating capacity. The cost of the conversions, including a second, smaller plant operated by Illinois Power, was announced as $125 million, which works out to be between $55 and $60 per kW^e. With a 100% switch, the emission rate after the conversion will be about 0.50 lb/mmBtu, one-tenth the Phase I rate. Moreover, Illinois Power and its Baldwin units will change from being the largest sources of demand for allowances to cover emissions in Phase I to being an important net supplier of allowances in Phase II.

Switching to Lower-Sulfur Bituminous Coals

Boilers built for bituminous coals can switch to lower-sulfur bituminous coals with relatively little additional capital expenditure for boiler modifications and coal handling or environmental control equipment. Depending on the coals and the boiler, the additional investment can range from 0 to $20/$kW^e$, but the typical capital expenditure is between $5/$kW^e$ and $10/$kW^e$.

The relative ease of switching to other bituminous coals has several implications for Phase I units switching to these coals. First, the lower-sulfur, bituminous coal to which the Phase I unit could switch is more expensive than the coal used in the generating unit prior to 1995; otherwise, the lower-sulfur coal would be used. Second, the higher cost, or premium, for the lower-sulfur, bituminous coal constitutes almost all of the cost of switching to that coal. Whether a Phase I unit will switch to a lower-sulfur coal will depend upon the comparison between the premium and the expected or actual cost of an allowance.[29] Third, unless constrained by contract, switching to a lower-sulfur, bituminous coal is reversible. Thus, if allowance values fall or coal sulfur premiums rise, a unit that had switched to a lower-sulfur, bituminous coal could be expected to switch back to a higher-sulfur coal. All this implies that the short-run margin for Title IV compliance consists of the units capable of switching among bituminous coals of differing sulfur content.

29. The comparison between coal premiums and allowance value is done by dividing the premium, expressed in $/mmBtu, by the difference in emissions, expressed as lb/mmBtu, and multiplying by 2,000.

Table 9.4. *Changes in abatement at Phase I units, 1996 and 1997*

Source of abatement	1995 to 1996 (thousand tons)	1996 to 1997 (thousand tons)
Switching	−531	+107
Scrubbing	+167	+58
Title IV effects	−364	+165
Exogenous PRB trend	+205	+206
Total for Phase I units	−159	+371

Sources: Derived from Pechan (1995), EPA (1996b, 1997, 1998), and Appendix to this book.

The response of the bituminous coal switching units on the short-run margin is readily identifiable in the changes in abatement at Phase I units, as calculated by the econometrically estimated counterfactual. As shown in Table 9.4, abatement attributable to Title IV declines in 1996, compared to 1995, along with allowance prices, and all the increase in emissions is due to units that had switched to lower-sulfur coals in 1995. Allowance prices were slightly higher in 1997 than they had been in 1996, and Title IV abatement from switching increased, although it was still some 400,000 tons less than in 1995. During the same period of time abatement from scrubbing increased steadily, in 1996 because of the six additional scrubbers and in 1997 because of improved utilization. At the same time, the PRB trend continued, independently of Title IV, to reduce aggregate emissions and the amount of abatement required to meet the Title IV cap.

Switching to bituminous coals differs from switching to a PRB coal in another important respect. The range of lower-sulfur bituminous coals that can be used is very wide with respect both to sulfur content and geographic location. This diversity and geographic breadth explain why switching to lower-sulfur bituminous coals has been the most frequent choice of abatement technique among Phase I units. As with scrubbing and switching to PRB coals, there were some surprises that deserve particular note.

First, the low-sulfur coal in greatest demand was not the type known as "compliance coal," that with sufficiently low-sulfur content it could meet the pre-1978 New Source Performance Standard (NSPS) of 1.2 lb/mmBtu without scrubbing. Rather, the coal in greater demand was the slightly higher-sulfur coals from Central Appalachia, 1.5–2.0 lb/mmBtu, which cannot serve the conventional compliance coal market. Compliance coal could be used in Phase I units, but it commands an extra premium from the specialized market of pre-1978 NSPS units that makes it less attractive to Phase I units.

The second surprise was the appearance of low- to mid-sulfur coals, primarily in the Midwest, where none had been produced previously. Prior to Title IV, all coals with sulfur content greater than 1.2 lb/mmBtu were generally treated as equivalent under U.S. environmental policy, even though their sulfur content varied considerably. Consequently, there was no premium for a low- to mid-sulfur coal (1.5 lb/mmBtu to 3.0 lb/mmBtu) that competed with a coal having 5.0 lb/mmBtu, for instance. Title IV created a premium for lower sulfur content among these "noncompliance coals," which is to say, among most of the coals produced in the United States.[30] As a result, low- and mid-sulfur coals that had not been able to compete with high-sulfur coals on a cost basis before became economically attractive to produce with the appearance of the Title IV premium for lower-sulfur content.

The third surprise was the extent of switching to lower-sulfur coals that were not low-sulfur coal at all. Many Phase I units in the Midwest and northern Appalachia were burning coals with SO_2 content of 5 lb/mmBtu or higher, even to 7 lb/mmBtu. Many of these units did not switch to what would be considered a low-sulfur coal, but they did reduce cost and SO_2 emissions by switching to locally available coals in the 3–4 lb/mmBtu range.

Both of these latter two responses to the coal sulfur premium account for the geographic diversity of the abatement observed and the unexpectedly large contributions from the predominantly

30. The appearance of a premium over the entire range of sulfur content in coal has also led to changes in mining practice and coal preparation that have resulted in a lower-sulfur product being delivered to market. Sulfur content varies somewhat even within the same seam, and some of the sulfur fraction of the coal can be removed in the preparation plants that separate rock and other impurities from raw, run-of-mine coal to make it marketable. Although a 4.0 lb/mmBtu coal cannot be changed into a 1.0 lb/mmBtu coal, the Title IV premium – about 5% for each pound of SO_2 per million Btu of heat content – provides the incentive to make what would otherwise have been a 4.0 lb/mmBtu coal into a 3.5 lb/mmBtu, or even 3.0 lb/mmBtu coal.

high-sulfur coal-producing regions of northern Appalachia and the Midwest.

MONITORING COSTS

Every regulatory program incurs administrative costs that are usually not included in estimates of direct compliance cost, and we have made no attempt to estimate the cost of personnel and equipment for administering Title IV at electric utilities or at the EPA.[31] Nevertheless, one very important part of Title IV compliance deserves particular note: the cost of installing and operating a continuous emission monitoring system (CEMS) on the stack of every affected unit. As its name indicates, a CEMS monitors flue gas emissions continuously, by means of electronic probes in the exhaust stack of generating units. These monitors are critical to the successful operation of Title IV's cap and trade system since they measure the emissions for which allowances must be surrendered.

The requirement to install continuous emissions monitoring systems at every coal-fired Title IV unit was controversial because CEMS are costly, and they may provide no better estimates of emissions than conventional methods. Prior to Title IV, most stacks did not have CEMS, and compliance with emission rate limits imposed by state implementation plans was determined by sampling of fuel input that is performed routinely to ensure the quality of fuel delivered to the plant. There is little doubt about the accuracy of these measurements, since billions of dollars of coal supply transactions rely on the commercial protocols for measuring in-fuel sulfur content, and a materials balance approach could have been adopted to estimate the mass of emissions exiting the stack. Adjustments would have been required to account for sulfur retained in the bottom ash and for sulfur reductions achieved by the use of additives or sorbents in combustion (as with fluidized beds) or in the exhaust stack (as with scrubbers), but such factors are well known based on engineering studies. Moreover,

31. A very detailed ex ante estimate of these costs is contained in the EPA's Regulatory Impact Analysis that was issued with the regulations implementing Title IV (EPA, 1992). To our knowledge, no attempt has been made to estimate administrative cost ex post; however, the factors cited by Kruger, McLean, and Chen (1998) would suggest that this cost has also been less than had been anticipated.

similar adjustments would be required to translate the data recorded by the CEMS probes to tons of SO_2 emitted, for instance, assumptions concerning the homogeneity and velocity of the flue gas stream. Still, notwithstanding the adequacy of the materials balance approach to measurement, the CEMS requirement was included in the legislation. In part, this requirement was the price of assuaging environmentalist concerns about emissions trading, but it also simplified administration of the program.

Whatever the comparative merits of the assumptions required to estimate emissions by the two approaches, a CEMS does reduce transaction costs by allowing operators to pursue flexible, cost-effective emission reductions without renegotiating the adjustments required by a materials balance approach to get from in-fuel sulfur content to SO_2 emissions. Such adjustments could be renegotiated, but the costs involved in doing so would dampen the extent to which they would be sought, including changes that reduced emissions. Moreover, measurement in the stack greatly simplifies the regulator's task of determining compliance. Translating measured stack gas flows into mass measures is profoundly technical in nature and relatively independent of operator control. In contrast, scrubber removal efficiency, ash content of the fuel, or other factors that affect how much of the in-coal sulfur content goes up the stack, are under the control of plant operators. Instead of simply matching recorded emissions with allowances, determining compliance would be complicated by the more problematic requirements of ensuring that the indicated sulfur-reduction methods are indeed removing sulfur by at least the specified percentage. In effect, use of a CEMS separates the problem of estimating emissions from the operator's actions to control emissions.

Information concerning the capital and operating costs of CEMS was solicited in the confidential questionnaire that MIT/CEEPR sent to electric utilities as part of this research project.[32] Table 9.5 presents the initial capital cost and the annual operating cost as reported by the respondents for all 130 Phase I units operated by respondents. The initial capital costs can be divided by the number of units or by the generating capacity of the units to obtain averages of approximately \$700,000 per generating unit (at 371 MW^e per unit) or slightly

32. See Note 3 supra.

Table 9.5. *Cost of CEMS*

Cost category	Total ($\times 10^3$)	Per unit	Per kW^e
Initial capital cost	$92,135	$709,000	$1.91
Annualized @ 11%	$10,135	$77,227	$0.21
Annual operating cost	$6,080	$46,780	$0.13
Total cost for 1995	$16,215	$124,007	$0.34

Source: MIT/CEEPR Title IV Questionnaire (1996).

less than $2 per kW^e of generating capacity. Annual operating costs work out to about $47,000 for this average 371 MW^e unit, or $0.13 per kW^e. When the initial capital charge is annualized into an amortization charge at 11%, the total annual cost of the CEMS is indicated at $125,000 per unit or about $0.34 per kW^e.

Assuming these costs are representative of the whole, the additional cost of monitoring for Title IV in 1995 amounted to $44–54 million, depending on whether extrapolation is made by capacity or by the number of active Phase I units that installed CEMS that year (i.e., 432).[33] At about 7% of the estimated direct cost of compliance, the cost of this extra requirement is noticeable, but it is not overwhelming.

In the end, CEMS represents an additional administrative cost that may have encouraged more emissions trading and greater cost savings than would have been the case otherwise. Emissions trading requires low transaction costs and confidence that the tradable permit will be regarded as valid when presented for compliance. To the extent that CEMS has imbued the environmental regulator with sufficient confidence in the accuracy of emissions accounting to dispense with ancillary review and approval of emission reductions, transaction costs have been reduced and greater emissions trading enabled. And, if more trading implies greater cost savings, as we believe it does, what began as political expediency may prove to be a worthwhile investment.

33. Title IV also required that CEMS be installed by 1995 on 447 Phase II units, totaling 98.6 GW^e of capacity, that will be subject to Title IV controls beginning in the year 2000. By the same methods of extrapolation described above, another $36–55 million in compliance costs were incurred in 1995 for Phase II monitoring.

PART THREE
Questions and Implications

10　Cost Savings from Emissions Trading

COST SAVINGS IS THE GOAL

Emissions trading is advocated as a means for achieving environmental goals because the flexibility it provides to affected sources promises lower costs than do the usual source-specific mandates, standards, and other forms of prescription broadly characterized as "command-and-control" (CAC). With the choices made possible by a market-based emissions control policy, the costs of achieving any given level of environmental protection can be reduced below those incurred by CAC regulation. Alternatively, more environmental protection can be obtained for the same cost.

The magnitude of the cost savings potentially available through use of emissions trading has been the subject of study for a number of years, but the results have varied widely. Estimated ratios of the cost of an observed CAC program to that of a least-cost market-based alternative have ranged from just over 1 to over 20.[1] The implication is that emissions trading could lead to negligible or enormous savings, depending on the costs of the CAC program to which the efficient, market-based alternative is compared. These earlier studies were performed with the considerable handicap of being able only to compare the unappealing, observed reality of CAC programs with simulated and often idealized market-based alternatives. This defect was

---

1. See Tietenberg (1996), Table 15.2, p. 362. For the air pollutant studies that are cited in this table, the ratio ranges from 1.07 to 22. See also Tietenberg (1985), Table 5, p. 46, for ratios from studies of water pollutants, which range from 1.12 to 3.13.

unavoidable because so few market-based alternatives have been available to observe, and, with one or two exceptions, these few have not been notably successful.[2] Now Title IV provides the opportunity to compare a real, market-based alternative, with all of its inevitable imperfections, with some hypothetical CAC alternative.

This chapter is primarily devoted to just such a comparison. Because the precision of the cost savings estimated in such cases is fundamentally limited by unavoidable ignorance of the unobserved alternative regulatory regime, our goal is to produce reasonable, approximate estimates in a way that clarifies the concepts and assumptions involved. Before embarking on this exercise, however, it is instructive to consider briefly the substantial prima facie evidence of cost-saving behavior that has accumulated in the first three years of Phase I.

EVIDENCE OF COST SAVINGS

Perhaps the most compelling evidence that emissions trading has reduced compliance costs is the significant divergence between the control levels adopted by Phase I units and those that would have been required in the absence of emissions trading. If emissions trading is made available when abatement costs vary widely among affected units, as they surely do, and if operators take advantage of the trading opportunity, then a considerable divergence between allowance allocations and emissions should regularly be observed at the unit level. That has been exactly the case with Title IV, as illustrated earlier by Figure 6.1. The use of allowances additional to those allocated to a unit clearly indicates the avoidance of abatement costs that are higher than those experienced elsewhere. Similarly, sizable emissions reductions that would be overcontrol in a no-trading context have little other explanation than being the "production" of allowances for use elsewhere or later, either internally or through sale in the external market.[3]

2. See Oates et al. (1989) for an excellent discussion of comparisons between CAC and market-based alternatives. Hahn (1989), Hahn and Hester (1989), and NERA (1994) provide reviews of pre-Title IV experience with emissions trading. The relatively small lead phase-out program is the principal success among earlier experiments with emissions trading.
3. Some Phase I units must meet lower emission rates than required by Title IV because of state or local emission limits. However, little of the emission reduction in Phase I comes from these units, which are located mostly in Wisconsin, Minnesota, New York, and Massachusetts.

The emergence of an external allowance market, as discussed in Chapter 7, provides further evidence of cost-saving behavior. The allowance market has been characterized by transparent prices, ease of price discovery, low transaction costs, and substantial trading volumes since mid-1994. All this indicates active selling and buying interest on each side of the market. Since an allowance ultimately has no other use than to meet the Title IV requirement to cover emissions, it is hard to envisage any other basis for observed allowance prices than the current abatement cost and perceptions of future cost. As is true of any commodity or financial instrument, perceptions and prices change over time, and the allowance market has experienced some notable volatility since 1994. Still, well-defined bottoms and ceilings have always emerged as buyers and sellers appear at their respective sides of the market. It is certainly not proven that all utilities are fully participating in this market and thereby eliminating all arbitrage opportunities, but this standard is met in few real markets. In fact, a significant number of utilities have been active players in the allowance market. For many utilities, especially those with Phase II units but no Phase I units, the allowance market is the only means to take advantage of lower abatement-cost opportunities in Phase I. The allowance market provides a relatively cheap source of compliance for all who face or expect to face high marginal costs of abatement, and it is a source of potential profit for all who can abate on the margin for less than the going price of allowances. The emergence of a vibrant allowance market and the significant participation in it indicate that utilities with Phase I and Phase II units are taking extensive, though not necessarily full, advantage of the cost-saving opportunities presented by emissions trading.

A third set of evidence concerning cost savings is supplied by the convergence of the premium paid for lower-sulfur coal with allowance prices, together with the related changes in abatement at Phase I units. If operators of Phase I units were seeking to achieve the cost savings possible through emissions trading, they would compare allowance prices with the premium paid for lower-sulfur coals, translated into an equivalent allowance value (EAV),[4] and

4. The calculation of equivalent allowance value (EAV) typically requires information on the price, SO_2 content and heat content of the coals being compared. EAV is computed by multiplying the ratio of the difference in price between the two coals to the difference in SO_2 content (both differences expressed per millions of Btu of heat content) by the number of pounds in a short ton, 2000. Although sulfur content is now increasingly expressed as pounds of SO_2 per millions of Btu of heat input, coal prices continue to be

choose coals accordingly. If the EAV premium to be paid for a lower-sulfur coal were less than the cost of an allowance, utilities' coal buyers would purchase a lower-sulfur coal instead of a cheaper but otherwise comparable higher-sulfur coal. Conversely, when allowances are cheaper than the EAV premium for lower-sulfur coal, utilities' coal buyers would choose the higher-sulfur coal and use more allowances. If utility coal buyers were performing this type of cost-saving arbitrage between the real and paper markets for SO_2 abatement, two related phenomena should be observed. First, allowance prices and the EAV coal-sulfur premium would tend to converge. Second, when allowance prices fall, as they did between 1994 and 1996, emission rates at Phase I units should increase on average, and when allowance prices increase, as they have since 1996, emission rates should decline, on average. Both phenomena have been observed.

A good example of the convergence of the coal-sulfur premium with allowance values is shown in Figure 10.1. Prior to the emergence of the allowance market in 1994 and going back as far as 1987, the premium between low- and mid-sulfur coals from central Appalachia had fluctuated, when stated in equivalent allowance value, from a peak of $400 to a negative $140. Since 1994, the relationship between these two coals has been much more stable, with one very interesting exception.[5]

On the eve of Phase I, the EAV premium for low-sulfur coal from central Appalachia rose to $400, well above the contemporaneous allowance price, but the explanation for this exception and its quick disappearance demonstrate the convergence of these two markets. In late 1994, many thought that allowance prices were below equilibrium levels. A corollary of that belief was that allowance prices would increase once Phase I took effect and utilities would have to start covering emissions with allowances. Facing such a prospect, no coal producer would want to sell cheaply in the last quarter of 1994 what would be worth much more in the first quarter of 1995. As a result, the price of low-sulfur coal from central Appalachia rose relative to

quoted in dollars per ton of coal. It is necessary therefore to divide the coal price by the heat content of the coal, expressed as millions of Btus, to obtain the numerator for the ratio of differences needed to calculate equivalent allowance value.

5. Other coal-producing regions exhibit similar patterns, although none is quite so clear as the pattern in central Appalachia, which is moreover the predominant source of low- and mid-sulfur coals in the eastern part of the United States.

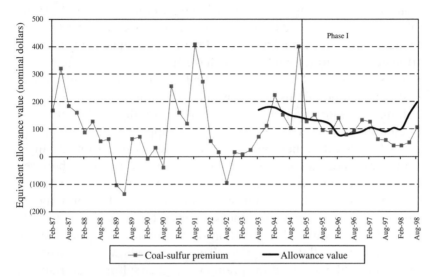

Figure 10.1. Allowance value vs. coal-sulfur premium, central Appalachia, 12,500 Btu/lb, 1.5 to 2.0 lb/mmBtu.
Source: Fieldston (1997, 1998).

the price of the competing mid-sulfur coal. When Phase I began and the price of allowances did not rise, however, it became quickly evident that utility coal buyers would not pay the equivalent of $400 for compliance that could then be obtained in the allowance market for about $125. Given the price of the higher-sulfur coal and allowance values, producers of low-sulfur coal had no alternative but to return to the previous price and premium. If utilities' coal buyers had not been alive to the cost-saving opportunities afforded by using more allowances and purchasing higher-sulfur coal, the price of lower-sulfur coal would not have collapsed. Since then, this coal-sulfur premium and the allowance price have remained very close to each other, although there was a tendency in 1998 for the coal premium to lag behind allowance prices.

The effects of such cost-saving arbitrage between allowances and lower-sulfur coal should also be evident in observed emission rates. So long as the sulfur premium embedded in coal prices does not adjust instantaneously to changes in allowance prices, falling allowance prices should be associated with rising average emission rates, as it becomes more attractive to shift away from lower-sulfur coal to bundles of higher-sulfur coal and allowances. Similarly, rising allowance prices should be associated with falling emission rates. This tendency will not be observed at all Phase I units since many are constrained by contract, and not all have access to both higher- and lower-sulfur coals; however, those that can respond to differences between coal premiums and allowance prices do so.

Emission rates will also change as a result of the bundling of allowances with coal deliveries in coal-supply contracts. Coal suppliers bundle allowances with coal deliveries in part to make high-sulfur coal more attractive, but also to conduct arbitrage between the allowance and coal markets.[6] They do so by contracting to deliver a 2.5 lb/mmBtu coal, for instance, and deliver either that or a higher-sulfur coal with enough allowances to make it the Title IV equivalent to a 2.5 lb/mmBtu coal, depending on the relation of prices in the coal market to allowance prices. Thus, when allowance prices are lower than the coal-sulfur premium, higher-sulfur coal bundled with allowances will be delivered. Conversely, when the sulfur premium is less than current allowance value, lower-sulfur coal will be delivered.

Figure 10.2 presents a histogram of the changes in emission rates observed at the 401 continuously affected units between 1995 and 1997. The first column reflects changes in emission rates from 1995 to 1996 and the second column, changes from 1996 to 1997. The categories represent the changes occurring between partitions established at ±0.20 lb/mmBtu, ±0.50 lb/mmBtu, ±1.00 lb/mmBtu, and ±2.00 lb/mmBtu. The middle pair of columns, labeled "no change," includes all units with an observed change in the annual emission rate of less than ±0.20 lb/mmBtu, which is what could be expected in any year-to-year comparison as a result of the natural variability of any given coal's sulfur content.[7] Observed changes greater than this "no change" category are designated "slight," "modest," "large," and "very large," according to the intervals between the values just cited. Thus, very large changes in emission rate are those more than ±2.00 lb/mmBtu.

---

6. A number of coal suppliers have opened accounts with the Allowance Tracking System and regularly move allowances in and out of these accounts as they buy allowances and bundle them with coal supplies. For a discussion of bundling coal and allowances, see Doucet and Strauss (1994).
7. The average absolute deviations for the mean change in emission rates from 1995 to 1996 and from 1996 to 1997 are 0.293 and 0.218, respectively.

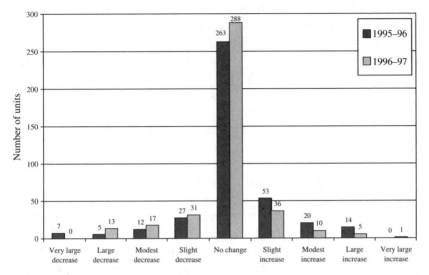

Figure 10.2. Distribution of changes in emission rates, 1995–97.
Sources: Derived from Pechan (1995) and EPA (1996b, 1997, 1998).

The most prominent feature of these distributions is the large number of units that made little change in their emission rate regardless of the period of comparison. A number of explanations can be offered for such stability. Operators of some of these units may simply not be responsive to allowance price changes, but the fixity of abatement choices and locational or plant-specific restrictions limit many units' ability to respond to allowance price changes. For instance, eighteen of the twenty-one retrofitted scrubbers that were operating for all of 1995 are included in this group. Similar fixity would obtain for fuel-switching units that had signed long-term coal contracts extending throughout these three years.

The tails of these distributions reveal the cost-saving arbitrage of units capable of switching among bituminous coals. Given procurement and contracting lag times, the effect of declining allowance prices throughout 1995 would appear in the comparison of emission rates between 1995 and 1996, and the subsequent rise in allowance prices would show up in the change between 1996 and 1997. The number of units increasing emissions slightly or more between 1995 and 1996 outnumbers those reducing their emissions, 87 to 51, while between 1996 and 1997 the relation is reversed, with 52 increasing versus 61 decreasing. The heat-input weighted average emission rate shows a similar pattern, rising from 1.70 lb/mmBtu in 1995 to 1.75 lb/mmBtu in 1996 and then falling to 1.71 lb/mmBtu in 1997. The 1998 data were not available at the time of this writing, but the sharp rise in allowance prices in 1998 and the disparity between allowance prices and coal premiums for 1998 in Figure 10.1 imply further reduction of emission rates in 1998.

In short, various indicators suggest that electric utilities have taken advantage of the opportunities to reduce compliance cost afforded by Title IV's allowance-trading system. Operators of Phase I units have not taken allowance allocations as the effective limits on individual units' emissions; a reasonably efficient and robust allowance market has developed, and convergence between the value of lower-sulfur content in coal and allowance prices can be observed. Exceptions and qualifications to these indicators can be cited, but the general tendency is clear. The simplest and most obvious explanation for the observed behavior is that utilities are taking advantage of the cost-saving opportunities afforded by emissions trading.

BASIC ANALYTIC FRAMEWORK

A Command-and-Control Alternative to Title IV

Any estimate of the cost savings from emissions trading will depend greatly upon the choice of the hypothetical CAC alternative to which it is compared. There would be little point in choosing an implausibly costly CAC alternative that would generate large cost savings for even a poorly implemented market-based system. Accordingly, the first task is to define a plausible CAC alternative against which to measure the cost savings from emissions trading.

Legislative proposals to enact acid rain legislation throughout the 1980s provide one CAC alternative. These proposals typically mandated scrubbers at a certain number of units, required other units to meet a prescribed standard (1.2 lb SO_2/mmBtu), and provided limited "bubbling," usually only at the state level. Still, these proposals are not particularly useful, in part because many involved different levels of aggregate SO_2 abatement than does Title IV, but also because none proposed the two-phase approach ultimately adopted. A further problem is that none of the earlier proposals were able to muster enough legislative support to warrant a floor vote in the House of Representatives and the Senate, so there is some question about their plausibility as a CAC alternative.

A more plausible alternative can be derived by reference both to Title IV itself and to the conventional approach to air-emission regulation in the United States. As noted in Chapter 3, the legislative jostling for allowances proceeded on the implicit assumption that little allowance trading would be observed, so that each utility would be limited in its emissions by the allowances it initially received. Yet, source- or unit-specific emission limits have long been the preferred approach to emissions control under the Clean Air Act. For instance, all units affected by Title IV are subject to source-specific emission rate limits imposed either through a state implementation plan or the New Source Performance Standards. Title IV imposed a quantity rather than a rate limit, but otherwise a source-specific approach would not have been inconsistent with past practice.

In this chapter, we define the CAC alternative as a *unit*-level tonnage limit equal to the amount of allowances received, as a compromise between these two referents. This unit-level alternative is more limiting than what was widely expected when the legislation was being debated; however, a utility-level limitation would have been a significant change in the regulation of utility air emissions and thus hardly what most would have viewed as traditional "command-and-control." Defining the CAC alternative to include intrautility emissions trading would also exclude what would be both a significant innovation and a source of significant cost savings.

A Simple Two-Period Model of Cost Savings

The cost savings from Title IV emissions trading are depicted schematically in Figure 10.3. Two periods are represented. A certain amount of abatement is mandated in each, with more required in the second period than in the first. The quantity of abatement required in each period is represented on the x-axis, from O_1 to R_{NT} for the first period and from O_2 on the right to R_{NT} for the second period. The y-axes represent the per ton cost of abatement in each period, with the Period 2 cost stated in present-value terms at an appropriate discount rate. The two lines originating at both the left and right

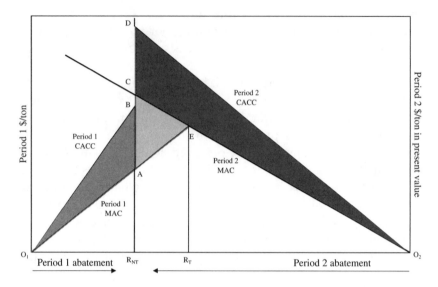

Figure 10.3. Illustrative two-period cost-savings diagram.

origins represent the marginal abatement cost (MAC) and what we shall call the command-and-control cost (CACC) for each of the two periods. The MACs, the two lower lines, have the conventional economic meaning in that (a) they indicate the marginal cost at which a given quantity of abatement can be achieved efficiently (i.e., at least cost), and (b) the area under the plot represents the total cost of abatement.

The two upper lines, O_1B for Period 1 and O_2D for Period 2, represent the command-and-control costs of abatement required of all affected units, R_{NT}. Each affected unit can be represented by a column, the base of which equals the abatement required at that unit, and the height of which is the average cost incurred to realize that abatement. Some units' mandated abatement would be very cheap, while abatement at other units would be very expensive; which units abate how much is determined by the details of command-and-control regulation, not, as in the construction of the MAC, by minimization of total cost. If these columns are arrayed along the abatement axis from least to most costly, the succession of columns will cover an area equal to total abatement cost, and the tops of columns can be connected to create a line looking like a MAC. As such, the CACC has no economic meaning; it simply depicts the cost of mandated abatement levels at each affected unit in a way that facilitates comparison with the area under the economically meaningful MAC.

For each period, the MAC and CACC plots represent alternative combinations of abatement at affected units that achieve the same aggregate reduction of emissions. The difference in the total cost associated with the alternative arrangements is the cost savings achievable by rearranging amounts of abatement undertaken by affected units. Such a rearrangement might be achieved by issuing rights for allowed emissions to each affected unit after the mandated reduction, and letting the affected units trade those rights among themselves. Under such circumstances, both the units facing lower incremental costs and those facing higher incremental costs would find it in their interest to exchange rights to emit at a price that makes the deal worthwhile to both, and to modify their abatement plans accordingly. When all economically attractive exchanges have been consummated, the most efficient arrangement of abatement for any given level of aggregate abatement will have been achieved. The resulting array of unit-specific compliance cost columns would represent a true marginal abatement cost curve.

Accordingly, the area between the CACC and the MAC plots up to the aggregate mandated emissions reduction represents the cost savings that can be obtained by a more efficient allocation of abatement across generating units in each period, or by the spatial trading of emissions rights. (This area is positive because the MAC corresponds to minimum-cost abatement, but the CACC does not.) These areas are denoted in Figure 10.3 by the shaded triangles.

Further cost savings are available if emissions trading between the two time periods, via allowance banking, is permitted.[8] We refer to such trading in what follows as "intertemporal trading." Given an efficient allocation of abatement across sources in each period, if the present value of the expected marginal cost of abatement in the second period is higher than the marginal cost of abatement in the first period, then it is worth abating more in the first period and

8. For the trading discussed here to be environmentally benign, it must be the case that a ton-for-ton shift of emissions from the first period to the second does no environmental harm. This is generally thought to be the case for acid rain because damages apparently depend primarily on cumulative emissions, but it would not necessarily hold if damages depended instead, for instance, on the highest per-period emissions level.

less in the second, until present and discounted future marginal costs are equal. As drawn in Figure 10.3, the slopes of the MAC plots and the required abatement levels are such that the present value cost of the last increment of required abatement is higher in the second period than in the first period. If trading were permitted between the two periods, so that additional abatement in the first period could be "banked" to relieve abatement requirements in the second, affected units would trade between periods until marginal costs were equal. Such an intertemporal equilibrium is represented in Figure 10.3 by the point E, which is determined by the intersection of the two MAC plots. With intertemporal trading, the additional abatement under-taken in the first period is the amount $R_T R_{NT}$, and a corresponding amount of abatement would be avoided in the second period. Affected units would incur additional abatement costs equal to the area $R_{NT} A E R_T$ in the first period, thereby avoiding the cost repre-sented by the area $R_{NT} C E R_T$ in the second. Consequently, the trian-gle ACE represents the cost savings from the intertemporal trading of emissions and abatement requirements.

The total cost savings from emissions trading is the sum of these three components: spatial trading in the first period, spatial trading in the second period, and banking, represented by the three triangles in Figure 10.3. This sum is the difference between what would be the total cost of abatement without either spatial or intertemporal trading, the area $O_1 BCDO_2$, and the total cost of abatement with trading, the area $O_1 AEO_2$. While this total is unambiguous, the shares of total savings attributable to spatial trading in the second period and to banking are arbitrary. As presented in Figure 10.3, spatial trading is assumed first so that the additional savings from banking is the small triangle ACE. In actuality, because of banking, the abate-ment that creates the savings from spatial trading does not occur. Because of this, it could be said that the savings from banking are greater than indicated by triangle ACE; however, the magnitude of this additional amount cannot be estimated uniquely since there is no correspondence between the MAC and CACC segments.[9]

9. All that can be said for abatement represented by marginal cost of $200, for instance, in the MAC is that it avoided the cost of some abatement in the CACC that cost more than $200. Whether the avoided abatement would have cost $201 or $400 cannot be determined. By the same token, the cost savings from spatial trading that would have been associated with the efficient Phase II abatement avoided by banking cannot be uniquely determined.

Some Simplifying Assumptions

Applying this basic framework to the observed data of Phase I compliance with Title IV requires a number of simplifying assumptions. Two are fundamental: The operators of Phase I units are assumed to act rationally, in the sense that they seek to minimize costs, and they are assumed to have full information about the future. These assumptions imply that (a) observed Phase I compliance costs correspond exactly to the efficient MAC and (b) observed banking accurately reflects cost differences between Phase I and Phase II. Neither assumption is likely to be literally correct in any real setting, but both are extremely useful here, and we do not know how to model imperfect rationality or imperfect foresight in an objective, tractable manner.[10] Moreover, variations on our basic assumptions can be employed to examine the sensitivity of the estimated cost savings to errors in expectation.

Two other assumptions are more specific to the particular framework of analysis presented above. They are that the MAC and CACC curves are linear and pass through the origin, and that the costs of Phase I and Phase II can be depicted as two representative, average years. Since these two assumptions are more particular to this analysis, both require justification.

The assumption that marginal and average costs rise linearly with abatement is intended only as a convenient approximation. Economic theory and reasoning impose relatively few restrictions on the shape of the MAC: Zero abatement should correspond to zero cost, and the MAC should rise with increased abatement. The second of these holds for the CACC by construction, but the first need not hold. (Suppose, for instance, that only units with high control costs are constrained in the no-trading case.) A schedule similar to a MAC is given in Figure 9.1 for average unit cost at the 200 or so units that made noticeable emission reductions in 1995, and it is convex over some regions and concave over others. Other studies of the cost of Title IV, such as EPRI (1993) and GAO (1994), exhibit similar curves, with both concave and convex sections. The assumption of linearity (and,

---

10. Thus we are treating actual Phase I behavior in some respects as if it were fully efficient, even though it almost surely has not been. As this assumption is employed in what follows, however, we believe it is a useful approximation and not likely to be a source of significant bias.

for the CACC, passage through the origin) enables us to fix the positions of the MAC and the CACC plots using data drawn from the experience in Phase I. Moreover, we are unaware of any reason why this assumption should bias our results in any particular direction.

The second simplifying assumption is the use of only two representative years to depict costs and cost savings, rather than a full multiyear model. This assumption is primarily an expositional device. The same results could be obtained by a more laborious and less intuitive calculation of the costs and cost savings in all relevant years of Phases I and II. If one had perfect foresight or were looking back from some Phase II year with complete information, the annual costs and cost savings could be summed and averaged for the five years of Phase I and for some set of years in Phase II.

Since Phase II extends infinitely into the future, some terminal point must be chosen if any sum or average is to be calculated. A natural terminal point is the Phase II year in which the allowance bank is drawn down and all cost savings from intertemporal trading have been realized. (Savings from spatial trading in Phase II will, of course, continue indefinitely.) Summing the cost savings over those years would provide a present-value sum, which could be divided by the number of Phase II years covered to provide an average. Although it is most natural to think of that average as the number of years over which the bank is drawn down, perhaps eight, the present-value sum could be divided by any number to yield a different average. Doing so effectively divides the banking period into $(N/5) \times 12$ months, where N is the number of years over which the allowances banked in Phase I are used. Comparison of the two periods in the two-way diagram is made much easier when the discounted Phase II sum is divided by 5. For instance, with an eight-year draw-down, the allowances accumulated in each average Phase I year will avoid a like number of emissions over every 19.2 months of the Phase II draw-down. The 12-month year is, after all, a convention, and any more appropriate period of time can be used to simplify the analysis.

An Optimal Multiyear Banking Program

The concept of a "representative year" can be made more understandable by illustrating what each year in two multiyear periods, such as Phase I and Phase II, might look like.[11] With perfect information and rational behavior, aggregate emissions and allowance prices would follow optimal paths such as depicted in the two panels of Figure 10.4. The top panel shows a hypothetical optimal emissions path and its relationship to counterfactual emissions and the annual allowance distribution for the Phase I and Phase II periods. The bottom panel shows a possible optimal allowance price path associated with this emissions path. In both panels, the horizontal axis represents years from the start of Phase I, t_0, to the start of Phase II, t', to the year when the bank is exhausted, t_T, and beyond. The vertical axis for the top panel shows the quantity of emissions or allowances, and the vertical axis for the optimal allowance price path in the bottom panel is stated in *nominal* (i.e., nondiscounted) dollars.

In the top panel, the aggregate allowance distribution is stipulated by law, and counterfactual emissions are assumed to be rising, as they would with increasing demand for coal-fired electricity over time. The annual Phase I allocation is shown roughly as it was in reality, with more allowances in 1995 and 1996 than in the remaining three years of Phase I. (The small number of extra allowances distributed in the first ten years of Phase II is ignored for the sake of simplicity.) With no banking, the required reduction in aggregate emissions would be the distance from the level of counterfactual emissions in each year to the corresponding quantity of allowances distributed that year. Note that there would be two sharp, discontinuous increases in abatement: the first in 1997, since most Phase I extension allowances were distributed in 1995 and 1996, and the second in the year 2000, with the start of Phase II. Finally, with a rising level of counterfactual emissions over time, the amount of abatement required in each succeeding year would increase even with an unchanging distribution of allowances.

The optimal emissions path is downward sloping from t_0 to t_T, at a rate determined by the pattern of required reductions (the differences between counterfactual emissions and the aggregate allowance allocation), abatement costs, the discount rate, and the number of affected units. With the sharp increase in required abatement at the

11. See Chapter 7 and especially Note 29 there. For a more complete development of the economic theory of Title IV banking, see Schennach (1998).

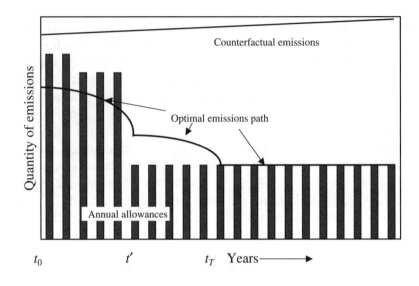

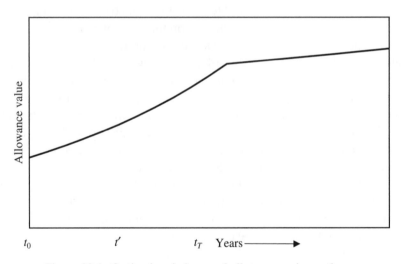

Figure 10.4. Optimal emissions and allowance price paths.

end of Phase I, marginal abatement cost will increase at a rate greater than the discount rate and thus it will be optimal to bank at least some allowances in Phase I to avoid the higher-cost abatement in Phase II. In a world without surprises, the optimal emissions path would begin below the first annual allowance distribution and decline continuously over time until the bank is exhausted. After the bank is exhausted, optimal emissions each year would equal the number of allowances issued for that year (i.e., the permanent de facto cap on annual emissions). The distance between the quantity of allowances issued for each year and the optimal emissions path represents the number of allowances banked during each year of Phase I. The same distance during the Phase II period represents the draw-down of the bank. The quantities banked in Phase I and used in Phase II must equal one another.

The second panel of Figure 10.4 presents the optimal allowance price path corresponding to the optimal emissions path in the top panel. With a fixed, more stringent Phase II cap and no surprises, the equilibrium price of allowances will rise smoothly at the rate of interest throughout the banking period from t_0 to t_T. With a rising level of counterfactual emissions and a roughly constant quantity of allowances issued each year, the price will continue rising after the bank is exhausted, but at a rate less than the discount rate: hence, the kink at t_T. Briefly, if the marginal cost of abatement in Phase II is expected to be higher in present value than today's marginal cost, then costs would be minimized over time by abating more today and using the allowances thus produced to cover emissions in Phase II. With marginal cost rising as a function of abatement, such action would increase Phase I marginal cost of abatement and lower expected Phase II marginal cost, and the process would continue until marginal cost is brought into equivalence on a present-value basis for every year over the banking period. Another way to visualize this is to note that, were the allowance price to rise more slowly (faster) than the rate of interest, making allowances inferior (superior) to other stores of value, market participants would sell (buy) allowances in large quantities, thus shifting the price path. If there is no banking, allowances are not serving as a store of value, and the allowance price can rise more slowly than the rate of interest.

The price and quantity data from this multiyear optimal banking program provide the data that are averaged and compressed into two representative years for purposes of the simplified representation provided in Figure 10.3 and the computations that follow. One key computational issue must be addressed to work with the two representative Phase I and Phase II years. The equilibrium price path in Figure 10.4 is expressed in nominal dollars. If those prices were instead expressed at their discounted present value in the initial year, t_0, the equilibrium price path would be flat from t_0 to t_T and decline thereafter. The equality of the discounted equilibrium allowance price in all years of the banking period permits both the representation of Phase II costs in present-value terms and the use of the point of intertemporal equilibrium depicted by point E in Figure 10.3.

The optimal quantities, on the other hand, need not be discounted, so they can be read off the optimal emissions path and averaged as appropriate for the two-period diagram. The quantity $O_1 R_{NT}$ in Figure 10.3 is the average of the distance from counterfactual emissions to the allowance distribution for each year of Phase I, and the quantity $O_2 R_{NT}$ is the corresponding average for Phase II years from t' to t_T. The average of the annual differences between the allowance distribution and the optimal emissions path in Phase I will define the distance $R_{NT} R_T$, which is the average annual additional abatement in Phase I for banking. This sum will, of course, equal the sum of the comparable differences during the Phase II banking period.

POSITIONING THE TITLE IV COST CURVES

The framework for measuring cost savings from the Title IV allowance-trading system relative to a plausible command-and-control alternative can be implemented by "fitting" the CACC and MAC relationships depicted in Figure 10.3 to observed data from the first three years of Phase I, using the economic reasoning embodied in the optimal banking program discussed above. Observed emission quantities and prices are not as smooth as the lines drawn in Figure 10.4, largely because costs and expectations change over time, but the economic reasoning presented above still applies. Periods 1 and 2 in Figure 10.3 are, of course, Phases I and II, and the abatement quantity axis is denominated in millions of tons from the periods' respective origins. The vertical axes represent dollars per ton (or per allowance), with the Phase I axis on the left stated in initial Phase I dollars (1995$) and the Phase II axis on the right in Phase II dollars discounted to initial Phase I present value.

Table 10.1. *Data for average Phase I year*

Phase I year	Counterfactual emissions	Allowance allocation	Emissions	Required reduction	Abatement	Banking
		(All data in millions of tons)				
1995	9.26	8.69	5.30	0.57	3.96	3.39
1996	9.51	8.27	5.43	1.24	4.08	2.84
1997	9.73	7.11	5.47	2.62	4.26	1.64
1998	9.88	7.11	5.52	2.77	4.36	1.59
1999	10.02	7.11	5.57	2.91	4.45	1.54
Total	48.40	38.29	27.29	10.11	21.11	11.00
Average	9.68	7.66	5.46	2.02	4.22	2.20

Required Abatement in Phases I and II

The entire length of the horizontal axis in Figure 10.3 is the sum of the amount of emissions abatement required without emissions trading in the representative Phase I and Phase II years, which is equal to the quantities O_1R_{NT} and O_2R_{NT}, counting from the respective origins. The data for Phase I are more than half complete so that a fairly accurate estimate of the quantity O_1R_{NT} can be made. Table 10.1 provides the actual data for 1995–97 and our estimates for counterfactual emissions, allowances, and actual emissions in the remaining two years of Phase I.[12] The amount of abatement required in 1995 was very small, 0.57 million tons, primarily because of the distribution of bonus allowances. However, the amount of abatement required has risen steadily to what is estimated to be 2.91 million tons of required abatement in 1999. When averaged over the five years of Phase I, the required abatement without trading for the Phase I representative year is 2.02 million tons, which corresponds to the quantity O_1R_{NT} in Figure 10.3.

The required reduction in aggregate emissions for the Phase II representative year is the average difference between the allowance distribution and counterfactual emissions in these years. Table 10.2 provides an accounting of allowances and emissions for Phase II similar to that just presented for Phase I; the sources of these

---

12. The data for 1995–97 are drawn from Table 5.2 for all affected units. Note that the allowance distribution includes 150,000 allowances sold at auction in each year. The 1998–99 estimates assume a 1.5% annual increase in counterfactual emissions from 1997, the same allowance distribution as in 1997, and an end-of-Phase I bank of 11 million allowances.

Table 10.2. *Data for average Phase II year*

Phase II year	Counterfactual emissions	Allowance allocation	Emissions	Required reduction	Abatement	Banking
	(All data in millions of tons)					
2000	17.80	9.40	11.80	8.40	6.00	−2.40
2001	18.06	9.40	11.60	8.66	6.46	−2.20
2002	18.34	9.40	11.40	8.94	6.94	−2.00
2003	18.61	9.40	11.10	9.21	7.51	−1.70
2004	18.89	9.40	10.70	9.49	8.19	−1.30
2005	19.17	9.40	10.30	9.77	8.87	−0.90
2006	19.46	9.40	9.80	10.06	9.76	−0.40
2007	19.75	9.40	9.50	10.35	10.25	−0.10
	Totals and averages					
Total	150.08	75.20	86.20	74.88	63.88	−11.00
8-year average	17.76	9.40	10.78	9.36	7.99	−1.38
5-year average	30.01	15.04	17.24	14.97	12.77	−2.20
	Reference years					
1997	17.02	NA	12.59	NA	NA	NA
2008	20.05	9.40	9.40	10.65	10.65	0.00

numbers are described below. In addition to the simulated data for the eight years over which we assume the bank will be drawn down, Table 10.2 provides sums of the quantities shown over the eight years of the Phase II banking period, as well as the five- and eight-year averages. The final panel in the table provides comparable data for 1997, the Phase I year used as the basis for predicting counterfactual emissions, and for 2008, the first Phase II year in which we assume the bank will be fully exhausted.[13]

The number of allowances to be issued for each Phase II year is already known. A second quantity that can be identified with reasonable accuracy is the size of the bank at the end of Phase I: about 11 million allowances. Given these two quantities and assuming that the allowance bank will be drawn down in the first eight years of Phase II, the average level of emissions can be quickly calculated. As

13. The most recent detailed analysis of Phase II compliance took as a "medium" case a nine-year draw-down for a bank of 12.35 million tons (EPRI, 1997). Our assumption of eight years for the draw-down reflects the smaller size of the predicted bank. EPRI (1997) was published before 1996 or 1997 compliance data were available. Load growth has also been quite strong since 1995 so that, in the absence of significant further abatement in Phase I, the predicted bank is smaller than might have been expected on the basis of 1995 data alone.

shown in Table 10.2, there will be 75.2 million allowances distributed over these eight years. When the 11 million banked allowances are included, total emissions over the period can be predicted to be 86.2 million tons, or 10.8 million tons, on average, over these eight years. The amount by which the bank is drawn down will decline with each passing Phase II year, but the average over the eight years will be 1.38 million allowances, or five-eighths of the average annual amount banked in Phase I.

The only other quantity needed to fill in the rest of the cells in Table 10.2 is an estimate of counterfactual emissions, which cannot be more than a prediction from an observed year. Our estimate of counter-factual emissions for all Title IV units in 1997 is 17.02 million tons: 9.73 million tons for the Phase I units (as indicated in Table 5.2, using the simple counterfactual) and 7.29 million tons for the units that will become subject to Title IV in Phase II (actual 1997 emissions for these units as reported by EPA's Emissions Monitoring System). Emissions at Phase II units have risen at an average annual rate of 2.2% over the period from 1985 to 1997, which included the recession of 1992. Since the recession, the rate of emissions increase has risen to 3.6%. For Phase I units, the rate of increase in counterfactual emissions is significantly less because of the cost-driven trend to more intensive use of Powder River Basin coal, discussed in Chapter 4. Since 1993, counterfactual emissions at Phase I units have increased at an annual rate of 1.7%, about half that of the Phase II units, most of which are located beyond the reach of the PRB or are already using PRB coals.[14] Counterfactual emissions from Phase I units were also still below the level of emissions in 1985. When the Phase I and Phase II units are taken together, any annual growth rate between 1% and perhaps 2.5% per annum could be justified for the entire 1997–2007 decade. We chose 1.5%, to give the numbers displayed in Table 10.2, which are comparable to the growth rates assumed by others.[15]

The remaining numbers in Table 10.2 follow from the assumptions made above about the number of allowances distributed annually, the size and time profile of the bank draw-down, and the growth in coun-

14. This rate of growth is based upon the econometrically estimated counterfactual because it takes the PRB trend into account.
15. EPRI (1997) notes a range of forecasts for the growth in coal-fired generation over this period between 1% and 2.5% per annum. This latest study by EPRI researchers picked 2% as the base case and 1% as a low growth alternative.

terfactual emissions. The average required reduction in emissions over the assumed eight-year banking period is 9.4 million tons, which becomes 15.0 million tons when converted to a five-year average comparable to the representative Phase I year. The average "withdrawal" from the aggregate allowance bank is 1.38 million tons, which becomes 2.2 million tons when converted to a five-year average, and which then equals the average annual "deposit" into the bank during Phase I. Put another way, the five-year average statistics in Table 10.2 indicate that every 2.2 million tons of allowances banked in Phase I will avoid 2.2 million tons of abatement in Phase II, and this saving will occur on average over a 1.3 ($= 8/5$)-year period during which 15.0 million tons of Phase II abatement would otherwise have been required. This last quantity corresponds to the distance O_2R_{NT} in Figure 10.3, which is needed to complete the horizontal axis for calculating the cost savings from emissions trading.

Observed Intertemporal Equilibrium

The Phase I and Phase II MACs can be located by reference to the point of intertemporal equilibrium represented by point E in Figure 10.3. This is the point at which the marginal abatement cost in Phase I equals the discounted marginal abatement cost in Phase II. On the quantity axis, this point corresponds to the average amount of abatement observed in Phase I, and the corresponding point on the vertical axis is the long-run marginal cost of abatement in Phase I. Intertemporal arbitrage implies that this point is observed in Phase I. The point R_T on the quantity axis has already been determined; it is the 4.22 million tons of average annual abatement observed in Phase I, as shown in the next-to-last column of Table 10.1.

The corresponding ordinate can be taken from Figure 9.1, which shows the schedule of the average cost of abatement, by unit, for the aggregate emission reduction observed in 1995. Since capital cost is included in the 1995 estimates and the capital is still in place, this schedule can be seen as depicting the long-run marginal cost of abatement for Phase I. As presented, this schedule has some peculiar features, notably, a stretch of zero-cost abatement for the first 500,000 tons and a very high-cost tail rising to as much as $800/ton of SO_2 abated. For the present purpose, we ignore both of these extremes and focus on the long-run marginal cost in the segment of the curve just before the high-cost tail. Abatement opportunities appear to be relatively continuous up to about $350 per ton of SO_2 removed. Thus, the intertemporal equilibrium, point E in Figure 10.3, is defined as [4.2, $350], and lines drawn from this point of intertemporal arbitrage to the Phase I and Phase II origins represent the Phase I and Phase II MACs.[16] In the case of the Phase II MAC, we assume it extends linearly beyond this point to the full amount of abatement that would be required in Phase II without banking. The implied average total abatement cost for the representative Phase I year, the area under the Phase I MAC up to R_T, is $735 million, which is virtually identical to the estimate of Phase I abatement cost presented in Chapter 9, $726 million.

The distance between the point on the horizontal (abatement) axis corresponding to the assumed intertemporal equilibrium, R_T, and the no-trade point, R_{NT}, measures the amount of additional abatement undertaken in an average Phase I year and, thus, the amount of required abatement avoided in each representative Phase II "year." That amount is 2.2 million tons, so that for every 15.0 million tons of Phase II abatement required during the banking period (O_2R_{NT}), 12.8 million tons (O_2R_T) will actually be abated. As Table 10.2 indicates, when expressed as annual averages over the expected *eight*-year draw-down of the allowance bank, the corresponding figures are 9.4 million tons of required abatement without banking, 1.4 million tons of abatement avoided because of banking, and 8.0 million tons of abatement performed.

Positioning the CACCs

Excess allowances introduce a methodological complication into the positioning of the CACC and the consequent estimate of cost savings from spatial trading. The usual assumption in tradable-permit programs is that each affected unit is constrained by its allowance allocation, so that the aggregate emission reduction is the same whether trading occurs or not. When some units receive allowances in excess of their counterfactual (i.e., unconstrained) emissions, however, the aggregate abatement required in the emissions trading and command-and-control cases is no longer the same. This difference in

---

16. Given the approximate nature of these estimates, we work in tenths of million tons and thus round down from the previously cited 4.22 million tons.

the quantity of abatement involves a difference in the benefits from abatement as well as in the cost of abatement. In a no-trading regime, excess allowances that cannot be used effectively tighten the aggregate emissions cap.

The ability to reallocate excess allowances through spatial and intertemporal trading would clearly be welfare enhancing on balance if the cap represented optimal abatement. In this case, trading would both reduce costs and move emissions (upward!) to their optimal level. More generally, however, a correct calculation of the net benefits of trading excess allowances must take into account both the cost savings from avoiding abatement in aggregate and the reduced benefits due to increased emissions.[17] Counting the cost savings but not the fall in benefits would be justified only if marginal benefit of abatement were zero. If this were the case, however, it would represent a very serious problem with the program. Since we cannot compare the benefits of different levels of emissions reduction, the best we can do is to avoid overstating the cost savings from emissions trading by ignoring the savings associated with reallocation of excess allowances. Formally, we do this by adjusting the level of abatement required in the no-trading command-and-control case to equal the amount of abatement required in the observed allowance-trading case.

Holding aggregate abatement constant between the trading and no-trading cases gives rise to a two-step process for estimating the CACC. First, the Phase I CACC is located based on observed data, as if abatement were not being held constant. Then, an adjustment is made as if the regulatory authority had reallocated allowances to affected units in order to avoid the tightening of the cap that would have occurred because excess allowances had been created (for whatever reasons) at some affected units.

Table 10.3 provides the numbers for accomplishing the first step. The key variable is the amount of required abatement avoided by trading. Where observed emissions are greater than the allowance allocation to a Phase I unit, abatement has been avoided by emissions trading. For instance, in 1995, 152 out of 263 Table A units received fewer allowances than their respective estimated counterfactual emissions, using the simple counterfactual from Chapter 5.

17. On this point, see Oates et al. (1989).

Table 10.3. *Data for positioning CACC*

	(Millions of tons)			
	Trading case	No-trading case		
Year	Required reduction	Required reduction	Avoided by trading	Abated with trading
1995	0.57	1.94	0.45	1.49
1996	1.24	2.29	0.66	1.63
1997	2.62	3.29	1.12	2.17
1998	2.77	3.65	1.30	2.35
1999	2.91	3.83	1.36	2.47
Total	10.11	15.00	4.89	10.11
Average	2.02	3.00	0.98	2.02

Without trading, these 152 constrained units would have been required to reduce emissions by a total of 1.94 million tons, considerably more than was required in the aggregate with trading, as shown in the first column of Table 10.3. About half of these units reduced emissions by more than would have been required without emissions trading. The other half acquired a total of 0.45 million additional allowances to avoid abating emissions by that amount. On the assumption that the operators of affected units were minimizing cost, it follows that the 0.45 million tons of abatement avoided by purchasing allowances would have cost more to abate than the assumed long-run marginal cost of $350 a ton. For years after 1995, the required abatement similarly avoided by these and other Table A units increases because of the reduced allowance allocations and the rising counterfactual. In Table 10.3, actual data are given for 1995 through 1997, and estimates are provided for 1998 and 1999. For the average Phase I year, the required reduction with no trading has been 3.00 million tons, and the average amount of that abatement avoided by trading has been 0.98 million tons.

Figure 10.5 illustrates the Phase I cost curves, as derived using the data in Table 10.3 and the Phase I MAC. The latter extends linearly from the origin to the observed point of intertemporal equilibrium [4.2, $350], as previously explained. If there had been no emissions trading, Table A units that were constrained by the allowance allocation would have been required to reduce emissions by 3.0 million. In fact, that is, with trading, these units reduced emissions by 2.0

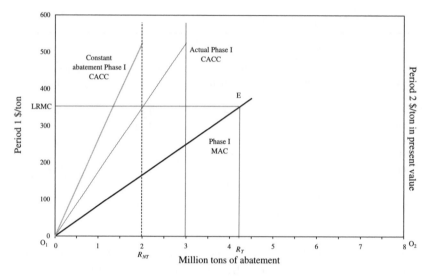

Figure 10.5. The Phase I cost curves.

million tons. The clear implication is that the 2.0 million tons of abatement cost less than $350 a ton and the 1.0 million tons of abatement avoided through emissions trading cost more than $350 a ton. Accordingly, assuming a linear relation between abatement and cost when the command-and-control abatement opportunities at Table A units are arrayed from least to most costly, the Phase I CACC passes through the point [2.0, $350] and extends out to 3.0 million tons of abatement.

The second step in positioning the CACC is to reduce the required aggregate abatement so as to maintain the same aggregate level of abatement, 2.0 million tons, in the command-and-control (no-trading) case and the emissions-trading case. If this were done by avoiding only the most expensive abatement measures, the new CACC plot in Figure 10.5 would coincide with the actual Phase I CACC up to 2.0 million tons of abatement. Alternatively, if the aggregate constraint were relaxed by exempting those units with the lowest abatement costs, the new CACC curve would begin on the vertical axis at about $175 and run parallel to the actual Phase I CACC curve until it reached the same height at 2.0 million tons as the actual curve reaches at 3.0 million tons. Neither of these extreme cases has much appeal, however, and we assume instead a randomly administered relaxation of unit-specific constraints, so that high-cost and low-cost units are affected similarly. This implies the Constant Abatement Phase I CACC in Figure 10.5; a line through the origin that reaches the same height at 2.0 million tons of abatement as the actual Phase I CACC reaches at 3.0 million tons. The Constant Abatement Phase I CACC is the adjusted Phase I CACC that will be used for estimating the cost savings from spatial trading in Phase I.

A full accounting of the cost savings from Title IV emissions trading also requires that cost savings from spatial trading in Phase II be included. No data exist by which the Phase II CACC can be calibrated, but the method used to position the Phase I CACC can be extrapolated in a rough-and-ready way to Phase II. To see how this can be done, note first that moving from the MAC to the actual CACC in Figure 10.5 involves rotating the former line upward to reflect the cost implications of economically efficient trades that would be blocked in our hypothetical no-trading regime. A natural summary measure of the relative importance of such trades is the ratio of the slope of the actual CACC to the slope of the MAC. For instance, a ratio of 1 indicates no blocked trades, since the CACC and MAC would be identical. A ratio of 2 implies that half the economically efficient trades would be blocked and only half the abatement mandated by the CACC would be performed with trading. A ratio of 3 implies that only one-third of the mandated abatement would be performed and two-thirds of the economically efficient trades would be blocked, and so forth.

The easiest way of extrapolating the Phase I method to Phase II is to assume that blocked trades would be of the same relative importance in both phases, so that the ratio of the slope of the Phase II CACC to that of the Phase II MAC is the same as the corresponding ratio in Phase I.[18] If economically attractive trading is expected to be relatively more important in Phase II, then the ratio of slopes will be greater in Phase II, the Phase II CACC will be steeper, and

18. Consideration of excess allowances in Phase II is not necessary in this analysis because the abatement required in Phase II was calculated assuming efficient emissions trading. In fact, there will be some excess allowances so that the required abatement from constrained units in Phase II will be greater than $O_2 R_{NT}$ in Figure 10.3. Also, it could be argued that the presence of voluntary, non-Table A units in Phase I would cause the ratio of slopes to be greater in Phase I than in Phase II. As we showed in Chapter 8, their contribution to Phase I emission reduction is small (at best 5% of the total) and sufficiently so that we believe this consideration can be ignored.

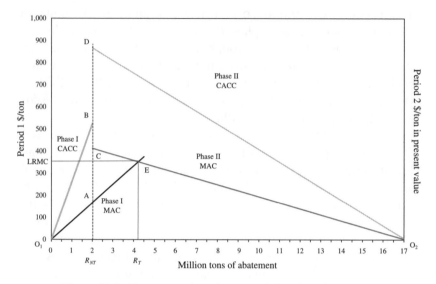

Figure 10.6. The cost-savings framework fitted to Title IV.

(from the discussion of Figure 10.3) the gains from spatial trading in Phase II will be greater. Conversely, a smaller proportion of optimally traded allowances implies less divergence between the two curves and less cost savings from spatial trading.

Figure 10.6 illustrates the analytic framework for estimating the cost savings from Title IV when fitted to observed data using the assumptions and reasoning previously explained. In particular, the placement of the Phase II CACC assumes that the proportion of optimally traded allowances will be the same in Phase II as in Phase I. These four curves provide all the information necessary to calculate the cost savings produced by emissions trading.

COST-SAVING ESTIMATES

Spatial Trading and Banking

Calculating the cost savings from emissions trading is now just a matter of computing costs by calculating areas beneath the CACCs and the MACs and comparing the results. In Phase I, the required annual abatement is 2.0 million tons, and the area under the adjusted

Phase I CACC implies that the total cost of achieving this level of aggregate abatement without trading would be $525 million. With the more efficient arrangement of abatement represented by the Phase I MAC, the same level of emission reduction could be achieved for $167 million. The indicated cost savings for spatial trading in Phase I is the difference, $358 million per year, about twice the cost of efficient abatement. The implied CAC to Title IV cost ratio is 3.14, which implies a cost savings of about two-thirds of the cost of this CAC alternative.

The prospective gains from spatial trading in Phase II appear to be very large. The costs associated with abating 15 million tons by the Phase II CACC and MAC are $6,460 million and $3,076 million, respectively, as depicted in Figure 10.6. Alternatively, when stated as eight-year averages, the costs are $4,037 million and $1,923 million, respectively. The indicated cost savings are $3,384 million on average for each five 19.2-month periods, or an annual average of $2,115 million over the eight years of the assumed Phase II banking period. The CAC to Title IV cost ratio for Phase II spatial trading is 2.10, which implies a cost savings from emissions trading of about half the cost of the CAC alternative.[19]

The cost savings from banking, the triangle *ACE* in Figure 10.6, are $268 million for each year of banking in Phase I, or $167 million for each of the eight years of Phase II in which the Phase I bank is assumed to be drawn down. Calculating a CAC to Title IV cost ratio for this component of the cost savings from emissions trading is not very meaningful. Unlike the cost ratios for spatial trading, which remain constant at varying levels of abatement with our assumption of rising, linear cost curves, the ratio of cost without banking to cost with banking does not remain constant but diminishes as the quantity of abatement approaches the optimal level. Nevertheless, when calculating a ratio for the cost of the CAC alternative to Title IV that includes all components of cost savings from emissions trading, banking must be included, and we do so in what follows.

The three components of cost savings from Title IV emissions trading are presented in condensed form, along with abatement costs

---

19. The CAC to Title IV ratio is lower for Phase II because the assumed angle between the Phase II MAC and CACC is less than the angle between the *adjusted* Phase I CACC and MAC. The adjustment to the Phase I CACC to hold abatement constant effectively increased the angle between the two cost curves and thus the cost savings.

Table 10.4. *Abatement cost and cost savings from emissions trading*

| | | (Millions of present-value 1995 dollars) | | | |
| | | Cost savings from emissions trading | | | |
	Abatement cost	Phase I spatial trading	Banking	Phase II spatial trading	Total cost savings
Average Phase I year (1995–99)	735	358	—	—	358
Average Phase II year (2000–07)	1,400	—	167	2,115	2,282
13-year sum	14,875	1,792	1,339	16,919	20,050

in Table 10.4. Most of the cost savings will take place in Phase II, not only because that is when the cost savings from banking are realized, but also because the cost savings from spatial trading in Phase II are very large. This single component accounts for 84% of the total cost savings over this thirteen-year horizon. On a present-value basis, cost savings of $20 billion are indicated, compared with $16 billion expended for abatement with emissions trading. The implied CAC to Title IV cost ratio for the thirteen years as a whole, taking into account banking savings, is 2.35, which indicates a cost savings of about 55% relative to the assumed CAC alternative.

Sensitivity Analysis of the Cost Savings

Calibrating our basic analytic framework to Title IV required three important point estimates: the point of intertemporal equilibrium, the number of years over which the bank will be drawn down, and the angle between the CACC and MAC plots. Varying any of these can produce significant changes in abatement costs and predicted cost savings, though the ratio of the two, savings as a percentage of cost, is relatively insensitive to these variations. In fact, as we now discuss, the only plausible variation in assumption to produce nonnegligible changes in the percentage cost savings is variation of the CACC/MAC angle.

Perhaps the most questionable of the assumptions on which the estimates in Table 10.4 rest is that the level of Phase I abatement and the associated long-run marginal cost constitute an intertemporal equilibrium based on perfect foresight. As will be discussed in more detail in the next chapter, there is strong evidence that, in building scrubbers and signing long-term contracts for expensive low-sulfur

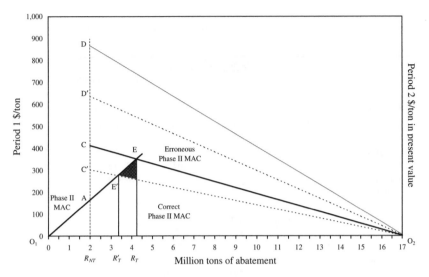

Figure 10.7. The effect of overinvestment.

coal, operators of Phase I units in aggregate overinvested in Phase I abatement. Otherwise, it is hard to explain the steady collapse of allowance prices, from about $150 in mid-1994 to a low of $70 in early 1996. Such overinvestment would imply that the assumed point of intertemporal equilibrium lies to the right of the true intertemporally efficient point on the Phase I MAC. For instance, suppose that without overinvestment in Phase I, the equilibrium long-run marginal cost would have been about $275 per ton instead of $350.[20] In this case, our erroneous assumption that the two MACs intersected at a price of $350 would produce an upwardly biased estimate of the location of the Phase II MAC. The effect of such an error, failing to recognize overinvestment, is depicted in Figure 10.7.[21] The efficient intertemporal equilibrium, E', would have led to 3.3 million tons of Phase I abatement instead of 4.2 million, and the total cost of this optimal level of Phase I abatement would have been $454 million instead of $735 million.

20. We do not pretend to know what would have been the right equilibrium level. An equilibrium price of $275 is chosen here simply to illustrate the point.
21. The Phase II CACC/MAC slope ratio is preserved. Also, the Phase I CACC is not shown since it is unnecessary for this analysis.

Table 10.5. *Alternative estimates of abatement cost and cost savings from emissions trading*

| | | (Millions of present-value 1995 dollars) | | | |
| | | Cost savings from emissions trading | | | |
	Abatement cost	Phase I spatial trading	Banking	Phase II spatial trading	Total cost savings
		With originally estimated Phase II MAC ($350 equilibrium)			
Phase I year	735	358	—	—	358
Phase II year	1,400	—	167	2,115	2,282
13-year sum	14,875	1,792	1,339	16,919	20,050
Ratio and %	2.35	9%	7%	84%	100%
		With alternative Phase II MAC ($275 equilibrium)			
Phase I year	454	358	—	—	358
Phase II year	1,177	—	55	1,553	1,607
13-year sum	11,688	1,792	437	12,420	14,649
Ratio and %	2.25	12%	3%	85%	100%

Two questions arise from this potential (and probable) error. First, by assuming the equilibrium to be $350, might we overstate the cost savings from emissions trading? For instance, with less banking and less abatement cost to be incurred in Phase II, the cost savings could be expected to be less. Second, and forgetting about what might have been optimal, how does overinvestment change the cost-saving estimate? Overinvestment implies unnecessary expenditure, so there must be some cost.

Table 10.5 presents a comparison of the indicated cost savings and total abatement cost when equilibrium long-run marginal cost is $350 per ton and when it is $275 per ton. At the $275 equilibrium, optimal abatement expenditure is less in both Phase I and Phase II. The cost savings from spatial trading in Phase I are not changed, but the other two components are.[22] With only 1.3 million allowances banked annually in Phase I, the savings from banking, the small triangle $AC'E'$ in Figure 10.7, is one-third of what it was when the point of intertem-

---

22. If the Phase I MAC had been shifted downward, then the cost savings from spatial trading in Phase I would be changed. Overinvestment does not question the existence of the "observed" point [4.2, $350], only whether it is the correct point of intertemporal equilibrium. It may be that the "observed" Phase I MAC is not the most efficient, but that is another variation on the analysis, which we do not perform here.

poral equilibrium was assumed to lie on the Phase I MAC at $350.[23] The cost savings from spatial trading in Phase II are about 27% lower because maintaining the slope ratio with a less steeply sloping Phase II MAC implies a smaller angle and area between the two curves. The total cost savings are smaller, $14.6 billion instead of $20.1 billion; however, significantly for this analysis, so are the predicted abatement costs. The cost of efficient abatement is 21% less, while the cost savings are 27% less. As a result, the cost ratio of CAC to Title IV abatement is only slightly lower, 2.25 versus 2.35 before, as indicated by the first entry in the last row in each panel of Table 10.5.

Now, is the estimate of cost savings significantly reduced by over-investment? The answer is that some cost savings are lost, but the amount is small. Most of this suboptimal expenditure can be recouped in Phase II, since the excess allowances produced by over-investing can be banked and then used to reduce abatement during the first few years of Phase II. In the example depicted by Figure 10.7, the 0.9 million tons of excessive Phase I abatement involves an expenditure of $281 million, but the avoided Phase II abatement would cost $204 million in present value. The net present-value loss is thus $77 million, the area represented by the shaded triangle, or $385 million when summed over the five years of Phase I. This loss is less than 3% of the total cost savings from emissions trading, but it virtually wipes out the cost savings from banking at the $275 equilibrium, and it constitutes a significant portion of the cost savings from banking at the $350 equilibrium.

This analysis suggests, in general, that banking of allowances is a relatively minor source of cost savings from emissions trading. This example, however, brings out an important property of banking: its ability to avoid the much larger losses associated with meeting fixed targets in an uncertain world. Comparison of the loss from overinvestment with the potential gain from banking could lead to the conclusion that the small potential savings hardly justify the risk of the loss associated with this extra flexibility. The conclusion is unjustified, however, because it implies that the uncertainty can be resolved or that the costs associated with uncertainty can be completely avoided.

23. The reduction in marginal cost implies not only less banking, but also a shorter banking period in Phase II. To simplify the comparison, we keep the Phase II banking period unchanged at eight years. As will be noted later, the cost savings are not significantly affected.

The nature of the problem and the role of banking can best be appreciated by imagining a regime without banking. The abatement required to meet the fixed cap each year will remain uncertain until the last day of the year. If abatement actions were reversible, quickly adjustable, and nondiscrete, operators could tune abatement to the cap as December 31 approached, but few abatement options meet these criteria, and those that do are unlikely to be cheap. If the target is fixed and unyielding, operators will likely build in some margin of error, but in so doing they will be abating more than is required and presumed optimal. In effect, they will have overinvested in abatement, the difference being that without banking, there is no recoupment of any of the costs of this overinvestment. Alternatively, operators might not run a margin of safety, but they would then have to be prepared to undertake costly short-term abatement measures as the year draws to a close. Moreover, these extra costs for the margin of error or for last-minute, short-term abatement would be repeated to varying degrees every year.

The real cost-saving contribution of banking allowances arises from its ability to reconcile a fixed cap with uncertainty. With the cumulative ceiling and banking, any shortfall in abatement in one year would have to be made up, and any overcompliance can be recouped. The costs associated with not possessing perfect foresight and complete flexibility, as represented by the small triangle in Figure 10.7 and its equivalent for underinvestment, will be incurred, but it is difficult to imagine another mechanism that would result in still smaller losses and still meet the cap. By ignoring this irreducible uncertainty, conventional CAC systems force continual overinvestment without any recoupment, or, worse yet, the cap is "busted" by exceptions and exemptions that recognize the exceptional and unanticipated. In the end, banking minimizes the costs associated with uncertainty while holding cumulative emissions unchanged at what is presumed to be the optimal level.

The second major assumption underlying our estimate of cost savings concerns the number of years during which the bank that was accumulated during Phase I will be drawn down in Phase II. The optimal number of years is uniquely determined by the discount rate, required abatement, and abatement cost functions, as well as by the number of allowances accumulated when any of these variables change. Although reasonable estimates can be made concerning these

Table 10.6. *Effect of banking periods on abatement cost and cost savings from emissions trading*

	Abatement cost	Cost savings from emissions trading (Millions of present-value 1995 dollars)			
		Phase I spatial trading	Banking	Phase II spatial trading	Total cost savings
		Bank drawn down over 6 years			
Phase I year	735	358	—	—	358
Phase II year	1,269	—	249	2,191	2,440
10-year sum	11,288	1,792	1,495	13,144	16,431
Ratio and %	2.46	11%	9%	0%	100%
		Bank drawn down over 8 years			
Phase I year	735	358	—	—	358
Phase II year	1,400	—	167	2,115	2,282
13-year sum	14,875	1,792	1,339	16,919	20,050
Ratio and %	2.35	9%	7%	84%	100%
		Bank drawn down over 10 years			
Phase I year	735	358	—	—	358
Phase II year	1,496	—	126	2,097	2,222
15-year sum	18,638	1,792	1,256	20,966	24,014
Ratio and %	2.29	7%	5%	87%	100%

variables, no analyst could confidently say that the Phase II banking period will be eight years, as opposed to six or ten. The effect on our estimates of varying the Phase II draw-down period is to change the amount of Phase II abatement over which each year of banking in Phase I will be spread. Graphically, the effect is to shorten or lengthen the distance O_2R_T in Figure 10.6, which has the effect of making the 2.2 million allowances banked in an average Phase I year more or less important in the representative Phase II year.

Numerically, the effect of varying the banking period is shown in Table 10.6. Phase I abatement cost and cost savings from emissions trading are not affected at all. As the Phase II banking period increases, annual Phase II abatement cost increases as a result of spreading the banked allowances over more Phase II abatement and the annual and total savings from banking diminish. The relative importance of banking is diminished further as more years of Phase II abatement cost and savings from spatial trading are included in the sums over the lengthening banking period. As was the case with overinvestment, total abatement cost and total cost savings change together so that the CAC to Title IV cost ratio does not change greatly. The ratio rises slightly with a shorter banking period because the cost savings from banking loom larger in total costs and cost savings; the converse is true when the banking period is lengthened.

The third key assumption underlying our estimates of cost savings from trading involves the ratio between the slopes of the CACC and the MAC in Figure 10.6. As noted before, the transfer of the Phase I CACC/MAC slope ratio to Phase II implies both that half of the abatement provided at the unit level in Phase II would have been required without trading and that half the allowances distributed to units will be traded spatially. Geometrically, for any given present-value price on the right-hand-side vertical axis, the Phase II CACC will lie about half the distance from the origin to the Phase II MAC.

When the Phase II CACC/MAC slope ratio is lower, there is less divergence between the two cost curves and less cost savings, because less spatial trading will be called for. When the ratio is higher, there is more divergence, more cost savings, and more spatial trading. The effect of this variation in the assumption about the CACC/MAC ratio on cost savings from emissions trading is shown in Table 10.7 for a 50% variation, plus and minus, in the ratio between the CACC and MAC in Phase II. In this instance, abatement cost in both phases is not affected, nor are the cost savings from Phase I spatial trading and banking changed.[24] When the CACC/MAC slope ratio is halved, the cost savings from Phase II spatial trading are also halved. Given the importance of Phase II spatial trading, the effect on the overall cost ratio, comparing the cost of the CAC and least cost alternatives, is considerable. It falls from 2.35 to 1.78, which implies a reduction of the cost savings from emissions trading from 57% of the CAC alternative to 44%. Increasing the CACC/MAC *slope* ratio by half again has exactly the opposite effect. The cost ratio rises from 2.35 to 2.92, implying cost savings of 66% of this more expensive CAC alternative.

Figure 10.8 illustrates the effect of varying our assumptions con-

---

24. Variations in the Phase I CACC/MAC slope ratio could also be performed, but the changes in cost savings will be hardly noticeable compared to the effect of similar variations on the Phase II cost curves.

Table 10.7. *Effect of Phase II CACC on abatement cost and cost savings from emissions trading*

| | (Millions of present-value 1995 dollars) | | | | |
| | | Cost savings from emissions trading | | | |
	Abatement cost	Phase I spatial trading	Banking	Phase II spatial trading	Total cost savings
	Phase II CACC/MAC slope ratio half of Phase I ratio				
Phase I year	735	358	—	—	358
Phase II year	1,400	—	167	1,057	2,225
10-year sum	14,875	1,792	1,339	8,459	11,590
Ratio and %	1.78	15%	12%	73%	100%
	Phase II CACC/MAC slope ratio equal to Phase I ratio				
Phase I year	735	358	—	—	358
Phase II year	1,400	—	167	2,115	2,282
13-year sum	14,875	1,792	1,339	16,919	20,050
Ratio and %	2.35	9%	7%	84%	100%
	Phase II CACC/MAC slope ratio 1.5 times Phase I ratio				
Phase I year	735	358	—	—	358
Phase II year	1,400	—	167	3,172	3,340
15-year sum	14,875	1,792	1,339	25,378	28,509
Ratio and %	2.92	6%	5%	89%	100%

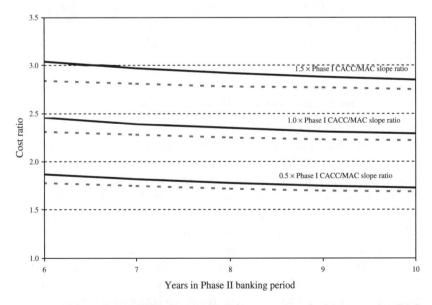

Figure 10.8. Effect of assumptions on cost ratio between the CAC alternative and Title IV.

cerning the intertemporal equilibrium, the number of years over which the Phase I bank is drawn down, and the slope of the Phase II CACC. The vertical axis represents the overall cost ratio of the CAC alternative to Title IV, and the horizontal axis indicates the number of years in the Phase II banking period. The solid lines represent an intertemporal equilibrium at an observed long-run marginal cost of $350/ton, while the dashed lines represent the overinvestment case in which the true intertemporal equilibrium is $275/ton. The cost ratio does not change much as the length of the optimal banking period is varied or as the Phase I equilibrium departs from the true intertemporal equilibrium. What does make a difference is the slope ratio between the Phase II CACC and MAC curves.

Clearly, changing the assumptions that underlie our estimates of the cost savings from trading yields estimates of costs and cost savings that vary significantly in absolute amount. However, when normalized to the predicted level of no-trading costs, the cost savings are remarkably stable. Variations in the assumed CACC/MAC angle have a considerable effect on cost savings as a percentage of CAC cost, but even so, the plausible range of percentage savings is small relative to the range of estimates in the literature. For Title IV, the cost savings from emissions trading appear unlikely to be greater than two-thirds of the CAC alternative, or less than 40%. Cost savings of 50%, implying a cost ratio of 2.0, seems a reasonable point estimate.

Other Estimates of Title IV Cost Savings

Nearly every study of the expected cost of Title IV has made some estimate of the value of the extra flexibility provided by emissions trading, but the definitions and assumptions about emissions trading were often very different from those that have been adopted here. For instance, all of these prior studies counted the abatement costs avoided by use of excess allowances in the trading case as savings attributable to emissions trading, and they ignored the corresponding increase in emissions. Moreover, none distinguished clearly between spatial and intertemporal trading. Some studies, such as ICF (1989) and EPRI (1993), assumed *intra*utility trading and estimated only the savings that would occur from *inter*utility trading.

Three pre-1995 studies are sufficiently detailed that reasonable comparisons can be made with the estimates developed above. Two of these studies, EPRI (1993) and GAO (1994), provided estimates of Phase I cost for the comparison in Chapter 9. The third study, EPA's Regulatory Impact Analysis (RIA), was not used in Chapter 9 because it measured the emission reduction from 1980 instead of from a counterfactual.[25] However, it does provide an estimate of the cost savings from emissions trading, and its CAC alternative is nearly identical to the one we adopted, namely, a unit-by-unit limitation defined by the allowances issued to each unit. There has been one post-1995 attempt at estimating the cost savings attributable to Title IV emissions trading, by a group of analysts associated with Resources for the Future (Carlson et al., 1998; henceforth, RFF98).

Table 10.8 presents the cost savings estimated by these four studies, as well as our estimates, for representative years in three periods: Phase I, Phase II during the banking period, and Phase II after the bank has been exhausted.[26] The first panel presents the cost estimates as given by each source, expressed in 1995 dollars.[27] All of these studies provide an estimate of the cost savings after the bank has been exhausted, that is, for Phase II spatial trading around the end of the first decade of the twenty-first century. Estimates prior to this time are not always provided and when they are, they are more difficult to interpret. For instance, EPRI93 provides no estimate of the cost savings in Phase I because emissions trading is defined as interutility trading only, and little was expected to occur in Phase I. RFF98 provides no estimate of the cost savings from banking because their econometric model is static and their focus is on the gains from spatial trading. Where estimates are provided, they are usually only partial. For instance, GAO94 provides an estimate of the cost savings from intrautility trading in Phase I, but none for interutility trading, while EPRI93 provides an estimate for interutility trading in early

25. A Regulatory Impact Analysis is required for any regulation that will cost $100 million or more. The authors of this RIA noted wryly that these regulations implementing the emissions trading system would *reduce* costs compared to what would obtain if the statute were otherwise enforced.

26. Note that in all cases, the "Phase II Banking" estimates include savings from both Phase II spatial trading and from banking. Our estimate for "Phase II Postbank" is the area between the Phase II CACC and MAC out to abatement level R_{NT}.

27. The estimates in RFF98 were given in 1995 dollars, RIA92 in 1990 dollars, and the other two in 1992 dollars. The latter figures were inflated, using the consumer price index, by factors of 1.166 for 1990 and 1.086 for 1992.

Table 10.8. *Estimates of Title IV cost savings*

Year	(Billions of 1995 dollars)		
	Phase I	Phase II banking	Phase II post-bank
	As given by each estimate		
RIA92	0.47	2.45	1.51
EPRI93	NA	1.47[b]	3.15[c]
GAO94	0.24[a]	3.32	3.17
RFF98	0.25	NA	0.78
	After adjustment for excess allowances		
RIA92			1.36
EPRI93			1.19
GAO94			1.63
RFF98			NA[d]
	Table 10.4 estimate for reference		
MIT99	0.36	2.28	1.92

[a]Intrautility trading only.

[b]Does not include intrautility trading.

[c]Intrautility, $1.84 billion; interutility, $1.29 billion.

[d]CAC emissions are recognized as being lower than with trading, but the magnitude of the difference in emissions is not provided.

Sources: RIA (1992), EPRI (1993), GAO (1994), and Carlson et al. (1998).

Phase II, but none for intrautility trading. Only RIA92 provides estimates for Phase I and Phase II during the bank draw-down that include both intra- and interutility trading. Despite these differences, all these studies find that the major cost savings from emissions trading will be realized in Phase II.

Another difference between our estimates and those provided by these other studies is the treatment of the reduction in abatement cost from trading excess allowances. Recall that our analysis constrains the aggregate emissions reductions in Phase I and Phase II to be the same in the trading and no-trading cases. We do not take credit for the cost reduction associated with using excess allowances to avoid the tightening of the emissions cap that is implied by the no-trading assumption. The middle panel of Table 10.8 provides adjusted estimates of the postbanking cost savings based on differences in aggregate emissions between the trading and no-trading cases.[28] With the exception of RIA92, the adjustments for excess allowances are considerable, amounting to about half of the large cost savings otherwise projected by EPRI93 and GAO94. This adjustment also brings these estimates closer to the comparable estimate derived from our analysis, namely, average Phase II cost without banking. Over all, Table 10.8 indicates that our estimates of cost savings from emissions trading are roughly comparable to others in the literature.

It is worth noting that the estimates of total cost (not cost savings) in these studies differ substantially. For instance, the RIA and Carlson et al. predict the postbanking Phase II total cost to be about $1.2 billion and $1.04 billion, respectively, whereas the EPRI and GAO studies predict costs for the same period of $2.4 billion and $2.2 billion, respectively.[29] When the CAC cost in these studies is expressed as a ratio to the cost in emissions-trading cases, there is much closer agreement. These ratios are 2.30 for the RIA, 1.75 for GAO94 and RFF98, and 1.50 for EPRI93. These ratios bracket the CAC to Title IV cost ratio of 2.10 that would obtain for Phase II spatial trading in our own estimate.[30] Despite the many differences in approach and assumption, these studies suggest the same conclusion that emerges from our analysis: Emissions trading will reduce the cost of achieving Title IV's emission-reduction goal by about half.[31]

28. The adjustment consisted of fitting a linear marginal cost function to the data provided in each study and adjusting the cost estimate for the amount of excess allowances used. These adjustments were considerable for the EPRI and GAO estimates. Comparable adjustments to the Phase I and Phase II banking period estimates could not be made because the sources did not indicate how much of the change in emissions between trading and no-trading cases was due to banking and how much to the use of excess allowances under trading.
29. Much of the variation results from differing assumptions about the amount of abatement required. These range from 6.0 million tons (RFF98) to 8.5 million tons (RIA92). Our estimate of $1.92 billion for the postbank Phase II cost savings corresponds to abatement of 9.4 million tons.
30. The CAC alternatives also vary among these estimates. The EPRI93 and GAO94 alternatives are the least clearly specified as "traditional" or "conventional" command-and-control. RFF98 specifies the CAC alternative more clearly, a uniform emission rate standard, but this alternative is less stringent than that assumed by us and RIA92.
31. A similar conclusion is reached in a study by Bernstein et al. (1994) that addresses Phase I only.

SUBSTANTIAL AND REAL COST SAVINGS

The goal of reducing abatement costs lies at the core of arguments in favor of emissions trading and market-based approaches to environmental regulation, more generally. This is the primary advantage of the trading mechanism embodied in Title IV that its proponents have emphasized. Early estimates of the expected cost of complying with the emissions caps in Title IV emphasized that those costs would depend on the extent to which the operators of affected units would or could take advantage of the flexibility inherent in Title IV's allowance-trading mechanism. With three years of well-documented compliance and abatement behavior and associated allowance and coal-market activity, the evidence is overwhelming that utilities have made good use of the flexibility afforded by emissions trading. As such, Title IV provides an unparalleled opportunity to gauge the magnitude of cost savings that can be realized from emissions trading.

The approach we have taken to estimating these cost savings differs from those adopted by earlier studies of the cost of compliance with Title IV. Our approach is decidedly macro in orientation, and rests heavily on the application of economic reasoning to empirically observable aggregate data reflecting the abatement undertaken by Phase I units during the 1995–97 period. In effect, we seek to determine what cost savings are indicated by observed abatement behavior, on the assumption that operators are rationally pursuing the cost-saving opportunities available to them. RFF98 shares our macro orientation, but uses econometric techniques in attempting (heroically) to estimate aggregate marginal abatement curves from observed fuel-price and emission-rate data. In contrast, the pre-1995 efforts adopted micro-, bottom-up, cost-engineering approaches that simulate likely behavior and costs under various scenarios that vary the extent of emissions trading.

Two particular features of our approach deserve note. First, little reference has been made to allowance prices in forming these estimates of cost savings. Although allowance prices do reflect emissions-trading activity, the observed price equilibria indicate short-run marginal costs, which are, of course, influenced by (changing) expectations of long-run marginal-cost and counterfactual-emissions trajectories. At any point in time, allowance prices may be above or below their long-run equilibrium levels. Whatever the short-run price, the costs and cost savings associated with Title IV will include the capital and other fixed costs that constitute a significant proportion of long-run marginal cost. Thus, an estimate of cost savings must be based on long-run marginal cost, and for that we have relied on the bottom-up estimate of cost presented in Chapter 9 rather than on allowance prices.

A second feature of our estimation approach worth noting is that no attempt has been made to distinguish between static and dynamic efficiency. While the former takes technology as given, the latter incorporates any cost-reducing changes in technology that emissions trading may have induced. The existing theoretical literature, however, does not demonstrate that market-based instruments generally provide stronger or weaker incentives to innovate than do command-and-control regimes.[32] Accordingly, without an empirical study, it is not possible to claim a priori that Title IV has provided additional cost savings by inducing faster innovation than an alternative command-and-control regime would have done. Moreover, because we cannot observe the alternative CAC regime directly, it is unclear in principle how to perform the requisite empirical study.

As we have noted, the observed total cost of abatement has been on the low side (but not outside) of expectations, and much of that lower cost has been due to the much lower than anticipated cost of scrubbing. With each succeeding announcement of a new Phase II scrubber – undertaken without benefit of bonus allowances or, as the electric utility industry is being deregulated, guaranteed recovery of capital costs – it is increasingly obvious that a significant drop in cost of this abatement technology has occurred. Whether the reduction in scrubbing cost was induced by emissions trading or has been due instead to the application of exogenous advances in information processing and control technology is a fascinating and difficult question but one we do not attempt to answer here.[33]

32. See Magat (1978), Malueg (1989), and Montero (1997).
33. See Burtraw (1996) and Burtraw and Swift (1996) for a discussion of various innovations that have accompanied the implementation of Title IV. Carlson et al. (1998) find that marginal abatement cost curves have declined significantly since 1985, but they attribute the shift to a fall in low-sulfur coal prices and to technical change, not to allowance trading.

The inclusion of any dynamic gains from emissions trading is essentially a matter of the ratio between the CACC and MAC curves. Our approach has been one in which whatever improvements are reflected in the MACs would also be observed in the CACCs, which is effectively to assume that there are no dynamic gains. Thus, to the extent that dynamic gains can be shown to exist, our approach provides an underestimate of the cost savings from emissions trading.

Estimates of the absolute level of the costs of complying with Title IV and of the cost savings from emissions trading have varied greatly; however, when expressed as a percentage of estimated costs, the cost-saving estimates are remarkably robust. Whether the comparison is made across studies or across variations in the same study, the cost ratio of some CAC alternative to Title IV's emissions-trading provisions falls between 1.5 and 3.0, indicating cost savings from 33% to 67% of the CAC alternative. The obvious single number that emerges from this range, 50%, is definitely at the lower end of the range of cost-saving estimates encountered in the literature for emissions trading more generally, as noted at the beginning of this chapter. Nevertheless, this estimate is based on a real, large-scale program in which affected parties do appear to be taking good advantage of emissions trading. Although the evidence from Title IV indicates that emissions trading cannot make the costs of abatement nearly vanish, as suggested by CAC to least-cost ratios of 20 that appear in the literature, emissions trading can produce still significant and real cost savings.

11 Errors, Imperfections, and Allowance Prices

UNEXPECTED BEHAVIOR AT
ALLOWANCE PRICES

The experience with Title IV has largely confirmed the expectations of those who argued at the time of its passage that emissions trading would work well. A significant reduction of SO_2 emissions was implemented, a robust allowance market developed, utilities took advantage of flexibility to reduce costs, and neither hot spots nor regulatory interference materialized. However, neither the proponents of emissions trading nor the skeptics anticipated anything like the observed evolution of allowance prices over time. As Figure 11.1 (which appeared earlier as Figure 7.1) shows, spot allowance prices declined sharply from the first observed trades until early 1996, when they reached a low of around $70/ton. Thereafter they moved irregularly upward until early 1998, when they ran up rapidly to as high as $210. From then until March 1999, they have remained in the vicinity of $200/ton. While compliance costs have been somewhat below earlier estimates, as Chapter 9 discussed, allowance prices in the 1995–97 period were far below expectations. Even after the run-up in early 1998, allowance prices have been lower than expected.

From the beginning, it was widely anticipated that there would be excess abatement during Phase I, with allowances banked for use in Phase II. And, as we noted in Chapter 10, in a world of certainty, allowance prices during such a period of banking would rise smoothly at the rate of interest. In such a world, the price for current-vintage

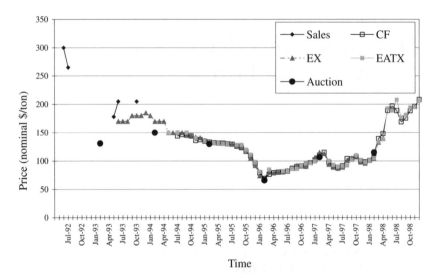

Figure 11.1. Allowance prices, 1992–98 (1995 or current vintage).

Sources: Allowance Price Indications, 1993–97* Cantor Fitzgerald Environmental Brokerage, NY, NY; *Compliance Strategy Review*, 1992–97* Fieldston, Washington, DC; *Exchange Value*, 1993–97* Emission Exchange Corp., Escandido, CA. *Selected issues.

allowances (allowances that can be used to offset current emissions) should equal at every instant both the marginal cost of reducing current emissions and the discounted marginal cost of reducing emissions when the allowance bank is exhausted in Phase II.

What would observed allowance prices imply about the marginal costs of abatement in Phase II if allowance prices, abatement investments, and emissions were on their long-run equilibrium paths? Focusing just on results of the EPA spot auctions, prices in 1995 dollars fell from $154 to $64 between March 1994 and March 1996, rose to just over $100 in 1997 and 1998, and jumped to $200 in March 1999.[1] Supposing the allowance bank is expected to be exhausted in 2008 (in March, for convenience), and taking the real rate of interest to be 5%, these auction results imply a fall in expected Phase II marginal costs (in 1995 dollars) at the time of exhaustion from $310 to $117 per ton, a plateau at about $175, and a jump back to just under

---

1. The actual clearing prices in nominal dollars were $150 in 1994, $66 in 1996, $107 in 1997, $115 in 1998, and $201 in 1999.

$290. No changes of which we are aware in current costs or in plausibly expected future costs are nearly large enough to explain such substantial changes in observed prices and implied future costs. (As we will discuss, however, expected future costs have almost certainly fallen noticeably over the relevant period.)

The explanation must lie in departures from the textbook world of perfect rationality, perfect competition, and perfect certainty, in which the system always follows the long-run equilibrium path – that is, in mistakes, market imperfections, and forecasting errors. The rest of this chapter is devoted to exploring explanations of these sorts for the observed behavior of allowance prices. It is important to establish a context first, however. Any real emissions-trading program, like any real market, will be affected by errors and imperfections of various sorts, if only because future outputs and abatement costs are necessarily uncertain. By attempting to explain this program's failure to achieve perfection, we do not intend to suggest that any other design would have done better. That remains an important, open question.

SOME UNCONVINCING HYPOTHESES

Skeptics of Title IV's tradable-emissions approach have commonly attributed the low allowances prices early in Phase I to defects in allowance markets and surrounding institutions. These include:

1. The design flaws of EPA auctions (Cason, 1993, 1995; Cason and Plot, 1996)
2. Uncertainty regarding the rate-making treatment of allowances traded (Burtraw, 1996; Rose, 1994; Bohi and Burtraw, 1992)
3. Barriers to trading (Winebrake et al., 1995) and transaction costs (Doucet and Strauss, 1994)

None of these explanations is persuasive, however.

As we discussed in Chapter 7, after mid-1994 the EPA auctions were a small factor in the overall market for allowances. Moreover, the critics argued that auction prices would be depressed because private sellers would set reservation prices too low, while in fact private sellers have tended to set their reservation prices too high to produce sales. And, partly as a consequence, private sales have been of very little importance in the EPA auctions. Similarly, we noted in Chapter 7 that the action or inaction of public utility commissions seemed to have little or no impact on the allowance market in its critical early years. Finally, while some barriers to trading and transaction costs surely are present in allowance markets, as in all real markets, they do not appear to be substantial. And it is not clear a priori whether transaction costs raise or lower market prices of allowances (Stavins, 1995; Montero, 1998b).

A second explanation, popular for a time with those claiming that use of emissions trading would drastically reduce the costs of reducing U.S. emissions of greenhouse gases, is that allowance prices were much lower than expected simply because control costs were much lower than expected. There certainly were unanticipated innovations that reduced the costs of controlling SO_2 emissions. For example, as we discussed in Chapter 9, the observed per ton cost of scrubbing in Phase I has been substantially below earlier estimates. Our investigation indicates that this difference has reflected unanticipated improvements in instrumentation and control that reduce personnel requirements, innovative sludge-removal techniques, and higher than expected availability and utilization of scrubbed units (which reduces capital cost per ton of sulfur removed). In addition, new ways were found to adapt midwestern boilers to blends of local and Powder River Basin coals. Although such adaptation was underway prior to 1990, it may well have been accelerated by the passage of Title IV.

Nonetheless, this second explanation for the low early prices of allowances is not persuasive either. The unanticipated innovations we have been able to identify are simply not important enough to explain the difference between expected allowance prices of around $300/ton and actual prices early in Phase I of around $100. Moreover, while Phase I scrubber costs were less than had been anticipated, they were well above $100/ton of sulfur removed.

A third factor that has been associated with unexpected features of allowance-price determination is the failure of utilities to minimize costs when making compliance decisions. Some have argued that utilities were slow to shift from traditional "autarkic" approaches to compliance with environmental requirements to embrace fully and take advantage of the flexibility provided by a cap-and-trade system. That is, it took some time for firms to learn how to use the new system effectively. Others have argued that as regulated public utilities, the owners of affected sources had little incentive to minimize costs and were subject to political pressures to protect local coal or mine labor interests.

We saw in Chapter 9 that average abatement costs differ substantially across generating units, and long-run marginal costs likely follow a similar pattern. In part, this reflects a tendency, made very clear in numerous conversations, for utilities to plan for Phase I compliance as if they faced a utility-specific cap, within which they created their own implicit market for allowances. The price implicit in this internal market often bore little relation to the outside, market price for allowances, however.

In addition, some have argued that compliance costs were increased because some utilities were forced by political pressures, reinforced by the utilities' status as regulated monopolies subject to cost-plus regulation, to invest in high-cost scrubbers to permit their continued use of local high-sulfur coal and thereby protect local businesses and jobs. Indeed, Title IV itself explicitly encouraged the use of scrubbers through special bonus-allowance provisions, described in Chapter 3.

In theory, excessive scrubbing would have two effects. First, it would increase compliance costs above the "least-cost" level and make it difficult to identify a textbook least-cost marginal compliance cost curve. Second, since scrubbers remove about 95% of the sulfur in flue gas, units installing scrubbers would require many fewer allowances to cover emissions than they were issued for Phase I. Thus, excessive scrubbing, *all else equal*, would effectively increase the supply of allowances available for sale or banking for future use and thus reduce allowance prices.

Some of the investment in Phase I scrubbing has no doubt been driven by a combination of political pressures and subsidies provided by Title IV; however, we do not believe this has been a major determinant of allowance prices. Many scrubbers that had been planned at the time Title IV was passed were subsequently canceled for economic reasons – including scrubbers in areas where there was substantial pressure to continue using local high-sulfur coal. Moreover, implementation of Title IV coincided with the introduction of public policies for increasing competitive pressures on traditional, regulated-monopoly utilities. This in turn increased utilities' reluctance to make long-lived investments that might not be recovered in a competitive market.

More generally, factors that raise compliance costs (including planning errors by utilities) cannot by themselves explain low allowance prices. Investments in scrubbing, in particular, are very visible, and utilities' planning processes are subject to regulatory oversight. With good information, utilities could calculate the impact of others' scrubbing investments on allowance prices and adjust their own decisions accordingly. All else being equal, irrational scrubbing by some utilities should result in less scrubbing and less fuel switching by others. Aggregate compliance costs would be increased, but there is no reason to think that allowance prices should be forced down.

EXPECTATION ERRORS AND OVERINVESTMENT

Not only do none of these hypotheses provide satisfactory explanations for the low allowance prices observed in the 1995–97 period, but they shed no light at all on the gap between allowance prices and long-run marginal abatement costs. As presented in Chapter 9, the average total cost and the long-run marginal cost of abatement in 1995 were approximately $200 and $350 per ton, respectively; yet, from the beginning of Phase I until shortly after the March 1998 auctions, allowance prices have ranged from only $70 to $130.

We believe that both low allowance prices and the gap between allowance prices and observed abatement costs reflect two factors. First, there was a general underestimation of the extent to which cost-based shifts to Powder River Basin coal after 1990 reduced the amount of abatement necessary to comply with Title IV. Second, long-lived investments in compliance technology and long-term fuel commitments were made well in advance of compliance deadlines, when future allowance and fuel prices, abatement costs, and electricity prices were all still uncertain. The durability of these investments prolonged the depressing effects of expectation errors on allowance prices.

Many utilities subject to Phase I committed to abatement strategies by making investment and contractual decisions in the early 1990s based on expectations then prevailing about Phase I allowance and fuel prices. In 1993, these decisions seemed economical because allowance prices were expected to be well above their actual 1995–97 levels, and costs for low-sulfur coal and transportation were expected to be higher than they turned out to be. As time passed, allowance prices and abatement costs proved to be lower than expected, and alternatives to scrubbing now look much more attractive than they did when commitments to build scrubbers were made and long-term coal-supply contracts were signed. However, once the investment and contractual commitments had been made, the supply of allowances from these sources was fixed, so that when the demand for allowances turned out to be less than expected, the current market was oversupplied. As a result, both short-run allowance prices and (because of banking) the trajectory of future allowance prices are below what they would have been, had investment and contracting decisions been made in a world where decision-makers had perfect foresight.

One of the two principal means of abatement under Title IV – scrubbing – is capital intensive, and the contracting and construction lead time for placing a scrubber in service is two to three years. Consequently, decisions to comply with Title IV by scrubbing required commitments in 1992–93, when information about allowance prices was not very good. In particular, it is now evident that there was a general failure to appreciate the extent to which switching to PRB coals for purely economic reasons would reduce the demand for abatement and increase the supply of allowances.[2] Many scrubbers may have looked economic in 1992, when allowance prices were expected to be $300 or higher. With allowance prices around $100 in 1995, however, the ex ante economics of building scrubbers were much less favorable. But if a scrubber had been begun in 1992 (and not cancelled), the capital involved was sunk by 1995. And, with mar-

2. A good example is provided by one of ICF's early studies, which assumed no PRB displacement but which also included a prophetic qualification: "These analyses assume that no subbituminous coals can be used in boilers designed for bituminous coals. However, many boilers in the Midwest have begun to experiment with subbituminous coals (either wholly or in blends), and this could be a low-cost emissions reduction option in many applications. As such, compliance costs could be lower than presented herein, and coal market impacts different. Recent analysis conducted by ICF Resources suggests that about 40–50 million tons of subbituminous coals could penetrate the bituminous boiler markets, largely displacing bituminous coal shipments from the West, but also displacing some Midwestern high-sulfur coal use" (ICF, 1990, p. 36). As it turned out, Phase I units burned 70 million tons of PRB coal in 1995.

ginal operating costs at about $65 per ton abated, it made sense
ex post to operate scrubbers throughout almost all the 1995–99
period.[3] As a result, today's supply of allowances reflects pre-1995
expectations about allowance prices, now embedded in irreversible
investments.

The role of expectations in the choice to scrub is clearly indicated
by responses to the MIT/CEEPR questionnaire discussed in Chapter
9. Respondents accounted for about half of the total retrofitted Phase
I scrubber capacity. Of this group, operators representing 5,000 MW^e
of retrofitted capacity (75% of the retrofitted capacity operated by
respondents) indicated that expectations of allowance prices of
$300 to $400 were "very important" in decisions to scrub, which were
made before the EPA auction in March 1993 offered the first signal
that allowance prices might be significantly lower than expected.
Responses also identified about 3,600 MW^e of capacity for which
scrubbing had been the initial – but not the final – choice; one-third
of these responses stated that the initial decision was reversed due to
"low allowance prices."[4]

Although fuel switching is generally a more flexible form of compliance, coal contracts can and do contain irreversible elements that
operate analogously to those complicating investments in scrubbers.
Any utility fuel manager planning to comply at a Phase I-affected
unit by switching to lower-sulfur coal would be faced with the decision of whether to sign a contract prior to 1995 for low-sulfur coal
supplies during part or all of Phase I, procure low-sulfur coal on the
spot market during Phase I, or do some of both. A premium would
be paid for the lower-sulfur coal in either case, and the choice would
be whether to lock in a premium (and the Btu value of the coal) in
1993 or 1994, or pay whatever the spot market required in 1995
and thereafter. Fears of "fly-ups" in low-sulfur coal prices (cf. ICF,

---

3. We are informed that in early 1996, when allowance prices fell to around $70, some
   scrubbers were pulled off line for maintenance, and other operators considered shut
   down or actually reduced removal efficiencies.
4. Among those who initially planned to scrub but decided otherwise, two-thirds stated
   that the decision was based upon a fall in low-sulfur coal prices relative to scrubber
   costs. The CEEPR/MIT questionnaire responses also make it clear that allowance
   prices were not the only consideration in deciding to retrofit a scrubber. One-quarter
   of respondents with scrubbers stated that allowance prices were not an important consideration in the choice to scrub; for instance, one operator made the commitment to
   scrub prior to passage of the 1990 CAAA, as the result of a Clean Coal Technology
   Program award.

1990, p. 37) and other uncertainties motivated many to sign contracts for low-sulfur coal in 1992–94 at the premiums then prevailing. Although such contracts do provide the buyer protection against price increases, they also prevent the buyer from taking advantage of lower-than-expected prices – in this case, purchasing less low-sulfur coal and using more allowances. As a result, the supply of compliance from such sources was, like that from scrubbers, more a reflection of price expectations when contracting and investment decisions were made than a response to fuel and allowance prices realized ex post.

Evidence for the oversupply of abatement can be seen in the evolution of the spot-market premium for lower-sulfur coal. As discussed in Chapter 10, the difference in price between low- and high-sulfur coal in central Appalachia dropped by half at the beginning of 1995, when the emissions limits of Title IV first came into effect. A reduction in the premium paid for lower-sulfur coal was not a predicted effect of Title IV. Rather, it was expected that increased spot-market purchases of low-sulfur coal would increase the premium. The collapse of the sulfur premium reflected the realization that spot purchases of low-sulfur coal would not be needed for compliance. Alternatively, as we discussed in Chapter 10, since buying low-sulfur coal and buying allowances are substitutable methods of abatement, the sulfur premium had to fall to align with the low and declining allowance prices. The coal-sulfur premium on the eve of Phase I was in line with earlier predictions of allowance price, but not with actual allowance prices. Suppliers of low-sulfur coal may have been hoping that the onset of actual compliance with Title IV would justify the expectation-based premium that existed prior to 1995. But that premium would be sustained only if allowance prices rose. When they did not, because there was more than enough current abatement being supplied at the existing allowance price, the absence of demand for low-sulfur coal left no alternative but to reduce spot prices for low-sulfur coals so that the sulfur premium was consistent with the value being accorded additional abatement by the (spot) allowance market.

It is also instructive to compare actual abatement and allowance banking with published forecasts. Figure 11.2 presents a comparison of earlier predictions of compliance in early Phase I by ICF, EPRI, and GAO with our estimate of what actually happened in 1995, 1996,

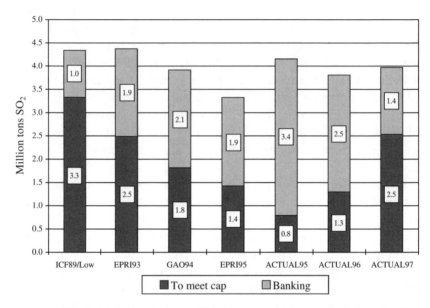

Figure 11.2. Mandatory and banking components of 1995–97 reduction.
Sources: ICF (1989), EPRI (1993, 1995), GAO (1994) and data in Table
5.1 and Table 3 of the Appendix of this book.

and 1997.[5] The height of the columns indicates the reduction in
emissions attributable to Title IV, which is then split into two parts:
that required to reduce emissions to the aggregate cap and the extra
amount attributable to banking.

In 1989, ICF's forecast for the case of low electricity growth (which
is close to what actually happened) was a 3.3-million-ton reduction of emissions to meet the cap and an additional 1.0 million tons
banked. Subsequent studies, with better information, predicted less
abatement required to meet the cap, twice as much banking, and,
according to two later studies, less total abatement. Obviously, expectations about the amount of emission reduction that would be
required to meet the cap were being revised as Phase I approached.
The EPRI95 forecast was an average for the years 1995–97, so it can

5. See ICF (1989), EPRI (1993, 1995), GAO (1994), and Ellerman et al. (1997). Our estimates employ the econometrically estimated counterfactual developed in the Appendix.

be compared directly with the average for actual abatement during these years. The estimate of the amount of abatement required was about right (the actual average was 1.52 million tons), but the estimate of the total abatement to which operators of Phase I units were already committed was about a half-million tons too low, annually. The difference was added to the allowance bank, with consequent effect on allowance prices and the sulfur premium.

In a quantitative analysis, Montero and Ellerman (1998) use the expected 1995 allowance price provided by EPRI (1993) as the benchmark against which to assess the importance of the different expectation errors. EPRI (1993) stands out among the early studies of compliance with the U.S. Acid Rain Program for the detail of its forecast and its explicit assumptions, with which the later actual data can be compared. It also predicted an expected equilibrium allowance price of $273 under favorable trading conditions.[6] This expectation was well above actual prices in early Phase I, but it was a well-informed estimate that reflected expected prices at the time when electric utilities were defining their compliance strategies for Phase I.[7]

Montero and Ellerman (1998) find that, after controlling for expectation errors and the irreversibility of some abatement investments, EPRI's 1995 equilibrium price of $273 drops to $106 – almost equal to the actual 1995–96 average of $105. Unanticipated cost-based expansion of PRB coal accounts for 60% of the drop, while irreversibility accounts for 27%. The remaining 13% is divided almost evenly between two other factors not included in EPRI (1993): voluntary participation from nonaffected sources and the more intensive utilization of units retrofitted with scrubbers. Thus, expectation errors and irreversibility provide a reasonable quantitative explanation for the observed gap between projected and observed allowance prices early in Phase I.

Many of the unconvincing explanations for low pre-1998 allowance prices imply that allowance prices should remain low more or less indefinitely. Our preferred explanation, discussed in the preceding section, is at least consistent with a rise in price after market partic-

---

6. The estimate in EPRI (1993) is $250 in 1992 dollars.
7. The price is within the range established by the earliest bilateral trades. Furthermore, a number of respondents to the MIT/CEEPR questionnaire discussed in Chapter 9 cited expectations of early Phase I allowance prices in this range.

ipants have had a chance to recognize the aggregate overinvestment disequilibrium and, subject to the constraints imposed by durability of contracts and tangible assets, to work through it.

Lower allowance prices justify less current abatement and increase the demand for allowances. The convergence of the central Appalachian low-sulfur coal premium to the allowance price in early 1995 indicated that coal buyers were prepared to use more allowances and buy higher-sulfur coal rather than purchase spot low-sulfur coal at a premium equivalent to a $400 allowance value. Another indication of this short-term adjustment is provided by comparison of 1996 abatement with 1995. A noticeable change in emission rate ($> \pm 0.20$ lb SO_2/mmBtu) is observed at about one-third of the Phase I units, and twice as many of these units increased emission rates as decreased them (87 vs. 45).[8] As a result, the heat-input weighted average SO_2 emission rate for the 358 Phase I units without scrubbers increased from 2.25 lb/mmBtu to 2.30 lb/mmBtu.

This switching back to higher-sulfur coal in 1996, and the concomitant use of more allowances, provides clear evidence that utilities were willing to base compliance decisions on the allowance market. Utilities that continued to disregard allowance prices would not have increased emissions during Phase I. If anything, they would have reduced emissions even more as Phase II approached. Not all utilities responded to lower allowance prices in this manner, but some of those that adhered to previous plans were constrained to do so by long-term coal contracts.

The more important adjustment to overinvestment in compliance during Phase I is the long-term response. Banked allowances permit the deferral of compliance with Phase II emission limits for a few years, and the extent of deferral depends on the amount of banking. Early studies did not contain precise forecasts about the size of the allowance bank at the end of Phase I. In the first years of Phase I, however, it became widely recognized that the bank would be bigger than previously anticipated. For instance, EPRI (1995) noted that then-recent projections of bank size ranged from 7 to 15 million allowances. Their own best estimate at that time was 9.4 million, but that estimate was increased to 12.3 million allowances two years later (EPRI, 1997). At the same time, estimates of when

---

8. The six units completing scrubber retrofits are excluded in this comparison.

the bank would be exhausted have been pushed out by several years. Obviously, costs that would have been incurred in, say, 2005, when the smaller bank was expected to run out, can now be put off for a few more years.

If some electric utilities are arbitraging between current Phase I and discounted expected Phase II compliance costs, then a deferral of the time when the bank runs out will affect current allowance prices. The value of an allowance not used today will be the present value of the marginal cost of future abatement. If future abatement is pushed off several years, because of an unexpected access of allowances, the present value will fall, not because the expected expenditure is any less, but because it will take place later. Thus, overinvestment in Phase I compliance will depress allowance prices, but Phase II requirements will prevent allowance prices from falling to zero.

PUZZLES AND FUTURE PRICE TRENDS

Still, it is difficult to reconcile pre-1998 allowance prices with most estimates of marginal abatement costs in Phase II. The latest available EPRI study (EPRI, 1997), for instance, predicts exhaustion of the allowance bank in 2009, with marginal abatement cost (and allowance price) at that time of $437. (All prices in this paragraph are in 1995 dollars.) With a real discount rate of 4–7%, this corresponds to a discounted cost of $176–260 at the time of the 1996 auction, which cleared at a price of $64. Subsequent allowance price increases have served to close the gap: by early 1999, allowance prices were around $183, while the range of discounted EPRI cost estimates was from $217 to $293. This raises two questions, neither of which can be definitively answered. First, why did the large gap between allowance prices and discounted estimates of Phase II costs persist until 1998 and then close, at least partially? Second, does a gap remain, and if so, why?

Both theory and experience make clear that explaining price movements in markets in which speculators are active is a tricky business, and allowances are bought and sold in such a market. We do not pretend to know why allowance prices rose rapidly during 1998 rather than, for instance, rising gradually over a longer period or rising rapidly earlier or later than they did. Preliminary analysis that we have been able to conduct as of the time of this writing suggests that the cause was a change in expectation concerning Phase II needs. The quantity of allowances purchased or sold through mid-1998 was predicted fairly well by comparing 1997 abatement levels projected to 2000 with the Phase II allowance allocations at the utility level in the year 2000. Net purchasers tended to be utilities facing larger abatement requirements in Phase II, while net sellers were those facing smaller abatement requirements or, more typically, none at all. This relationship is discernible for the period 1994 to 1998 as a whole and for particular subperiods, but it is particularly noticeable for allowance transactions during the months leading up to and during the price spike of 1998 (Andrin, 1999). Although no single, precipitating event can be identified to mark the change in expectation, the cumulative effect of the continuing (as we write) miracle of the post-1992 expansion of the American economy on the demand for electricity and coal-fired generation may have been recognized at about the time of the price spike. The 3.5% annual rate of growth in the demand for coal-fired electricity since 1993 has been higher than anything witnessed since the early and mid-1980s, when oil prices were high and new coal-fired power plants were coming on line.

Just as it is hard to explain price movements in speculative markets, it is difficult to forecast marginal costs a decade hence. It may be that early-1999 allowance prices are still on average below long-run equilibrium, but it is not obvious what market forces would produce this. A second possibility is that current allowance prices incorporate a discount for the likelihood that future environmental programs, particularly those relating to NO_x and CO_2 emissions, may indirectly depress sulfur emissions and thus reduce the value of allowances. This hypothesis is plausible, but, unfortunately, untestable.

It also seems possible that current allowance prices may be accurately forecasting that future abatement costs will be below current projections. Two bits of evidence are relevant here.

First, projections of Phase II allowance prices have tended to fall over time. As noted above, discounting the EPRI (1997) allowance-price projection for 2009 to early 1999, using discount ranges between 4% and 7%, gave a range of $217 to $293 for discounted marginal abatement cost. This is well below the $298–$378 range implied by the central-case allowance-price forecast in EPRI (1993), published four years earlier.

In the second place, recent announcements of new scrubbers scheduled to come online in early Phase II suggest that costs of this technology have fallen substantially below the unexpectedly low costs of Phase I scrubbers. As noted in Chapter 9, decisions have been announced to retrofit scrubbers at five Phase II units since July 1998. Before 1998, Phase II scrubbers had not been expected to be built until well after 2000. However, at the investment cost reported for four of these units, the new Phase II scrubbers will remove sulfur at around $167 1995 dollars per ton – clearly economic at current allowance price levels, about 40% of the average for Phase I scrubbers, and well below the $437 projection in EPRI (1997).[9] If these units are at all representative, Phase II compliance costs may be substantially below current estimates and close to what is being indicated by allowance prices in early 1999.

Finally, the possibility that an allowance price of $200 in early 1999 is *above* the (discounted) long-run equilibrium cannot be entirely discounted. The allowance market is clearly driven by expectations concerning Phase II compliance. Expectations in 1999 concerning Phase II are no doubt better informed than were similar ones in 1995, but they are not thereby necessarily correct. The eventual Phase II equilibrium price when the bank is exhausted will depend, among other things, upon the difference between counterfactual emissions and the number of allowances issued. Only the latter is known currently. Just as the strength and durability of the economic recovery in the United States from the 1992 recession has been underestimated, so it would not be surprising if current estimates of future

---

9. The recently announced scrubbers at the Mt. Storm plant in West Virginia provide a good comparison of Phase I and Phase II scrubber cost (*Clean Air Compliance Review*, "Virginia Power to Add Scrubbers at Mt. Storm," February 24, 1999). Using the consumer price index to convert to 1995 dollars, the total announced cost for the scrubbers at units 1 and 2 is $109 million, or $99/KW^c of capacity. This compares very favorably with the Phase I scrubber installed on unit 3, which cost $272/KW^c of capacity in 1995 dollars. Virginia Power announced that the new scrubbers would remove 110,000 tons of sulfur per year. At 100 tons/MW^c, this is not a particularly high yield per unit of capacity (the Phase I average was 133). Nonetheless, at a 11.33% real capital charge rate, the surprisingly low capital cost implies a fixed cost of $102 per ton. Adding a $65/ton variable cost yields the $167/ton figure in the text.

growth err in the opposite direction, leading to higher estimates of required abatement and equilibrium allowance prices than otherwise would have been made.

At the same time, there has been little experience with abatement responses to higher and lower allowance prices. Utilities did respond to lower allowance prices during the first years of Phase I, but that response was limited by the fixity of scrubber investments and long-term contracts for low-sulfur coal. Experience with higher allowance prices is only now being gained, but the announcement of new scrubbers at five units, without benefit of bonus allowances, guaranteed cost recovery, or local political bias, suggests that up-side response may not be similarly limited. Finally, non-price-responsive compliance actions taken to coincide with the start of Phase II may lead to more abatement than is warranted, with consequent downward adjustment in allowance prices, similar to what occurred with the start of Phase I.[10]

A BETTER ALTERNATIVE POLICY?

We have argued that allowance prices were unexpectedly low early in Phase I because of prior overinvestment in compliance. That overinvestment was triggered by a general underestimation of the extent to which declines in rail rates would drive down the delivered prices of Powder River Basin coal and reduce the need for abatement to meet the aggregate Phase I constraint. Because overinvestment involves long-term contracts and long-lived scrubbers with low marginal operating costs, its effects on allowance markets have persisted.

All this confirms that the allowance and coal markets, like all real

---

10. For instance, as noted in Chapter 9, Illinois Power's Baldwin plant has announced plans to switch to Powder River Basin coal beginning in the year 2000. This decision converts what has been the largest source of demand for allowances in Phase I into a net supplier of allowances in Phase II. The timing of the switch is dictated in part by the expiration of one of two preexisting long-term coal contracts for the supply of high-sulfur coal to this plant at the end of 1999. Still, the justification provided for changing the source of supply for the remaining contract from the nearby high-sulfur mine to the Powder River Basin is the reduction in the number of allowances allocated to the plant with the start of Phase II. In theory, the year-to-year distribution of allowances within the total cumulative allocation would not affect the timing of abatement actions; however, where public relations or political considerations intrude, the start of Phase II provides a convenient exogenous focal point.

markets, are neither perfectly informed nor continually in long-run equilibrium. Were they so, allowance prices would have been higher in Phase I, and the average total cost of abatement in Phase I would have been somewhat lower. Any alternative policy, however, would also have involved long-lived investments and long-term contracts in the face of expectations that proved to be substantially wrong. Title IV had the considerable merit of allowing Phase II costs to be reduced, through banking of allowances, as a consequence of Phase I overinvestment. It is far from obvious that any feasible alternative policy could have done noticeably better in this regard.

12   Concluding Observations

The U.S. Acid Rain Program – Title IV of the 1990 Clean Air Act Amendments – was passed by Congress and signed by President Bush to reduce SO_2 emissions that contribute to acid rain. Neither Congress, nor President Bush, nor most of Title IV's other supporters conceived of the program as a policy experiment. Our analysis indicates that the Acid Rain Program has thus far been a notable success. Title IV more than achieved the SO_2 emissions-reduction goal established for Phase I, and it did so on time, without extensive litigation, and at costs lower than predicted. Moreover, there has been 100% compliance by all affected sources. Not only have there been no violations of the law, but no administrative exemptions or exceptions have been granted to permit noncompliance. After all, no affected source has been able to claim that compliance would be a special hardship, since it could always meet its compliance obligations simply by purchasing allowances on the open market. We are unaware of any other U.S. environmental program that has achieved this much,[1] and we find it impossible to believe that any feasible alternative command-and-control program could have done nearly as well. This performance justifies emission trading's recent emergence as a star on the environmental policy stage.

But, just as no single actor can excel in all roles, neither emissions

---

1. It has been suggested to us that the program to remove lead from U.S. gasoline may have performed nearly as well, but we do not believe existing research suffices to establish this (see NERA, 1994, Chapt. 2). Trading was, of course, a central feature of the lead phase-out program.

trading nor any other approach to environmental policy can provide low-cost solutions to all environmental problems. We have analyzed the performance of Title IV in depth here in large part to learn about the potential for using emissions trading in other contexts and about how the design of future emissions-trading systems should be affected by the performance of the SO_2 trading program. We believe our analysis of the U.S. Acid Rain Program supports a number of general lessons, and we devote the remainder of this brief final chapter to what seem to us to be the most important.

TRADING CAN WORK

The experience thus far with Title IV clearly establishes that large-scale tradable-permit programs can work more or less as textbooks describe.[2] By providing flexibility to polluters along with rigorous emissions measurement and enforcement, such programs can both achieve stated environmental objectives and reduce compliance costs. Title IV has gone well beyond the Phase I environmental objectives. Chapters 5 and 6, in particular, make clear that owners of affected sources have taken advantage of the flexibility Title IV provided and focused on reducing emissions when and where it was cheapest to do so – even though some observers had contended that regulated electric utilities would never be agile enough to do this.[3] Chapter 9 showed that Phase I compliance costs were significantly below expectations. More importantly, though it is difficult in both principle and practice to quantify the cost savings achieved thus far by trading under Title IV compared to a plausible command-and-control alternative, we believe the analysis in Chapter 10 establishes that those savings have been substantial. Finally, while we cannot

2. See, for instance, Tietenberg (1996, Chapt. 14).
3. Of course, it doesn't take much agility to move allowances between commonly owned generating units. Similarly, an allowance market makes "environmental dispatch" both desirable and easy to implement. Under Title IV, cost-minimizing utilities consider both fuel cost and allowance cost per kilowatt hour in deciding which generating units to run, and it is fairly simple to modify standard dispatch procedures to do this. Thus, under Title IV, generating units that emit more SO_2 per kilowatt hour are run less, all else being equal. And, as indicated in the analysis of heat input in the Appendix, this is what happened. Given the irreducible role of judgment in dispatch decisions, it would be very difficult to write a workable regulation to implement an equally effective form of environmental dispatch in a command-and-control regime.

demonstrate that Title IV accelerated innovation in scrubber technology, the fall in scrubber costs observed since the early 1990s, particularly when contrasted with the earlier technological stagnation reported by Bellas (1998), suggests that Title IV has stimulated progress in abatement technology. Given the controversy that Title IV sparked when first proposed, it is heartening that experience under this program is generally viewed as having established the workability of emissions trading.

On the other hand, it is important not to forget that textbooks also tell us that the emissions-trading approach is not well suited to some environmental problems. If a specific, isolated plant is emitting toxic chemicals that put nearby residents at excessive risk, emissions trading has no obvious role. It may be possible to use emission fees or taxes to deal with problems of this sort, but direct regulation is likely to have more appeal – even to economists. In other cases in which actual emissions are expensive or impossible to measure, or enforcement of emission limits would be impractical, emissions trading may not be a sensible policy approach. In still other cases, emissions trading may be practical but (in general or as embodied in some particular proposal) inferior to other approaches.[4] A fair conclusion to be drawn from experience to date with Title IV is that the tradable emissions approach is a valuable policy tool but not a panacea or even necessarily the best approach to all environmental challenges.

POLITICS DON'T MATTER

In Chapters 2 and 3, we described the political history of federal acid rain legislation and analyzed the complex legislative provisions that determined the allocation of allowances to hundreds of electric utilities located throughout the United States. The process of crafting the ultimate legislative provisions embodied in Title IV was clearly marked by the sort of rent seeking that is both regularly deplored by nonpoliticians and universally present when the gov-

---

4. For instance, see Schmalensee (1998a) for an argument that a particular emissions-trading proposal is unlikely to be the most efficient approach to meeting the limits on U.S. greenhouse-gas emissions contained in the Kyoto Protocol.

ernment is doling out things of value. We found support for no simple models of distributive politics, however.

Perhaps the most important lesson of this analysis in the present context is that all that rent seeking didn't matter in terms of program performance. That is, the complex political process that led to the allowance allocations in Title IV has had no significant adverse effect on the operation of the Acid Rain Program.[5] There is some irony here. Most U.S. environmental programs follow from legislation with strong language requiring regulators to pursue noble objectives, like protecting human health or eliminating risk, without regard to cost. The economic and environmental performance of these programs is regularly deplored in the policy literature.[6] Elegant language and noble intentions, in this context at least, have tended to produce bad results. In contrast, Title IV is built on more or less arbitrary emission limits, trading to reduce cost, and an allowance-allocation scheme that is at least as messy as most tax legislation and that has a history with no more nobility. Still, Title IV has effective provisions for emissions measurement and enforcement; active allowance markets with low transaction costs have developed; and Title IV has performed well in both economic and environmental terms.

MARKETS CAN DEVELOP

Efficient, competitive markets for tradable permits (allowances) can develop when program design and implementation are favorable. Title IV was signed into law in November 1990, and its final rules were adopted in January 1993. The analysis in Chapter 7 indicates that by around the middle of 1994, a reasonably efficient market for allowances had emerged. That is, prices for allowances were easily available to buyers and sellers, transaction costs were low, arbitrage opportunities were quickly exploited, and buyers and sellers were taking advantage of the opportunities to reduce compliance costs by

---

5. The one important qualification that must be noted is that the provisions in Title IV that allocated bonus allowances to utilities using "technology" to reduce emissions in Phase I likely resulted in overinvestment in scrubbing. Since scrubbing may have been economic, at least ex ante, in some cases even without this subsidy, it is unclear how much overinvestment the bonus provisions induced.

6. See, for instance, Portney (1990).

engaging in trading activity. Important factors contributing to the development of this market were the fundamental design of an "allowance" and the subsequent enlightened implementation of the Acid Rain Program by the EPA. The key design elements were, first, that de facto rights to emit SO_2 were being traded rather than reductions of SO_2 emissions, and second, that each allowance was worth the same amount (one ton of SO_2) regardless of when or between whom it was traded.

The distinction between trading "rights" and trading "reductions" may seem sophistical, since the number of permits implies a significant emissions reduction. However, the distinction is important for the development of a market. Emissions are what damage the environment, and measuring them is, at least in this case, a relatively routine engineering problem. Specifying and fixing emissions *reductions* cannot be done so easily, though, unless it is known in advance what emissions would have been absent the control program being implemented. Such counterfactual emissions levels are never easily ascertained; and the need for administrative review and approval of counterfactual emissions baselines increases transaction costs enormously.[7]

In its implementation of Title IV, the EPA deserves significant credit for resisting opportunities to review and approve compliance and trading decisions by private parties and for focusing instead on the integrity of emissions monitoring and on a strict, no-excuse, banker-type accountability for emissions and allowances. The commendable focus on results, without regard to intent or effort, minimized transaction costs and further encouraged the development of the allowance market. Finally, regardless of the theoretical strengths and weaknesses in the design of the EPA-administered allowance auction, the simple fact that a transparent mechanism existed in the early stages of implementation to facilitate the revelation of allowance prices encouraged the development of a private market.

7. Tietenberg (1985) provides examples of (relatively unsuccessful) programs in which emissions reductions rather than emissions are traded. The Clean Development Mechanism adopted in principle as part of the Kyoto Protocol on global climate change appears to have this same structure. See UNCTAD (1998), especially Section VI, for a complete discussion of the problem in the context of global greenhouse-gas trading.

TRADING HANDLES SURPRISES

One can expect a tradable allowance program both to produce surprises and to adapt reasonably efficiently to them. The more flexible a regulatory program, the more unexpected behavior it will produce as regulated firms exercise ingenuity in adapting to the new requirement and to unexpected events in related markets that affect efficient control strategies and optimal emission levels. Fundamentally, the fixed emissions ceiling of a tradable allowance program minimizes the potential environmental harm that such cleverness can produce.

The big surprise (or exogenous shock) in the SO_2 case was the rapid expansion of the market area for low-sulfur Powder River Basin coal, discussed in Chapter 4. This expansion was due mostly to the reduction in rail rates caused by the deregulation of railroads in the 1980s and by the introduction of rail competition into the Powder River Basin. As a result, low-sulfur coal became the fuel of choice based on cost rather than regulatory requirement for a larger number of sources than was anticipated when Title IV was passed. Thus, the emissions reduction required in the Midwest to meet the Phase I constraint was less than expected. The Title IV Program did not adapt perfectly to this surprise. As discussed in Chapter 11, more investment in compliance occurred before 1995 than would have been optimal if the required emission reductions and allowance prices had somehow been predicted more accurately ex ante, and the durability of those investments meant that they affected allowance and coal markets in much of Phase I.

In an ideal, textbook world, allowance price discovery would be instantaneous, resulting in no "overinvestment," even from the perspective of 20/20 hindsight. However, while one can imagine program design changes that would move toward this ideal, there is no way to reach the textbook ideal in the real world, in which future costs and prices are uncertain, information becomes available over time, and its discovery and dissemination are costly. However, since command-and-control programs do not generally embody any significant incentives for information discovery and dissemination, a command-and-control program would likely have translated the initial expectation error into even greater excess compliance costs.

In the case of Title IV, the owners of affected sources did in fact react to the information contained in the allowance prices revealed by the first EPA auction, and orders for some scrubbers were canceled. The provisions for banking allowances then ensured that the investments that had been made were used efficiently. Emissions were reduced well beyond what was required to meet the Phase I cap, without new legislation or regulation, because these reductions were cheap ex post and because the allowances thus saved could be banked for use in Phase II, when marginal compliance cost was expected to be higher. Thus, banking provided an important mechanism for mitigating the cost consequences of overinvestment, since these "excess" allowances could be used to avoid additional control costs in Phase II.

It is hard to imagine any command-and-control regime adapting as sensibly to such an important exogenous event. The response here was not only cost effective, but also environmentally beneficial, particularly for a pollutant whose effects are thought to be cumulative rather than dependent on ambient concentrations at particular points in time. The Title IV experience suggests that banking may generally be a potentially important source of cost savings in tradable-permit programs – particularly in the context of exogenous shocks.

OPT-IN PROVISIONS ARE TRICKY

"Opt-in" provisions need to be carefully considered, as they may not always be advantageous. As Chapter 8 has indicated, many of the complexities and administrative difficulties encountered thus far in the Acid Rain Program reflect the fact that Phase I covers some – but not all – sources of SO_2 emissions. The program includes substitution and compensation provisions for electric utility generating units and opt-in provisions for industrial sources to permit the substitution of lower-cost emissions reductions, where possible. The response by electric utility units has been substantial; however, the overall contribution of these units to emissions reduction early in Phase I was small, as was the cost savings from emissions trading with these units.

The widespread participation by electric utility sources appears to have been induced by overgenerous allowance allocations that will result, in all likelihood, in some increase in emissions. This slight increase over the course of the program will occur because any "opt-in" provision that is attractive to some emitters for cost-saving reasons is almost certain to involve provision of unneeded allowances to at least a few who are likely also to opt in. In retrospect, it appears that the most cost-effective Title IV emission reductions were to be found at the dirtiest large units – which were, by design, those required to participate in Phase I.

EXTRAPOLATE WITH CARE

All of our analysis suggests one final observation: Experience with and lessons learned from the Acid Rain Program must be applied with care to other environmental objectives. Though it can be described relatively simply, the operation of the U.S. Acid Rain Program was in fact fairly complicated, and details of the legislation and related regulations have mattered. There is a potentially large distance between embracing emissions trading in principle and producing a detailed program that will perform well in practice.

Because accurate emissions monitoring and strict enforcement seem feasible, we are inclined to argue that the Titlè IV experience provides considerable support for the careful use of emissions trading to control regional emissions of oxides of nitrogen (NO_x). Even here, though, nontrivial design problems must be solved if a trading-based program is to achieve both economic and environmental goals. The gap between principle and practice appears quite large in the climate change context though.[8] The Title IV Program was built on accurate emissions monitoring and strong penalties for violations – elements almost certain to be absent from international agreements on climate. Title IV covered a relatively small number of relatively large sources of SO_2: U.S. electric utility generating units. Carbon dioxide and other so-called greenhouse gases, however, are emitted by many more sources worldwide, most of which are too small to make direct measurement of emissions practical. In addition, much of the complexity in Phase I of the Acid Rain Program stems from its partial coverage of relevant sources, a key element in the Kyoto Protocol. Finally, the Acid Rain Program was designed to specify emission

8. See Schmalensee (1998b).

limits once and for all; any sensible climate-change regime must permit emission limits to be changed several times, at least, over the course of a century or so. These and other differences can have major impacts on both optimal design and program performance.

Appendix   Effect of Title IV on SO_2 Emissions and Heat Input

Susanne M. Schennach

INTRODUCTION

This appendix presents the econometric analysis of the effect of Title IV on emissions and heat input, on which much of the discussion in Chapter 5 is based. Panel data regression techniques are applied to a large data sample, including more than Phase I units alone and more years than 1995–97, to account for the most important factors determining SO_2 emissions. Three factors are particularly important.

- *Title IV* can be expected to reduce SO_2 emissions through a reduction in the emission rate as well as through a change in dispatch among units. Some of the effect may have taken place even prior to 1995.
- The greater availability of low-sulfur *PRB coals* throughout 1995, 1996, and 1997, due to further reductions in rail rates or contract expirations, has to be considered.
- *Changes in electricity demand* are a natural cause of fluctuations in heat input and emissions.

The model presented here is not intended to be a structural model of the electricity-generating sector to be used for testing the effect of a variety of economic and regulatory factors, as well as for forecasting. Rather, the model is tuned to answer a specific question, namely, the amount of SO_2 abatement that can be attributed to Title IV.

This appendix is organized as follows. The next sections describe the database; introduce the econometric model and describe its features; present the results; address the effect of Title IV on utilization; and draw conclusions.

DATA

The data for this analysis are taken from the Pechan database provided by EPA's Acid Rain Division, which contains detailed information on all Phase I-affected units as well as units that will be subject to Phase II of Title IV. Information on emissions, heat input, and fuel use for these units is provided for the period from 1988 through 1997. The specific sample used for this analysis includes all fossil fuel-fired units subject to Title IV – that is, those greater than 25 MW, located in states with at least one Phase I-affected unit and in some adjacent states with closely integrated electrical systems, such as Connecticut, Delaware, Rhode Island, and Virginia.[1] In the end, the sample consists of 13,640 observations, representing 1,364 units in 26 states, of which 457 units have been subject to Phase I in at least one year.

The inclusion of Phase II units in the sample is essential to evaluation of the impact of Phase I of Title IV. The units not affected by Phase I provide a "control group," which helps to identify the effect of all factors not related to Title IV. If these units were not included, only the pre-Title IV experience of the affected units could be used to differentiate between the effect of Title IV and the effects of unrelated factors.

SPECIFICATION OF THE MODEL

Estimating Equation

Counterfactual emissions are estimated using the following model, which relates SO_2 emissions of a unit i in year t to various explana-

---

1. Five Phase I substitution units in Utah and Wyoming are excluded because of the lack of interconnection between power plants in these two western states and the midwestern and eastern states where all other Phase I units are located.

tory variables, associated with Title IV and other factors that affect emissions.

$$SO2_{it} = SO2_{i0}(b_1 TA95_{it} + b_2 TA96_{it} + b_3 TA97_{it} + \qquad \text{(A.1)}$$
$$b_4 TIVScr95_{it} + b_5 TIVScr96_{it} + b_6 TIVScr97_{it} +$$
$$b_7 SubCom_{it} + b_8 pre1\_TA_{it} + b_9 pre2\_TA_{it} +$$
$$b_{10} pre\_Scrub + b_{11}\, t\, prbvar_i + b_{12}\, t\, oilgas_i +$$
$$\left(\sum_j htinpt_{jt} - \sum_j htinpt_{j0} \right) \Big/ \left(\sum_j htinpt_{j0} \right))$$
$$+ u_i + \varepsilon_{it},$$

where

$t = 1 \ldots T$, with $t = 0$ corresponding to year 1988 and $\mathrm{var}(\varepsilon_{it}) = a_1\, SO2_{i0} + a_2\, (SO2_{i0})^2$.

$SO2_{i0}$: Since changes in emissions are to be expressed as percentages rather than absolute amounts, the right-hand-side variables are multiplied by the SO$_2$ emissions in a reference year during which Title IV had no effect (here, 1988).

TA95, TA96, and *TA97* = dummy variables equal to 1 for Table A units without a Title IV scrubber in the respective years.

TIVScr95, TIVScr96, and *TIVScr97* = dummy variables set to 1 for Table A units that operated a retrofitted Title IV scrubber in the respective years.

SubCom = dummy variable set to 1 for Phase I units under the Substitution/Compensation Provisions. The number of units for which this dummy applies varies from year to year.

pre1_TA and *pre2_TA* = dummy variables equal to 1 in 1993 and 1994, respectively, for Table A units that potentially could switch to lower-sulfur coals (i.e., excluding one Table A unit with a pre-1990 scrubber and those retrofitting Title IV scrubbers in Phase I.

pre_Scrub = dummy included to account for three units that installed Title IV scrubbers prior to 1995.

prbvar = dummy set to 1 for all years for all coal units (oil/gas units excluded) located between 600 and 1,200 miles from the Powder River Basin. This dummy is multiplied by t because the penetration of PRB coal is expected to increase over the years.

oilgas = dummy equal to 1 for all the oil/gas units, and multiplied by t to allow for a gradual shift away from oil/gas units toward coal-fired generating capacity.

$(\Sigma_j \, htinpt_{jt} - \Sigma_j \, htinpt_{j0})/(\Sigma_j \, htinpt_{j0})$: The variable *htinpt* gives a unit's heat input. The sum $(\Sigma_j \, htinpt_{jt})$ is used as a proxy for electricity demand at time t. It is then normalized by $(\Sigma_j \, htinpt_{j0})$, the total heat input in 1988, so that fluctuations in demand are measured as deviations from the demand in 1988.

u_i = unit-specific fixed effect

ε_{it} = error term for which the variance is assumed to depend on unit size, as measured by SO_2 emissions in 1988 $(SO2_{i0})$, in order to account for heteroskedasticity. A two-step FGLS (feasible generalized least squares) procedure is used to obtain efficient estimates of the regression coefficients.

Several important considerations underlie this specification of the model. First, each generating unit possesses specific, time-invariant characteristics that play an important role in determining emissions, such as its size, location, or position in the dispatch order of its electricity generating system. The model therefore contains a unit-specific effect to measure these time-invariant factors. Moreover, units that have a large unit-specific effect, and thus "naturally" higher emissions, are more likely to have been selected as Table A units, for which emission reductions have to be estimated. Since this consideration introduces a possible correlation of the unit-specific effect with the other regressors, a fixed-effect model is the most appropriate choice to avoid bias in the regression results.

Second, a linear specification is used to relate each unit's SO_2 emissions to various explanatory variables. This choice guarantees that the estimate of counterfactual emissions is a linear function of the regression coefficients, so that the unbiased coefficients translate directly into an unbiased estimate of abatement, without requiring further assumptions. The two most obvious alternatives (log-linear regression or separate regressions of heat input and emission rate before multiplication of the results) do not possess this desirable property.[2]

---

2. Fitting the rate and the heat input separately would also create a simultaneous equation problem, which introduces difficulties of its own, such as the problem of finding good instruments.

Finally, since emissions are the product of heat input and emission rate, the regression coefficients measure the combined effect of the explanatory variables on this product. For example, to the extent that Title IV causes heat input to shift among Phase I units, the regression coefficients measure the effect on emissions of the change in utilization at Phase I units, as well as the effect of the change in emission rate.[3]

Title IV-Related Variables

A set of explanatory variables is included to model the impact of Title IV on various types of units. Separate dummy variables are used for affected units with retrofitted scrubbers, all other Table A units, and substitution units, since different types of Phase I units are likely to choose different levels of abatement. Scrubbed units typically achieve a much higher rate of abatement than do units that rely on fuel switching. Also, substitution and compensation units volunteering for Phase I may have different abatement strategies, as they differ from Table A units in size, utilization, and pre-Title IV emission rates.[4] Using separate dummy variables for the Table A units for each year allows us to observe the evolution of the abatement level as Phase II approaches.

The inclusion of the dummies *pre1_TA* and *pre2_TA* allows for the possibility that Table A units switching to lower-sulfur coals may have reduced emissions prior to the onset of Title IV in 1995, for instance by experimenting with lower-sulfur coals or renegotiating existing coal contracts. The *pre_Scrub* dummy is included in a similar spirit, to account for scrubbers installed before 1995.

Non-Title IV-Related Variables

Other factors, independent of Title IV, that are expected to affect SO₂ emissions prompt the inclusion of additional explanatory variables in the model. An accurate counterfactual for Title IV is crucially depen-

---

3. Title IV-induced shifts of heat input among heat-input groups are another matter, which will be discussed later.
4. According to the provisions of Title IV, a unit's decision to enter Phase I as a substitution or compensation unit in a particular year can directly depend on its emissions for that year, since a unit can withdraw until fairly late in the year. This potential endogeneity problem in the specification is less of a concern, to the extent that substitution and compensation units make their decision based on factors other than their current emissions, such as NO_x grandfathering.

dent on controlling for the decreases in emissions due to the expansion of PRB coal into the Midwest as a result of the deregulation of railroads during the 1980s, as discussed in more detail in Chapter 4. This trend is expected to continue into Phase I as more long-term coal contracts expire or are renegotiated, enabling more units to switch to the now cheaper PRB coal. The increasing importance of PRB coal is simulated by including a linear time trend for all units located between 600 and 1,200 miles of the PRB. The inclusion of Phase II units in the sample and the start of this time trend in the late 1980s, well before any early compliance with Title IV, make separation of the PRB and Title IV effects possible, even though both factors tend to decrease emissions. More flexible functional forms for the time dependence of the PRB coal effect were tried, but they do not improve the fit sufficiently to justify the loss in precision of the estimated coefficients.

A similar time-trend variable is included for oil- and gas-fired units to allow for the reduction in utilization of these units as the price of oil and gas increased relative to that of coal from 1988 through 1997. While this trend is not expected to affect the level of emissions greatly, ignoring it would mask the effect of Phase I, since the proportion of oil and gas units is much greater among Phase II units in the "control group" than among Table A units.

SO_2 emissions follow trends in electricity demand, which fluctuates for reasons independent of Title IV. The sum of the heat input of all Title IV-affected units in a given year provides a measure of the net electricity demand for fossil fuel-fired units subject to Title IV. While the distribution of heat input among the units may be affected by Title IV, the total heat input to these units can safely be assumed to be exogenous, which validates its use as a proxy for electricity demand. As with the other regressors, the changes in heat input are measured relative to 1988. The variable entering the specification thus takes the form $(\Sigma_j \, htinpt_{jt} - \Sigma_j \, htinpt_{j0})/(\Sigma_j \, htinpt_{j0})$, based on the assumption that, other things being equal, a 1% increase in total heat input (relative to 1988) causes a 1% increase in emissions at each unit (relative to 1988). The coefficient of $(\Sigma_j \, htinpt_{jt} - \Sigma_j \, htinpt_{j0})/(\Sigma_j \, htinpt_{j0})$ is not evaluated from the regression. The units as a whole must produce their own total heat input, which constrains this coefficient to be one.

An assumption that fluctuations in demand are absorbed uniformly by all units would be unnecessarily restrictive, and a failure to account either for major changes in the demand for electricity by region or for other characteristics would obscure the effects of Title IV. For this reason, four mutually exclusive subgroups of units are identified, and each is assigned its own growth trend in heat input. This assignment is, of course, based on the assumption that Title IV does not cause a shift in heat input from one group of units to another group, only shifts within the groups. The first partitioning of units is based on geographic location. In particular, units located within 1,200 miles from the PRB differ significantly in their heat input trends from other units, with units in the Midwest exhibiting much higher growth rates than their counterparts farther east.

A second partitioning of the units separates Phase I from Phase II units, to be consistent with the use of Phase II units as a control group unaffected by Title IV. Hence, the regression results will not measure the effect on emissions of any potential heat input shifts between Phase I and Phase II units due to Title IV. As long as the heat input shifts do not affect emission rates in Phase I and Phase II units, the Title IV abatement estimated by the regression will err only to the extent that the average emission rate for Phase I units differs from that for Phase II units. Shifts in generating load from Phase I to Phase II units will be analyzed separately and will be shown to have a negligible effect on abatement.[5]

In short, a separate electricity demand trend is defined for each of the four subgroups: Phase I and Phase II units located either within or beyond 1,200 miles from the PRB. For every unit in a given subgroup, the growth trend in heat input is assumed to be the same as the percentage increase of the aggregate heat input for the subgroup.

RESULTS

The results of the regression, shown in Table A.1, indicate that all factors included in the model have a statistically significant impact on

---

5. If the regression were to assign a common heat input trend to affected and unaffected units, Phase II units could no longer be used as a control group. The resulting regression coefficients would incorrectly measure the magnitude of shifts from Phase I to Phase II units, leading to a bias in estimated abatement that would be difficult to correct. In contrast, the assumption of no heat-input shifts between Phase I and Phase II units made in the current regression allows for this potential weakness to be corrected in a straightforward way later in this Appendix.

Table A.1. *Estimated coefficients of Equation (A.1)*

Variable	Coefficient	Std. Dev.	t-Stat.
TA95	−0.3454	0.0293	−11.80
TA96	−0.2871	0.0304	−9.45
TA97	−0.3009	0.0312	−9.65
TIVSr95	−0.9032	0.0769	−11.75
TIVSr96	−0.8863	0.0696	−12.73
TIVSr97	−0.9206	0.0699	−13.17
SubCom	−0.2131	0.0378	−5.63
t prbvar	−0.0414	0.0040	−10.27
t oilgas	−0.0448	0.0084	−5.33
pre1_TA	−0.0478	0.0287	−1.66
pre2_TA	−0.0669	0.0292	−2.30
pre_Scr	−0.6716	0.1627	−4.13

Number of obs = 10,305
$F(12, 9148)$ = 97.42
Prob > F = 0
R^2 = .8528
Adj R^2 = .8342
Root MSE = 41.129

SO_2 emissions. Note that the coefficient measuring the effect of a given factor represents the difference between a unit's actual emissions level and the level of emissions that would be observed in the absence of this effect, as a percentage of the unit's emissions in 1988.

As expected, the effect of Title IV is substantial. The results show that Table A units reduced their emissions between 29% and 35%, measured as a percentage of their 1988 emissions. Not surprisingly, units that installed a scrubber are characterized by a significantly larger reduction in emissions (from 89% to 92%). Substitution and compensation units, on the other hand, are associated with a smaller reduction, of about 21%.

What is perhaps even more interesting is the fact that Title IV had a substantial impact prior to 1995, as indicated by the *Pre1_TA* and *Pre2_TA* dummies. Table A units reduced their emissions by 5% in 1993, and by 7% in 1994. Since relatively few Table A units were subject to other regulations requiring emission reductions prior to 1995, this abatement results mostly from early compliance with Title IV.

Finally, the crucial effect of the greater penetration of PRB coal can be clearly identified. Units located between 600 and 1,200 miles from the PRB steadily reduced their emissions by about 4% per year during the time period covered by the sample.

Thanks to the linearity of the model, these regression results can be readily converted into tons of SO_2 abatement by Phase I units, by multiplying the regression coefficients associated with a given dummy variable by the total emissions in 1988 of units for which this dummy is equal to one. The results of this exercise, shown in Table A.2 and illustrated in Figure A.1, emphasize important features of the effect of Title IV. The impact of early compliance, most of which occurred at Table A units that did not install a Title IV scrubber, amounts to a nonnegligible 398,000 and 537,000 tons in 1993 and 1994, respectively. The aggregate emissions reduction by Phase I units was about 4 million tons of SO_2 per year of compliance. More specifically, the abatement at Phase I units amounted to 4.2 million tons in the first year of compliance, then decreased to 3.8 million in 1996, before rising to 4.0 million in 1997.

Perhaps the most remarkable feature of Title IV abatement has been the contribution by scrubbed units. Despite the relatively small number of scrubbed units (21 in 1995, and 27 afterward), they contributed 37% of overall Title IV abatement at Phase I units from 1995 through 1997. The importance of scrubbed units arises both from their large size and from the high removal efficiency of scrubbers. At the other extreme, substitution and compensation units contributed little to the aggregate emissions reductions during this time period (less than 7%).

Table A.3 and Figure A.2 show the evolution over time of actual, predicted, and counterfactual emissions. Predicted emissions were obtained by substituting the estimated regression coefficients and the

Table A.2. *SO₂ abatement (in thousands of tons), for each type of Phase I unit*

Year	Unscrubbed Table A	Scrubbed Table A	Voluntary units	All Phase I
1992	0	50	0	50
1993	344	55	0	398
1994	482	55	0	537
1995	2,563	1,326	265	4,153
1996	2,068	1,493	229	3,791
1997	2,167	1,551	237	3,955

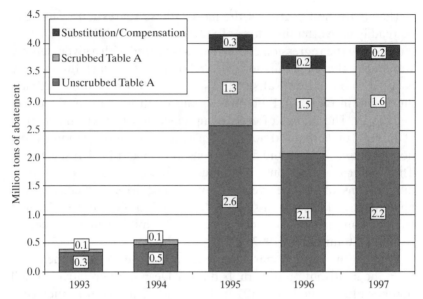

Figure A.1. Title IV abatement, by unit type.
Sources: Derived from Pechan (1995) and EPA (1996b, 1997, 1998).

Table A.3. *Actual, predicted, and counterfactual emissions (in thousands of tons),*
for units subject to Phase I in at least one year

Year	Actual	Predicted	Counterfactual
1989	10,200	10,200	10,200
1990	9,989	9,837	9,837
1991	9,585	9,417	9,417
1992	9,206	8,984	9,033
1993	8,615	8,614	9,013
1994	8,415	8,488	9,025
1995	5,383	5,314	9,468
1996	5,681	5,747	9,538
1997	5,628	5,686	9,641

Sources: Derived from Pechan (1995), EPA (1996b, 1997, 1998), and
Appendix to this book.

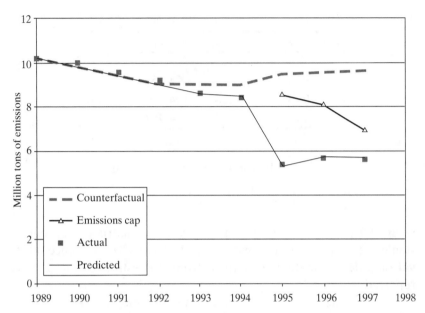

Figure A.2. Actual, predicted, and counterfactual emissions, for units subject to Phase I in at least one year.

Sources: Derived from Pechan (1995) and EPA (1996b, 1997, 1998).

estimated fixed effects into Equation (A.1). Counterfactual emissions were obtained in a similar fashion, after setting all Title IV-related dummies to zero. (Alternatively, one could calculate the counterfactual by adding the Title IV abatement previously derived to the predicted emissions.)

How accurate is this estimate of aggregate Title IV abatement, setting aside the effect of any shift of heat input to non-Phase I units for the moment? The very close correspondence between predicted emissions and actual emissions (always within 2.5%) indicates that the specification includes the most important factors determining emissions at Phase I units. Under the assumption that the model is correctly specified, standard statistical techniques provide a confidence interval on the predicted aggregate Title IV abatement. If the Title IV abatement a_i of unit i is related to a vector x_i of Title IV-related variables by a vector of coefficients b:

$$a_i = x_i'b$$

Table A.4. *95% confidence interval of Title IV abatement (in thousands of tons)*

Year	Min	Max
1995	3,652	4,654
1996	3,281	4,301
1997	3,430	4,481

then the variance of the total abatement is given by:

$$Var\left(\sum_i a_i\right) = \left(\sum_i x_i'\right) Var(b)\left(\sum_i x_i\right)$$

where $Var(b)$ denotes the variance-covariance matrix of the regression coefficients associated with Title IV. The 95% confidence interval of Title IV abatement derived from this estimated variance is reported in Table A.4.

Finally, while the previous graphs only illustrate the effect of Title IV, the abatement due to Title IV can be compared to the emissions reductions at Phase I units resulting from the expansion of PRB coal. Following the discussion in Chapter 4, the effect of the PRB trend is assumed negligible in 1985. Consequently, the estimate of PRB abatement is obtained by multiplying the regression coefficient associated with the PRB effect by the number of years elapsed since 1985 and by the total emissions in 1988 of all Phase I coal-fired units located between 600 and 1,200 miles from the PRB. Table A.5 and Figure A.3 compare PRB abatement at Phase I units to Title IV abatement. It is immediately apparent why the effect of PRB coal is so important. PRB coal contributes a substantial one-third of the emission abatement observed at Phase I units in 1995–97. It is worth noting that, while PRB abatement includes emission reductions that would have occurred without Title IV, Title IV abatement also includes switching to PRB coal at units where Title IV allowance value made a difference in the choice between PRB coal and competing higher-sulfur coals.

EFFECT OF TITLE IV ON UTILIZATION

One final factor must be taken into consideration in evaluating the effect of Title IV on SO_2 emissions. While the model of emissions pre-

Table A.5. *PRB abatement by coal-fired Phase I units located between 600 and 1,200 miles from the PRB (in thousands of tons); total Title IV abatement also shown*

Year	PRB abatement	Title IV abatement
1989	821	0
1990	1,026	0
1991	1,231	0
1992	1,436	50
1993	1,641	398
1994	1,846	537
1995	2,051	4,153
1996	2,256	3,791
1997	2,462	3,955

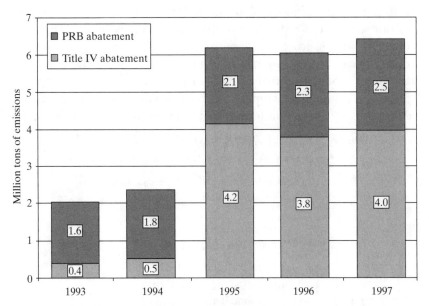

Figure A.3. Relative magnitudes of Title IV abatement and PRB abatement by coal-fired Phase I units located between 600 and 1,200 miles from the PRB.

Sources: Derived from Pechan (1995) and EPA (1996b, 1997, 1998).

sented above properly incorporates the emissions effects of Title IV-induced shifts in heat input among Phase I units, it fails to account for changes in emissions resulting from shifts in heat input from Phase I to Phase II units. Accordingly, this section presents a regression analysis of the heat input trends at the unit level. The results of this analysis are used to determine the magnitude of the heat input transfers and of any consequent emissions "leakage."

Two types of heat input shifts can be expected. First, the added cost of allowances or of the premium for lower-sulfur coal will unavoidably create an incentive to shift generation from affected to non-affected units. For this reason, extensive "reduced utilization provisions" were developed to ensure that Phase I units did not reduce utilization below baseline (average 1985–87 levels) by shifting generation to other SO_2-emitting sources. In fact, demand was sufficiently robust in 1995–97 that few units had any trouble with the reduced utilization provisions. Nevertheless, the incentive is still present, even when demand is above baseline levels, and some shifting of heat input and emissions would be expected.

Second, although this was not widely anticipated, Table A units retrofitted with scrubbers experienced a noticeable increase in utilization coincident with the installation of the scrubbers. This shift reflects both the lower marginal cost of abatement with scrubbing (once the capital cost is sunk) and the typically lower prices for high-sulfur coals that result from the sulfur premium imposed by Title IV.

The regression of heat input at each unit on a set of explanatory variables takes a form similar to the one used to study trends in emissions.

$$htinpt_{it} = htinpt_{i0}(c_1 TA95_{it} + c_2 TA96_{it} + c_3 TA97_{it} +$$
$$c_4 TIVScr95_{it} + c_5 TIVScr96_{it} + c_6 TIVScr97_{it} +$$
$$c_7 SubCom_{it} + c_8\, t\, prbdum_i + c_9\, t\, oilgas_i +$$
$$c_{10}\, pre\_Scrub_{it} + \mu_t Phase I_{it} + \tau_t) + \alpha_i + e_{it} \qquad (A.2)$$

where

$$Var(e_{it}) = d_1\, htinpt_{i0} + d_2\, (htinpt_{i0})^2$$

$$TAnn = \begin{cases} +1 \quad \text{for unscrubbed Table A units} \\[4pt] -\dfrac{\left(\begin{array}{c}\text{Sum of 1988 heat input at} \\ \text{unscrubbed Table A units}\end{array}\right)}{\left(\begin{array}{c}\text{Sum of 1988 heat input} \\ \text{at Phase 2 units}\end{array}\right)} \quad \text{for Phase 2 units} \end{cases}$$

$$SubCom = \begin{cases} +1 & \text{for Sub. Com. units} \\ -\dfrac{\left(\begin{array}{l}\text{Sum of 1988 heat input} \\ \text{at Sub. Com. units}\end{array}\right)}{\left(\begin{array}{l}\text{Sum of 1988 heat input at} \\ \text{Phase 2 units}\end{array}\right)} & \text{for Phase 2 units} \end{cases}$$

$$TIVScrnn = \begin{cases} +1 & \text{for scrubbed units} \\ -\dfrac{\left(\begin{array}{l}\text{Sum of 1988 heat input} \\ \text{at scrubbed units}\end{array}\right)}{\left(\begin{array}{l}\text{Sum of 1988 heat input at} \\ \text{unscrubbed Phase 1 units}\end{array}\right)} & \begin{array}{l}\text{for unscrubbed} \\ \text{Phase 1 units}\end{array} \end{cases}$$

(where "scrubber" denotes a Title IV scrubber only)

oilgas and *pre_Scrub*: Defined as in equation (A.1)

prbdum = dummy equal to 1 for all units located within 1,200 miles of the PRB

PhaseI = dummy equal to 1 for Phase I units in all years before 1995

μ_t = time-specific effect for Phase I units before 1995

τ_t = time-specific effect common to all units

α_i = fixed effect

e_{it} = error term

The modifications made to the Title IV-related dummies (*TAnn*, *SubCom*, and *TIVScrnn*) have a simple origin. Under the reasonable assumption that Title IV changes only the distribution of the load among all fossil fuel-fired units, but not the total load, every decrease in heat input at some units has to be exactly absorbed by an increase at other units.[6] Each of these variables measures a change in emissions at one type of unit, due to a transfer to (or from) another type of unit. The *TAnn* variables model the drop in heat input at unscrubbed Table A units resulting from a possible shift to Phase II

6. In particular, the utilization of nuclear and hydro units in a given year is assumed to be unaffected by Title IV. Typically, these units are fully utilized to the extent they are available. Thus, any heat input shift away from Phase I units would increase the demand for fossil fuel-fired, Phase II units.

units, as does the *SubCom* variable for substitution and compensation units. The *TIVScrnn* variable represents the increase in load at Phase I units with a Title IV scrubber due to a transfer from unscrubbed Phase I units, whether Table A or substitution units. In each case, the regressors take opposite signs for the two types of units participating in the transfer. A normalization factor is included so that, for any value of the regression coefficients, there is no change in the total heat input as a result of each type of transfer.[7] For example, the aggregate heat input of Table A units amounts to about half of the aggregate heat input of Phase II units. The *TAnn* variable thus takes the value +1 for Table A units and about –0.5 for Phase II units, which means that every 1% decrease in the heat input of Table A units can be absorbed by a 0.5% increase at Phase II units.

The heat input growth associated with units located near PRB is modeled by a simple linear trend: $t\, prbdum_i$. The inclusion of the time dummies for Phase I units, μ_t, provides an answer to the important question of whether there was any significant heat input shift from Phase I to Phase II units with the onset of Title IV, after controlling for all other factors influencing heat input.

The results of this regression analysis, shown in Table A.6, reveal the following:

- There is no significant difference in heat input trends between Phase I and Phase II units prior to 1995, as seen from the low *t*-statistics of the μ_t coefficients.
- Unscrubbed Phase I units, whether Table A or substitution units, exhibited a significant 8% to 12% decrease in heat input due to a transfer to other units in the first three years of Title IV.[8] In contrast, scrubbed units experienced a significant 15% increase in heat input in 1995 as a result of a transfer from unscrubbed Phase I units, which declined to 9% in 1996 and 7% in 1997.

The regression results can be readily converted into heat input transfers as follows. The transfer in heat input from unscrubbed Phase I units to Phase II units is estimated by multiplying the sum of the heat input at Table A and substitution units in 1988 by the corre-

7. The normalization factors are, for 1995 through 1997, respectively, for *TAnn*, .602, .557, and .559; for *SubCom*, .278, .221, and .225; and for *TIVScrnn*, .116, .148, and .147.
8. Approximately 6% to 11% was shifted to Phase II units, and another 1% to 2% to Table A units with retrofitted scrubbers.

Table A.6. *Estimated coefficients of Equation (A.2)*

Variable	Coef.	Std err.	t-stat		
				Number of obs =	10,341
				$F(31,\ 9161) =$	40.97
τ_5	−0.024	0.019	−1.275	Prob > F =	0
τ_6	−0.038	0.019	−1.954	$R^2 =$	.9225
τ_7	−0.088	0.020	−4.503	Adj $R^2 =$	.9126
τ_8	−0.026	0.020	−1.311	Root MSE =	0.65266
τ_9	−0.016	0.020	−0.794		
τ_{10}	0.039	0.016	2.399		
τ_{11}	0.076	0.017	4.455		
τ_{12}	0.122	0.018	6.848		
μ_5	0.006	0.026	0.215		
μ_6	−0.017	0.026	−0.630		
μ_7	0.000	0.026	0.012		
μ_8	−0.045	0.026	−1.693		
μ_9	−0.041	0.026	−1.555		
pre_Sr	0.337	0.130	2.603		
TA95	−0.070	0.018	−3.813		
TA96	−0.077	0.019	−4.021		
TA97	−0.112	0.019	−5.843		
SubCom	−0.064	0.020	−3.194		
TIVSr95	0.153	0.052	2.938		
TIVSr96	0.093	0.047	1.971		
TIVSr97	0.071	0.047	1.507		
t prbvar	0.027	0.003	9.816		
t oilgas	−0.059	0.004	−15.011		

sponding regression coefficients, *TAnn* and *SubCom*. The heat-input transfer from unscrubbed units to scrubbed Phase I units is evaluated by multiplying the 1988 sum of the heat input at units that were to retrofit scrubbers by the regression coefficients *TIVScrnn*. The transfers thus estimated, shown in Figure A.4, reveal that most of the decrease in heat input at unscrubbed Phase I units was absorbed by Phase II units rather than by scrubbed Phase I units. More specifi-

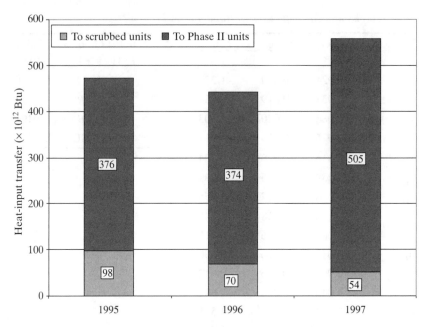

Figure A.4. Transfers of heat input from unscrubbed Phase I units.
Sources: Derived from Pechan (1995) and EPA (1996b, 1997, 1998).

cally, scrubbers absorbed only 20% of the decreased utilization of unscrubbed Phase I units in 1995, and even less, 10%, in 1997.

While the model of emissions accounts for the emission-reducing transfer from unscrubbed to scrubbed Phase I units, it neglects the transfer in heat input from Phase I to Phase II units, which results simultaneously in lower emissions at Phase I units and higher emissions at Phase II units. The decrease in emissions at unscrubbed Phase I units caused by this transfer, shown in Table A.7, is obtained by multiplying the heat-input transfer to Phase II units by the heat-input weighted average emission rate of Phase I units. The increase at Phase II units is similarly derived using the heat input weighted average rate at Phase II units. The net emissions effect of the shift in heat input, as shown in Table A.7, is emission reducing, since the average emission rate of unscrubbed Phase I units is on average higher than that of Phase II units.[9]

9. The heat input weighted average emission rates for unscrubbed Phase I units were 1.831 lb/mmBtu, 1.886 lb/mmBtu, and 1.834 lb/mmBtu for 1995 through 1997, respectively. The comparable rates at Phase II units were 1.147 lb/mmBtu, 1.158 lb/mmBtu, and 1.189 lb/mmBtu for the same years.

Table A.7. *Changes in emissions at Phase I and Phase II units (in thousands of tons) resulting from a heat-input transfer from Phase I to Phase II units*

Year	Decrease at Phase I	Increase at Phase II	Net effect
1995	344	216	−129
1996	353	216	−136
1997	463	300	−163

The aggregate emissions reduction attributable to Title IV should be increased by the additional abatement resulting from the shift in load to Phase II units. However, as shown in Table A.7, this correction is only of the order of 150,000 tons per year, which is less than 5% of total abatement. The accuracy of the previous approach is thus only minimally affected.

CONCLUSION

The estimate of counterfactual emissions is based on a regression of the unit-level SO_2 emissions on a set of explanatory variables both related and unrelated to Title IV. Accounting for factors unrelated to Title IV is crucial to obtain unbiased estimates of the abatement due to Phase I of Title IV. Notably, the greater availability of PRB coal and fluctuations in electricity demand arising from business cycles led to important changes in emissions. The inclusion of unaffected Phase II units in the data sample greatly facilitates the estimation of these effects.

A similar regression analysis of the generating load dispatch found that a heat-input shift from Phase I to Phase II units did occur. The magnitude of the shift away from unscrubbed Phase I units is considerable, on the order of 10% of what generation would otherwise have been. The heat-input shift was emissions reducing since the emission rates for the Phase II units benefiting from the shift were lower on average than those for the unscrubbed Phase I units. The additional emissions reduction resulting from the heat-input shift to Phase II units is small and well within the error bounds for this estimate of Title IV abatement.

The level of abatement resulting from Title IV is estimated to be about 4.1 million tons of SO_2 per year, after accounting for the heat-input shift to Phase II units. The annual amounts attributable to unscrubbed Table A units, units retrofitted with scrubbers, and substitution units are approximately 2.3 million tons, 1.5 million tons, and 0.2 million tons, respectively. Moreover, early compliance at Table A units contributed another 0.4 million tons of abatement annually in the two years preceding the onset of Title IV (1993 and 1994).

Bibliography

Ackerman, Bruce A., and Hassler, William T. 1981. *Clean Coal and Dirty Air.* New Haven, CT: Yale Univ. Press.

Allowance Price Indications. 1993–97. Cantor Fitzgerald Environmental Brokerage.

Andrin, Estelle. 1999. "The Price Behavior of Tradable Permits: The SO_2 Allowance Price Spike of 1998." Unpublished thesis for completion of requirements for S.M. degree in Technology and Policy, Massachusetts Institute of Technology.

Arora, Seema, and Cason, Timothy C. 1996. "Why Do Firms Volunteer to Exceed Environmental Regulations? Understanding Participation in EPA's 33/50 Program." *Land Econ.* 72, no. 4 (November): 413–32.

Atkeson, Erica. 1997. "Joint Implementation: Lessons from Title IV's Voluntary Compliance Programs." Working Paper no. MIT-CEEPR 97-003 WP. Cambridge, MA: MIT Center for Energy and Environmental Policy Research (CEEPR). May.

Bailey, Elizabeth M. 1998a. "Allowance Trading Activity and State Regulatory Rulings: Evidence from the U.S. Acid Rain Program." Working Paper no. MIT-CEEPR 98-005 WP. Cambridge, MA: MIT CEEPR. March.

1998b. "Intertemporal Pricing of Sulfur Dioxide Allowances." Working Paper no. MIT-CEEPR 98-006 WP. Cambridge, MA: MIT CEEPR. March.

Baron, David P. 1990. "Distributive Politics and the Persistence of Amtrak." *J. Politics* 52, no. 3 (August): 883–913.

1991. "Majoritarian Incentives, Pork Barrel Programs, and Procedural Control," *American J. Political Science,* 35: 57–90.

Bartels, Carlton W. 1997. "Recent Trends in the SO_2 Allowance Marketplace." Mimeo, Cantor Fitzgerald Environmental Brokerage Services (22 January).

Baumol, William J., and Oates, Wallace E. 1988. *The Theory of Environmental Policy: Externalities, Public Outlays, and the Quality of Life.* Englewood Cliffs, NJ: Prentice-Hall.

Bellas, Allen S. 1998. "Empirical Evidence of Advances in Scrubber Technology." *Resource and Energy Economics* 20, no. 4 (December): 327–43.

Bernstein, Mark; Farrell, Alex; and Winebrake, James. 1994. "The Environment and Economics: The Impact of Restricting the SO_2 Allowance Market." *Energy Policy* 22, no. 9: 748–54.

Bohi, Douglas. 1994. "Utilities and State Regulators Are Failing to Take Advantage of Emissions Allowance Trading," *Electricity J.* (March): 20–27.

Bohi, Douglas R., and Burtraw, Dallas. 1992. "Utility Investment Behavior and the Emission Trading Market." *Resources and Energy* 14, nos. 1–2 (April): 129–53.

Braine, Bruce H. 1991. "Allowance Market Implications of Acid Rain Regulation." In *The New Clean Air Act: Compliance and Opportunity*, edited by Reinier Locke and Dennis P. Harkawik. Arlington, VA: Public Utilities Reports.

Burtraw, Dallas. 1996. "The SO_2 Emissions Trading Program: Cost Savings without Allowance Trades." *Contemporary Econ. Policy* 14, no. 2 (April): 79–94.

Burtraw, Dallas, and Swift, Byron. 1996. "A New Standard of Performance: An Analysis of the Clean Air Act's Acid Rain Program." *Environmental Law Review News and Analysis* XXVI, no. 8 (August): 26 ELR 10411–23.

Carlson, Curtis; Burtraw, Dallas; Cropper, Maureen; and Palmer, Karen L. 1998. *Sulfur Dioxide Control by Electric Utilities: What Are the Gains from Trade?* Policy Research Working Paper 1966. The World Bank, Development Research Group, August.

Cason, Timothy N. 1993. "Seller Incentive Properties of EPA's Emission Trading Auction." *J. Environmental Econ. and Management* 25, no. 2 (September): 177–95.

　　1995. "An Experimental Investigation of the Seller Incentives in EPA's Emission Trading Auction." *American Economic Rev.* 85, no. 4 (September): 905–22.

Cason, Timothy N., and Plott, Charles R. 1996. "EPA's New Emissions Trading Mechanism: A Laboratory Evaluation." *J. Environmental Econ. and Management* 30, no. 2 (March): 133–60.

Clean Air Act Amendments (CAAA 1990). As available in Moyer, Craig A., and Francis, Michael A. 1992. *Clean Air Act Handbook: A Practical Guide to Compliance.* 2d ed. Deerfield, Il: Clark Boardman Callaghan.

Cohen, Richard E. 1990. "When Titans Clash on Clean Air." *National J.* 22, no. 14 (7 April): 849–50.

　　Washington at Work: Back Rooms and Clean Air. New York: Macmillan, 1992. *The Congressional Quarterly Almanac* (Washington: Congressional Quarterly, Inc.): *1982*, pp. 425–34; *1983*, pp. 340–41; *1984*, pp. 340–42; *1986*, p. 137; *1987*, pp. 299–301; *1988*, pp. 142–48.

Cox, Gary W., and Mathew D. McCubbins. 1993. *Legislative Leviathon: Party Government in the House.* Berkeley: University of California Press.

Crandall, Robert W. 1984. "An Acid Test for Congress?" *Regulation* 8 (September/December): 21–28.

Dales, J. H. 1968. *Pollution, Property & Prices: An Essay in Policy-making and Economics.* Toronto: University of Toronto Press.

Davis, Joseph A. 1986. "Acid Rain to Get Attention as Reagan Changes Course." *Congressional Q.* 44, no. 12 (22 March): 675–76.

DOE. *See* U.S. Department of Energy.

Doucet, Joseph A., and Strauss, Todd. 1994. "On the Bundling of Coal and Sulfur Dioxide Emissions Allowances." *Energy Policy* 22, no. 9: 764–70.

Electric Power Research Institute (EPRI). 1993. *Integrated Analysis of Fuel, Technology and Emission Allowance Markets: Electric Utility Responses to the Clean Air Act Amendments of 1990.* EPRI TR-102510. Palo Alto, CA.

———. 1995. *The Emission Allowance Market and Electric Utility SO_2 Compliance in a Competitive and Uncertain Future.* EPRI TR-105490s. Palo Alto, CA.

———. 1997. *SO_2 Compliance and Allowance Trading: Developments and Outlook.* EPRI TR-107897 4129. Palo Alto, CA.

Ellerman, A. Denny, and Montero, Juan-Pablo. 1996. "Why Are Allowance Prices So Low? An Analysis of the SO_2 Emissions Trading Program." Working Paper no. MIT-CEEPR 96-001 WP. Cambridge, MA: MIT CEEPR. February.

———. 1998. "The Declining Trend in Sulfur Dioxide Emissions: Implications for Allowance Prices." *J. Environmental Econ. and Management* 36, no. 1 (July): 26–45.

Ellerman, A. Denny; Schmalensee, Richard; Joskow, Paul L.; Montero, Juan-Pablo; and Bailey, Elizabeth M. 1997. *Emissions Trading under the U.S. Acid Rain Program: Evaluation of Compliance Costs and Allowance Market Performance.* Cambridge, MA: MIT CEEPR, October.

EPA. *See* U.S. Environmental Protection Agency.

EPRI. *See* Electric Power Research Institute.

Exchange Value. Emission Exchange Corp. (various issues).

FERC. *See* U.S. Federal Energy Regulatory Commission.

Ferejohn, John A., and Morris P. Fiorina. 1975. "Purposive Models of Legislative Behavior." *American Economic Review Papers and Proceedings* 65 (May):407–14.

Fieldston Publications, Inc. *Compliance Strategy Review.* Selected issues. Washington.

———. 1994. *Fieldston's Guide to Phase I and Phase II Units,* 4th ed. Washington.

———. 1994–98. *Clean Air Compliance Review* (previously *Compliance Strategy Review*). Selected issues. Washington.

———. 1997. *Coal Markets PriceLine.* Washington.

———. 1998. *Coal Markets PriceLine: Fieldston Coal Markets Link* (disk update). Washington, Summer.

Fullerton, Don; McDermott, Shaun P.; and Caulkins, Jonathan P. 1996. "Sulfur Dioxide Compliance of a Regulated Utility." Working Paper 5542. Cambridge, MA: National Bureau of Economic Research, April.

GAO. *See* U.S. General Accounting Office.

Gas Research Institute (GRI). 1991. Clean Air Act Amendments of 1990:

Impacts on Natural Gas Markets (Summary of the 12th Annual GRI Energy Seminar). Chicago: Gas Research Institute.

Gollop, Frank M., and Roberts, Mark J. 1983. "Environmental Regulations and Productivity Growth: The Case of Fossil-Fueled Electric Power Generation." *J. Political Economy* 91, no. 4 (August): 654–74.

Greene, William H. 1993. *Econometric Analysis*. Englewood Cliffs, NJ: Prentice Hall.

Greenwald, Judith M. 1998. *Labor and Climate Change: Getting the Best Deal for American Workers*. Washington: Progressive Policy Institute, October, pp. 18, 22.

Hahn, Robert W. 1989. "Economic Prescriptions for Environmental Problems: How the Patient Followed the Doctor's Orders." *J. Econ. Perspectives* 3, no. 2 (Spring): 95–114.

Hahn, Robert W., and Hester, Gordon L. 1989. "Marketable Permits: Lessons for Theory and Practice." *Ecology Law Q.* 16: 361–406.

Hanley, Robert. 1983. "Turning Off Acid Rain at the Source." *New York Times*, 11 December.

Hartman, Raymond S. 1988. "Self-Selection Bias in the Evaluation of Voluntary Energy Conservation Programs." *Rev. Econ. and Statis.* 70, no. 3 (August): 448–58.

Hausker, Karl. 1992. "The Politics and Economics of Auction Design in the Market for Sulfur Dioxide Pollution." *J. Policy Analysis and Management* 11, no. 4 (Fall): 553–72.

ICF Resources Inc. 1989. "Economic Analysis of Title IV (Acid Rain Provisions) of the Administration's Proposed Clean Air Act Amendments," H.R.3030/S.1490. Washington, September.

——— 1990. *Comparison of the Economic Impacts of the Acid Rain Provisions of the Senate Bill (S. 1630) and the House Bill (S. 1630 [sic])*. Draft report prepared for the U.S. Environmental Protection Agency, July.

Joskow, Paul L. 1985. "Vertical Integration and Long-Term Contracts: The Case of Coal-Burning Generating Plants." *J. Law, Econ., and Organization* 1, no. 1 (Spring): 33–80.

——— 1987. "Contract Duration and Relationship-Specific Investments: Empirical Evidence from Coal Markets." *American Economic Rev.* 77, no. 1 (March): 168–85.

——— 1988. "Price Adjustment in Long-Term Contracts: The Case of Coal." *J. Law and Econ.* 31, no. 1 (April): 47–83.

——— 1989. "Regulatory Failure, Regulatory Reform and Structural Change in the Electric Power Industry." *Brookings Papers on Economic Activity: Microeconomics*, pp. 125–99.

——— 1990. "The Performance of Long-Term Contracts: Further Evidence from Coal Markets." *Rand J. Econ.* 21, no. 2 (Summer): 251–74.

——— 1997. "Restructuring, Competition, and Regulatory Reform in the U.S. Electricity Sector." *J. Econ. Perspectives* 11, no. 3 (Summer): 119–38.

Joskow, Paul L.; Rose, Nancy L.; and Wolfram, Catherine D. 1996. "Political Constraints on Executive Compensation: Evidence From the Electric Utility Industry." *Rand J. Econ.* 27, no. 1 (Spring): 165–82.

Joskow, Paul L., and Schmalensee, Richard. 1986. "Incentive Regulation for Electric Utilities," *Yale J. Regulation.*

1998. "The Political Economy of Market-Based Environmental Policy: The U.S. Acid Rain Program." *J. Law and Econ.* 41, no. 1 (April): 37–83.

Joskow, Paul L.; Schmalensee, Richard; and Bailey, Elizabeth M. 1998. "The Market for Sulfur Dioxide Emissions." *American Economic Rev.* 88, no. 4 (September): 669–85.

Kalt, Joseph P., and Zupan, Mark. 1984. "Capture and Ideology in the Economic Theory of Politics." *American Economic Rev.* 74, no. 3 (June): 279–300.

Kete, Nancy. 1993. "The Politics of Markets: The Acid Rain Control Policy in the 1990 Clean Air Act Amendments." Unpublished Ph.D. dissertation, Johns Hopkins University.

Kiel, Lisa J., and McKenzie, Richard B. 1983. "The Impact of Tenure on the Flow of Federal Benefits to SMSAs." *Public Choice* 41: 285–93.

Kiewiet, D. Roderick, and Mathew D. McCubbins. 1991. *The Logic of Delegation: Congressional Parties and the Appropriations Process.* Chicago: University of Chicago Press.

Kriz, Margaret E. 1989. "Politics in the Air." *National J.* 21 (6 May): 1098–102.

1990. "Dunning the Midwest." *National J.* 22 (14 April): 893–97.

Kruger, Joe; McLean, Brian; and Chen, Rayenne. 1998. "A Tale of Two Revolutions: Administration of the SO_2 Trading Program." Xeroxed copy available from Acid Rain Division, U.S. EPA. Forthcoming in Richard F. Kosobud, ed., *Emissions Trading: Environmental Policy's New Instrument,* New York: John Wiley & Sons.

Kuntz, Phil, and Hager, George. 1990. "Showdown on Clean-Air Bill: Senate Says 'No' to Byrd." *Congressional Q.* (31 March): 983–87.

Laffont, Jean-Jacques, and Tirole, Jean. 1993. *A Theory of Incentives in Procurement and Regulation.* Cambridge, MA: MIT Press.

Levitt, Steven D., and Poterba, James M. Forthcoming. "Congressional Distributive Politics and State Economic Performance." *Public Choice.*

Locke, Reinier, and Harkawik, Dennis P., eds. 1991. *The New Clean Air Act: Compliance and Opportunity.* Arlington, VA: Public Utilities Reports.

Magat, Wesley. 1978. "Pollution Control and Technological Advance: A Dynamic Model of the Firm." 1978. *J. Environmental Econ. and Management* 5: 1–25.

Malm, Eric. 1996. "An Actions-Based Estimate of the Free Rider Fraction in Electric Utility DSM Programs." *Energy J.* 17, no. 3: 41–48.

Malueg, D. 1989. "Emission Credit Trading and the Incentive to Adopt New Pollution Abatement Technology." *J. Environmental Econ. and Management* 16: 52–57.

McLean, Brian J. 1996. "Evolution of Marketable Permits: The U.S. Experience with Sulfur Dioxide Allowance Trading." Unpublished manuscript. Washington: U.S. EPA, Acid Rain Division, December.

MIT/CEEPR Title IV Questionnaire. 1996. Cambridge, MA: Massachusetts Institute of Technology / Center for Energy and Environmental Policy Research.

Montero, Juan-Pablo. 1997. "Environmental Regulation and Technology Innovation." Chapter 1 in Ph.D. dissertation, Massachusetts Institute of Technology, March.

1998a. "Voluntary Compliance with Market-Based Environmental Policy: Evidence from the US Acid Rain Program," Working paper #98-001, CEEPR, MIT, January.

1998b. "Marketable Pollution Permits with Uncertainty and Transaction Costs." *Resource and Energy Econ.* 20, no. 1 (March): 27–50.

1999. "Voluntary Compliance with Market-Based Environmental Policy: Evidence from the US Acid Rain Program." *J. Political Econ.* 107 (October): 998–1033.

2000. "Optimal Design of a Phase-in Emissions Trading Program." *J. Public Econ.* 75, no. 2: 273–91.

Montero, Juan-Pablo, and Ellerman, A. Denny. 1998. "Explaining Low Sulfur Dioxide Allowance Prices: The Effect of Expectation Errors and Irreversibility." Working Paper no. MIT-CEEPR 98-012 WP. Cambridge, MA: MIT CEEPR. October.

Montgomery, W. David. 1972. "Markets in Licenses and Efficient Pollution Control Programs." *J. Economic Theory,* 3: 395–418.

NAPAP. *See* U.S. National Acid Precipitation Assessment Program.

National Coal Association (NCA; now National Mining Association). 1987. *Reduction in Sulfur Dioxide Emissions at Coal-Fired Electric Utilities: The Trend Continues.* Washington: National Coal Association.

Coal Data. Washington: National Coal Association, various years.

National Economic Research Associates, Inc. (NERA). 1994. *Key Issues in the Design of NO_x Emission Trading Programs to Reduce Ground-Level Ozone.* Palo Alto, CA: Electric Power Research Institute.

NERA. *See* National Economic Research Associates.

Noll, Roger G. 1989. "Economic Perspectives on the Politics of Regulation." In *Handbook of Industrial Organization,* vol. 2, edited by R. Schmalensee and R. D. Willig. New York: North-Holland.

Oates, Wallace E.; Portney, Paul R.; and McGartland, Albert M. 1989. "The Net Benefits of Incentive-based Regulation: A Case Study of Environmental Standard Setting." *American Economic Rev.* 79, no. 5 (December): 1233–42.

Pasha Publications, Inc. 1993. *1993 Guide to Coal Contracts.* Arlington, VA.

1995. *1995 Guide to Coal Contracts.* Arlington, VA.

Pashigian, B. Peter. 1984. "The Effects of Environmental Regulation on Optimal Plant Size and Factor Shares." *J. Law and Econ.* 27: 1–28.

1985. "Environmental Regulation: Whose Self-Interests Are Being Protected?" *Econ. Inquiry* 23: 551–84.

Pechan, E. H., and Associates, Inc. 1989. *Comparison of Acid Rain Control Bills.* EPA Contract no. 68-WA-0038, Work Assignments 94 and 116, OTA Contract L3-5480.0. Washington, November.

1993. The National Allowance Data Base Version 2.11: Technical Support Document, prepared for the US Environmental Protection Agency's Office of Atmospheric Programs–Acid Rain Division, Washington.

1995. The Acid Rain Data Base Version 1 (ARDBV1). Contract no. 68-D3-

0005, prepared for the US Environmental Protection Agency's Office of Atmospheric Programs – Acid Rain Division, Washington.

Peltzman, Sam. 1976. "Toward a More General Theory of Regulation." *J. Law and Econ.* 19 (August): 211–40.

1990. "How Efficient Is the Voting Market?" *J. Law and Econ.* 33: 27–63.

Portney, Paul R. 1990. "Air Pollution Policy." In *Public Policies for Environmental Protection*, edited by Paul R. Portney. Washington: Resources for the Future, pp. 27–96.

Pytte, Alyson. 1990. "A Decade's Acrimony Lifted in the Glow of Clean Air." *Congressional Q.* 48, no. 43 (27 October): 3587–92.

Roberts, Leslie. 1991a. "Learning from an Acid Rain Program." *Science* 251, no. 4999 (15 March): 1302–05.

1991b. "Acid Rain Program: Mixed Review." *Science* 252, no. 5004 (19 April): 371.

Rose, Kenneth. 1994. "The SO$_2$ Emissions Trading Program: Events and Lessons So Far." *PUR Utility Weekly*, 4th Quarter Supplement: 1–8.

Schennach, Susanne M. 1998. "The Economics of Pollution Permit Banking in the Context of Title IV of the 1990 Clean Air Act Amendments." Working Paper no. MIT-CEEPR 98-007 WP. Cambridge, MA: MIT CEEPR. May.

Schmalensee, Richard. 1998a. "Tradable Emissions Rights and Joint Implementation for Greenhouse Gas Abatement: A Look under the Hood." In *The Impact of Climate Change Policy on Consumers: Can Tradable Permits Reduce the Cost?* C. E. Walker, M. A. Bloomfield, and M. Thorning, eds. Washington: American Council for Capital Formation, pp. 39–55.

1998b. "Greenhouse Policy Architectures and Institutions." In *Economics and Policy Issues in Climate Change,* edited by William D. Nordhaus. Washington: Resources for the Future, pp. 137–58.

Schmalensee, Richard; Joskow, Paul L.; Ellerman, A. Denny; Montero, Juan-Pablo; and Bailey, Elizabeth M. 1998. "An Interim Evaluation of Sulfur Dioxide Emissions Trading." *J. Econ. Perspectives* 12, no. 3 (Summer): 53–68.

Schmidt, Peter, and Strauss, Robert P. 1975. "Estimation of Models with Jointly Dependent Qualitative Variables: A Simultaneous Logit Approach." *Econometrica* 43, no. 4 (July): 745–55.

Sharp, Richard G. 1991. "The Clean Air Act Amendments: Impacts on Rail Coal Transportation." *Public Utilities Fortnightly* 127, no. 5 (1 March): 26–30.

Shepsle, Kenneth A., and Weingast, Barry R. 1984. "When Do Rules of Procedure Matter?" *J. Politics* 46: 206–21.

1987. "The Institutional Foundations of Committee Power." *A. P. Sci. Rev.* 81: 85–104.

Smith, Anne E.; Platt, Jeremy; and Ellerman, A. Denny. 1998. *The Costs of Reducing Utility SO$_2$ Emissions – Not as Low as You Might Think.* Working Paper no. MIT-CEEPR 98-010 WP. Cambridge, MA: MIT CEEPR. August.

Solomon, Barry. 1994. "SO$_2$ Allowance Trading: What Rules Apply?" *Public Utilities Fortnightly* 132, no. 17 (15 September): 22–25.

Stavins, Robert N., ed. 1988. Project 88 – Harnessing Market Forces to Protect Our Environment: Initiatives for the New President. A Public Policy Study sponsored by Senator Timothy E. Wirth, Colorado, and Senator John Heinz, Pennsylvania. Washington DC, December.

1995. "Transaction Costs and Tradeable Permits." *J. Environmental Econ. and Management* 29 (September): 133–48.

1998. "What Can We Learn from the Grand Policy Experiment? Lessons from SO_2 Allowance Trading." *J. Economic Perspectives*, vol. 12, no. 3 (Summer), pp. 69–88.

Stern, Amy. 1986a. "House Acid Rain Legislation Criticized from Several Sides." *Congressional Q.* (3 May): 970.

1986b. "Acid Rain Measure Faces Very Cloudy Future." *Congressional Q.* (30 August): 2041.

Stigler, George J. 1971. "The Theory of Economic Regulation." *Bell J. Economics and Management Science* 2 (Spring): 3–21.

Suro, Roberto. 1989. "Concern for the Environment." *New York Times* (2 July).

Tietenberg, Thomas H. 1985. *Emissions Trading: An Exercise in Reforming Pollution Policy*. Washington, DC: Resources for the Future.

1992. *Environmental and Natural Resource Economics*, 3d ed. New York: Harper Collins Publishers.

1996. *Environmental and Natural Resource Economics*, 4th ed. Reading, MA: Addison Wesley Longman Publishing Company.

Tietenberg, Thomas H., and Victor, David. 1994. "Possible Administrative Structures and Procedures for Implementing a Tradeable Entitlement Approach to Controlling Global Warming." In *Combating Global Warming*, edited by the United Nations. New York: United Nations, December.

United Nations Conference on Trade and Development (UNCTAD). 1998. *Greenhouse Gas Emissions Trading: Defining the Principles, Modalities, Rules and Guidelines for Verification, Reporting & Accountability*. Geneva: Draft dated July.

U.S. Council of Economic Advisers. 1998. *Economic Report of the President*. Washington: U.S. Government Printing Office, February.

U.S. Department of Energy (DOE). 1991. *Trends in Contract Coal Transportation: 1979–1987*. Report DOE/EIA-0549. Washington: Energy Information Administration.

1994a. *Costs and Quality of Fuels for Electric Utilities 1993*. Report DOE/EIA-0191(93). Washington: Energy Information Administration.

1994b. *Electric Utility Phase I: Acid Rain Compliance Strategies for the Clean Air Act Amendments of 1994*. Report DOE/EIA-0582. Washington: Energy Information Administration.

1995. *Energy Policy Act Transportation Rate Study: Interim Report on Coal Transportation*. Report DOE/EIA-0597. Washington: Energy Information Administration.

1997. *Effects of Title IV of the Clean Air Act Amendments of 1990 on Electric Utilities: An Update*. Report DOE/EIA-0582(97). Washington: Energy Information Administration, March.

U.S. Environmental Protection Agency (EPA). 1991. *Retrofit Costs for SO_2 and*

NO$_x$ Control Options at 200 Coal-fired Plants. Report EPA/600/S7-90/021. Research Triangle Park, NC: Air and Energy Engineering Research Laboratory, March.

1992. *Regulatory Impact Analysis of the Final Acid Rain Implementation Regulations.* Washington: Acid Rain Division, as prepared by ICF Incorporated, October 19.

1993. *Technical Documentation for Phase II Allowance Allocations.* Report EPA-430-R-93-002. Washington: Acid Rain Division, March.

1994. *National Air Pollutant Emission Trends, 1900–1993.* Report EPA-454/R-94-027. Washington: Office of Air Quality Planning and Standards, October.

1995a. *The Opt-in Program.* Report EPA 430-F-95-032. Washington: Office of Air and Radiation, March.

1995b. *Human Health Benefits from Sulfate Reductions under Title IV of the 1990 Clean Air Act Amendments.* Contract no. 68-D3-0005. Washington: Office of Air and Radiation, November.

1995c. *Allowance Transactions, TRANSmmdd.* (Data is available in print from the Acid Rain Division or can be found on the Acid Rain homepage on the Internet.) Washington: Acid Rain Division.

1996a. *Acid Rain Program Update No. 3: Technology and Innovation.* Report EPA 430-R-96-004. Washington: Acid Rain Division, May.

1996b. *1995 Compliance Results: Acid Rain Program.* Report EPA/430-R-96-012. Washington: Office of Air and Radiation, July.

1997. *1996 Compliance Report: Acid Rain Program.* Report EPA 430-R-97-025. Washington: Office of Air and Radiation, June.

1998. *1997 Compliance Report: Acid Rain Program.* Report EPA-430-R-98-012. Washington: Office of Air and Radiation, Acid Rain Division, August.

Emissions Monitoring System (ongoing reports).

U.S. Federal Energy Regulatory Commission (FERC). Form 423: USDOE/EIA, Cost and Quality of Fuels Consumed at Electric Powerplants. Washington (issued monthly).

U.S. General Accounting Office (GAO). 1984. *An Analysis of Issues Concerning Acid Rain.* GAO/RCED-85-13. Washington: GAO, December.

1994. *Allowance Trading Offers Opportunity to Reduce Emissions at Less Cost.* GAO/RCED-95-30. Washington: GAO, December.

U.S. House of Representatives Committee on Energy and Commerce, Subcommittee on Energy and Power. 1990. *Hearings on "Clean Air Reauthorization (Part 2)," September 12, October 4 and 11, 1989.* Serial no. 101–14. Washington: Government Printing Office.

U.S. National Acid Precipitation Assessment Program (NAPAP). 1990. *1989 Annual Report to the President and Congress.* Washington: NAPAP Office of the Director, June.

1991. *The U.S. National Acid Precipitation Assessment Program: 1990 Integrated Assessment Report.* Washington: NAPAP Office of the Director, November.

1998. *NAPAP Biennial Report to Congress: An Integrated Assessment.* Silver Spring, Maryland, May.

Van Dyke, Brennan. 1991. "Emissions Trading to Reduce Acid Deposition." *Yale Law J.* 100: 2707–26.

Weingast, Barry, and Marshall, W. J. 1988. "The Industrial Organization of Congress: Or, Why Legislatures, Like Firms, Are Not Organized as Markets." *J. Political Economy* 96: 132–63.

Weingast, Barry, and Moran, M. 1983. "Bureaucratic Discretion or Congressional Control? Regulatory Policymaking by the Federal Trade Commission." *J. Political Economy* 91: 765–800.

White, H. 1980. "A Heteroskedasticity-Consistent Covariance Matrix Estimator and a Direct Test for Heteroskedasticity." *Econometrica* 48: 817–38.

Williams, Jeffrey C., and Brian D. Wright. 1991. *Storage and Commodity Markets*, Cambridge: Cambridge Univ. Press.

Wilson, James Q. 1980. "The Politics of Regulation." In *The Politics of Regulation*, edited by J. Q. Wilson. Cambridge, MA: Harvard Univ. Press.

Winebrake, James J.; Farrell, Alexander E.; and Bernstein, Mark A. 1995. "The Clean Air Act's Sulfur Dioxide Emissions Market: Estimating the Costs of Regulatory and Legislative Intervention." *Resource and Energy Economics* 17, no. 3 (November): 239–60.

Index

abatement. *See also* emissions reduction
  coal-switching effects on cost of, 242–248
  costs of, 228–231, 284
  distribution among Phase I units, 123–126
  emissions trading effects on, 141–166
  geographic distribution of, 130–136
  impact of Powder River Basin coals on, 122
  scrubbing effects on cost of, 235–242
  by technique, 126–130
acid rain
  areas affected by, 5
  controversies over, 15–17
  as environmentalist concern, 18–21
  historical legislation on, 13–30
  legislation proposed for, 19–21
  state laws controlling, 38
  sulfur dioxide as major cause of, 4
Acid Rain Advisory Committee (EPA), 38
Acid Rain Program, 3, 45, 54, 68, 69, 76, 168,
    314, 317, 320
  in coal-mining and -burning states, 34
  costs of, 78, 221
  description of, 5–9
  legislative history of, 21–30, 33–35, 318
  lessons learned from, 321–322
Acid Rain Title. *See* Title IV
Adirondacks, acid rain in, 5
adverse selection, 11, 198, 217, 219–220
aggregate emissions
  control of, 6, 82, 111
  prediction of, 114
air pollution, early U.S. legislation on, 13–16
Alabama
  as allocation loser, 59
  allowance allocations for, 41
  emission reduction in, 132, 135
  sulfur dioxide emissions of, 19
Alaska, 6
ALCOA, 139
  allowance sales by, 174(n15)

Allegheny Power, 128(n11), 150, 157
  allowance sources and uses of, 163
allowance-allocation rule, 218(n19)
allowance allocations
  EPA methods for, 38
  political economy of, 31–76
allowance "pie," 36–39
allowances
  banking of, 7, 8, 121, 146, 161–165
  brokerage of, 7
  bundling of, 258
  current demand for, 154–161
  excess, 151–154
  individual buyers of, 182
  intertemporal market for, 185–190
  market development for, 167–196
  offer curve for, 179(n24)
  Phase I allocations of, 36(n9), 39–43
  price trends of, 309–312
  private market for, 172–190
  public auction of, 149(n9)
  retained, 162
  for substitution units, 152(n10)
  swapping of, 178, 185(n28)
  unexpected behavior at prices of, 297–
    299
Allowance Tracking System, use by coal
    suppliers, 258(n6)
AMAX Energy, allowance purchases by,
    177(n21)
Ameren, 156(n13)
American Electric Power (AEP), 60(n40),
    128(n11), 150, 151, 157, 158
  allowance demands of, 160
  allowance sources and uses of, 163, 164
Appalachia and Appalachian states, 28
  Acid Rain Program in, 34
  coal prices in, 305
  coal-switching in, 247
  "dirty" generating units in, 56